"APIs are eating the world. Organizations and  and more on APIs. For all these APIs to be designed way of tackling design challenges. *Patterns for A* sign their APIs more effectively: They can focus nain while standard design issues are solved with patterns. If you're working in the API space, this book will change how you design APIs and how you look at APIs."

—*Erik Wilde, Catalyst at Axway*

"The authors have captured design patterns across the API lifecycle, from definition to design, in an approachable way. Whether you have designed dozens of web APIs or you are just starting out, this book is a valuable resource to drive consistency and overcome any design challenge you may face. I highly recommend this book!"

—*James Higginbotham*
Author of Principles of Web API Design: Delivering value with APIs and Microservices *and Executive API Consultant, LaunchAny*

"APIs are everywhere in today's software development landscape. API design looks easy but, as anyone who has suffered a poorly designed API will attest, it is a difficult skill to master and much subtler and more complex than it initially appears. In this book, the authors have used their long experience and years of research work to create a structured body of knowledge about API design. It will help you to understand the underlying concepts needed to create great APIs and provides a practical set of patterns that you can use when creating your own APIs. It is recommended for anyone involved in the design, building, or testing of modern software systems."

—*Eoin Woods, CTO, Endava*

Application programming interfaces (API) are among the top priority elements to help manage many of the trade-offs involved in system design, in particular distributed systems, which increasingly dominate our software ecosystem. In my experience, this book removes the complexities in understanding and designing APIs with concepts accessible to both practicing engineers and those who are just starting their software engineering and architecting journey. All who aspire to play a key role in system design should understand the API design concepts and patterns presented in this book."

—*Ipek Ozkaya*
Technical Director, Engineering Intelligence Software System
Software Solutions Division
Carnegie Mellon University Software Engineering Institute
Editor-in-Chief 2019–2023 IEEE Software Magazine

.

"It is my belief that we are entering into an era where API-first design will become the dominant form of design in large, complex systems. For this reason, *Patterns for API Design* is perfectly timed and should be considered essential reading for any architect."

—*Rick Kazman, University of Hawaii*

"Finally, the important topic of API design is addressed systematically! I wish I would have had this great pattern collection a few years earlier."

—*Dr. Gernot Starke, INNOQ Fellow*

"I observed software projects fail because middleware technology hid a system's distributed nature from programmers. They designed problematic APIs of a non-distributed gestalt exercised remotely. This book embraces the required dispersal of software in an interdependent world and provides timeless advice on designing interfaces between its separated parts. The Patterns guide beyond specific middleware technology and will not only help with creation and understanding but also with necessary evolution of the interconnected software systems we grow today and in the future. Those systems not only span the globe for international business, but also work within our cars, houses, and almost any technology our daily lives depend on."

—*Peter Sommerlad, independent consultant, author of*
Pattern-Oriented Software Architecture: A System of Patterns *and* Security Patterns

"The book *Patterns for API Design* is the Swiss army knife for software engineers and architects when it comes to designing, evolving, and documenting APIs. What I particularly like about the book is that it does not just throw the patterns at the reader; instead, the authors use realistic examples, provide hands-on architecture decision support, and exemplify patterns and decisions using a case study. As a result, their pattern language is very accessible. You can use the book to find solutions for specific problems or browse entire chapters to get an overview of the problem and solution spaces related to API design. All patterns are well-crafted, well-named, and peer-reviewed by the practitioner community. It's a joy."

—*Dr. Uwe van Heesch, Practicing Software Architect and*
Former Vice President Hillside Europe

"This comprehensive collection of API patterns is an invaluable resource for software engineers and architects designing interoperable software systems. The introduction into API fundamentals and numerous case study examples make it excellent teaching material for future software engineers. Many of the patterns discussed in this book are extremely useful in practice and were applied to design the APIs of integrated, mission-critical rail operations centre systems."

—*Andrei Furda, Senior Software Engineer at Hitachi Rail STS Australia*

Patterns for API Design

Pearson Addison-Wesley
Signature Series

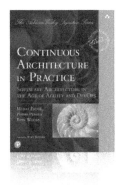 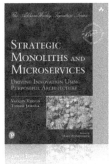  

Visit informit.com/awss/vernon **for a complete list of available publications.**

The Pearson Addison-Wesley Signature Series provides readers with practical and authoritative information on the latest trends in modern technology for computer professionals. The series is based on one simple premise: great books come from great authors.

Vaughn Vernon is a champion of simplifying software architecture and development, with an emphasis on reactive methods. He has a unique ability to teach and lead with Domain-Driven Design using lightweight tools to unveil unimagined value. He helps organizations achieve competitive advantages using enduring tools such as architectures, patterns, and approaches, and through partnerships between business stakeholders and software developers.

Vaughn's Signature Series guides readers toward advances in software development maturity and greater success with business-centric practices. The series emphasizes organic refinement with a variety of approaches—reactive, object, and functional architecture and programming; domain modeling; right-sized services; patterns; and APIs—and covers best uses of the associated underlying technologies.

Make sure to connect with us!
informit.com/socialconnect

Pearson
Addison-Wesley

informIT.com
the trusted technology learning source

Patterns for API Design

Simplifying Integration with Loosely Coupled Message Exchanges

Olaf Zimmermann

Mirko Stocker

Daniel Lübke

Uwe Zdun

Cesare Pautasso

✦✦ Addison-Wesley

Boston • Columbus • New York • San Francisco • Amsterdam • Cape Town
Dubai • London • Madrid • Milan • Munich • Paris • Montreal • Toronto • Delhi • Mexico City
São Paulo • Sydney • Hong Kong • Seoul • Singapore • Taipei • Tokyo

Pearson's Commitment to Diversity, Equity, and Inclusion

Pearson is dedicated to creating bias-free content that reflects the diversity of all learners. We embrace the many dimensions of diversity, including but not limited to race, ethnicity, gender, socioeconomic status, ability, age, sexual orientation, and religious or political beliefs.

Education is a powerful force for equity and change in our world. It has the potential to deliver opportunities that improve lives and enable economic mobility. As we work with authors to create content for every product and service, we acknowledge our responsibility to demonstrate inclusivity and incorporate diverse scholarship so that everyone can achieve their potential through learning. As the world's leading learning company, we have a duty to help drive change and live up to our purpose to help more people create a better life for themselves and to create a better world.

Our ambition is to purposefully contribute to a world where:

- Everyone has an equitable and lifelong opportunity to succeed through learning.

- Our educational products and services are inclusive and represent the rich diversity of learners.

- Our educational content accurately reflects the histories and experiences of the learners we serve.

- Our educational content prompts deeper discussions with learners and motivates them to expand their own learning (and worldview).

While we work hard to present unbiased content, we want to hear from you about any concerns or needs with this Pearson product so that we can investigate and address them.

- Please contact us with concerns about any potential bias at https://www.pearson.com/report-bias.html.

Contents

Foreword by Vaughn Vernon, Series Editor

My signature series emphasizes organic growth and refinement, which I describe in more detail below. It only makes sense to start off by describing the organic communication that I experienced with the first author of this book, Professor Dr. Olaf Zimmermann.

As I often refer to Conway's Law of system design, communication is a critical factor in software development. Systems designs not only resemble the communication structures of the designers; the structure and assembling of individuals as communicators is just as important. It can lead from interesting conversations to stimulating thoughts and continue to deliver innovative products. Olaf and I met at a Java User Group meeting in Bern, Switzerland, in November 2019. I gave a talk on reactive architecture and programming and how it is used with Domain-Driven Design. Afterward, Olaf introduced himself. I also met his graduate student and later colleague, Stefan Kapferer. Together they had organically designed and built the open-source product Context Mapper (a domain-specific language and tools for Domain-Driven Design). Our chance meeting ultimately led to this book's publication. I'll tell more of this story after I describe the motivation and purpose of my book series.

My Signature Series is designed and curated to guide readers toward advances in software development maturity and greater success with business-centric practices. The series emphasizes organic refinement with a variety of approaches—reactive, object, as well as functional architecture and programming; domain modeling; right-sized services; patterns; and APIs—and covers best uses of the associated underlying technologies.

From here, I am focusing now on only two words: *organic refinement*.

The first word, *organic*, stood out to me recently when a friend and colleague used it to describe software architecture. I have heard and used the word *organic* in connection with software development, but I didn't think about that word as carefully as I did then when I personally consumed the two used together: *organic architecture*.

Think about the word *organic*, and even the word *organism*. For the most part, these are used when referring to living things, but they are also used to describe inanimate things that feature some characteristics that resemble life forms. *Organic* originates in Greek. Its etymology is with reference to a functioning organ of the body. If you read the etymology of *organ*, it has a broader use, and in fact organic followed suit: body organs; to implement; describes a tool for making or doing; a musical instrument.

We can readily think of numerous organic objects—living organisms—from the very large to the microscopic single-celled life forms. With the second use of organism, though, examples may not as readily pop into our mind. One example is an organization, which includes the prefix of both *organic* and *organism*. In this use of *organism*, I'm describing something that is structured with bidirectional dependencies. An organization is an organism because it has organized parts. This kind of organism cannot survive without the parts, and the parts cannot survive without the organism.

Taking that perspective, we can continue applying this thinking to nonliving things because they exhibit characteristics of living organisms. Consider the atom. Every single atom is a system unto itself, and all living things are composed of atoms. Yet, atoms are inorganic and do not reproduce. Even so, it's not difficult to think of atoms as living things in the sense that they are endlessly moving, functioning. Atoms even bond with other atoms. When this occurs, each atom is not only a single system unto itself, but becomes a subsystem along with other atoms as subsystems, with their combined behaviors yielding a greater whole system.

So then, all kinds of concepts regarding software are quite organic in that nonliving things are still "characterized" by aspects of living organisms. When we discuss software model concepts using concrete scenarios, or draw an architecture diagram, or write a unit test and its corresponding domain model unit, software starts to come alive. It isn't static because we continue to discuss how to make it better, subjecting it to refinement, where one scenario leads to another, and that has an impact on the architecture and the domain model. As we continue to iterate, the increasing value in refinements leads to incremental growth of the organism. As time progresses, so does the software. We wrangle with and tackle complexity through useful abstractions, and the software grows and changes shapes, all with the explicit purpose of making work better for real, living organisms at global scales.

Sadly, software organics tend to grow poorly more often than they grow well. Even if they start out life in good health, they tend to get diseases, become deformed, grow unnatural appendages, atrophy, and deteriorate. Worse still is that these symptoms are caused by efforts to refine the software that go wrong instead of making things better. The worst part is that with every failed refinement, everything that goes wrong with these complexly ill bodies doesn't cause their death. Oh, if they could just die! Instead, we have to kill them and killing them requires nerves, skills, and the intestinal fortitude of a dragon slayer. No, not one, but dozens of vigorous dragon slayers. Actually, make that dozens of dragon slayers who have really big brains.

That's where this series comes into play. I am curating a series designed to help you mature and reach greater success with a variety of approaches—reactive, object, and functional architecture and programming; domain modeling; right-sized services; patterns; and APIs. And along with that, the series covers best uses of the associated underlying technologies. It's not accomplished in one fell swoop. It requires organic refinement with purpose and skill. I and the other authors are here to help. To that end, we've delivered our very best to achieve our goal.

Now, back to my story. When Olaf and I first met, I offered for him and Stefan to attend my IDDD Workshop a few weeks later in Munich, Germany. Although neither were able to break away for all three days, they were open to attend the third and final day. My second offer was for Olaf and Stefan to use time after the workshop to demonstrate the Context Mapper tool. The workshop attendees were impressed, as was I. This led to further collaboration on into 2020. Little did any of us expect what that year would bring. Even so, Olaf and I were able to meet somewhat frequently to continue design discussions about Context Mapper. During one of these meetings, Olaf mentioned his work on API patterns that were provided openly. Olaf showed me a number of patterns and additional tooling he and others had built around them. I offered Olaf the opportunity to author in the series. The result is now in front of you.

I later met on a video call with Olaf and Daniel Lübke to kick off product development. I have not had the chance to spend time with the other authors—Mirko Stocker, Uwe Zdun, Cesare Pautasso—but I was assured of the team's quality given their credentials. Notably, Olaf and James Higginbotham collaborated to ensure the complementary outcome of this book and *Principles of Web API Design*, also in this series. As an overall result, I am very impressed with what these five have contributed to the industry literature. API design is a very important topic. The enthusiasm toward the book's announcement proves that it is right in the topic's sweet spot. I am confident that you will agree.

—*Vaughn Vernon, series editor*

Foreword by Frank Leymann

APIs are everywhere. The API economy enables innovation in technology areas, including cloud computing and the Internet of Things (IoT), and is also a key enabler of digitalization of many companies. There hardly is any enterprise application without external interfaces to integrate customers, suppliers, and other business partners; solution-internal interfaces decompose such applications into more manageable parts, such as loosely coupled microservices. Web-based APIs play a prominent role in these distributed settings but are not the only way to integrate remote parties: queue-based messaging channels as well as publish/subscribe-based channels are widely used for backend integration, exposing APIs to message producers and consumers. gRPC and GraphQL have gained a lot of momentum as well. Thus, best practices for designing "good" APIs are desirable. Ideally, API designs persist across technologies and survive when those change.

Patterns establish a vocabulary for a problem-solution domain, finding a balance between being abstract and concrete, which gives them both timelessness and relevance today. Take *Enterprise Integration Patterns* by Gregor Hohpe and Bobby Woolf from the Addison Wesley Signature Series as an example: I have been using it in teaching and industry assignments since my time as lead architect of the IBM MQ family of products. Messaging technologies come and, sometimes, go—but the messaging concepts such as Service Activator and Idempotent Receiver are here to stay. I have written cloud computing patterns, IoT patterns, quantum computing patterns, even patterns for patterns in digital humanities myself. And Martin Fowler's *Patterns of Enterprise Application Architecture*, also from the Addison Wesley Signature Series, gives us the Remote Façade and the Service Layer. Hence, many parts of the overall design space of distributed applications are covered well in this literature—but not all. Therefore, it is great to see that the API design space is now supported by patterns too, the request and response messages that travel between API client and API provider in particular.

The team who wrote this book is a great mix of architects and developers composed of deeply experienced industry professionals, leaders in the patterns community, and academic researchers and lecturers. I have been working with three of the authors of this book for many years and have been following their MAP project since its inception in 2016. They apply the pattern concept faithfully: Each pattern text follows a common template that takes us from a problem context, including design forces, to a conceptual solution. It also comes with a concrete example (often

RESTful HTTP). A critical discussion of pros and cons resolves the initial design forces and closes with pointers to related patterns. Many of the patterns went through shepherding and writers workshops at pattern conferences, which helped to incrementally and iteratively improve and harden them over several years, capturing collective knowledge as a result from this process.

This book provides multiple perspectives on the API design space, from scoping and architecture to message representation structure and quality attribute-driven design to API evolution. Its pattern language can be navigated via different paths, including project phases and structural elements such as API endpoint and operation. As in our *Cloud Computing Patterns* book, a graphical icon for each pattern conveys its essence. These icons serve as mnemonics and can be used to sketch APIs and their elements. The book takes a unique and novel step in providing decision models that collect recurring questions, options, and criteria regarding pattern applications. They provide stepwise, easy-to-follow design guidance without over-simplifying the complexities inherent to API design. A stepwise application to a sample case makes the models and their advices tangible.

In Part 2, the patterns reference, application and integration architects will find the coverage of endpoint roles such as Processing Resource and operation responsibilities such as State Transition Operation useful to size APIs adequately and make (cloud) deployment decisions. State matters, after all, and several patterns make state management behind the API curtain explicit. API developers will benefit from the careful consideration given to identifiers (in patterns such as API Key and Id Element), several options for response shaping (for instance, with Wish Lists and a Wish Template that abstracts from GraphQL), and pragmatic advice on how to expose metadata of different kinds.

I have not seen life-cycle management and versioning strategies captured in pattern form in other books so far. Here, we can learn about Limited Lifetime Guarantees and Two in Production, two patterns very common in enterprise applications. These evolution patterns will be appreciated by API product owners and maintainers.

In summary, this book provides a healthy mix of theory and practice, containing numerous nuggets of deep advice but never losing the big picture. Its 44 patterns, organized in five categories and chapters, are grounded in real-world experience and documented with academic rigor applied and practitioner-community feedback incorporated. I am confident that patterns will serve the community well, today and tomorrow. API designers in industry as well as in research, development, and education related to API design and evolution can benefit from them.

—Prof. Dr. Dr. h. c. Frank Leymann, Managing Director
Institute of Architecture of Application Systems
University of Stuttgart

Preface

This introduction to our book covers the following:

- The context and the purpose of the book—its motivation, goals and scope.
- Who should read the book—our target audience with their use cases and information needs.
- How the book is organized, with patterns serving as knowledge vehicles.

Motivation

Humans communicate in many different languages. The same holds for software. Software not only is written in various programming languages but also communicates via a plethora of protocols (such as HTTP) and message exchange formats (such as JSON). HTTP, JSON, and other technologies operate every time somebody updates their social network profile, orders something in a Web shop, swipes their credit card to purchase something, and so on:

- Application frontends, such as mobile apps on smartphones, place requests for transaction processing at their backends, such as purchase orders in online shops.
- Application parts exchange long-lived data such as customer profiles or product catalogs with each other and with the systems of business partners, customers, and suppliers.
- Application backends provide external services such as payment gateways or cloud storage with data and metadata.

The software components involved in these scenarios—large, small, and in-between—talk to others to achieve their individual goals while jointly serving end users. The software engineer's response to this distribution challenge is application integration via *application programming interfaces (APIs)*. Every integration scenario involves at least two communication parties: API client and API provider.

API clients consume the services exposed by API providers. API documentation governs the client-provider interactions.

Just like humans, software components often struggle to understand each other when they communicate; it is hard for their designers to decide on an adequate size and structure of message content and agree on the best-suited conversation style. Neither party wants to be too quiet or overly talkative when articulating its needs or responding to requests. Some application integration and API designs work very well; the involved parties understand each other and reach their goals. They interoperate effectively and efficiently. Others lack clarity and thereby confuse or stress participants; verbose messages and chatty conversations may overload the communication channels, introduce unnecessary technical risk, and cause extra work in development and operations.

Now, what distinguishes good and poor integration API designs? How can API designers stimulate a positive client developer experience? Ideally, the guidelines for good integration architectures and API designs do not depend on any particular technology or product. Technologies and products come and go, but related design advice should stay relevant for a long time. In our real-world analogy, principles such as those of Cicero's rhetoric and eloquence or Rosenberg's in *Nonviolent Communication: A Language of Life* [Rosenberg 2002] are not specific to English or any other natural language; they will not go out of fashion as natural languages evolve. Our book aims to establish a similar toolbox and vocabulary for integration specialists and API designers. It presents its knowledge bits as *patterns* for API design and evolution that are eligible under different communication paradigms and technologies (with HTTP- and JSON-based Web APIs serving as primary sources of examples).

Goals and Scope

Our mission is to help overcome the complexity of designing and evolving APIs through proven, reusable solution elements:

> How can APIs be engineered understandably and sustainably, starting from stakeholder goals, architecturally significant requirements, and already proven design elements?

While much has been said and written about HTTP, Web APIs, and integration architectures in general (including service-oriented ones), the design of individual API endpoints and message exchanges has received less attention so far:

- How many API operations should be exposed remotely? Which data should be exchanged in request and response messages?

- How is loose coupling of API operations and client-provider interactions ensured?

- What are suitable message representations: flat or hierarchically nested ones? How is agreement reached on the meaning of the representation elements so that these elements are processed correctly and efficiently?

- Should API providers be responsible for processing data provided by their clients, possibly changing the provider-side state and connecting to backend systems? Or should they merely provide shared data stores to their clients?

- How are changes to APIs introduced in a controlled way that balances extensibility and compatibility?

The patterns in this book help answer these questions by sketching proven solutions to specific design problems recurring in certain requirements contexts. Focusing on remote APIs (rather than program-internal ones), they aim at improving the developer experience on both the client side and the provider side.

Target Audience

This book targets intermediate-level software professionals striving to improve their skills and designs. The presented patterns primarily aim at integration architects, API designers, and Web developers interested in platform-independent architectural knowledge. Both backend-to-backend integration specialists and developers of APIs supporting frontend applications can benefit from the knowledge captured in the patterns. As we focus on API endpoint granularity and the data exchanged in messages, additional target roles are API product owner, API reviewer, and cloud tenant and provider.

> This book is for you if you are a medium-experienced software engineer (such as developer, architect, or product owner) already familiar with API fundamentals and want to improve your API design capabilities, including message data contract design and API evolution.

Students, lecturers, and software engineering researchers may find the patterns and their presentation in this book useful as well. We provide an introduction to API fundamentals and a domain model for API design to make the book and its patterns understandable without first having to read a book for beginners.

Knowing about the available patterns and their pros and cons will improve proficiency regarding API design and evolution. APIs and the services they provide will be simpler to develop, consume, and evolve when applying patterns from this book suited for a particular requirements context.

Usage Scenarios

Our objective is to make API design and usage a pleasant experience. To that end, three main use cases for our book and its patterns are as follows:

1. *Facilitate API design discussions and workshops* by establishing a common vocabulary, pointing out required design decisions, and sharing available options and related trade-offs. Empowered by this knowledge, API providers are enabled to expose APIs of quality and style that meet their clients' needs, both short term and long term.

2. *Simplify API design reviews and speed up objective API comparisons* so that APIs can be quality assured—and evolved in a backward-compatible and extensible way.

3. *Enhance API documentation with platform-neutral design information* so that API client developers can grasp the capabilities and constraints of provided APIs with ease. The patterns are designed to be embeddable into API contracts and observable in existing designs.

We provide a fictitious case study and two real-world pattern adoption stories to demonstrate and jumpstart this pattern usage.

We do not expect readers to know any particular modeling approach, design technique, or architectural style already. However, such concepts—for instance, the Align-Define-Design-Refine (ADDR) process, domain-driven design (DDD), and responsibility-driven design (RDD)—have their roles to play. They are reviewed briefly in Appendix A.

Existing Design Heuristics (and Knowledge Gaps)

You can find many excellent books that provide deep advice on specific API technologies and concepts. For instance, the *RESTful Web Services Cookbook* [Allamaraju 2010] explains how to build HTTP resource APIs—for example, which HTTP method such as POST or PUT to pick. Other books explain how asynchronous messaging works in terms of routing, transformation, and guaranteed delivery [Hohpe 2003]. Strategic DDD [Evans 2003; Vernon 2013] can get you started with API endpoint and service identification. Service-oriented architecture, cloud computing, and microservice infrastructure patterns have been published. Structuring data storages (relational, NoSQL) is also documented comprehensively, and an entire pattern language for distributed systems design is available as well [Buschmann 2007]. Finally, *Release It!* extensively covers design for operations and deployment to production [Nygard 2018a].

The API design process, including goal-driven endpoint identification and operation design, is also covered well in existing books. For instance, *Principles of Web API Design: Delivering Value with APIs and Microservices* [Higginbotham 2021] suggests four process phases with seven steps. *The Design of Web APIs* [Lauret 2019] proposes an API goal canvas, and *Design and Build Great Web APIs: Robust, Reliable, and Resilient* [Amundsen 2020] works with API stories.

Despite these invaluable sources of design advice, the remote API design space still is not covered sufficiently. Specifically, what about the structures of the request and response messages going back and forth between API client and provider? *Enterprise Integration Patterns* [Hohpe 2003] features three patterns representing message types (event, command, and document message) but does not provide further details on their inner workings. However, "data on the outside," exchanged between systems, differs from "data on the inside" that is processed program-internally [Helland 2005]. There are significant differences between the two types of data in terms of their mutability, lifetime, accuracy, consistency, and protection needs. For instance, increasing a local stock-item counter internal to an inventory system probably requires somewhat less architecture design than product pricing and shipment information that is exchanged between manufacturers and logistics companies jointly managing a supply chain via remote APIs and messaging channels.

Message representation design—data on the outside [Helland 2005] or the "Published Language" pattern [Evans 2003] of an API—is the main focus area of this book. It closes the knowledge gaps regarding API endpoint, operation, and message design.

Patterns as Knowledge Sharing Vehicles

Software patterns are sophisticated knowledge-sharing instruments with a track record of more than 25 years. We decided for the pattern format to share API design advice because pattern names aim at forming a domain vocabulary, a "Ubiquitous Language" [Evans 2003]. For instance, the enterprise integration patterns have become the lingua franca of queue-based messaging; these patterns were even implemented in messaging frameworks and tools.

Patterns are not invented but are mined from practical experience and then hardened via peer feedback. The patterns community has developed a set of practices to organize the feedback process; shepherding and writers' workshops are two particularly important ones [Coplien 1997].

At the heart of each pattern is a problem-solution pair. Its forces and the discussion of consequences support informed decision making, for instance, about desired and achieved quality characteristics—but also about the downsides of certain designs. Alternative solutions are discussed, and pointers to related patterns and possible implementation technologies complete the picture.

Note that patterns do not aim at providing complete solutions but serve as sketches to be adopted and tailored for a particular, context-specific API design. In other words, patterns are soft around their edges; they outline possible solutions but do not provide blueprints to be copied blindly. How to adopt and realize a pattern to satisfy project or product requirements remains the responsibility of API designers and owners.

We have been applying and teaching patterns in industry and academia for a long time. Some of us have written patterns for programming, architecting, and integrating distributed application systems and their parts [Voelter 2004; Zimmermann 2009; Pautasso 2016].

We found the pattern concept to be well suited for the usage scenarios stated earlier under "Goals and Scope" and "Target Audience."

Microservice API Patterns

Our pattern language, called *Microservice API Patterns (MAP)*, provides comprehensive views on API design and evolution from the perspective of the messages exchanged when APIs are exposed and consumed. These messages and their payloads are structured as representation elements. The representation elements differ in their *structure* and meaning because API endpoints and their operations have different architectural *responsibilities*. The message structures strongly influence the design time and runtime *qualities* of an API and its underlying implementations; for instance, few large messages cause network and endpoint workloads (such as CPU consumption and network bandwidth usage) that differ from those caused by many small messages. Finally, successful APIs *evolve* over time; the changes over time have to be managed.

We chose the metaphor and acronym MAP because maps provide orientation and guidance, just as pattern languages do; they educate their readers on the options available in an abstract solution space. APIs themselves also have a mapping nature, as they route incoming requests to the underlying service implementations.

We admit that "Microservice API Patterns" might come across as click-bait. In case microservices are no longer fashionable shortly after this book is published, we reserve the right to rename the language and repurpose the acronym. For instance, "Message API Patterns" outlines the scope of the language well too. In the book, we refer to MAP as "the pattern language" or "our patterns" most of the time.

Scope of the Patterns in This Book

This book is the final outcome of a volunteer project focused on the design and evolution of Web APIs and other remote APIs addressing endpoint and message responsibility, structure, and quality concerns as well as service API evolution. The project started in the fall of 2016. The resulting pattern language, presented in this book, helps answer the following questions:

- What is the architectural role played by each API endpoint? How do the endpoint roles and the responsibilities of operations impact service size and granularity?

- What is an adequate number of representation elements in request and response messages? How are these elements structured? How can they be grouped and annotated with supplemental information?

- How can an API provider achieve a certain level of API quality while at the same time using its resources in a cost-effective way? How can quality trade-offs be communicated and accounted for?

- How can API professionals deal with life-cycle management concerns such as support periods and versioning? How can they promote backward compatibility and communicate unavoidable breaking changes?

We collected our patterns by studying numerous Web APIs and API-related specifications and reflecting on our own professional experience (before writing any pattern). We observed many occurrences of the patterns—known uses—both in public Web APIs and in application development and software integration projects in industry. Intermediate versions of many of our patterns went through the shepherding and writers' workshop processes at EuroPLoP[1] from 2017 to 2020; they were later published in the respective conference proceedings.[2]

---

1. https://europlop.net/content/conference.
2. We decided not to include big collections of known uses in the book; such information is available online and in the EuroPLoP conference proceedings from 2016 to 2020. In some of the supplemental resources, you can find extra implementation hints as well.

Entry Points, Reading Order, and Content Organization

When maneuvering a complex design space to solve wicked problems [Wikipedia 2022a] (and API design certainly qualifies as sometimes wicked), it is often hard to see the forest for the trees. It is neither possible nor desirable to serialize or standardize the problem-solving activities. Therefore, our pattern language has multiple entry points. Each book part can serve as a starting point, and Appendix A suggests even more.

The book has three parts: **Part 1, "Foundations and Narratives," Part 2, "The Patterns,"** and **Part 3, "Our Patterns in Action (Now and Then)."** Figure P.1 shows these parts with their chapters and logical dependencies.

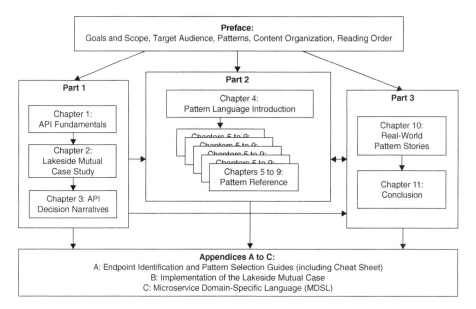

Figure P.1 *Book parts and their dependencies*

Part 1 introduces the domain of API design conceptually, starting with **Chapter 1, "Application Programming Interface (API) Fundamentals."** Lakeside Mutual, our case study and primary source of examples, appears for the first time with its business context, requirements, existing systems, and initial API design in **Chapter 2, "Lakeside Mutual Case Study."** We provide decision models that show how the patterns in our language relate to each other in **Chapter 3, "API Decision Narratives."** Chapter 3 also provides pattern selection criteria and shows how the featured decisions were made in the Lakeside Mutual case. These decision models may serve as navigation aids when reading the book and when applying the patterns in practice.

Part 2 is the pattern reference; it starts with **Chapter 4, "Pattern Language Introduction,"** followed by five chapters full of patterns: **Chapter 5, "Define Endpoint Types and Operations," Chapter 6, "Design Request and Response Message Representations," Chapter 7, "Refine Message Design for Quality," Chapter 8, "Evolve APIs,"** and **Chapter 9, "Document and Communicate API Contracts."** Figure P.2 illustrates these chapters and possible reading paths in this part; for instance, you can learn about basic structure patterns such as ATOMIC PARAMETER and PARAMETER TREE in Chapter 4 and then move on to element stereotypes such as ID ELEMENT and METADATA ELEMENT found in Chapter 6.

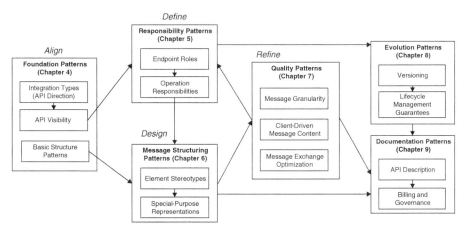

Figure P.2 *Über-pattern map: Chapter flows in Part 2 of the book*

Each pattern description can be seen as a small, specialized article on its own, usually a few pages long. These discussions are structured identically: First, we introduce when and why to apply the pattern. Then we explain how the pattern works and give at least one concrete example. Next, we discuss the consequences of applying the pattern and direct readers to other patterns that become eligible once a particular one has been applied. The names of our patterns are set in SMALL CAPS (example: PROCESSING RESOURCE). This pattern template, introduced in detail in Chapter 4, was derived from the EuroPLoP conference template [Harrison 2003]. We refactored it slightly to take review comments and advice into account (thank you Gregor and Peter!). It puts particular emphasis on quality attributes and their conflicts, as our patterns deal with architecturally significant requirements; consequently, trade-offs are required when making API design and evolution decisions.

Part 3 features the application of the patterns in two real-world projects in rather different domains, e-government and offer/order management in the construction industry. It also reflects, draws some conclusions, and gives an outlook.

Appendix A, "Endpoint Identification and Pattern Selection Guides," provides a problem-oriented cheat sheet as another option to get started. It also discusses how our patterns relate to RDD, DDD, and ADDR. **Appendix B, "Implementation of the Lakeside Mutual Case,"** shares more API design artifacts from the book's case study. **Appendix C, "Microservice Domain-Specific Language (MDSL),"** provides a working knowledge of MDSL, a language for microservices contracts with built-in pattern support via decorators such as `<<Pagination>>`. MDSL provides bindings and generator support for OpenAPI, gRPC protocol buffers, GraphQL, and other interface description and service programming languages.

You will see some (but not much) Java and quite a bit of JSON and HTTP (for instance, in the form of curl commands and responses to them) as you find your way through the book. Very little, if any, gRPC, GraphQL, and SOAP/WSDL might also come your way; if so, it is designed to be simple enough to be understandable without expertise in any of these technologies. Some of our examples are described in MDSL (if you are wondering why we created yet another interface description language: OpenAPI in its YAML or JSON renderings simply does not fit on a single book page when going beyond HelloWorld–ish examples!).

Supplemental information is available through the Web site companion to this book:

https://api-patterns.org

We hope you find the results of our efforts useful so that our patterns have a chance to find their way into the body of knowledge of the global community of integration architects and API developers. We will be glad to hear about your feedback and constructive criticism.

Olaf, Mirko, Daniel, Uwe, Cesare
June 30, 2022

Acknowledgments

We thank Vaughn Vernon for all his feedback and encouragement during our book project. We feel honored to be part of his Addison Wesley Signature Series. Special thanks also go to Haze Humbert, Menka Mehta, Mary Roth, Karthik Orukaimani, and Sandra Schroeder from Pearson for their excellent support and to Frank Leymann for providing the foreword and valuable feedback on our work. Our copy editor, Carol Lallier of Clarity Editing, made this late activity a rewarding, even pleasant experience.

The real-world pattern stories in this book would have not been possible without the cooperation of development projects. Thus, we'd like to thank Walter Berli and Werner Möckli from Terravis and Phillip Ghadir and Willem van Kerkhof from innoQ for their inputs and work on these stories. Nicolas Dipner and Sebnem Kaslack created the initial versions of the patterns icons in their term and bachelor thesis projects. Toni Suter implemented large parts of the Lakeside Mutual case study applications. Stefan Kapferer, developer of Context Mapper, also contributed to the MDSL tools.

We want to thank all the people who provided feedback on the content of this book. Special thanks go to Andrei Furda, who provided input to the introductory material and reviewed many of our patterns; Oliver Kopp and Hans-Peter Hoidn, who applied patterns, provided feedback, and/or organized several informal workshops with peers; James Higginbotham and, again, Hans-Peter Hoidn, who reviewed the book manuscript.

In addition, many colleagues provided helpful feedback, especially the shepherds and writer's workshop participants from EuroPLoP 2017, 2018, 2019, and 2020. We thank the following individuals for their valuable insights: Linus Basig, Luc Bläser, Thomas Brand, Joseph Corneli, Filipe Correia, Dominic Gabriel, Antonio Gámez Díaz, Reto Fankhauser, Hugo Sereno Ferreira, Silvan Gehrig, Alex Gfeller, Gregor Hohpe, Stefan Holtel, Ana Ivanchikj, Stefan Keller, Michael Krisper, Jochen Küster, Fabrizio Lazzaretti, Giacomo De Liberali, Fabrizio Montesi, Frank Müller, Padmalata Nistala, Philipp Oser, Ipek Ozkaya, Boris Pokorny, Stefan Richter, Thomas Ronzon, Andreas Sahlbach, Niels Seidel, Souhaila Serbout, Apitchaka Singjai, Stefan Sobernig, Peter Sommerlad, Markus Stolze, Davide Taibi, Dominic Ullmann, Martin (Uto869), Uwe van Heesch, Timo Verhoeven, Stijn Vermeeren, Tammo van Lessen, Robert Weiser, Erik Wilde, Erik Wittern, Eoin Woods, Rebecca Wirfs-Brock, and Veith Zäch. We also would like to thank the students of several editions of the HSR/OST lectures "Advanced Patterns and Frameworks" and "Application Architecture" and of the USI lecture on "Software Architecture." Their discussion of our patterns and additional feedback are appreciated.

About the Authors

Olaf Zimmermann is a long-time service orienteer with a PhD in architectural decision modeling. As consultant and professor of software architecture at the Institute for Software at Eastern Switzerland University of Applied Sciences, he focuses on agile architecting, application integration, cloud-nativity, domain-driven design, and service-oriented systems. In his previous life as a software architect at ABB and IBM, he had e-business and enterprise application development clients around the world and worked on systems and network management middleware earlier. Olaf is a Distinguished (Chief/Lead) IT Architect at The Open Group and co-edits the Insights column in *IEEE Software*. He is an author of *Perspectives on Web Services* and the first IBM Redbook on Eclipse. He blogs at ozimmer.ch and medium.com/olzzio.

Mirko Stocker is a programmer by heart who could not decide whether he liked frontend or backend development more, so he stayed in the middle and discovered that APIs hold many interesting challenges as well. He cofounded two startups in the legal tech sector, one of which he still chairs as managing director. This path has led him to become a professor of software engineering at the Eastern Switzerland University of Applied Sciences, where he researches and teaches in the areas of programming languages, software architecture, and Web engineering.

Daniel Lübke is an independent coding and consulting software architect with a focus on business process automation and digitization projects. His interests are software architecture, business process design, and system integration, which inherently require APIs to develop solutions. He received his PhD at the Leibniz Universität Hannover, Germany, in 2007 and has worked in many industry projects in different domains since then. Daniel is author and editor of several books, articles, and research papers; gives training; and regularly presents at conferences on topics of APIs and software architecture.

Uwe Zdun is a full professor of software architecture at the Faculty of Computer Science, University of Vienna. His work focuses on software design and architecture, empirical software engineering, distributed systems engineering (microservices, service-based, cloud, APIs, and blockchain-based systems), DevOps and continuous delivery, software patterns, software modeling, and model-driven development. Uwe has worked on many research and industry projects in these fields, and in addition to his scientific writing is co-author of the professional books *Remoting Patterns—Foundations of Enterprise, Internet, and Realtime Distributed Object Middleware, Process-Driven SOA—Proven Patterns for Business-IT Alignment,* and *Software-Architektur.*

Cesare Pautasso is a full professor at the Software Institute of the USI Faculty of Informatics, in Lugano, Switzerland, where he leads the Architecture, Design, and Web Information Systems Engineering research group. He chaired the 25th European Conference on Pattern Languages of Programs (EuroPLoP 2022). He was lucky to meet Olaf during a brief stint at the IBM Zurich Research Lab back in 2007, after receiving his PhD from ETH Zurich in 2004. He has co-authored *SOA with REST* (Prentice Hall, 2013) and, self-published the Beautiful APIs series, *RESTful Dictionary,* and *Just Send an Email: Anti-patterns for Email-centric Organizations* on LeanPub.

Part 1

Foundations and Narratives

The three chapters in Part 1 prepare you to make the best use of *Patterns for API Design*. Chapter 1, "Application Programming Interface (API) Fundamentals," introduces basic API concepts and motivates why remote APIs are important and rather hard to design well. This chapter sets the stage for the following ones.

Chapter 2, "Lakeside Mutual Case Study," introduces a fictitious case study from the insurance domain that supplies running examples for the book. The systems of Lakeside Mutual feature our patterns in action.

Chapter 3, "API Decision Narratives," gives an overview of the patterns in the form of decisions required. (The patterns are then covered in depth in Part 2.) Each decision answers an API design question; the patterns provide the solution alternatives (options). Examples of decision outcomes from the Lakeside Mutual case are given as well. The decision model presented in this chapter can help you organize your API design work and/or serve as a checklist in API design reviews.

Chapter 1

Application Programming Interface (API) Fundamentals

This chapter first establishes the context of remote APIs. Next, it motivates why APIs are so important today. It also calls out the main design challenges for APIs, including coupling and granularity concerns. Finally, it introduces an API domain model to establish the terminology and concepts used throughout the book.

From Local Interfaces to Remote APIs

Hardly any fully disconnected application exists today; even standalone applications typically offer some kind of external *interface*. A simple example is file export and import, often text based; even copy-paste capabilities leveraging the operating system clipboard can be seen as interfaces. Looking inside applications, every software component provides an interface as well [Szyperski 2002]. These interfaces describe which operations, properties, and events a component exposes, but they do not unveil component-internal data structures or implementation logic. To use a component, developers have to learn and understand the interface that it provides. A selected component might consume the services of other components; in such cases, it has an outbound dependency on one or more required interfaces.

Some interfaces are more exposed than others. For instance, middleware platforms and frameworks typically provide APIs. APIs with a platform character originally appeared in operating systems to separate the user application software from the operating system implementation; POSIX and the Win32 API are two examples of such platform APIs. These APIs have to be sufficiently general and expressive for developers to build different kinds of applications; they also should be stable over multiple operating system releases so that old applications continue working unchanged after operating system upgrades. Promoting the internal interface of an operating system component to become part of a published API imposes strong requirements on the quality of its documentation and tight constraints on the kind of changes it may undergo over time.

APIs not only can cross the boundaries of operating system processes but also can be exposed on the network. This allows applications running on different physical or virtual hardware nodes to communicate with each other. Enterprises have been using such *remote APIs* to integrate their applications for a long time [Hohpe 2003]. Nowadays, such APIs are commonly found at the boundary between the frontends of mobile apps or Web applications and the server-side backends of these applications, often deployed in cloud data centers.

Application frontends often work with shared data managed by their backends. Hence, the same API may support different kinds of API clients (for example, mobile apps and rich desktop clients) as well as multiple client instances running concurrently. Some APIs even open systems to external clients developed and operated by other organizations. This openness raises security concerns, for instance, regarding the application clients or end users that are allowed to access the API. It also has strategic implications. For example, data ownership and service levels have to be agreed upon.

Both local component interfaces and remote APIs connecting applications assume *shared knowledge*. Two or more parties require this knowledge to write interoperable software. Just like it is possible to plug cables into matching electrical sockets seamlessly, APIs are meant to enable the integration of compatible systems. The shared knowledge covers:

- Exposed operations and the computation or data manipulation services they provide.
- Representation and meaning of data exchanged when operations are invoked.
- Observable properties such as information about component state and valid state transitions.
- Handling of event notifications and error conditions such as component failure.

Remote APIs also have to define:

- Communication protocols to transfer messages across networks.
- Network endpoints, including location and other access information (addresses, security credentials).

- Policies regarding failures specific to distribution, including those caused by the underlying communication infrastructure (examples: timeouts, transport errors, network and server outages).

API contracts express the expectations of the interacting parties. Following basic information-hiding principles, the implementation is kept secret. Only a minimum amount of information on how to contact the API and how to consume its services is revealed. For example, the developer of a software engineering tool that integrates with GitHub is informed how to create and retrieve issues and which attributes (or fields) an issue contains. The GitHub API does not unveil the programming language, database technology, component structure, or database schema within the issue management application that serves the public API.

It is worth noting that not all systems and services feature APIs from the start; APIs may also disappear over time. For example, Twitter opened its Web API to third-party client developers to increase its popularity; soon, an entire client ecosystem emerged that attracted many users. To monetize its user-generated content, Twitter later closed down the API and acquired some client applications to continue maintaining them in-house. We can conclude that API *evolution* over time has to be managed.

A Bit of Distribution and Remoting History

Remote APIs come in many different forms. Over the last 50 years, many concepts and technologies to decompose applications into *distributed systems* appeared to let system parts communicate with each other:

- The transport and networking protocols TCP/IP along with their *socket API,* the backbone of the Internet, were developed in the 1970s. The same holds for file transfer protocols such as FTP and basic file input/output (from/to shared drives or mounted network file systems), arguably available in all programming languages past and present.

- *Remote Procedure Calls (RPCs),* such as the distributed computing environment (DCE), and object-oriented request brokers, such as CORBA and Java RMI, added abstraction and convenience layers in the 1980s and 1990s. Recently, newer variants of RPC, such as gRPC, became popular.

- *Queue-based, message-oriented application integration,* such as IBM MQSeries and Apache ActiveMQ, help to decouple communication parties in the time dimension. They are about as old as RPCs, with new implementations and flavors emerging since the 2000s. For instance, major cloud providers offer their own messaging services today. Cloud tenants can also deploy other messaging middleware to cloud infrastructures; RabbitMQ is a frequent choice in practice.

- Due to the popularity of the World Wide Web, *hypermedia-oriented protocols* such as HTTP have risen in the last two decades. To qualify as RESTful would require respecting all architectural constraints of the Representational State Transfer (REST) style. While not all HTTP APIs do so, HTTP seems to dominate the public application integration space at present.

- Data processing pipelines built over continuous *data streams,* such as those built with Apache Kafka, have their roots in classical UNIX pipes-and-filters architectures. They are particularly popular in data analytics scenarios (for example, analysis of Web traffic and online shopping behavior).

While TCP/IP, HTTP, and asynchronous queue-based messaging are as important and common as ever today, distributed objects went out of fashion again; some legacy systems still use them. File transfer via protocols or shared drives is very common still. Time will tell whether the currently available options are here to stay; new ones are likely to appear.

All remoting and integration technologies share a common goal—connecting distributed applications (or their parts) so that they can trigger remote processing or retrieve and manipulate remote data. Without APIs and API descriptions, these applications would not know how to connect and talk to remote partner systems or how to receive and process the replies from these systems.

Remote API: Access to Services via Protocol for Integration

We introduce the API terminology used throughout the book under "A Domain Model for Remote APIs" later in this chapter. But let us generalize the preceding observations into a single definition now.

API stands for *application programming interface* due to the roots of the term in program-internal decomposition (via local APIs). APIs have a dual nature—they connect and separate at the same time. In our remoting context, API could therefore just as well mean *access* to server-side resources such as data or software services via a communication *protocol* for application *integration.*

Figure 1.1 illustrates the remote messaging concepts that came our way so far.

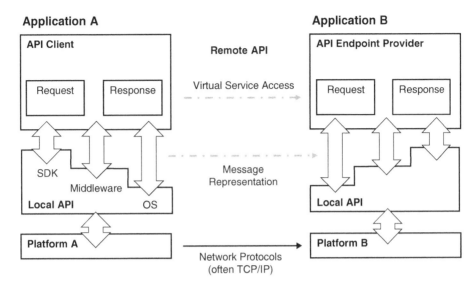

Figure 1.1 *Message-based integration and concepts in remote APIs (OS: operating system, SDK: software development kit)*

Remote APIs provide a virtual, abstract connection between the integrated application parts. Each remote API is realized by at least three other APIs: a local one both on the client side and on the provider side plus a remote interface on the next lower layer of the communication stack. The two local interfaces are provided by operating system, middleware, or programming language libraries and software development kits (SDKs); they are consumed by the applications on both the API client and the API provider sides. These local interfaces expose the networking/transport protocol services, such as HTTP over TCP/IP sockets, to application components, subsystems, or entire applications requiring integration.

To reach the common goal of interoperable communication, a shared understanding between the communication participants has to be established in an *API contract*. When defining API contracts, protocols and endpoints supporting them are one side of the coin; the exposed data is the other. Request and response *message representations* have to be structured somehow.[1] Even file import/exports or transfers require careful message design; the files contain these messages in that case. Clipboard-based integration has similar properties. The API contract describes the

---

1. It depends on the message exchange pattern in use whether a response message is present (our API domain model, introduced later in this chapter, covers this topic).

shared knowledge about message syntax, structure, and semantics that connects—but also separates—the two parties.

Our definition of remote API follows from these thoughts:

A remote API is a set of well-documented network endpoints that allow internal and external application components to provide services to each other. These services help achieve domain-specific goals, for instance, fully or partially automating business processes. They allow clients to activate provider-side processing logic or support data exchanges and event notifications.

This definition establishes the design space of our book. Note that our book is on remote APIs; hence, the term *API* refers to remote APIs from now on—unless we explicitly say that we mean a local API.

Designing APIs is highly challenging. Many decision drivers, also called *forces* or *quality attributes,* play vital roles in their design. "Decision Drivers in API Design," later in this chapter, discusses these desired qualities.

APIs Matter

Let us now visit some business domains and technology areas in which we find many APIs today.

Real-World APIs from A to Z

APIs today deal with advertising, banking, cloud computing, directories, entertainment, finance, government, health, insurance, jobs, logistics, messaging, news, open data, payments, QR codes, real estate, social media, travel, URL shortening, visualization, weather forecasting, and zip codes. On the Web, there are thousands of APIs providing access to reusable components delivered as a service. Following are examples from the previous domains:

- Create and manage ad campaigns. Obtain the status of keywords and ads. Generate keyword estimates. Generate reports about campaign performance.

- Open bank accounts with customer identity verification.

- Manage and deploy applications on virtual machines and track resource consumption.

- Identify a single person. Find their phone numbers, email addresses, locations, and demographics.

- Collect, discover, and share your favorite quotes.

- Retrieve information on forex (foreign exchange market), stocks, and commodities. Access real-time prices from the markets.

- Access public datasets such as air quality surveillance, parking facilities, electric and water consumption, COVID cases daily counts, and emergency service requests.

- Enable health and fitness data sharing while keeping the user's privacy and control.

- Return quotes to travel, home, and car insurance policies. Deliver instant insurance cover to customers.

- Integrate a job database with your software or Web site using methods for basic job searching, retrieving data for a specific job, and applying to a job.

- Aggregate information from multiple freight carriers, with freight class rating, shipping cost quotes, and shipment booking and tracking functions with the ability to arrange for pickup and delivery.

- Send text messages worldwide.

- Harness published content, including news, video, pictures, and multimedia articles.

- Access online payment solutions featuring invoice management, transaction processing, and account management.

- Provide access to home valuation services, property details (including historical sales prices, city and neighborhood market statistics), mortgage rates, and monthly payment estimates.

- Explore how claims spread across social media. A claim may be a fake news article, hoax, rumor, conspiracy theory, satire, or even an accurate report.

- Get webcams by categories, country, region, or just nearby your location. Get timelapse slideshows for every webcam. Add your own webcam.

- Provide programmatic access to current observations, forecasts, weather watches/warnings, and tropical cyclone advisories using the Digital Weather Markup Language (DWML).

In all these examples, API contracts define where and how to call the API, which data to send, and how received responses look. Some of these domains and services actually depend on APIs and would not exist without them. Let us now investigate some of these domains and services in more depth.

Mobile Apps and Cloud-Native Applications Consume and Provide Many APIs

The way software is built and made available to end users has changed dramatically since smartphones such as the iPhone and public clouds such as Amazon Web Services (AWS) appeared about 15 years ago. The availability of JavaScript in Web browsers and the XMLHttpRequest specification[2] also played their role in the paradigm shift toward rich clients such as single-page applications and smartphone apps.

The backends of applications serving mobile apps or other end-user frontend often are deployed to public or private clouds nowadays. Countless cloud services in different as-a-service (XaaS) models exist today that can be deployed, rented, scaled, and billed independently. This massive modularization and (possibly) regional distribution require APIs, both cloud-internal ones and APIs consumed by cloud tenants. As of 2021, AWS comprises more than 200 services, closely followed by Microsoft Azure and the Google Cloud.[3]

When cloud providers offer APIs to their tenants, applications deployed to clouds start to depend on these cloud APIs but also expose and consume application-level APIs themselves. Such application-level APIs may connect cloud-external application frontends to cloud-hosted application backends; they also may componentize the application backends so that these backends can benefit from cloud properties such as pay-per-use and elastic scaling and become true *cloud-native applications (CNAs)*. Figure 1.2 illustrates a typical CNA architecture.

From an architectural point of view, Isolated State, Distribution, Elasticity, Automation, and Loose Coupling (IDEAL) are desired properties of CNAs [Fehling 2014]. IDEAL is one of several sets of principles in the literature that characterize cloud applications. As a superset of IDEAL, the following seven traits summarize what enables CNAs to operate successfully and to exploit the benefits of cloud computing [Zimmermann 2021a]:

1. Fit for purpose

2. Rightsized and modular

3. Sovereign and tolerant

4. Resilient and protected

---

2. Known as *AJAX*, short for Asynchronous JavaScript and XML: https://developer.mozilla.org/en-US/docs/Web/Guide/AJAX. Note that JSON is preferred over XML these days, and the Fetch API is more powerful and flexible than the XMLHttpRequest object.

3. The exact numbers are difficult to pin down and depend on how services are distinguished from one another.

5. Controllable and adaptable

6. Workload-aware and resource-efficient

7. Agile and tool-supported

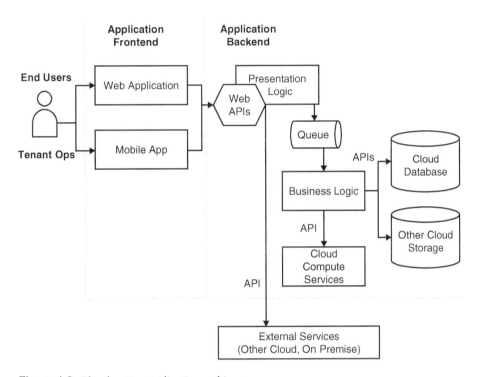

Figure 1.2 *Cloud-native application architecture*

Trait 2, rightsized and modular, directly calls for the introduction of APIs. Cloud application management (trait 5) also requires APIs, and DevOps tool chains (trait 7) benefit from them, too.

The cluster management software Kubernetes, for example, has become a popular choice for running applications and orchestrating the underlying computing resources both on premises and in the cloud. It addresses the problem of having to deploy many individual applications and services repeatedly. All these application services communicate with each other and with their clients through APIs. The Kubernetes platform itself also exposes management APIs [Kubernetes 2022] as well as command-line interfaces. Its operator concept, exposed via API and an SDK on top of it, promotes extensibility. Application APIs can even be managed with Kubernetes.

As another example, software-as-a-service providers typically not only provide customizable, multitenant end-user applications but also open up their application functionality to third parties via HTTP. An example is Salesforce, offering data access and integration in HTTP APIs. At the time of writing, 28 APIs were available, covering rather diverse domains such as marketing, business-to-consumer commerce, and customer data management.

Microservices Communicate via APIs

It has been hard to escape the term *microservices* in recent years. Much has been said about this rather advanced approach to system decomposition since James Lewis and Martin Fowler's early online article in April 2014 [Lewis 2014]. They emerged as service-oriented architectures (SOAs) entered the age of continuous software delivery and cloud computing. Beyond the hype, microservices are positioned as a substyle or implementation approach to SOA, emphasizing independent deployability, scalability, and changeability of services—as well as themes such as decentralized, autonomous decision making and container orchestration [Pautasso 2017a].

Each microservice has a single responsibility; this responsibility should represent a domain-specific business capability. Microservices are often deployed in lightweight virtualization containers (such as Kubernetes and Docker), encapsulate their own state, and communicate via remote APIs (often using HTTP but also other protocols). These service APIs help to ensure a loose coupling with each other and therefore their ability to evolve or be replaced without affecting the rest of the architecture [Zimmermann 2017].

Microservices facilitate software reuse thanks to their limited scope focusing on the implementation of individual business capabilities. They support agile software development practices with continuous delivery. For example, each microservice is typically owned by a single team, allowing this team to independently develop, deploy, and operate its microservices. Microservices are also well suited for implementing IDEAL CNAs (discussed earlier). When deployed independently, horizontal on-demand scalability can be achieved through container virtualization and elastic load balancing. By keeping an existing service API unchanged, they allow an incremental migration of monolithic applications, which reduces the risk of failure of software modernization efforts.

Microservices also bring new challenges. Their distributed, loosely coupled nature requires carefully designed APIs and comprehensive systems management. The communication overhead within a distributed architecture combined with poor API design choices can impact the performance of microservice architectures.

Data consistency and state management challenges are introduced, for example, when decoupling monolithic, stateful applications into independent, autonomous microservices [Furda 2018]; single points of failure or cascading failure proliferation effects have to be avoided. Autonomy and consistency for the whole microservice architecture cannot be guaranteed at the same time when employing a traditional backup and disaster recovery strategy [Pardon 2018]. Scaling the architecture to include a large number of microservices requires a disciplined approach to their life cycle management, monitoring, and debugging.

Some of these challenges can be overcome with adequate infrastructures. For example, load balancers introduce (managed) redundancy and circuit breakers [Nygard 2018a] reduce the risk that failing downstream microservice instances bring down upstream ones (and, eventually, the entire system). The service APIs still have to be rightsized and evolved properly over time.

In this book, we are not concerned with microservices infrastructures but with service rightsizing on the API level (in terms of endpoint granularity and operation/data coupling). However, infrastructure design is eased when API services have adequate sizes; so indirectly, we are also concerned about infrastructure design.

APIs Are Products and May Form Ecosystems

A software *product* is a physical or virtual asset that can be purchased (or licensed). Paying customers have certain expectations regarding longevity, quality, and usability of their acquisitions. We already saw examples of APIs that are products in their own right; others come with software products (for instance, to load these products with master data or configure and tailor them for a particular user group). Even APIs that do not have their own business model or any ambitions to contribute to a business strategy directly should be "treated as products" [Thoughtworks 2017]. They are supposed to have a dedicated businessowner, a governance structure, a support system, and a roadmap.

As an example, a data lake powered by deep-learning algorithms requires data, which has to come from somewhere. If data is the new oil in the digital era, message channels and event streams form the pipelines, with middleware/tools/applications being the refineries. APIs then are valves located between the pipelines, producers, and consumers in this metaphor. The data lake can be a marketed product exposing APIs but also a company-internal asset that is managed just like a marketed product.

A software *ecosystem* "is the interaction of a set of actors on top of a common technological platform that results in a number of software solutions or services." [Manikas 2013]. They consist of organically growing, independent yet related parts and players. They either are fully decentralized or center on a market maker.

Open-source marketplaces such as the Cloud Foundry Ecosystem qualify as software ecosystems; another form are *resale software ecosystems* such as the App Store from Apple. APIs play a key role to success for both types, allowing applications to join or leave the ecosystem, to let members communicate and collaborate, to analyze the health of the ecosystem, and so forth [Evans 2016].

Let's take a travel management ecosystem as an example. One API is required for onboarding (loading an ecosystem member such as a tenant of rooms or a transportation provider, that is). Another one might support the development of travel planning, reporting, and analysis apps (featuring destination rankings, accommodation reviews, and so on). These ecosystem parts communicate via APIs—with each other but also with the market/ecosystem maker when train trips and flights are booked or hotel rooms are reserved.

Ecosystem success depends on getting the API design and evolution right. The more complex and dynamic a software ecosystem is, the more challenging becomes the design of its APIs. Multiple messages travel between the actors, whose relationships are described in the API contracts; the messages form longer-running conversations. The members of the ecosystem have to agree on formats, protocols, conversation patterns, and so forth.

Wrap Up

All examples, scenarios, and domains we have visited in this section contain and depend on remote APIs and their contracts, and there are more. If you are up for a round of buzzword bingo: APIs are an *enabling technology* for most (if not all) major trends in recent years—not only mobile/Web and cloud, as mentioned earlier, but also artificial intelligence and machine learning, the Internet of Things, smart cities, and smart grids. Even quantum computing in the cloud relies on APIs; see, for example, the Quantum Engine API provided by Google Quantum AI.[4]

Decision Drivers in API Design

The rather unique connect-and-separate role of APIs in an architecture such as that shown in Figure 1.1 leads to many challenging, sometimes conflicting design concerns. For instance, a balance has to be found between exposing data (so that clients can make good use of it) and hiding their implementation details (so that they can be changed as the API evolves). The data representations exposed by APIs not only must meet the information and processing needs of their clients but also be designed and

---

4. Bingo!

documented in an understandable, maintainable way. Backward compatibility and interoperability are important qualities.

In this section, we introduce particularly important drivers that we will keep coming back to throughout the book. Let's start with critical success factors.

What Makes an API Successful?

Success is a relative and somewhat subjective measure. One position on API success might be

> Only an API designed and launched years ago, daily serving requests of billions of paying clients with minimal latency and zero downtime, qualifies as a successful one.

An opposing position could be

> A newly launched API, finally receiving and responding to the first request of an external client built entirely on the basis of its documentation with no help or interaction from the original implementation team, can be considered a success already.

If the API is used in a commercial setting, the success of an API can be assessed according to *business value* focusing on the economic sustainability of the service operating costs versus the revenues generated directly or indirectly from each API client. Different business models are possible, ranging from freely accessible APIs, funded by advertisers interested in mining the data willingly (or not willingly?) provided by users of the applications built on top of the API, to subscription-based APIs and pay-per-use APIs offered under different pricing plans. For example, Google Maps used to be a standalone Web application. The Google Maps API appeared only after users started to reverse engineer how to embed map visualizations in their own Web sites. Here, an initially closed architecture opened up following user demand. The initially freely accessible API was later turned into a lucrative pay-per-use service. OpenStreetMap, the open-source alternative to Google Maps, also provides several APIs.

A second success factor is *visibility*. The best API design will fail if its prospective clients do not know it exists. Public APIs, for instance, may be *discovered* via links to provided APIs in company products and product documentation or by advertising their existence within developer communities. Moreover, API directories such as ProgrammableWeb and APIs.guru exist. Either way, investments for making the API known should pay off eventually.

Time to market for APIs can be measured in terms of how long it takes to deploy new features or bug fixes to an API as well as in terms of how long it takes to develop a fully functional client for the API. The *time to first call* is a good indicator of the quality of the API documentation and the onboarding experience of client developers. To keep this measure low, the learning effort should be low, too. Another metric might be the *time to first level n ticket*—hopefully, it takes a long time for an API client developer to find a bug that requires level 1, 2, or 3 support to resolve.

Another success measure is the API *lifetime*. APIs may outlive their original designers. A successful API usually survives because it keeps attracting clients by adapting to their changing needs over time. However, a stable API that does not change for a long time can still be in active use by clients—including those not having an alternative, such as when fulfilling regulatory compliance requirements via stand-ardized, slow-moving e-government APIs.

In summary, APIs enable *rapid integration* of systems and their parts in the short term and have to support the autonomy and *independent evolution* of these systems in the long term. The goal of rapid integration is to decrease the cost of bringing two systems together; independent evolution has to prevent systems from becoming so entangled and coupled that they can no longer be separated (or replaced). These objectives conflict with each other to some extent—which will keep us busy through-out the book.

How Do API Designs Differ?

The design of APIs impacts all of software design and architecture. Under "From Local Interfaces to Remote APIs," we discussed that APIs rely on assumptions that independently developed and operated clients and service providers make about each other. Their success requires the involved parties to reach agreements and keep up with their end of the bargain for a long time. These assumptions and agreements concern issues and trade-offs such as the following:

- **One general versus many specific/specialized endpoints:** Should all clients use the same interface, or should some or all of them be provided with their own API? Which of these options makes the API easier to use—for instance, is a general-purpose API more reusable but also more difficult to apply in specific cases?

- **Fine- versus coarse-grained endpoint and operation scope:** How is balance found between breadth and depth of API functionality? Should the API match, aggregate, or split the underlying system functionality?

- **Few operations carrying much data back and forth versus many chatty interactions carrying little data:** Should request and response messages be elaborate or narrowly focused in their data content? Which of these two alter-natives leads to better understandability, performance, scalability, bandwidth consumption, and evolvability?

- **Data currentness versus correctness:** Is it better to share stale data than to share none at all? How should natural conflicts between reliable data consistency (within the API provider) and fast response times (as perceived by the API client) be resolved? Should state changes be reported via polling or pushed by event notifications or streaming? Should commands and queries be separated?

- **Stable contracts versus fast changing ones:** How are APIs kept compatible without sacrificing their extensibility? How are backward-compatible changes introduced in rich, long-lived APIs?

These questions, options, and criteria challenge API designers; different choices are made in different requirements contexts. Our patterns discuss possible answers and their consequences.

What Makes API Design Challenging?

Just as the design of an end-user interface will result in a pleasant or cumbersome human user experience, an API design will affect the *developer experience (DX)*— first and foremost, of client-side developers learning how to use the API to build distributed applications, but also of developers working on the provider-side API implementation. Once the API is initially released and runs in production, its design has a major impact on the performance, scalability, reliability, security, and manageability of the resulting integrated system. Conflicting stakeholder concerns must be balanced; DX extends into operator and maintainer experience.

The goals and requirements of API providers and clients may overlap but also conflict; a win-win model is not always achievable. Here are some nontechnical reasons why API design can be hard:

- **Client diversity:** The wants and needs of API clients differ from one client to another, and they keep changing. API providers have to decide whether they want to offer good-enough compromises in a single, unified API or try to satisfy specific, diverging client requirements individually.

- **Market dynamics:** Competing API providers trying to catch up on each other's innovations may cause more change and possibly incompatible evolution strategies than clients are able or willing to accept. Furthermore, clients look for standardized APIs as a means of preserving their independence from specific providers, while some providers may be tempted to lock clients in by offering enticing extensions. Wouldn't it be nice if Google Maps and OpenStreetMap APIs implemented the same set of APIs? Client and provider developers might answer this question differently.

- **Distribution fallacies:** Remote APIs are accessed through sometimes unreliable networks. What can go wrong will eventually go wrong. For example, even if a service is up and running, clients may be temporarily unable to reach it. This makes it particularly challenging to deliver access to an API with high quality-of-service (QoS) guarantees, for instance, concerning API availability and response times.

- **Illusion of control:** Any data exposed in an API can be used by the clients, sometimes in unexpected ways. Publishing an API means giving up some control and thus opening up a system to the pressure of external and sometimes unknown clients. The decision as to which internal system parts and data sources should become accessible via the API must be made carefully. Once lost, control is hard if not impossible to regain.

- **Evolution pitfalls:** While microservices are meant to enable frequent changes, for instance, in the context of DevOps practices such as continuous delivery, there is only one chance to get the design of an API right in the first place. When an API has been released and is successful with more and more clients depending on it, it will become increasingly expensive to apply corrections and improvements and impossible to remove features without breaking some clients. Still, APIs do evolve over time. Changing them requires resolving the tension between the need for design stability and the need for flexibility by adopting adequate versioning practices. Sometimes, the provider has enough market power to dictate the evolution strategies and rhythm; sometimes, the client community is the stronger end of the API usage relation.

- **Design mismatches:** What backend systems can do (in terms of functional scope and quality) and how they are structured (in terms of endpoint and data definitions) might be different from what clients expect. These differences have to be overcome by introducing some form of adapters that translate between mismatching parts. Sometimes, the backend systems have to be refactored or reengineered to be able to meet external client needs.

- **Technology shifts and drifts:** User interface technology keeps advancing, for example, from keyboard and mouse to touchscreen to voice recognition to motion sensors in virtual and augmented reality (and onward). These advances require rethinking how users interact with applications. API technology keeps changing as well—new data representation formats, improved communication protocols, and changes in the middleware and tools landscape all require continuously investing in keeping integration logic and communication infrastructure up to date.[5]

---

5. How many XML developers and tools are still out there?

In summary, API design can make or break software projects, products, and ecosystems. An API is not just a mere implementation artifact but an integration asset; APIs have to be architected well due to their dual connector-separator role and typically long lifetime. While technologies come and go, many of the underlying design problems for integration designers and solutions to them stay the same.

Related architecturally significant requirements, covered next, change somewhat, but a common set has stayed relevant for a long time.

Architecturally Significant Requirements

Quality goals for APIs come in three forms: *developmental, operational,* and *managerial.* An initial collection follows; more details on these goals are covered in later chapters.

- **Understandability:** One important developmental concern in API design is the structure of the representation elements in request and response messages. To ensure understandability and avoid unnecessary complexity, it is often advisable to follow the domain model closely both in the API implementation code and in the API. Note that "following" does not imply full exposure or exact copies here; hiding as much information as possible is in order.

- **Information sharing versus hiding:** APIs specify what clients can expect while abstracting how such expectations are met by the provider. It takes effort to separate the specification from the realization of a software component. While a quick solution to design the API may be to simply expose what is already there, such leaks of implementation details into the interface severely constrain how the implementation can change without affecting clients later on.

- **Amount of coupling:** *Loose coupling* is an internal quality of the structural design of a distributed system and its components; as an architectural principle, it can be seen to reside halfway between a requirement (problem) and a design element (solution). Loose coupling of communication parties has different dimensions: (a) reference autonomy dealing with naming and addressing conventions, (b) platform autonomy hiding technology choices, (c) time autonomy when supporting synchronous or asynchronous communication, and (d) format autonomy dealing with data contract design [Fehling 2014]. An API call, by definition, couples client and provider; however, the looser the coupling, the easier it is to evolve client and provider independently of each other. One reason is that the knowledge that must be shared by provider and consumer has an impact on changeability; rightsizing the exposed data structures, for instance, brings a certain amount of format autonomy. Moreover, two APIs from the same provider should not be coupled unnecessarily, for example, via hidden dependencies.

- **Modifiability:** Modifiability is an important sub-concern of supportability and maintainability. In the context of API design and evolution, it includes backward compatibility to promote parallel development and deployment flexibility.

- **Performance and scalability:** *Latency* from an API client point of view, influenced by network behavior such as bandwidth and low-level latency, and endpoint processing effort including marshalling and unmarshalling of the payload are important operational concerns. *Throughput* and *scalability* primarily are API provider concerns, meaning that response times do not degrade even if provider-side load grows because more clients use an API or because existing clients cause more load.

- **Data parsimony (or *Datensparsamkeit*):** This is an important general design principle in distributed systems that are performance- and security-critical. However, this principle is not always applied when iteratively and incrementally defining an API by specifying its request and response messages—it is typically easier to add things (in this case, information items or attributes of value objects) than to remove them.[6] Hence, the overall cognitive load and processing effort keep increasing during API design and evolution.

  Once something is added to an API, it is often hard to determine whether it can be safely removed, as many (maybe even unknown) clients might depend on it. Consequently, the API contracts exposed by an API might contain many possibly complex data elements (such as attributes of customer or product master data); and very likely, this complexity grows as the software evolves. Variability management and "option control" are required.

- **Security and privacy:** Security and privacy often are important considerations when designing an API, including access control as well as confidentiality and integrity of sensitive information. For instance, an API might require security and privacy to avoid exposing confidential elements from the backend services. To support observability and auditability, API traffic and runtime behavior should be monitored.

---

6. Think of business processes and corresponding forms to be filled out and approvals required in large enterprises: typically, many activities and data fields are added with good intentions, but these additions hardly ever replace existing ones.

To satisfy these sometimes conflicting (and ever-changing) requirements, architectural decisions choose between certain known or new options, with the requirements being among decision drivers (or criteria). Trade-offs exist and/or must be found/resolved; our patterns pick the requirements up as design forces and discuss trade-off resolution.

Developer Experience

The DX metaphor and analogy to user experience (UX) has become quite popular in recent years. According to Albert Cavalcante's blog post "What Is DX?" [Cavalcante 2019], the four pillars of a pleasant DX, combining input from UX with software design principles, are

DX = *function, stability, ease of use, and clarity.*

DX pertains to all things developers work with—tools, libraries and frameworks, documentation, and so on. The *function* pillar of DX states that the processing and/or data management features exposed by some software have a high priority simply because they are the reason that the client developer is interested in the API at hand; API features should meet goals of clients. *Stability* refers to satisfying the desired and agreed-upon runtime qualities such as performance, reliability, and availability. *Ease of use* (of software, for developers) can be achieved with documentation (tutorials, examples, reference material), community knowledge fora, as well as tool features (and other ways). The *clarity* pillar is about simplicity but also observability; the consequences of certain actions such as hitting a button in a tool, invoking a command-line interface (or command offered by an SDK), or generating code should always be clear. If things go wrong, client developers want to know why (invalid input or provider-side problem?) and what they can do about the problem (retry call later? correct the input?).

In this context, it is good to be reminded that we design APIs not for ourselves but for our clients and their software. That said, machine-to-machine communication is fundamentally different from human-computer interaction—simply because humans and computers work and behave differently. Programs might think (sort of) but do not feel and have no awareness of themselves and their environment.[7] Hence, some but not all UX advice applies to DX straightaway.

---

7. We might be able to train them in some constrained domains such as image recognition, but we cannot expect them to build a value system and behave morally/ethically as humans (hopefully) do.

While DX receives a lot of attention (rightfully) and can be seen to include maintainer experience and consultant/educator/learner experience, do we hear and know enough about the operator experience?

In conclusion, API success indeed has at least two facets, short-term positivity and long-term use:

First impressions last. The easier and clearer it is to successfully place the first call to an API, and to do something meaningful with the responses, the more client developers will use the API—and enjoy the experience (with regards to function, stability, ease of use, and clarity). Runtime qualities such as performance, reliability, and manageability decide whether a positive initial developer experience causes API usage to sustain.

The next and final section in this chapter introduces the API domain model that serves as our book vocabulary and glossary.

A Domain Model for Remote APIs

This book and its pattern language use a set of basic abstractions and concepts that form a *domain model* [Zimmermann 2021b] for API design and development. While we introduce all building blocks of our patterns in this domain model, we do not aim at painting a unified picture of all communication concepts and integration architectures that exist. The relation of the domain model elements to concepts in HTTP and other remoting technologies is explained though.

Communication Participants

At an abstract level, two kinds of *communication participants* (participants, for short) communicate via an *API*, the *API provider,* and the *API client*. An API client may use (or consume) any number of *API endpoints*. The communication is governed by the *API contract,* which is exposed by the API provider and consumed by its clients. This API contract contains information about the available endpoints that offer the functionality specified by the contract. Figure 1.3 visualizes these basic concepts and relations.

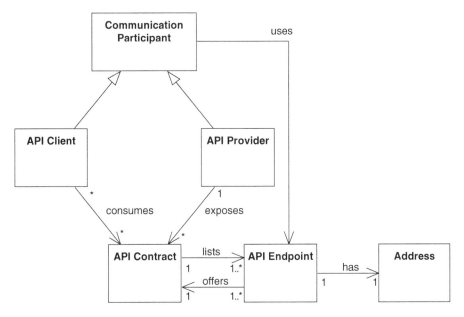

Figure 1.3 *Domain model for API design and evolution: Communication participants, API contract, API endpoint*

Note that the API as a whole is not shown in the figure; an API is a collection of endpoints with the contracts offered by them. An API endpoint represents the provider-side end of a communication channel; an API contains at least one such endpoint. Each API endpoint has a unique *address* such as a Uniform Resource Locator (URL), commonly used on the World Wide Web, RESTful HTTP, and HTTP-based SOAP. In the client role, a communication participant accesses an API via such an endpoint. A communication participant may play both the client role and the provider role. In that case, a communication participant offers certain services as an API provider but also consumes services offered by other APIs in its implementation.[8]

In service-oriented architecture terminology, the term *service consumer* is a synonym for API client; the API provider is called *service provider* [Zimmermann 2009]. In HTTP, an API endpoint corresponds to a set of related resources. A *home resource* with a prepublished URI is an entry-level URL to locate and access one or more related resources.

---

8. The client-side of a communication channel also requires a network endpoint, which is not depicted here due to our focus on APIs rather than communication channels or networking.

Endpoints Offer Contracts Describing Operations

As shown in Figure 1.4, an API contract describes *operations*. In addition to the endpoint address, an operation identifier distinguishes operations. For instance, the top-level XML tag in the body of a SOAP message has this duty. In RESTful HTTP, the name of the HTTP method (also called the *verb*) is unique within a single resource.[9]

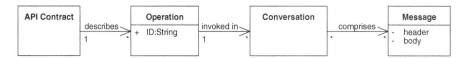

Figure 1.4 *Domain model: Operations, conversations, messages*

Messages as Conversation Building Blocks

The operations of an API, described by its contract and offered by its endpoints, can participate in *conversations*. Conversations differ in the way they combine and compose messages. Each conversation describes a sequence of messages exchanged between the involved communication participants. Figure 1.5 shows four main types of conversations. A *request-reply* message exchange consists of a single *request message* followed by a single *response message*. If there is no response, the conversation has a *one-way exchange* nature. A third form of conversation is an *event notification,* which features a single message containing the triggered event. Finally, a conversation can be long running; an initial single request is then followed by *multiple replies*. In this request–multiple replies case, one message, sent from the client to the provider, registers a callback, and one or more messages, sent from provider to client, perform the callback action.

Three types of messages are command message, document message, and event message [Hohpe 2003]. These three types match the conversation types naturally; document messages, for instance, can be transferred in a one-way exchange; command messages require request-reply conversations if the client cares about the command execution outcome. Messages can be delivered in multiple over-the-wire formats such as JSON or XML. In this book, we are primarily interested in the content and structure of these messages (of all three types).

---

9. In OpenAPI specifications, operations are identified by the HTTP method and its URI path; there also is an additional property, operationId [OpenAPI 2022].

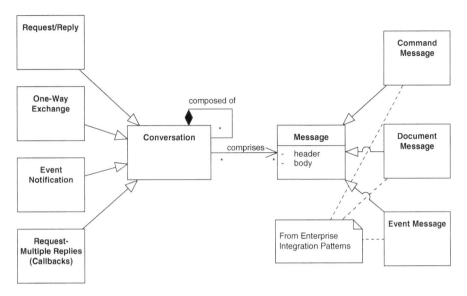

Figure 1.5 *Domain model: Conversation types and message types*

Many other kinds of conversations exist, including more complex ones like *publish-subscribe* mechanisms. Basic conversations can be composed into larger end-to-end conversations scenarios involving message exchanges between multiple API clients and providers up to managed *business processes* that run for days, months, or years. [Pautasso 2016; Hohpe 2017]. Such advanced conversations can commonly be found in software ecosystems, enterprise applications, and other API usage scenarios, but they are not our main focus in this book.

Message Structure and Representation

Figure 1.6 illustrates that one or more *representation elements,* also known as *parameters,* constitute the *representation* of a message sent over the wire (note that some technologies use the term operation *signature* to refer to parameters and their types). Messages carry data and metadata, which can be found in the message *header* and its *body.* The representation elements in addresses, headers, and body may or may not be ordered and further structured into hierarchies; they often are named and can be typed statically or dynamically. Messages may carry the address they are coming from (for instance, in order to enable sending a reply back to that address) and/or the addresses they are sent to. For instance, concepts such as return address and correlation identifier allow the message to participate in content-based message routing and complex, long-running conversations [Hohpe 2003]. In HTTP resource APIs, hypermedia controls (links) contain such address information. If addresses do not appear in a message, the communication channel solely takes care of the message routing.

We also call the message representations *data transfer representation (DTR)*. Such DTR should not make any assumption about client- and server-side programming paradigms (such as object-oriented, imperative, or functional programming); the client-server interactions are plain messages (for instance, they do not contain any remote object stubs or handlers).[10] The process of converting a programming language representation into a DTR that can be sent over the wire is called *serialization* (also known as marshalling); the opposite operation is called *deserialization* (or unmarshalling). These terms are commonly used in distributed computing technologies and middleware platforms [Voelter 2004]. Plain text as well as binary formats are often used to send and receive DTRs; as already mentioned, JSON and XML are common choices.

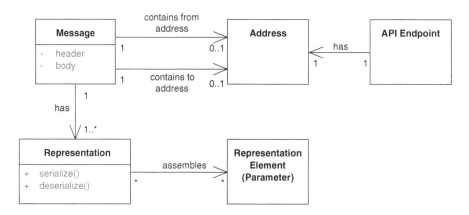

Figure 1.6 *Domain model: Message details*

API Contract

Figure 1.7 shows that all endpoint operations are specified in the API contract (which we introduced in Figure 1.3). Such a contract may detail all possible conversations and messages down to the protocol-level message representations (parameters, bodies) and network addresses. API contracts are necessary to realize any interoperable, testable, and evolvable runtime communication because API clients and API providers must agree on the shared knowledge specified in the contract in order to be able to communicate.

---

10. A DTR can be seen as a wire-level equivalent of a program-level pattern *data transfer object (DTO)* [Fowler 2002; Daigneau 2011].

In reality, this agreement can be highly asymmetrical because many APIs (especially public APIs) are offered as-is by the API provider. API clients can use it under those conditions or not at all; no negotiation or formal agreement on a contract between the participants takes place in such cases. This might be different if the API client pays for the service. In that case, the API contract might be the result of an actual negotiation and be accompanied by (or even part of) a legal contract. An API contract can either be documented minimally or be part of a more comprehensive API Description and/or Service Level Agreement (two of our patterns).

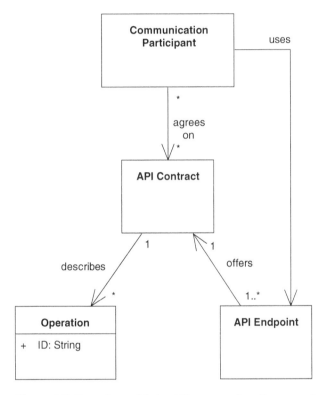

Figure 1.7 *Domain model: An API contract describes operations (that are invoked in conversations comprising messages)*

Domain Model Usage throughout the Book

The abstract concepts in the domain model form a vocabulary for the pattern language introduced in this book, as the pattern texts have to remain platform- and technology-independent by definition (except for their illustrative examples). Moreover, each concept and relationship in the domain model can potentially serve as a driver for a decision for or against a pattern. For instance, the parameter structure of each occurrence of a message has to be decided. Chapter 3, "API Decision Narratives," picks up these thoughts and guides us through the decision making about all domain model elements and patterns.

Finally, the Microservices Domain-Specific Language (MDSL) that we use to model some examples is designed according to this domain model. See Appendix C, "Microservice Domain-Specific Language (MDSL)," for reference information.

Summary

In this chapter, we discussed the following:

- What APIs are and why they are important—and challenging—to design well.

- Desired qualities in API design, including coupling and granularity considerations and elements of a positive developer experience (DX).

- The API domain terminology and concepts we use in this book.

APIs, both local APIs inside modular programs and remote APIs connecting operating system processes and distributed systems, have been around for a long time. Message-based protocols such as RESTful HTTP, gRPC, and GraphQL dominate the remote API realm at present. Remote APIs provide the means to access server-side resources via protocols for application integration. They play the role of an important intermediary, which connects multiple systems while keeping them as separate as possible to minimize the impact of future changes. An API and its implementations may even remain under separate control and ownership. Any API, whether local or remote, should address an actual client information or integration need and be *purposeful*.

A real-world metaphor would be to see the API as an *entrance door and hall* of a building, for instance, the lobby welcoming visitors to a skyscraper, routing them to the right elevator but also checking whether they are allowed to enter through the main door. First impressions last when entering a place for the first time—in real life between humans, when humans use software, or when API clients use APIs. An API portal, then, serves as a set of "business cards" (or building map) of the application behind the API, introducing services to developers potentially interested in using them to build their own applications. Both business cards and entrance hall influence the visitor experience (in this case, DX).

Getting local APIs right is one thing. For remote APIs, the fallacies of distributed computing come into play. Networks cannot be assumed to be reliable, for example, when end-user interfaces such as browser-based single-page applications as well as the backend services within distributed cloud applications require remote APIs to communicate with each other.

During the architectural decision making, a number of quality attributes have to be taken into account. The developmental qualities for APIs range from a pleasant client-side DX, affordable cost, and sufficient performance to sustainable and change-friendly operations and maintenance on the provider-side. Across the entire API life cycle, three types of quality attributes are particularly relevant:

1. *Development qualities:* APIs should be straightforward to discover, learn, and understand by developers and easily consumable to build applications. This is collectively referred to as providing a positive DX, defined via the four pillars function, stability, ease of use, and clarity.

2. *Operational qualities:* APIs and their implementations should be dependable and meet the performance, reliability, and security requirements that have been stated for them. They should be manageable at runtime.

3. *Managerial qualities:* APIs should be evolvable and maintainable over time, preferably being both extensible and backward compatible, so that changes are possible but do not break existing clients. Agility and stability have to be balanced here.

Why is it hard (and interesting) to get API design and evolution right?

- APIs are supposed to live long; API success has a short-term and a long-term perspective.

- APIs require different and diverse parties to reach agreements regarding exposed functionality and related qualities.

- The granularity of APIs is determined by the number of endpoints and operations exposed as well as by the data contracts of the request and response messages of these operations. An important decision point concerns choosing between a few rich operations and many narrow ones.

- Coupling control is required. Zero coupling means being disconnected; the more API client and API provider (have to) know about each other, the tighter they are coupled, and the harder it becomes to evolve them independently.

- While API technologies come and go, the fundamental concepts of API design and the related architectural decisions with their options and criteria stay.

Our focus in this book is on remote APIs connecting systems and their parts. API providers expose API endpoints, which have operations; operations are called via message exchanges. The messages in these exchanges form conversations; they contain flat or structured message representation elements. We defined these concepts in a domain model for API design and evolution. Bringing these concepts to life so that the resulting APIs meet the wants and needs of their clients with certain qualities is our task at hand.

What's up next? Chapter 2, "Lakeside Mutual Case Study," introduces a larger, fictitious yet realistic example of an API and service design. Chapter 3 picks up the design challenges and requirements from this section in the form of decision drivers. The forces and their resolution in the patterns in Part 2, the pattern reference, also elaborate on these success factors and quality properties.

Chapter 2

Lakeside Mutual Case Study

This chapter introduces the Lakeside Mutual case study that serves as our example scenario running through the book. To motivate the need for APIs in this scenario and to be able to justify API design decisions in later chapters, sample systems and the requirements they face are presented, along with an initial API design serving as an outline and preview.

Lakeside Mutual is a fictitious insurance company that provides several digital services to its customers, partners, and employees. Its company backend consists of several enterprise applications for customer, policy, and risk management; the application frontends serve multiple channels from smartphone apps for prospective and insured clients to rich client applications for company staff members and third-party sales agents.

Business Context and Requirements

One of the agile development teams in corporate IT of Lakeside Mutual has just been tasked with extending a customer application with a self-service capability. An early architectural spike has unveiled that the required customer and policy data are scattered across several backend systems. None of these systems offer suitable Web APIs or message channels that provide the required data.

The following analysis and design artifacts have already been created by the development team:

- User stories accompanied by desired system quality attributes and an analysis-level domain model

- A system context diagram/context map sketching available and required interfaces

- An architecture overview diagram showing the existing system parts and their relationships

Let us inspect these artifacts now. They provide valuable input to the API design.

User Stories and Desired Qualities

The next version of the customer application is supposed to support several new self-service features, one of which has been captured in the following user story:

> As a customer of Lakeside Mutual, I want to update my contact information myself online so that the data is current. I do not want to have to call an agent for that, which may involve long waiting times.

Requirements regarding desired system qualities (for example, performance, availability, and maintainability) have been gathered. The user story about contact information update should not take longer than two seconds in 80 percent of the executions. Lakeside Mutual expects 10,000 customers to use the new online service, 10 percent of which work with the system concurrently.

Usability is another significant concern. If the new self-service capability does not help clients achieve their self-service goals effectively, they might revert to more costly channels, defeating the whole purpose of the new capability. The same, although to a lesser degree, applies to reliability requirements. The interface should be available during extended office hours and on weekends and holidays when the clients of Lakeside Mutual might have time to take care of their insurance contracts.

Given these requirements, any chosen architecture and frameworks should support the development and operations teams at Lakeside Mutual effectively and efficiently. They should be able to monitor and manage the application and maintain it over time.

Analysis-Level Domain Model

Customers and their insurance policies constitute the core of the system (master data management). With the new self-service frontend, customers will not only be able to update their contact information, but will also be able to request quotations for different insurance policies, all without having to go to a branch office or schedule a home visit. The enterprise applications use domain-driven design (DDD) [Evans 2003; Vernon 2013] to structure their domain (business) logic. Figure 2.1 shows the three main aggregates Customer, InsuranceQuoteRequest, and Policy.[1]

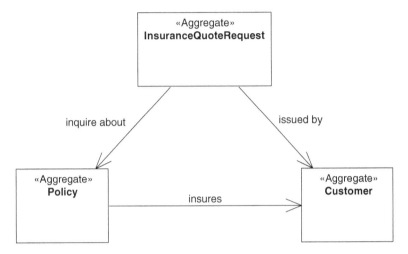

Figure 2.1 *Aggregate overview*

We now zoom into these three aggregates to explore additional DDD concepts. Insurance quote requests come from existing or prospective customers. They inquire about offers for new insurance policies (such as health care or car insurance). Offers and policies know about the customers who (will) pay for them and who may issue claims in the future.

Figure 2.2 shows the components of the InsuranceQuoteRequest aggregate, which is an example of short-lived operational data. It comprises several entities with an identity and life cycle and immutable value objects. An entity with a unique role is the InsuranceQuoteRequest aggregate root. It serves as an entry point into the aggregate and holds the components of the aggregate together. We can also see some outgoing references to other aggregates, pointing at the respective aggregate root entities. For example, an InsuranceQuoteRequest references a customer's existing policies that the customer now wishes to change. The request also includes CustomerInfo, which refers to one or more addresses, because a policy might pertain to several persons (and persons might have multiple residences too). For example, health insurance for children can be part of a parent's policy.

---

1. Aggregates are clusters of domain objects loaded and stored together, enforcing the related business rules.

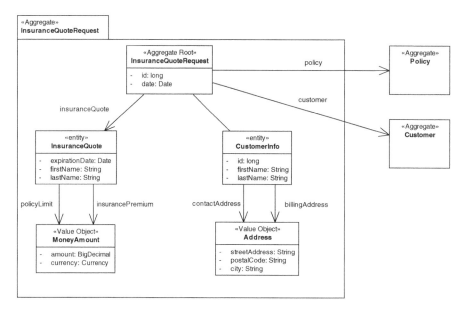

Figure 2.2 *Details of the InsuranceQuoteRequest aggregate*

Details of the Policy aggregate are shown in Figure 2.3. A policy deals primarily with value objects such as MoneyAmounts, types of policies, and date periods. Each policy also has an identifier (PolicyId) used to reference the aggregate from the outside. On the right, we can see the reference to the Customer aggregate.

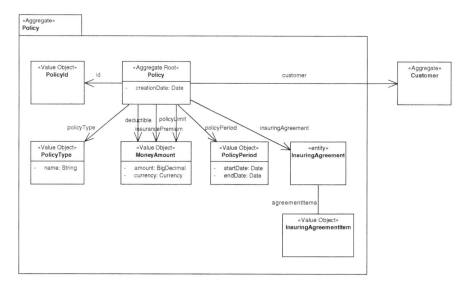

Figure 2.3 *Details of the Policy aggregate*

In Figure 2.4, we finally arrive at the Customer aggregate that holds the usual contact information and current and past addresses. Like policies, customers can be identified uniquely by their CustomerId.

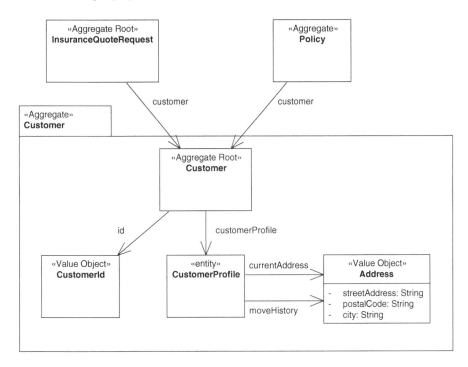

Figure 2.4 *Details of the Customer aggregate*

Architecture Overview

Now that we know about business context and requirements, let us investigate the existing systems at Lakeside Mutual and their architectures.

System Context

Figure 2.5 shows the current system context. Existing customers (not shown in the figure) should be able to use the Customer Self-Service frontend to update their contact information. This service retrieves the master data from the Customer Core service, which is also used by a Policy Management application and a company-internal Customer Management application.[2]

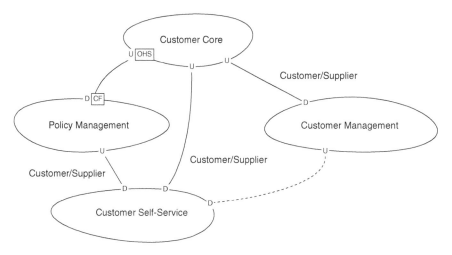

Figure 2.5 *Context map for Lakeside Mutual (solid lines: existing relations, dashed line: new interface)*

The four applications shown as Bounded Contexts in the figure are easy to trace back to the analysis-level domain model.[3] The Customer Self-Service context currently interacts only with Policy Management and Customer Core. To implement the new self-service capabilities, a new relationship to the Customer Management context will be added, which the dashed line in Figure 2.5 indicates. In the next section, we look at the software architecture that implements these bounded contexts.

Application Architecture

Refining the system context from Figure 2.5, Figure 2.6 shows an overview of the core components. These components are the building blocks for the services Lakeside Mutual provides to its customers and its employees. The Bounded Contexts from Figure 2.5 have led to the introduction of respective frontend applications and

---

2. Note that Customer/Supplier, Upstream (U), Downstream (D), Open Host Service (OHS), and Conformist (CF) are context relationships from DDD that call for API design and development [Vernon 2013].

3. The DDD pattern Bounded Context denotes a model boundary; it is an abstraction and generalization of teams, systems, and system parts (such as application frontends and backends).

supporting backend microservices (for instance, Customer Management frontend and Customer Management backend).

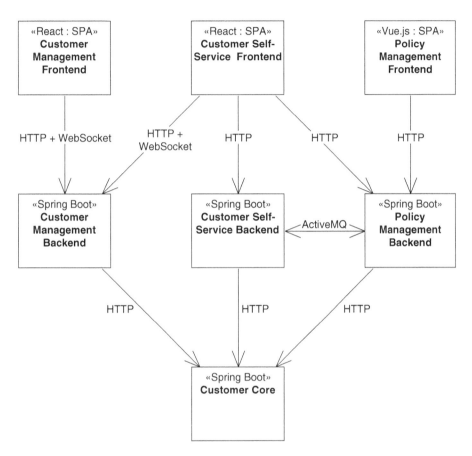

Figure 2.6 *Service components at Lakeside Mutual and their relationships*

The frontend strategy is to use rich Web clients; hence, single-page applications (SPAs) are implemented in JavaScript. Due to a strategic decision made on the company level several years ago, most backends are realized in Java, leveraging Spring Boot dependency injection containers to promote flexibility and maintainability. As a widespread and mature open-source messaging system, Apache ActiveMQ is used to integrate customer self-service and policy management.

- **Customer Core:** The Customer Core manages the personal data about the individual customers (for instance, name, email, current address, etc.). It provides this data to the other components through an HTTP resource API.

- **Customer Self-Service Backend:** The Customer Self-Service backend provides an HTTP resource API for the Customer Self-Service frontend. In addition, it connects to an ActiveMQ broker provided by the Policy Management backend to process insurance quote requests.

- **Customer Self-Service Frontend:** The Customer Self-Service frontend is a React application that allows users to register themselves, view their current insurance policy, and in the future, change their address (our exemplary user story).

- **Customer Management Backend:** The Customer Management backend is a Spring Boot application that exposes an HTTP resource API for the Customer Management frontend and the Customer Self-Service frontend. In addition, Web Sockets are used to implement the chat feature to deliver chat messages in real time between the call center agent using the Customer Management frontend and the customer logged into the Customer Self-Service Frontend.

- **Customer Management Frontend:** The Customer Management frontend is a React application that allows customer-service operators to interact with customers and help them resolve issues related to Lakeside Mutual's insurance products.

- **Policy Management Backend:** The Policy Management backend is a Spring Boot application that provides an HTTP resource API for the Customer Self-Service frontend and the Policy Management frontend.

- **Policy Management Frontend:** The Policy Management frontend is a JavaScript application built with vue.js that allows Lakeside Mutual employees to view and manage the insurance policies of individual customers.

Lakeside Mutual has decided to realize a microservices architecture. The rationale for this strategic architectural decision is to upgrade system parts more flexibly (in response to business change requests) and be prepared for business growth (which is expected to increase workload, possibly turning the backends into bottlenecks requiring independent scaling).

API Design Activities

We now turn back to our initial user story of providing a means for insurance customers to update their contact information.

The customer self-service team has just taken the above user story off its backlog and included it in the current sprint. During a sprint planning meeting, the teams identified the following activities for the next iteration:

1. Design a platform-independent API for the upstream Customer Management Backend, consumed by the downstream Customer Self-Service Frontend.

2. Specify the API endpoints (resources if we assume an HTTP-based Web API) and their operations (HTTP verbs/methods such as GET and POST), including request parameters and response structure (for example, object structure of JSON payloads).

3. Justify decisions based on the analysis and design artifacts listed or referenced earlier in this chapter.

How can patterns help the API designers at Lakeside Mutual when dealing with these tasks? This question will be answered in the following (and the remainder of the book). Appendix B, "Implementation of the Lakeside Mutual Case," collects some of the API implementation artifacts for the case.

Target API Specification

The following sketch of an API shows what an endpoint to update customer contact information *could* look like when performing the required API design activities (note that this sketch serves as a preview here; there is no need to understand all details already at this point):

```
API description CustomerManagementBackend
usage context SOLUTION_INTERNAL_API
  for FRONTEND_INTEGRATION

data type CustomerId ID
data type CustomerResponseDto D

data type AddressDto {
  "streetAddress": D<string>,
```

```
  "postalCode": D<string>,
  "city": D<string>
}

data type CustomerProfileUpdateRequestDto {
  "firstname": D<string>,
  "lastname": D<string>,
  "email": D<string>,
  "phoneNumber": D<string>,
  "currentAddress": AddressDto
}

endpoint type CustomerInformationHolder
  version "0.1.0"
  serves as INFORMATION_HOLDER_RESOURCE
  exposes
    operation updateCustomer
    with responsibility STATE_TRANSITION_OPERATION
     expecting
    headers
       <<API_Key>> "accessToken": D<string>
    payload {
       <<Identifier_Element>> "id": CustomerId,
       <<Data_Element>>
        "updatedProfile":
        CustomerProfileUpdateRequestDto
    }
    delivering
    payload {
      <<Data_Element>> "updatedCustomer": CustomerResponseDto,
      <<Error_Report>> {
        "status":D<string>,
        "error":D<string>,
        "message":D<string>}
    }
```

The API is specified in the MDSL specification language. MDSL, introduced in Appendix C, "Microservice Domain-Specific Language (MDSL)," is a domain-specific language (DSL) to specify (micro-)service contracts, their data representations, and API endpoints. OpenAPI specifications can be generated from it (the OpenAPI version of the preceding contract accounts for 111 lines in its YAML[4] rendering).

---

4. Originally, YAML stood for "Yet Another Markup Language." However, the name was later changed to "YAML Ain't Markup Language" to distinguish it as a data serialization language, not a true markup language.

At the top level, we can see the API description, two data type definitions, and an endpoint featuring a single operation. The <<API_Key>> stereotype, `SOLUTION_INTERNAL_API`, `FRONTEND_INTEGRATION`, `INFORMATION_HOLDER_RESOURCE`, and `STATE_TRANSITION_OPERATION` markers (and several others) all refer to patterns. In the next part of the book, these are explained in detail.

Summary

In this chapter, we introduced Lakeside Mutual, a fictitious case study that supplies us with running examples throughout the remainder of the book. Lakeside Mutual is an insurance company that implemented its core business capabilities for customer, contract, and risk management as a set of microservices with corresponding application frontends:

1. Web APIs connect the application frontends with the backends.

2. The backends also communicate via APIs.

3. API design starts with user requirements, desired qualities, system context information, and architectural decisions made already.

We elaborate on this initial API design in Chapter 3 and in Part 2 of the book, revisiting the patterns and the rationale for their application in the business and architectural context of the API design of the customer self-service API.

Some excerpts of the API implementation can be found in Appendix B. A complete implementation of the scenario is available at GitHub.[5]

---

5. https://github.com/Microservice-API-Patterns/LakesideMutual.

Chapter 3

API Decision Narratives

API endpoint, operation, and message design is multifaceted and therefore not easy. Requirements often conflict with each other, requiring balancing acts. Many architectural decisions and implementation choices have to be made, with numerous solution options available. The key to the success of an API is getting these decisions right. Sometimes the required choices are not known to developers, or developers know only a subset of the available options. Also, not all criteria may be obvious; for example, some quality attributes (such as performance and security) are more obvious than others (such as sustainability).

In this chapter, we identify pattern selection decisions by topical categories. The chapter walks through an API design iteration, starting with API scoping and then moving on to architectural decisions about endpoint roles and operations responsibilities. Decisions about quality-related design refinements and API evolution are covered as well. We call out the decisions required along with the most prevalent options (as covered by patterns from Part 2) and criteria for pattern selection that we have seen in practice.

Prelude: Patterns as Decision Options, Forces as Decision Criteria

Selecting a pattern is an architectural decision to be made and justified, as motivated, for instance, in *Continuous Architecture in Practice* [Erder 2021]. Hence, our narration identifies the architectural decisions required during API design and evolution. For each of these decisions, we discuss its decision-making criteria and design alternatives. These alternative options are provided by our patterns, which are covered in depth in Part 2 of the book.

To identify decisions required, we use the following format:

Decision: *Example of a decision required*

Which topic is addressed?

The eligible patterns are then presented in the following format:

	Pattern: PATTERN NAME
Problem	[Which design issue is addressed?]
Solution	[Overview of possible ways to address the issue]

The decision-making criteria, corresponding to the pattern forces from Part 2, are then summarized, and some good practice recommendations are given (which should not be followed word for word but should be put into the context of a particular API design effort).

Sample decision outcome. We also present examples of decisions from the Lakeside Mutual case introduced in Chapter 2, "Lakeside Mutual Case Study." We use the following architectural decision record (ADR) format:

In the context of [feature or component],

wanting to/facing the need for [requirement or quality goal],

we decided to [option chosen]

and neglected [alternatives]

to achieve [benefit],

accepting that [negative consequences].

This format, called a *why-statement* [Zdun 2013], is an example of an architectural decision record template. Popularized by Michael Nygard [Nygard 2011], such decision logs have a long history in research and practice.[1] In a nutshell, they keep track of decision outcomes and their justifications (rationale) in a given context.

An instance of the ADR template could be written as follows:

In the context of the pattern decision narratives,

facing the need to illustrate the options and criteria in examples,

---

1. See https://ozimmer.ch/practices/2020/04/27/ArchitectureDecisionMaking.html.

we decided to inject architectural decision records like this one

to achieve a balance of theory and practice,

accepting that the chapter gets longer and readers have to jump from concepts to their application when reading end to end.

Each why-statement is set in *italics* so that it is clearly distinguished from the conceptual content of this chapter (the decision points, options, and criteria, that is). The "neglected" part of the why-statement is optional, and not used in this example. In the remainder of the chapter, we cover the following decision topics:

- "Foundational API Decisions and Patterns" features API visibility, API integration types, and documentation of the API.

- "Decisions about API Roles and Responsibilities" discusses the architectural role of an endpoint, refining information holder roles, and defining operation responsibilities.

- "Selecting Message Representation Patterns" covers the choice between flat and nested structures of representation elements and introduces element stereotypes.

- "Governing API Quality" is multifaceted: identification and authentication of the API client, metering and charging for API consumption, preventing API clients from excessive API usage, explicit specification of quality objectives and penalties, communication of errors, and external context representation.

- "Deciding for API Quality Improvements" deals with pagination, other means of avoiding unnecessary data transfer, and handling referenced data in messages.

- "Decisions about API Evolution" has two parts: versioning and compatibility management and strategies for commissioning and decommissioning.

Two interludes cover "Responsibility and Structure Patterns in the Lakeside Mutual Case" and "Quality and Evolution Patterns in the Lakeside Mutual Case."

Foundational API Decisions and Patterns

In Chapter 1, "Application Programming Interface (API) Fundamentals," we saw that APIs are software interfaces that expose computing or information management services while decoupling the underlying service provider implementations from API clients. In this section, we introduce foundational architectural design decisions with patterns as decision options, detailing this relation between service implementations at the API provider side and the API clients. The patterns in this section have a managerial or organizational theme and also have a substantial impact on important technical considerations.

The decisions in this section answer the following questions:

- Where should the API be accessible from, or how *visible* is the API?
- Which *integration types* should be supported by the API?
- Should the API be *documented?* If so, how should it be documented?

Figure 3.1 shows how these decisions are related.

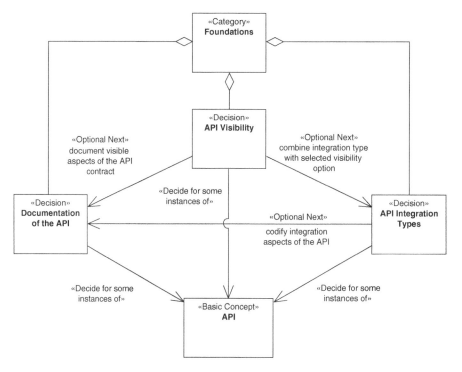

Figure 3.1 *Foundations category*

The first decision in this category is on API visibility. In different kinds of APIs, the API clients that are supposed to use the API might be vastly different, ranging from a large number of API clients residing in different organizations and locations to a few well-known API clients within a single organization and/or the same software system.

In addition, it has to be decided how the organization of a system in physical tiers is related to APIs, leading to different possible integration types. A frontend that is responsible for displaying and controlling an end user interface might be physically separated from its backends that are in charge of data processing and storage. Such backends might be split and distributed into several systems and/or subsystems, for instance, in service-oriented architectures. In both cases, frontend and backend, API-based integration is possible.

Finally, decisions about API documentation are required. When a service provider has decided to expose one or more API endpoints, clients must be able to find out where and how API operations can be called. This includes technical API access information, such as API endpoint locations or parameters in message representations, as well as documentation of operation behavior, including pre- and postconditions, and related quality-of-service guarantees.

API Visibility

You may want to provide a part of an application with a remote API exposing one or more API endpoints. In such a scenario, an early decision on each API pertains to its visibility. From a technical viewpoint, this visibility of an API is determined by the deployment location and its network connections (for instance, the Internet, an extranet, a company-internal network, or even a single data center). From an organizational viewpoint, the end users served by the API clients influence the required level of visibility.

This decision is not primarily technical but a managerial or organizational one. It is often related to budgets and funding considerations. Sometimes the API development, operations, and maintenance are funded by a single project or product; in other cases, several organizations (or units within one) contribute to the API funding.

The decision has important impacts on many technical aspects, however. Compare, for instance, an open, public API exposed on the Internet used by an arbitrary number of partially unknown API clients to a solution-internal API used by a small and stable number of other systems and/or subsystems of an organization. The possible workload that the open, public API has to tolerate might be rather high and contain numerous peaks; the workload of a solution-internal API with a few well-known API clients often is significantly lower. As a consequence, the performance and scalability requirements for the two kinds of API visibility can be very different.

The core decision to be taken is as follows:

Decision: *Visibility of the API*

Where should the API be accessible from: the Web, an access-controlled network such as an intranet or an extranet, or only the data center that hosts a particular solution?

Figure 3.2 illustrates the three decision options for this decision, described as patterns.

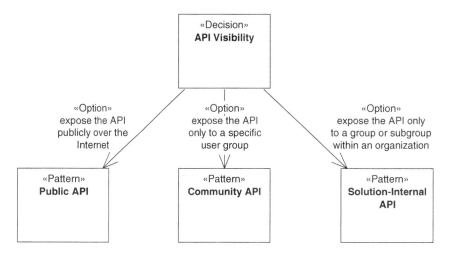

Figure 3.2 *API visibility decision*

The first option is the PUBLIC API pattern.

	Pattern: PUBLIC API
Problem	How can an API be made available to an unlimited and/or unknown number of API clients outside the organization that are globally, nationally, and/or regionally distributed?
Solution	Expose the API on the public Internet along with a detailed API DESCRIPTION that describes both functional and nonfunctional properties of the API.

Specifically for PUBLIC APIs, it is important to consider the target audience size, location, and diversity. The wants and needs of the target audience, possible development and middleware platforms they use, and other such considerations can help determine whether and how an API should be publicly offered. For example, the trend toward single-page applications that access APIs through the browser (in contrast to dynamic Web sites rendered on the server) has led to an increase in APIs that are accessible over the Internet.

PUBLIC APIs with high visibility often have to cope with continuously high workloads and/or peak loads. This can increase the complexity and require high maturity of backend systems and data stores. Possible loads the API has to take are dependent on the target audience size. The location of the target audience determines the level of Internet access and bandwidth required.

More visible APIs might have higher security demands than less visible ones. The use of API KEYS or, alternatively, authentication protocols usually indicates the difference between a PUBLIC API in general and its Open API variant: a truly *open* API is a PUBLIC API without an API KEY or other authentication means. Both API KEYS and authentication protocols can also be used in all other options of this decision, of course.

The costs of API development, operations, and maintenance have to be covered. Usually, an API must have a business model for generating funds. For PUBLIC APIs, paid subscriptions and per-call payments (see PRICING PLAN pattern) are common options. Another option is cross-funding, for instance, via advertising. Such considerations must go along with budget considerations. While it might be easy to fund the initial development of the first version of an API, its operations, maintenance, and evolution might be harder to fund in the long run, especially for a successful PUBLIC API with a large number of clients.

An alternative decision option with more limited visibility is COMMUNITY API.

	Pattern: COMMUNITY API
Problem	How can the visibility of and the access to an API be restricted to a closed user group that does not work for a single organizational unit but for multiple legal entities (such as companies, nonprofit/nongovernment organizations, and governments)?
Solution	Deploy the API and its implementation resources securely in an access-restricted location so that only the desired user group has access to it—for instance, in an extranet. Share the API DESCRIPTION only with the restricted target audience.

As for a Public API, the API development, operations, and maintenance of Community APIs must be funded. Thus, budgets play an equally important role, but here the specifics of the community and solutions they require determine how they are covered. In a community of product users, for example, license fees might cover the budget. A government or nonprofit organization might fund APIs for specific, restricted user groups to achieve certain community-specific goals. An essential difference to Solution-Internal APIs (explained shortly) is that it is often not a single project or product budget that pays for the API. The interests of those who pay for the API can be diverse.

More variants of the pattern exist, often observed in company contexts. An Enterprise API is an API that is available within a company-internal network only. A Product API ships with purchased software (or open-source software). Finally, Service APIs exposed by cloud providers and the application services hosted in cloud environments also qualify as variants of Community API if access to them is limited and secured.

The target audience size, location, and technical preferences play a role, too (often even related to the budget considerations, as members of the community might pay for the API). These community characteristics might be significantly more challenging and more diverse than those of individual teams or the public. In contrast to a Public API, where the API development organization often can set standards easily because the users are politically relatively weak, stakeholder concerns in bounded communities are often diverse and demanding. For example, the concerns of roles such as application owner, DevOps staff, IT security officer, and so on, might differ and conflict with each other. These considerations might also make API life-cycle management more demanding. For example, a paying customer of a Community API might have rather strong demands that an API version remains in operation.

Finally, the decision option with the most limited visibility is Solution-Internal API.

Pattern: Solution-Internal API

Problem	How can access to and usage of an API be limited to an application, for instance, components in the same or another logical layer and/or physical tier?
Solution	Decompose the application logically into components. Let these components expose local or remote APIs. Offer these APIs only to system-internal communication partners such as other services in the application backend.

As for the prior two patterns, the budget must be considered to fund the development, operations, and maintenance of the SOLUTION-INTERNAL API. This is usually less problematic for SOLUTION-INTERNAL APIs than for the two other API visibility types (which are more exposed) because a single project or product budget typically covers the costs of the API. This, in turn, means that the project can also decide about life-cycle considerations and supported target audience size, location, and technical preferences. Naturally, the significance of these concerns depends on the project goals. For example, consider an internal API developed to invoice product purchases in an online shop. It can be expected that the products and their billing requirements are known to the API development team; they change over time. If the team rolls out a new API version, it can notify the dependent teams, working on the same shop application, about the change.

Other technical concerns raised previously have a similar character. Workloads are typically better known than in PUBLIC APIs unless the SOLUTION-INTERNAL API receives its calls from a PUBLIC API. For example, in the billing scenario, if all company products themselves are offered via PUBLIC APIs, then the SOLUTION-INTERNAL API for billing has to cope with the loads coming from those PUBLIC APIs. Likewise, the complexity and maturity of backend systems and data stores, as well as security demands, have to fulfill only solution-internal demands and can follow best practices used in the organization that offers them.

Note that sometimes SOLUTION-INTERNAL APIs evolve into COMMUNITY APIs (or even PUBLIC APIs). Such graduation should not just happen as a form of scope creep but should be decided and planned consciously. Some API design decisions, such as those about API security, might have to be revisited when such graduation happens.

Also note that API visibility includes message and data structure visibility. API client and provider require a shared understanding of the data structures exchanged. In domain-driven design terms, these data structures are part of the Published Language [Evans 2003]. A rich Published Language has the potential to contribute to a positive developer experience; however, it also introduces coupling inherently.

Sample decision outcome. How did the case study team at Lakeside Mutual decide, and why?

In the context of the customer self-service channel,

facing the need to serve external users such as existing customers,

the API designers at Lakeside Mutual decided to evolve their SOLUTION-INTERNAL *API into a* COMMUNITY *API, neglecting* PUBLIC *API,*

to be able to address the wants and needs of a known user population and predict the API workload, accepting that unregistered users (prospective customers) cannot be served by this API.

API Integration Types

A second foundational decision is which integration types are supported by the API:

Decision: *Integration types supported by the API*

Do the API clients display forms and processing results to end users, for instance, in mobile apps, Web applications, and rich client applications? Or should they serve as wrappers and adapters in mid-tiers and backend tiers that host application components?

Figure 3.3 shows the two decision options, FRONTEND INTEGRATION (or vertical integration) and BACKEND INTEGRATION (or horizontal integration).[2]

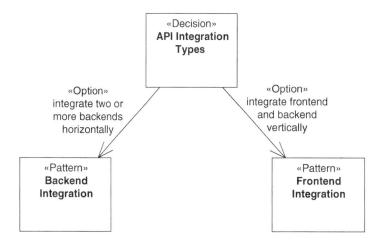

Figure 3.3 *API integration types decision*

---

2. The notion of horizontal versus vertical integration originates from the common visualization of distributed systems (and their layers and tiers) that places frontends at the top of diagrams and backends at the bottom.

Both integration types can be combined with any of the visibility patterns discussed earlier.

Pattern: FRONTEND INTEGRATION

Problem	How can client-side end user interfaces that are physically separated from server-side business logic and data storage be populated and updated with computing results, result sets from searches in data sources, and detailed information about data entities? How can application frontends invoke activities in a backend or upload data to it?
Solution	Let the backend of a distributed application expose its services to one or more application frontends via a message-based remote FRONTEND INTEGRATION API.

How to design a FRONTEND INTEGRATION API strongly depends on the information and business needs of the frontends. Especially if the frontend contains a user interface (UI), rich and expressive APIs might be required to address all the UI's needs (for example, the API should support the PAGINATION pattern to make it efficient for the UI to fetch additional information incrementally). This enables a pleasant API client developer experience. However, more expressive APIs are often costly to develop and might cause tighter coupling than simpler alternatives. Additional efforts and tight coupling might translate to higher risks.

For a FRONTEND INTEGRATION API security and data privacy considerations are usually important, as many application frontends work with sensitive data such as customer information.

Pattern: BACKEND INTEGRATION

Problem	How can distributed applications and their parts, which have been built independently and are deployed separately, exchange data and trigger mutual activity while preserving system-internal conceptual integrity without introducing undesired coupling?
Solution	Integrate the backend of a distributed application with one or more other backends (of the same or other distributed applications) by exposing its services via a message-based remote BACKEND INTEGRATION API.

For many backend integrations, runtime qualities such as performance and scalability have to be taken into account. For instance, some backends may in turn serve multiple frontends, or large amounts of data might have to be transferred between backends. Security might be an important consideration when backend integrations across organizational boundaries are required. Similarly, interoperability is an important force in some backend integration scenarios. For instance, application owners and system integrators of the involved systems might not know each other.

For integration tasks, Backend Integration in particular, the development budget might also be important to consider. As an example, the cost allocations of Solution-Internal APIs and Community APIs may not be clear, and only limited budgets can be spent on integration tasks. Integration of systems means that the development cultures and company politics of the systems to be integrated might clash or be incompatible.

For both patterns of this decision, Frontend Integration and Backend Integration, links to the decision options of the API visibility decision exist, such as the following:

- Public APIs often provide Frontend Integration capabilities to connect Web applications or mobile frontends. They can also be used to support Backend Integrations, for instance, to feed data lakes in big data scenarios with open data.

- Community APIs often support Backend Integration scenarios, for instance, data replication or event sourcing. They might also support Frontend Integration in portals and mashups.

- Finally, Solution-Internal APIs might support Frontend Integration to support API clients serving end user interfaces only used within the solution. They also might support Backend Integration in a local context, such as local extract, transform, and load (ETL) processes.

Sample decision outcome. Which Lakeside Mutual API design arose when going through this decision?

In the context of the customer self-service channel,

facing the need to supply external users with correct data through a user interface,

the Frontend Integration *pattern was chosen (and* Backend Integration *neglected) to achieve high data quality and productivity gains when customers serve themselves,*

accepting that the external interface has to be secured properly.

HTTPS and the API KEY pattern featured in a later decision are two options to deal with the "accepting that" consequence stated in the sample decision outcome.

Documentation of the API

In addition to the foundational decisions on API visibility and API integration types, it should be decided if and how the API should be documented. This decision is illustrated in Figure 3.4.

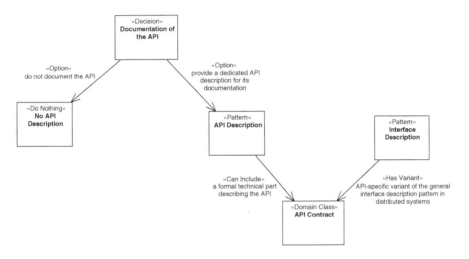

Figure 3.4 *API documentation decision*

The essential API-related pattern for this decision is API DESCRIPTION. A small or simple project, or prototype projects that are likely to change significantly in the near future, might choose not to apply this pattern and thus select the "no API DESCRIPTION" option.

Decision: *Documentation of the API*

Should the API be documented? If so, how should it be documented?

	Pattern: API DESCRIPTION
Problem	Which knowledge should be shared between an API provider and its clients? How should this knowledge be documented?
Solution	Create an API DESCRIPTION that defines request and response message structures, error reporting, and other relevant parts of the technical knowledge to be shared between provider and client. In addition to static and structural information, also cover dynamic or behavioral aspects, including invocation sequences, pre- and postconditions, and invariants. Complement the syntactical interface description with quality management policies as well as semantic specifications and organizational information.

An API DESCRIPTION contains the functional API contract that defines request and response message structures, error reporting, and other relevant parts of the technical knowledge to be shared between API provider and client. In addition to this syntactical interface description, it contains quality management policies as well as semantic specifications and organizational information. The API contract part is essentially a special case or variant of the "Interface Description" pattern [Voelter 2004], with the purpose of describing an API. For example, OpenAPI Specification (formerly known as Swagger), API Blueprint [API Blueprint 2022], Web Application Description Language (WADL), and Web Services Description Language (WSDL) are languages for specifying interfaces following the Interface Description pattern that can be used to describe the technical part of the API DESCRIPTION, the API contracts. Alternatively, more informal descriptions of the API contracts are possible, too, for example, in textual form on a Web site. Both options, description language and informal specification, can be combined. MDSL is an example of a machine-readable language that supports the pattern (see Appendix C, "Microservice Domain-Specific Language (MDSL)").

The other parts mentioned in the pattern solution (quality management policies, semantic specifications and organizational information, invocation sequences, pre- and postconditions, invariants, and so on) are often described informally in practice. For many of those, formal languages also exist, for example, to define pre- and post-conditions and invariants [Meyer 1997] or invocation sequences [Pautasso 2016].

A key aspect of the pattern is that an API DESCRIPTION helps to enable interoperability because it provides a common, programming-language-independent description of the API. In addition, it helps to support information hiding. Providers should not unveil details about the implementation of the API that clients do not require. At the same time, clients should not have to guess how to correctly invoke the API. That is, API designers should care for the consumability and understandability of the API. A clear and precise API DESCRIPTION is essential to reach this goal. The API DESCRIPTION can help to strike a balance between consumability, understandability, and information hiding.

Independence of API implementation details helps ensure loose coupling of API clients and providers. Both loose coupling and information hiding are essential to enable extensibility and evolvability of the API. If clients are not highly dependent on API implementation details, it is usually easy to change and evolve the API.

Sample decision outcome. Lakeside Mutual decided to apply the pattern:

In the context of the customer self-service channel,

wanting to improve the client developer experience,

the Lakeside Mutual API designers chose elaborate API DESCRIPTIONS *and the contract languages MDSL and OpenAPI,*

to achieve an interoperable API that is easy to learn and use,

accepting that its documentation has to be kept current as the API evolves.

In Part 2, the visibility and integration patterns presented in this section appear in Chapter 4, "Pattern Language Introduction." API DESCRIPTION is featured in Chapter 9, "Document and Communicate API Contracts."

Decisions about API Roles and Responsibilities

Two questions arise when designing API endpoints and their operations:

- Which architectural role should an API endpoint play?
- What is the responsibility of each API operation?

The drivers for API introduction and requirements for API design are diverse. As a consequence, the roles that APIs play in applications and service ecosystems differ widely. Sometimes, an API client wants to inform the provider about an incident or hand over some data; sometimes, a client requests provider-side data to continue client-side processing. Sometimes, the provider has to perform a lot of complex processing to satisfy the information needs of the client; sometimes, it can simply return a data element that already exists as part of its application state. Some of the provider-side processing, whether simple or complex, may change the provider-side state, some might leave it untouched.

Once the role of an endpoint has been defined (action- or data-oriented), more fine-grained decisions on the responsibilities of the endpoint operations are due. Operations can solely compute results, only read state, create new state without reading it, or realize a state transition. Clearly defining these responsibilities, for instance, in an API DESCRIPTION, can help developers to better design and choose deployment options for an API endpoint. For example, if only stateless computations and data reading are performed on an endpoint, their results can be cached and the corresponding implementation can be replicated to scale out more easily.

As illustrated in the category overview in Figure 3.5, the responsibility category contains two decisions. Usually, an (at least initial) architectural role decision is made during endpoint identification, and then operation responsibilities are designed. Note that architectural roles have to be decided for each endpoint (or resource), whereas operation responsibilities should be assigned to each API operation.

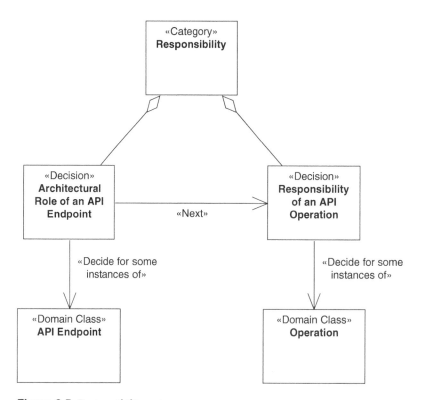

Figure 3.5 *Responsibility category*

Architectural Role of an Endpoint

The API requirement analysis might lead to a list of candidate API endpoints, for instance, HTTP resources. At the beginning of a project or product development, these interfaces are yet unspecified (or only partially specified). API designers have to address semantic concerns and find an appropriate business granularity for the services exposed by the API. Simplistic statements such as "services in a service-oriented architecture (SOA) are coarse-grained by definition, while microservices are fine-grained; you cannot have both in one system" or "always prefer fine-grained over coarse-grained services" are insufficient because project requirements and stakeholder concerns differ [Pautasso 2017a]. Context always matters [Torres 2015]; cohesion and coupling criteria come in many forms [Gysel 2016]. As a result, the nonfunctional requirements for service design often are conflicting [Zimmermann 2004].

In response to these general challenges, a major decision for the endpoints of an API is to decide which architectural role they should play. This, in turn, can help to improve the selection and decomposition of the (candidate) API endpoints.

Decision: *Architectural role of an endpoint*

Which technical role should an API endpoint play in the architecture?

Two main options can be chosen in this decision, illustrated in Figure 3.6.

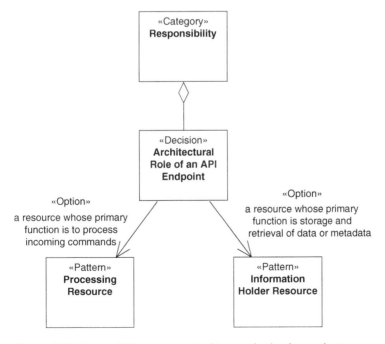

Figure 3.6 *Responsibility category: Architectural role of an endpoint*

PROCESSING RESOURCES are resources whose primary function is to handle incoming action requests (aka commands or activities).

Pattern: PROCESSING RESOURCE	
Problem	How can an API provider allow its clients to trigger an action in it?
Solution	Add a PROCESSING RESOURCE endpoint to the API exposing operations that bundle and wrap application-level activities or commands.

In contrast, INFORMATION HOLDER RESOURCES are resources whose primary function is to expose storage and management of data or metadata, including its creation, manipulation, and retrieval.

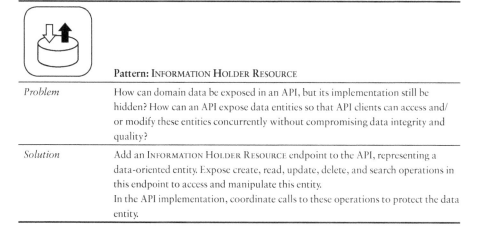

Pattern: INFORMATION HOLDER RESOURCE	
Problem	How can domain data be exposed in an API, but its implementation still be hidden? How can an API expose data entities so that API clients can access and/ or modify these entities concurrently without compromising data integrity and quality?
Solution	Add an INFORMATION HOLDER RESOURCE endpoint to the API, representing a data-oriented entity. Expose create, read, update, delete, and search operations in this endpoint to access and manipulate this entity. In the API implementation, coordinate calls to these operations to protect the data entity.

The basic decision between these two types of resources is relatively easy, as it is based on the functionalities required by clients. However, there is much freedom to determine which functions are offered on which resources and how to decompose the API well. For instance, API designers have to consider contract expressiveness and service granularity: simple interactions give the client good control and make processing efficient, but action-oriented capabilities can promote qualities such as consistency, compatibility, and evolvability. These design choices can be positive or negative for the learnability and manageability of the API. Also, semantic interoperability (including a joined understanding of the meaning of the data exchanged) must be ensured. If not done well, the chosen endpoint-operation layout can have a negative impact on response time and lead to chatty APIs.

A truly stateless Processing Resource can be hard to achieve in reality. API security and request/response data privacy can lead to the need for maintaining state, for example, when a full audit log of all API invocations and resulting server-side processing has to be maintained.

The underlying impact on coupling should be considered, particularly for stateful resources. Highly data-centric approaches tend to lead to create, read, update, delete (CRUD) APIs, which can negatively affect coupling. This is discussed later in more detail for the different kinds of information holder roles. The structure of some backends could lead to highly coupled APIs when followed as-is; however, API designers are free to design the API as an additional layer specifically to support the interactions between the API and its clients. Here, various quality attribute conflicts and trade-offs specific for API design but also in relation to backend services are to be considered, such as concurrency, consistency, data quality and integrity, recoverability, availability, and mutability (or immutability). Also, such decisions are often dependent on compliance with architectural design principles such as loose coupling [Fehling 2014], logical and physical data independence, or microservices tenets such as independent deployability [Lewis 2014].

> **Sample decision outcome.** How did our case study team resolve the forces of concern?
>
> *In the context of the customer self-service channel at Lakeside Mutual,*
>
> *facing the need to empower clients to update their contact information easily,*
>
> *the integration architects at Lakeside Mutual decided to introduce a data-oriented* Information Holder *and not an activity-oriented* Processing Resource
>
> *to provide expressive, easy-to-understand create, read, update, and delete functionality,*
>
> *accepting that the exposure of contact information couples the self-service channel to the customer management backend to some extent.*

Refining Information Holder Roles

Information Holder Resources have the primary function to expose storage and management of data or metadata, including its creation and retrieval. There are several patterns covering types of information holders, refining the general Information Holder Resource pattern. Figure 3.7 provides an overview.

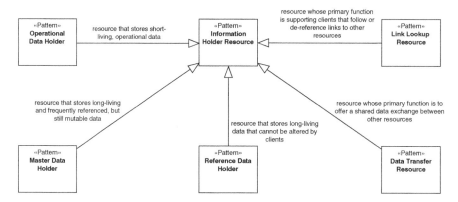

Figure 3.7 *Responsibility category:* INFORMATION RESOURCE HOLDER *types*

In the context of these information holder roles, we distinguish three types of data, which are the basis for defining the roles described in the first three patterns:

- *Operational data* covers the events in the transactions of an organization. For example, making an order to a business, shipping items to a customer, or hiring employees are all examples of business transactions that would form operational data. Operational data (also called *transactional data*) is usually short-living, transactional in nature, and has many outgoing relationships.

- *Master data* is essential information that supports the business transactions realized in a system. Typically, it covers the digital representation of the *parties* of an organization such as persons, customers, employees, or suppliers. It also covers the main *things* relevant to an organization, such as the products, materials, items, and vehicles. Finally, master data may represent physical or virtual places, such as locations or sites. Master data is usually long-living and frequently referenced.

- *Reference data* is inert data referenced and shared in one or more systems and among the microservices and components making up these systems. Examples are country codes, zip codes, and delivery status codes (such as pending, information received, in transit, out on delivery, failed attempt, delivered). Reference data is long-living, simple, and cannot be changed by clients directly.

The INFORMATION HOLDER RESOURCE role supporting operational data is OPER-ATIONAL DATA HOLDER. An important decision driver for this option usually is a high processing speed of the update operations. Services dealing with operational data must also be easy to change to support business agility and update flexibility. Nonetheless, the created and modified operational data must meet high accuracy and quality standards in many (business) scenarios. For example, qualities such as conceptual integrity and consistency must be supported.

	Pattern: OPERATIONAL DATA HOLDER
Problem	How can an API support clients that want to create, read, update, and/or delete instances of domain entities that represent operational data: data that is rather short-lived, changes often during daily business operations, and has many outgoing relations?
Solution	Tag an INFORMATION HOLDER RESOURCE as OPERATIONAL DATA HOLDER and add API operations to it that allow API clients to create, read, update, and delete its data often and fast.

Unlike operational data, master data is long-living and frequently referenced but still mutable. A MASTER DATA HOLDER stores such data. Here, master data quality is often a central decision driver, including master data consistency and its protection, for example, from attacks and data breaches. Very often, there are external dependencies such as data ownership by different organizational units that must be considered in the design of MASTER DATA HOLDER resources as well.

	Pattern: MASTER DATA HOLDER
Problem	How can I design an API that provides access to master data that lives for a long time, does not change frequently, and will be referenced from many clients?
Solution	Mark an INFORMATION HOLDER RESOURCE to be a dedicated MASTER DATA HOLDER endpoint that bundles master data access and manipulation operations in such a way that the data consistency is preserved and references are managed adequately. Treat delete operations as special forms of updates.

For both OPERATIONAL DATA HOLDERS and MASTER DATA HOLDER, a simple design is a CRUD resource for each identified interface element that exposes operational or master data. Use of the words "create, read, update, and delete" in the preceding pattern sketches should not indicate that such designs are the intended or only possible solution for realizing the patterns. Such designs quickly lead to chatty APIs with bad performance and scalability properties. They can also lead to unwanted coupling and complexity. Beware of such API designs! Instead, we recommend an incremental approach during resource identification. It aims to first identify well-scoped interface elements such as Aggregate roots in domain-driven design (DDD), business capabilities, or business processes. Even larger formations such as Bounded Contexts may serve as starting points. In infrequent cases, domain Entities can also be considered to supply endpoint candidates. For a deeper discussion on the relation of APIs and DDD, see [Singjai 2021a, 2021b, 2021c]. This approach leads to OPERATIONAL DATA HOLDER and MASTER DATA HOLDER designs that are semantically richer. In DDD terms, on the domain model side, we aim for a rich and deep domain model instead of an "anemic domain model" [Fowler 2003]; this model should be reflected, but not necessarily mirrored in the API design.

For some data, also long-living, we know that clients do not want to or should not be allowed to modify it. Such reference data should be offered via a REFERENCE DATA HOLDER. Caching of this data is possible, which leads to high performance. If caching is used, consistency versus performance trade-offs might have to be made. Since reference data rarely changes if at all, there is a temptation to simply hardcode it within the API clients or retrieve it once and then store a copy locally. Such designs violate the *do not repeat yourself (DRY)* principle and work well only in the short run.

Pattern: REFERENCE DATA HOLDER

Problem	How should data that is referenced in many places, lives long, and is immutable for clients be treated in API endpoints? How can such reference data be used in requests to and responses from PROCESSING RESOURCES or INFORMATION HOLDER RESOURCES?
Solution	Provide a special type of INFORMATION HOLDER RESOURCE endpoint, a REFERENCE DATA HOLDER, as a single point of reference for the static, immutable data. Provide read operations, but no create, update, or delete operations in this endpoint.

As a supporting role, there is the option to design LINK LOOKUP RESOURCES. They are resources whose primary function is supporting clients that follow or dereference links to other resources. Links are a primary means to improve coupling and cohesion between API consumers and providers, but there is also the coupling to the LINK LOOKUP RESOURCE to be considered. Links can also help to reduce message sizes by placing a link in the message instead of the content, as in the EMBEDDED ENTITY pattern. But if clients need all or part of the information, this practice increases the required number of calls. Both placing links in messages and including content in an EMBEDDED ENTITY influence the overall resource use. For links to work well, dynamic endpoint references that can change at runtime should ideally be established. LINK LOOKUP RESOURCES increase the number of endpoints in an API and can lead to higher API complexity; the severity of consequence depends on how *centralized* or *decentralized* LINK LOOKUP RESOURCES are. Finally, the consistency issue of dealing with broken links has to be considered: a link lookup provides the option to deal with the problem, whereas a broken link without a lookup usually immediately leads to an exception (i.e., a "resource not found" error).

	Pattern: LINK LOOKUP RESOURCE
Problem	How can message representations refer to other, possibly many and frequently changing, API endpoints and operations without binding the message recipient to the actual addresses of these endpoints?
Solution	Introduce a special type of INFORMATION HOLDER RESOURCE, a dedicated LINK LOOKUP RESOURCE endpoint that exposes special RETRIEVAL OPERATION operations that return single instances or collections of LINK ELEMENTS that represent the current addresses of the referenced API endpoints.

A DATA TRANSFER RESOURCE is an endpoint role pattern representing a resource whose primary function is to offer a shared data exchange between clients. This might help to reduce coupling between the communication participants interacting with the DATA TRANSFER RESOURCE; in terms of time—the API clients do not have to be up and running at the same time—and location—the API clients do not have to know the addresses of each other as long as they can locate the DATA TRANSFER RESOURCE. The pattern can help overcome certain communication constraints, such as if one party cannot be directly connected to another one. An asynchronous, persistent DATA TRANSFER RESOURCE is more reliable than, for example, client/server communication. It can also offer good scalability, but measures must be taken to deal with a possibly unknown number of recipients that can impede scalability. Indirect communication can introduce additional latency though. The data to be exchanged has to be stored somewhere, and sufficient storage space must be available. Finally, ownership of the shared information has to be established to achieve explicit control over the resource availability life cycle.

	Pattern: Data Transfer Resource
Problem	How can two or more communication participants exchange data without knowing each other, without being available at the same time, and even if the data has already been sent before its recipients became known?
Solution	Introduce a Data Transfer Resource as a shared storage endpoint accessible from two or more API clients. Provide this specialized Information Holder Resource with a globally unique network address so that two or more clients can use it as a shared data exchange space. Add at least one State Creation Operation and one Retrieval Operation to it so that data can be placed in the shared space and also fetched from it.

Sample decision outcome. The API designers at Lakeside Mutual decided for data holder specializations as follows:

In the context of the Customer Management backend,

facing the need to keep and use customer data for a long time,

the API designers at Lakeside Mutual decided to use the Master Data Holder *pattern, introducing a Customer Core service, and neglected the other four types of information holders,*

to achieve a single consolidated view on customer data across systems,

accepting that this Master Data Holder *might become a performance bottleneck and single point of failure if it is not architected and implemented properly.*

Defining Operation Responsibilities

Once an endpoint role is decided, more fine-grained decisions have to be made for its operations, covered in four patterns of widely used API operation responsibilities. These patterns are solution options in the decision illustrated in Figure 3.8.

Decision: *Operation responsibility*

What are the read-write characteristics of each API operation?

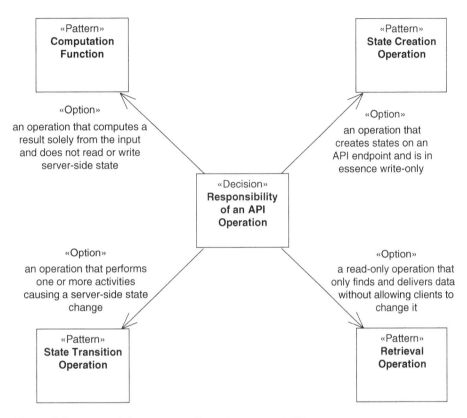

Figure 3.8 *Responsibility category: Operation responsibilities*

The first pattern is STATE CREATION OPERATION, modeling an operation that creates states on an API endpoint and is, in essence, write-only. Here, *in essence* means that such operations might need to read some provider-internal state—for example, to check for duplicate keys in existing data before creation. However, their main purpose is state creation.

In the design of STATE CREATION OPERATIONS, their impact on coupling should be considered. Because the provider state is not read, it can become difficult to ensure consistency. As incidents that clients report happen before they arrive at the provider, timing needs to be considered in the design as well. Finally, reliability is an important concern, as messages might appear in a different order or be duplicated at the API provider.

Pattern: State Creation Operation	
Problem	How can an API provider allow its clients to report that something has happened that the provider needs to know about, for instance, to trigger instant or later processing?
Solution	Add a State Creation Operation sco: in -> (out,S') that has a write-only nature to the API endpoint, which may be a Processing Resource or an Information Holder Resource.

The next option is a Retrieval Operation, representing a read-only access operation that only finds and delivers data without allowing clients to change any data. The data may be manipulated in the Retrieval Operation before sending it to clients, though, for instance, to optimize the transfer by aggregating data elements. Some retrieval operations search for data; others access single data elements. Data properties such as veracity, variety, velocity, and volume should be considered in the design of the operation, as data comes in many forms and client interest in it varies. In addition, workload management considerations should be made, especially if significant data volumes are transferred. Also, more information transferred from client to API provider (and back) can lead to higher coupling and larger message sizes.

Pattern: Retrieval Operation	
Problem	How can information available from a remote party (the API provider, that is) be retrieved to satisfy an information need of an end user or to allow further client-side processing?
Solution	Add a read-only operation ro: (in,S) -> out to an API endpoint, which often is an Information Holder Resource, to request a result report that contains a machine-readable representation of the requested information. Add search, filter, and formatting capabilities to the operation signature.

A State Transition Operation is an operation that performs one or more activities, causing a server-side state change. Examples of such operations are full and partial updates to server-side data as well as deletions of such data. Advancing the state of long-running business process instances also requires State Transition Operations. The data to be updated or deleted might have been created via a previous call of a State Creation Operation or initialized internally by the API provider (in other words, the creation might not be caused by and not be visible to the API client).

The selection of this pattern has the following decision drivers: service granularity is essential to consider, as large services may contain complex and rich state information, updated only in a few transitions, while smaller ones may be simple but chatty in terms of their state transitions. For longer-running process instances, it can be difficult to keep the client-side state and the states of provider-side backends consistent. In addition, it is important to consider whether there are dependencies on state changes made earlier in the process. For example, system transactions triggered by other API clients, by external events in downstream systems, or by provider-internal batch jobs might collide with a state change triggered by a STATE TRANSITION OPERATION. There is a trade-off between the two goals of *network efficiency* and *data parsimony:* the smaller messages are, the more messages have to be exchanged to reach a particular goal.

	Pattern: STATE TRANSITION OPERATION
Problem	How can a client initiate a processing action that causes the provider-side application state to change?
Solution	Introduce an operation in an API endpoint that combines client input and current state to trigger a provider-side state change `sto: (in,S) -> (out,S')`. Model the valid state transitions within the endpoint, which may be a PROCESSING RESOURCE or an INFORMATION HOLDER RESOURCE, and check the validity of incoming change requests and business activity requests at runtime.

A COMPUTATION FUNCTION is an operation that computes a result solely from the client input and does not read or write server-side state. The different performance and message size considerations elaborated previously are relevant for COMPUTATION FUNCTIONS as well. In many cases, COMPUTATION FUNCTIONS require reproducibility of executions. Some computations might require a lot of resources, such as CPU time and main memory (RAM); for such functions, workload management is essential. As many COMPUTATION FUNCTIONS change often, maintenance requires special consideration, in the sense that updating the provider side is easier than updating clients.

	Pattern: COMPUTATION FUNCTION
Problem	How can a client invoke side-effect-free remote processing on the provider side to have a result calculated from its input?
Solution	Introduce an API operation `cf` with `cf: in -> out` to the API endpoint, which often is a PROCESSING RESOURCE. Let this COMPUTATION FUNCTION validate the received request message, perform the desired function `cf`, and return its result in the response.

Sample decision outcome. The API designers at Lakeside Mutual decided as follows:

In the context of the Customer Core INFORMATION HOLDER RESOURCE,

facing the need to achieve a high level of automation and a wide range of clients,

the API designers at Lakeside Mutual decided to introduce operations realizing all four responsibility patterns (read, write, read-write, compute)

to achieve both read and write access to the customer master data plus validation support

accepting that concurrent access must be coordinated, and interactions might get rather chatty when too fine-grained create, read, update, write operations are specified.

In Part 2, the patterns covering the architectural roles of an endpoint appear in Chapter 5, "Define Endpoint Types and Operations." The operation responsibility patterns are featured in that chapter as well.

Selecting Message Representation Patterns

In addition to endpoints and operations, API contracts define the structure of the messages exchanged when invoking the operations. The structural representation category of our pattern language deals with how to design such message representation structures. It deals with the following design issues:

- What is the optimal number of API message parameters and body parts and an adequate structure of these representation elements?

- What are the meaning and stereotypes of the representation elements?

For instance, regarding the first question, an HTTP resource API typically uses the message body to send data to or receive data from the provider (for instance, rendered as JSON, XML, or another MIME type), and the query parameters of the URI specify the requested data. In a WSDL/SOAP context, we can interpret this design issue as how the SOAP message parts should be organized and which data types should be used to define the corresponding elements in the XML Schema Definition (XSD). In gRPC, this design issue is about the message structure defined with Protocol Buffer specifications, for example containing details such as messages and data types.

Decisions for this category likely have to be made whenever a message is designed or refactored. The representation elements transported in the message, including request parameters and body elements, are considerations in these decisions.

As illustrated in Figure 3.9, this category contains four typical decisions. The first is on the structure of the parameter representation. Based on this representation, it can be decided what the meaning and responsibility of message elements are. Next, it can also be decided whether multiple data elements require additional information. Finally, the whole message can or cannot be extended with context information.

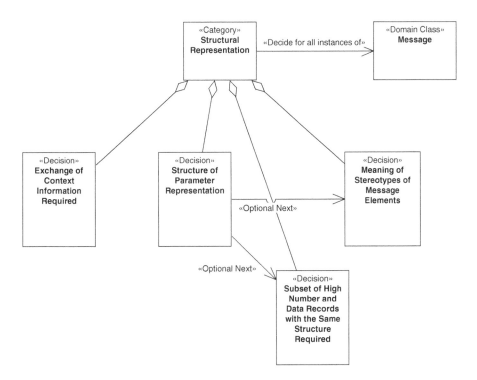

Figure 3.9 *Structural representation category*

Flat versus Nested Structure of Representation Elements

A major decision in structural representation design is as follows:

Decision: *Structure of parameter representation*

What is the adequate overall representation structure for the data elements to be transmitted in the message?

Figure 3.10 illustrates the typical decision-making options for this decision.

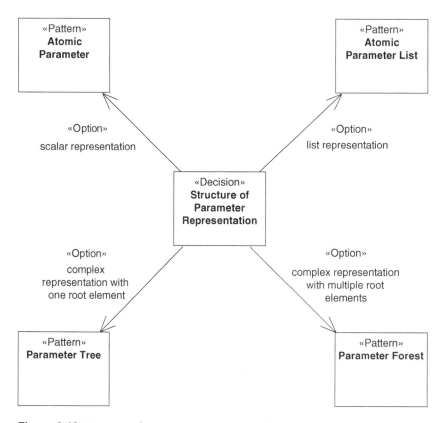

Figure 3.10 *Structure of parameter representation decision*

The simplest decision option is that a scalar representation is sufficient. In that case, the ATOMIC PARAMETER pattern should be chosen.

	Pattern: ATOMIC PARAMETER
Problem	How can simple, unstructured data (such as a number, a string, a Boolean value, or a block of binary data) be exchanged between API client and API provider?
Solution	Define a single parameter or body element. Pick a basic type from the type system of the chosen message exchange format for it. If justified by receiver-side usage, identify this ATOMIC PARAMETER with a name. Document name (if present), type, cardinality, and optionality in the API DESCRIPTION.

Sometimes, multiple scalars need to be transmitted. In such cases, a list representation usually is the best decision option, following the ATOMIC PARAMETER LIST pattern.

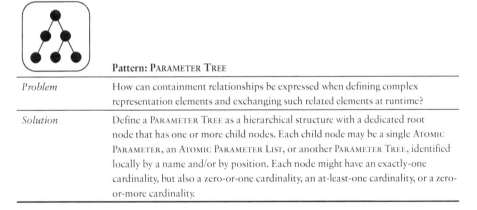

	Pattern: ATOMIC PARAMETER LIST
Problem	How can multiple related ATOMIC PARAMETERS be combined in a representation element so that each of them stays simple, but their relatedness becomes explicit in the API DESCRIPTION and the runtime message exchanges?
Solution	Group two or more simple, unstructured data elements in a single cohesive representation element to define an ATOMIC PARAMETER LIST that contains multiple ATOMIC PARAMETERS. Identify its items by position (index) or by a string-valued key. Identify the ATOMIC PARAMETER LIST as a whole with its own name as well if that is needed to process it in the receiver. Specify how many elements are required and permitted to appear.

If neither option (scalar or list representation) is applicable, one of two more complex representations should be chosen. If a single root element is present in the data or can easily be designed for the data to be transmitted, the representation elements can be wrapped in a hierarchical structure following the PARAMETER TREE pattern.

	Pattern: PARAMETER TREE
Problem	How can containment relationships be expressed when defining complex representation elements and exchanging such related elements at runtime?
Solution	Define a PARAMETER TREE as a hierarchical structure with a dedicated root node that has one or more child nodes. Each child node may be a single ATOMIC PARAMETER, an ATOMIC PARAMETER LIST, or another PARAMETER TREE, identified locally by a name and/or by position. Each node might have an exactly-one cardinality, but also a zero-or-one cardinality, an at-least-one cardinality, or a zero-or-more cardinality.

As any complex data structure can be placed under a single root element, the PARAMETER TREE option is always applicable but might not make much sense if the data elements are rather unrelated contentwise. If a single tree structure feels awkward or artificial for the data elements to be transmitted, several trees can be grouped into a list of such structures in the PARAMETER FOREST pattern.

Pattern: PARAMETER FOREST

Problem	How can multiple PARAMETER TREES be exposed as request or response payload of an API operation?
Solution	Define a PARAMETER FOREST comprising two or more PARAMETER TREES. Locate the forest members by position or name.

The more complex patterns in this category all use ATOMIC PARAMETERS to build up more complex structures. That is, ATOMIC PARAMETER LIST is a sequence of ATOMIC PARAMETERS, and the tree leaves in a PARAMETER TREE are ATOMIC PARAMETERS. The structures in a PARAMETER FOREST are built using the other three patterns. Those uses relations between the patterns are illustrated in Figure 3.11. As a consequence, the two decisions explained previously need to be recursively made again for the detailed structures in the complex patterns. For instance, for each data structure in a PARAMETER TREE, it must be decided again whether this structure itself is represented as a scalar, list, or tree. The technology mappings of the patterns are discussed in Chapter 4.

An ATOMIC PARAMETER LIST can be represented as a PARAMETER TREE as a wrapper structure for transport if the technology used supports no other way to transport multiple flat parameters. Such a tree has only scalar leaves underneath its root.

There are several shared decision drivers when selecting among the four patterns in the structure of parameter representation decision.

One obvious force is the inherent structure of the domain model and the system behavior. To ensure understandability and simplicity, and to avoid unnecessary complexity, it is advisable to stay close to the domain model, both in the code and in parameter representations in messages. It is important to apply this general advice carefully—only data that the receiver wants should be exposed to avoid unnecessary coupling. For instance, if the domain data element structure is a tree, applying PARAMETER TREE is a natural choice, enabling easy traceability from domain model or programming language data structures to message structures. Similarly, the intended behavior should be reflected closely: For an Internet of Things (IoT) scenario in which a sensor sends one data item frequently to an edge node, the most natural choice is an ATOMIC PARAMETER. Decisions on the number of messages and on each message structure require a careful analysis of when which data element is required. Sometimes this cannot be deduced analytically, and extensive testing is required to optimize the message structures.

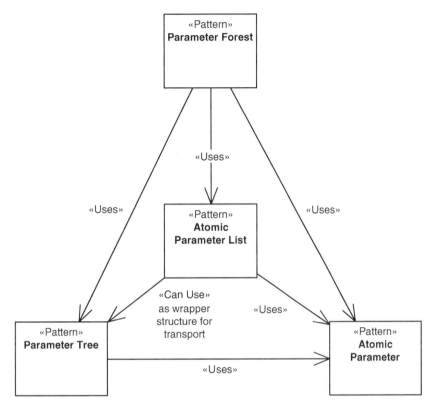

Figure 3.11 *Dependencies of patterns for the structure of parameter representation*

All kinds of additional data to be transmitted with the message, such as security-related data (for example, security tokens) or other metadata (for example, message and correlation identifiers or error codes), have to be considered here as well. Such extra information can actually change the structural representation of the message. For instance, if metadata has to be sent in addition to a Parameter Tree, it might make sense not to integrate the metadata in the tree but to use a Parameter Forest with two top-level tree elements instead, the message content and the metadata.

It is not always necessary to transmit entire data elements available in an underlying business logic or domain model. To enable better performance, only the relevant parts of the data elements should be transmitted. This optimizes the resource use (less bandwidth usage and lower memory consumption) and performance of message processing. For instance, if a client requires salary data stored in a set of employee data records to perform calculations unrelated to the specific employee, one could simply transmit all those records in a PARAMETER TREE. But as only the salary numbers are needed, sending only those numbers in an ATOMIC PARAMETER LIST would greatly reduce the message size.

On the other hand, breaking apart data into too many small messages can also negatively impact resource use, as it increases the network traffic and needs more bandwidth overall. Thus, a high number of small messages might require more performance for processing many messages overall. This situation gets even worse if the server has to restore the session state each time a message is processed. For instance, if the client in the preceding example requires other data from the set of employee records shortly after the first calculation and sends several successive requests, the total resource use and performance might be much worse than if the whole set of selected employee records had been transmitted in the first place.

Sometimes, a number of data elements can be grouped and sent in one message, again to improve resource use and performance. For instance, if an edge node of a cloud-based IoT solution collects data from sensors (such as a set of measurements in a certain time interval), it often makes sense to send this data to the cloud core in batches rather than sending each data element separately. When performing precalculations on the edge, their results might even fit into single ATOMIC PARAMETERS.

Considering the cacheability and mutability of message payload can help to improve performance and resource consumption.

Optimizing resource use and performance may have a negative influence on other qualities, such as understandability, simplicity, and complexity. For instance, an API that offers one message per specific task to be performed on an employee record would contain many more operations in the API endpoint than an alternative design that just allows for transmitting a specified set of employee records in their entirety. The former option might have a better resource utilization and performance, but the API design is also much more complex and thus harder to understand.

The request and response message structures are important elements of the API contract between API provider and API client; they contribute to the shared knowledge of the communication participants. This shared knowledge determines part of the coupling between API provider and API client, which is discussed as the *format autonomy* aspect of loose coupling [Fehling 2014]. For example, one could consider always exchanging strings or key-value pairs, but such generic solutions increase the knowledge that is implicitly shared between consumer and provider, leading to stronger coupling. This would complicate testing and maintenance. It also might bloat the message content unnecessarily.

Sometimes, only few data elements have to be exchanged in message structures to satisfy the information needs of the communication participants, for instance, when checking the status of a processing resource (in the form of a distinct value defined in an enumeration). If the API contract is underspecified, interoperability issues may arise, for instance, when dealing with optionality (which can be indicated by absence but also by dedicated `null` values) and other forms of variability (for example, choosing between different representations). If the contract is overspecified, it becomes inflexible with backward compatibility becoming hard to preserve. Simple data structures lead to fine-grained service contracts; complex ones are often used for coarse-grained services (that cover a large amount of business functionality).

In a few cases, interoperability concerns related to standardization might govern the decisions. If, for instance, a standard exchange format exists, the standard format might be chosen in order to save design effort even though a customized special-purpose format could be more understandable and more efficient to transfer.

Developer convenience and experience, including learning and programming effort, might also influence the decision on the structure of message representations. These aspects are closely related to understandability, simplicity, and complexity considerations. For instance, structures that are easy to create and populate might be difficult to understand or debug, whereas a compact format that is light in transfer might be difficult to document, understand, and parse.

Security (data integrity and confidentiality in particular) and data privacy concerns are relevant because security solutions might require additional message payload such as keys and tokens (often signed and/or encrypted). Another important consideration is which payload should actually be sent and how it should be protected. A thorough audit of all message content often is required. Data in transit should not be tampered with, and it should not be possible to pretend to be somebody else. Usually, it is enough to apply the security measures required for the most sensitive data elements of the message to the whole message. In some cases, such considerations might even lead to a different message structure or API refactoring (for instance, splitting endpoints or operations [Stocker 2021b]). For instance, when two data elements in a single message require different security levels (such as different permissions and roles), it might become necessary to split a complex message into two messages that are secured in different ways. Usage of Atomic Parameter requires the least design and processing work compared to the other more complex patterns with regard to the security level of the different parameters and their *semantic proximity,* as discussed in [Gysel 2016].

A problem with the decisions for the preceding patterns is that the API provider often does not know the use cases that API clients might have (in the future). For instance, when designing the API, the API provider offering the employee records in our example might not know which calculations different clients might want to perform. Hence, in real-life use, interface refactorings [Stocker 2021a; Neri 2020] and extensions are advisable. However, such continuous evolution of the API design has a negative impact on the stability of the API design. Important design considerations that are hard to get right in the first place are involved, one reason being the uncertainty about (future) use cases that API providers and API clients often experience.

> **Sample decision outcome.** The API designers at Lakeside Mutual decided as follows:
>
> *In the context of requests for the update customer* STATE TRANSITION OPERATION,
>
> *facing the need to aggregate information about customers,*
>
> *the API designers at Lakeside Mutual decided to combine the* PARAMETER TREE *and the* ATOMIC PARAMETER *patterns*
>
> *to achieve an expressive data contract exposing the desired view on the domain model,*
>
> *accepting that the nested tree structures have to be serialized and deserialized in an interoperable manner.*

Note that in addition to the more conceptual considerations called out in this section, many technology decisions also have to be made. This includes supported communication protocols (HTTP, HTTPS, AMQP, FTP, SMTP, and so on) and message exchange formats such as JSON, SOAP or plain XML, ASN.1 [Dubuisson 2001], Protocol Buffers [Google 2008], Apache Avro schemas [Apache 2021a], or Apache Thrift [Apache 2021b]. API query languages such as GraphQL [GraphQL 2021] can also be introduced.

Element Stereotypes

The decision on the structure of parameters, explained earlier, defines the data transfer representations (DTRs) for request and response messages. However, this decision does not yet define the meaning of the individual representation elements. Four element stereotype patterns, shown in Figure 3.12, define the typical design options for the element stereotypes decision.

> **Decision:** *Element stereotypes*
>
> What do the individual representation elements mean? Which purposes within the DTRs do they have?

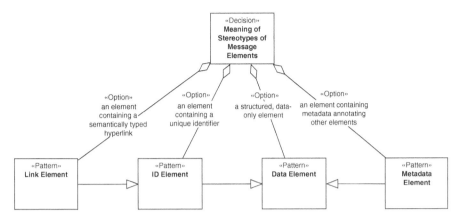

Figure 3.12 *Element stereotypes decision*

A rather common meaning or responsibility of a representation element is that it is used to transport ordinary application data. For example, consider the data of an Entity in the domain model if DDD [Evans 2003] is used to structure the business logic of an application.

	Pattern: DATA ELEMENT
Problem	How can domain/application-level information be exchanged between API clients and API providers without exposing provider-internal data definitions in the API? How can API client and API provider be decoupled from a data management point of view?
Solution	Define a dedicated vocabulary of DATA ELEMENTS for request and response messages that wraps and/or maps the relevant parts of the data in the business logic of an API implementation.

There are several decision drivers that apply to any kind of DATA ELEMENT. When designing API elements that represent data-centered domain elements such as Entities, the simplest and most expressive way to map them to APIs is to represent the Entity fully in the API. Often this is not a good idea, as it increases the number of processing options for communication participants, which limits the ease of processing the data. Interoperability can be at risk, and API documentation effort increases.

Unnecessary stateful communication might get introduced, violating SOA principles and microservices tenets [Zimmermann 2017] and leading to performance issues.

Security and data privacy concerns might also demand a careful selection of DATA ELEMENTS in an API. If communication partners receive a lot of detailed data, especially data elements they do not necessarily need, unwelcome security threats, such as the risk that data is tampered with, get introduced. In addition, extra data protection can cause configuration effort.

Any data in an API likely has to be maintained for a long period of time. Because backward compatibility is desired in many integration scenarios, APIs are hard to change. Continued testing of all API features is required. Flexibly adapting to continuously changing requirements comes with trade-offs regarding the maintainability and evolution of the API.

A type of DATA ELEMENT with metadata contained in it is METADATA ELEMENT.

	Pattern: METADATA ELEMENT
Problem	How can messages be enriched with additional information so that receivers can interpret the message content correctly, without having to hardcode assumptions about the data semantics?
Solution	Introduce one or more METADATA ELEMENTS to explain and enhance the other representation elements that appear in request and response messages. Populate the values of the METADATA ELEMENTS thoroughly and consistently; process them as to steer interoperable, efficient message consumption and processing.

The key decision drivers for METADATA ELEMENTS are similar to the ones for ordinary DATA ELEMENTS. However, a number of specific additional aspects have to be considered. If data travels with corresponding type, version, and author information, the receiver can use this extra information to resolve ambiguities, which improves interoperability. If runtime data is accompanied by additional explanatory data, it becomes easier to interpret and process; on the other hand, this may increase coupling between the communication parties. To improve ease of use, METADATA ELEMENTS may help the message recipient to understand the message content and process it efficiently. But messages become larger when METADATA ELEMENTS are included, so runtime efficiency may be negatively affected.

A type of DATA ELEMENT with a special meaning or responsibility are those elements that signify identifiers.

	Pattern: Id Element
Problem	How can API elements be distinguished from each other at design time and at runtime? When applying domain-driven design, how can elements of the Published Language be identified?
Solution	Introduce a special type of Data Element, a unique Id Element, to identify API endpoints, operations, and message representation elements that have to be distinguished from each other. Use these Id Elements consistently throughout API Description and implementation. Decide whether an Id Element is globally unique or valid only within the context of a particular API.

For an identification scheme used in Id Elements, it is important that they are accurate in multiple senses such that no ambiguities occur throughout the API life cycle. Simple schemes with low effort up front, such as flat, unstructured character strings as identifiers, can lead in the long run to stability issues and thus to more effort to fix the accumulated technical debt. For example, new requirements can lead to name changes of elements, and then API versions become incompatible with prior versions. Thus, if possible, universally unique identifiers (UUIDs) [Leach 2005] are usually better suited than simpler or only locally unique identifiers. Such identifiers are easily readable for machines but usually not for humans, which is another trade-off. Finally, there might be security concerns, as in many application contexts, it should be impossible or at least extremely difficult to guess instance identifiers. For UUIDs, this is the case, but it is not necessarily true for very simple identification schemes.

Remote addressability of identifiers is sometimes important. If so, URIs or other remote locators can be used as Id Elements. In their context, again, it must be decided whether speaking names or machine-readable unique identifiers are used (for example, a UUID can be part of a URI). This leads us to the next special type of Data Element, elements that provide links.

	Pattern: Link Element
Problem	How can API endpoints and operations be referenced in request and response message payloads so that they can be called remotely?
Solution	Include a special type of Id Element, a Link Element, to request or response messages. Let these Link Elements act as human- and machine-readable, network-accessible pointers to other endpoints and operations. Optionally, let additional Metadata Elements annotate and explain the nature of the relationship.

The LINK ELEMENT pattern shares its decision drivers with ID ELEMENT, as essentially all LINK ELEMENTS are remotely accessible ID ELEMENTS. The opposite does not hold; some identifiers used in APIs do not contain network-accessible addresses. For example, consider a domain data element that should not be remotely accessible by the client, but still has to be referenced (for instance, a key data element in the backend or in a third-party system). In such a situation, a URI cannot be used. It can be challenged whether or not such elements should be handed out to clients at all. Sometimes this might be a bad design choice, whereas in other cases, it might be necessary. Consider for instance a backend "Correlation Identifier" [Hohpe 2003] or a proxy (surrogate) for a Correlation Identifier: it must be passed along to the client in order to be applicable.

> **Sample decision outcome.** The API designers at Lakeside Mutual decided as follows:
>
> *In the context of the read customer* RETRIEVAL OPERATION,
>
> *facing the need to identify customers uniquely,*
>
> *the API designers at Lakeside Mutual decided to use a custom implementation of the* ID ELEMENT *pattern (example:* `"customerId"`: `"bunlo9vk5f"`)
>
> *to achieve a short, compact, and accurate form of customer identification,*
>
> *accepting that such ids are not network-addressable and not very readable for humans.*

Interlude: Responsibility and Structure Patterns in the Lakeside Mutual Case

We have already recorded several of the architectural decisions that the integration architects and API designers at Lakeside Mutual made. Let us now look at the resulting design (so far).

Turning the MDSL snippet from the initial API design in Chapter 2 into implementation-level classes—and walking through the decisions and pattern selection options we saw in this chapter so far—we might end up with the `CustomerInformationHolder` Spring Boot controller shown in Figure 3.13.

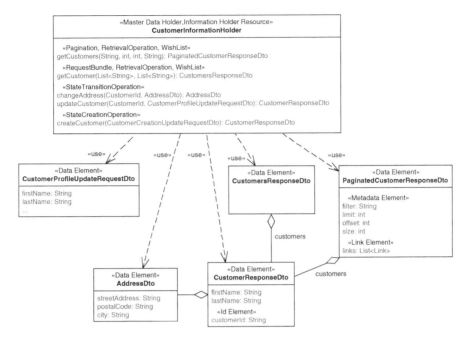

Figure 3.13 *Class diagram of the* CustomerInformationHolder *controller and its associated data transfer objects (DTOs)*

To let clients interact with the customer master data, the CustomerInforma-tionHolder is implemented as an INFORMATION HOLDER RESOURCE, specifically a MASTER DATA HOLDER that exposes several operations. In these operations, the request and response messages transport different DATA ELEMENTS, for example, of customer data. The implementation classes are not exposed directly; instead, DTOs are used. Unlike the entities, the DTOs also hold ID ELEMENTS and LINK ELEMENTS that let clients retrieve more data.

Because Lakeside Mutual serves a large number of customers, the result of the getCustomers RETRIEVAL OPERATION uses PAGINATION, a pattern we have not seen so far, to let API clients navigate the data in manageable chunks.

PAGINATION and other patterns related to API quality are featured later in the next two decision narratives.

Governing API Quality

An API provider must compromise between providing high-quality services and doing so in a cost-effective way. The patterns in the Quality category address or contribute to the following overarching design issue:

> *How can we achieve a certain level of quality of the offered API while at the same time utilizing the available resources in a cost-effective way?*

The quality of an API has many dimensions, starting with the functionality described in the API contract but also including reliability, performance, security, and scalability. Some of these technical qualities are referred to as *quality of service (QoS)* properties. QoS properties might be conflicting and almost always need to be balanced with economic requirements such as cost or time to market.

The guaranteed QoS does not have to be the same for all clients. Most decisions in this category have to be made for combinations of API clients and APIs accessed by these clients. Many decisions can be made for large groups of these combinations, such as all clients with freemium access to an API or all clients accessing a specific API.

The main decisions related to quality governance are shown in Figure 3.14.

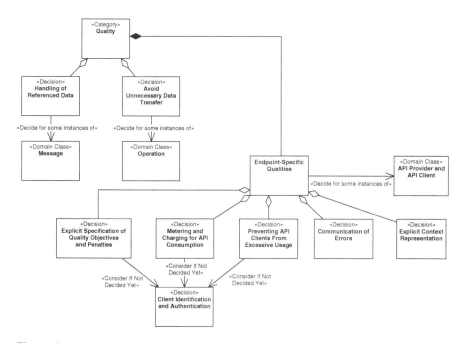

Figure 3.14 *Decisions about API quality and its governance*

API quality has to be governed and, as needed, improved. In this section, we look at governance and management; the next one suggests quality improvements. The themes of the decisions about the patterns in this category are as follows:

- Identification and authentication of the API client
- Metering and charging for API consumption
- Preventing API clients from excessive API usage
- Communication of errors
- Context representation

Identification and Authentication of the API Client

Identification means distinguishing which client is interacting with the API; *authentication* refers to validating an identity provided to the API. Identification and authentication are important for providers of APIs that are paid for (and/or use freemium models) in order to establish *authorization:* once an API client is identified and authenticated, the API provider grants access based on the API client's proven identity and its authorization rights. For example, an API provider of a commercial API offering must identify its clients to decide whether a call actually originates from a known client (such as a paying customer) or from an unknown one.

Authentication and authorization are important for ensuring security, but they also enable measures for ensuring many other qualities. For instance, the performance of the overall system can degrade if unknown clients can access the API without control or if known clients are able to make excessive use of the API. In such situations, reliability is threatened or operating costs may rise unexpectedly.

QoS-related factors such as performance, scalability, and reliability can be ensured or monitored to a certain extent by the API provider and API client. In addition, they can be guaranteed in QoS guarantees to the API client. Such guarantees are usually related to some notion of pricing scheme or subscription model of the client, and this requires API client identification and authentication as well.

In summary, client identification and authentication are the foundations for achieving certain security qualities and support many techniques to establish QoS and cost control. The typical decision to be made in this context is shown in Figure 3.15. Its link to other decisions and practices is apparent in Figure 3.14, which shows that several decisions require us to consider client identification and authentication.

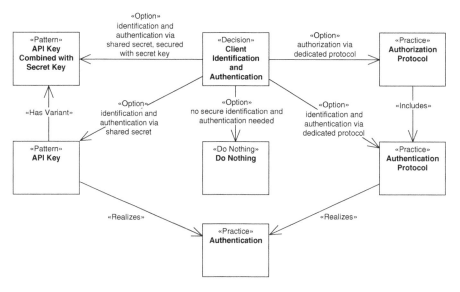

Figure 3.15 *Client identification and authentication decision*

The first and simplest option is to decide that secure identification and authentication are not needed, which is suitable, for instance, in nonproduction system APIs; for APIs in controlled, nonpublic networks with a limited number of clients; or for PUBLIC APIs with a limited number of clients and no great risks in case of abuse or excessive use.

The obvious alternative is to introduce an authentication mechanism for the API. An API KEY that identifies the client is a minimalistic solution to this problem.

	Pattern: API KEY
Problem	How can an API provider identify and authenticate clients and their requests?
Solution	As an API provider, assign each client a unique token—the API KEY—that the client can present to the API endpoint for identification purposes.

If security is an important issue, API KEYS are insufficient on their own. In conjunction with an additional secret key that is not transmitted, API KEYS can be used to securely authenticate an API client. The API KEY identifies the client, and an additional signature made with the secret key, which is never transmitted, proves the identity and ensures that the request was not tampered with.

Many complements and alternatives to API Keys exist, as security is a challenging, multifaceted topic. For instance, OAuth 2.0 [Hardt 2012] is an industry-standard protocol for authorization that is also the foundation for secure authentication through OpenID Connect [OpenID 2021]. Another example of a full-fledged authentication or authorization protocol is Kerberos [Neuman 2005], an authentication protocol that is often used inside a network to provide single sign-on. In combination with Lightweight Directory Access Protocol (LDAP) [Sermersheim 2006], it can also provide authorization. LDAP itself also offers authentication features, so LDAP can be used as authentication and/or authorization protocol. Examples of point-to-point authentication protocols are Challenge-Handshake Authentication Protocol (CHAP) [Simpson 1996] and Extensible Authentication Protocol (EAP) [Vollbrecht 2004].

A number of forces have to be considered in this decision. First of all, the level of required security is important. If secure identification and authentication are required, it is insufficient to choose either no secure identification and authentication needed or API Keys. API Keys help to establish basic security. Although they require following a registration process, API Keys bring only a slight degradation in terms of ease of use for clients once they have been obtained (compared to no secure identification and authentication). The other options are less easy to use, as they require dealing with more complex protocols and setting up the required services and infrastructure. The management of user account credentials required in authentication and authorization protocols can be tedious both on the client and provider side; this is avoided in all options using API Keys, including its combination with a secret key.

With regard to performance, the decision that secure identification and authentication is not needed has no overhead. API Keys have a slight overhead for processing the keys, and their combination with a secret key requires some more processing slightly reducing the performance. Authentication and authorization protocols tend to have more overhead, as they also offer additional features (such as contacting a trusted third party in Kerberos or authorization in OAuth or LDAP). Finally, the API Key option decouples the client making an API call from the client's organization, as using the customer's account credentials would needlessly give system administrators and developers full account access. This problem could be mitigated in authentication and authorization protocols by establishing subaccount credentials that only enable API access for an API client but do not offer any other privileges of the customer's account.

Sample decision outcome. The API designers at Lakeside Mutual decided as follows:

In the context of the Community API for Frontend Integration *for customer management,*

facing the need to protect sensitive personal information such as customer records,

the API designers at Lakeside Mutual decided for the API Key *pattern*

to achieve that only identified clients can access the API,

accepting that API Key *management is required, which adds operational cost, and also accepting that this is only a basic security solution.*

Metering and Charging for API Consumption

If the API is a commercial offering, the API provider might want to charge for its usage. Thus, a means for identifying and authenticating clients is required. Usually, existing authentication practices are used. Then the provider can monitor clients and assign a Pricing Plan for the API usage.

Pattern: Pricing Plan

Problem	How can the API provider meter API service consumption and charge for it?
Solution	Assign a Pricing Plan for the API usage to the API Description that is used to bill API customers, advertisers, or other stakeholders accordingly. Define and monitor metrics for measuring API usage, such as API usage statistics per operation.

Again, we can alternatively not meter and charge the customer.

Figure 3.17 illustrates possible variants of the Pricing Plan pattern: pricing can be based on actual usage, on some kind of market-based allocation (such as auctions), or on flat-rate subscriptions. Each of these variants can be combined with a freemium model. In the context of a Pricing Plan, sometimes a Rate Limit is used to ensure fair use. Figure 3.16 illustrates the metering and charging for API consumption decision.

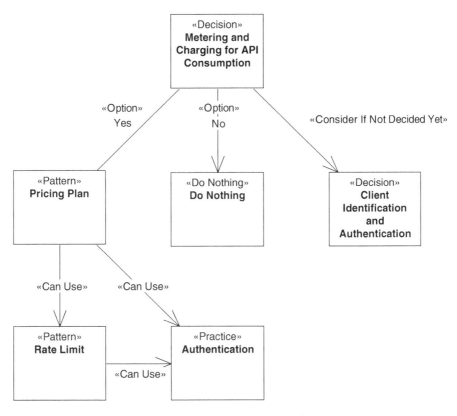

Figure 3.16 *Metering and charging for API consumption decision*

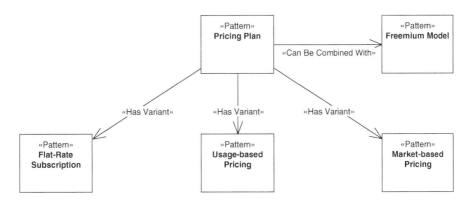

Figure 3.17 *PRICING PLAN variants*

The major drivers for this decision are usually economic aspects, such as pricing models and selecting a variant of the pattern that best suits the business model. The benefits of applying the pattern should be contrasted with the efforts and costs required to meter and charge customers. Accuracy is central, as API customers expect to be billed only for the services they actually have consumed. Accurate metering requires an adequate meter granularity. Because metering and charging records contain sensitive information about customers, extra protection has to be provided to ensure security.

Sample decision outcome. The API designers at Lakeside Mutual decided as follows:

In the context of the customer self-service channel,

facing the need to attract and retain customers,

the API designers at Lakeside Mutual decided not to introduce a Pricing Plan *but offer their API at no charge*

to achieve API acceptance and success,

accepting that the API has to be funded in other ways.

Preventing API Clients from Excessive API Usage

Excessive use of an API by a few clients can significantly limit the usefulness of the service for other clients. Simply adding more processing power, storage space, and network bandwidth to solve the problem is usually not viable economically. Therefore, preventing excessive API usage by clients often is in order. Once API clients can be identified, their individual usage of the API can be monitored; the typical way to perform identification is authentication of clients, as explained earlier. The Rate Limit pattern addresses the problem of excessive API use by limiting the number of requests per period of time allowed.

	Pattern: Rate Limit
Problem	How can the API provider prevent API clients from excessive API usage?
Solution	Introduce and enforce a Rate Limit to safeguard against API clients that overuse the API.

The alternative to using Rate Limits is to do nothing to prevent API clients from excessive API usage. This makes sense in situations in which the problem is assessed as unlikely to turn into a severe issue. For example, if all clients are in-house clients or trusted partners, the overhead of a Rate Limit might not be justified.

The two alternatives, as well as the link to client identification and authentication (and the authentication practices), are shown in Figure 3.18.

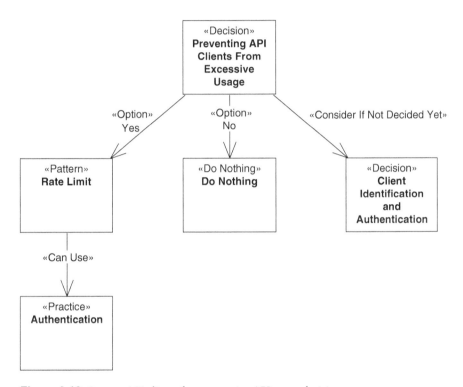

Figure 3.18 *Prevent API clients from excessive API usage decision*

The major forces to be considered in this decision are as follows: A certain level of performance has to be maintained by the provider (sometimes even formally guaranteed in a Service Level Agreement); performance could be compromised if clients abuse the API. Means for supporting client awareness of Rate Limits are required so that clients can find out how much of their limits they have used up at a given point in time. Establishing Rate Limits helps the provider to support qualities related to reliability because they make it harder for clients to abuse the API in a way that puts these qualities at risk. All these potential benefits must be contrasted to the impact and severity of risks of API abuse and economic aspects. Introducing RATE LIMITS produces costs and can be perceived negatively by clients. Thus, it has to be judged whether the risks of API abuse imposed by a few clients are higher than the risks and costs associated with introducing RATE LIMITS for all clients.

Sample decision outcome. The API designers at Lakeside Mutual decided as follows:

In the context of the customer self-service channel,

facing the need to attract and retain customers,

the API designers at Lakeside Mutual decided for the RATE LIMIT *pattern*

to achieve fair workload distribution,

accepting that the chosen RATE LIMIT *has to be enforced, which causes implementation effort and will slow down demanding API clients hitting their limits.*

Explicit Specification of Quality Objectives and Penalties

Quality objectives are kept implicit and vague for many APIs. If the client requires (or even pays for) stronger guarantees or the provider wants to make explicit guarantees, for instance, as differentiation from competitors, an explicit specification of quality objectives and penalties can be valuable. An instance of the SERVICE LEVEL AGREEMENT pattern as a more formal extension and complement of the API DESCRIPTION (and thus of the API contract) detailing measurable service-level objectives (SLOs) and (optionally) penalties in case of violations provides a way to compile such specifications.

Pattern: SERVICE LEVEL AGREEMENT

Problem	How can an API client learn about the specific quality-of-service characteristics of an API and its endpoint operations? How can these characteristics, and the consequences of not meeting them, be defined and communicated in a measurable way?
Solution	As an API product owner, establish a structured, quality-oriented SERVICE LEVEL AGREEMENT that defines testable service-level objectives.

The decision about introducing a service-level agreement (SLA) is shown in Figure 3.19. To make an SLA unambiguous, it must identify the specific API operation(s) that it pertains to and must contain at least one measurable SLO. An SLO specifies a measurable aspect of the API, such as performance or availability.

There are a number of typical variants of the pattern: SLAs only used for internal use, SLAs with formally specified SLOs, and SLAs with only informally specified SLOs.

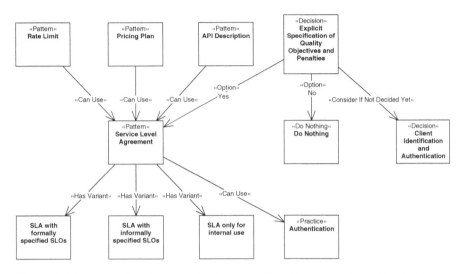

Figure 3.19 *SLAs and explicit specification of quality objectives and penalties decision*

A PRICING PLAN and RATE LIMIT should refer to the SERVICE LEVEL AGREEMENT if it is used. Like these patterns, a SERVICE LEVEL AGREEMENT requires means for identifying and authenticating clients; usually, authentication practices such as API KEYS or authentication protocols have to be used as well.

Several main decision drivers steer this decision. It relates to business agility and vitality, as the business model of an API client might rely on one or more of the previously named qualities of a particular service. Attractiveness from the consumer's point of view can be higher if guarantees about qualities are provided and communicated to the client. However, this must be contrasted with possible issues related to cost-efficiency and business risks from a provider point of view. Some guarantees are required by government regulations and legal obligations, such as those related to personal data protection. Typical aspects that are candidates for guarantees in SLAs are availability, performance, and security.

Sample decision outcome. The API designers at Lakeside Mutual decided as follows:

In the context of all insurance management APIs,

facing the need to coordinate API client and provider development,

the API designers at Lakeside Mutual decided against an explicit service-level agreement ("do nothing")

to achieve that the documentation and operations overhead is kept light,

accepting that clients' expectations might not match the QoS that they can actually experience.

Note that some architectural decisions typically are revised as a product or service evolves. In our insurance case, an SLA is actually introduced at a later stage, as we will see in the presentation of the SLA pattern in Chapter 9.

Communication of Errors

A common quality concern for APIs is how to report and handle errors, as this has direct impacts on aspects such as avoiding and fixing defects, costs of defect fixing, robustness and reliability problems due to unfixed defects, and so on. If an error occurs on the provider side, it can be due to an incorrect request, invalid permissions, or numerous other problems that could be the fault of the client, the API implementation, or the underlying IT infrastructure.

One option is not to report (and then handle) an error at all, but this is usually not advisable. A common solution if only one protocol stack is used (such as HTTP over TCP/IP) is to leverage the error-reporting mechanisms of these protocols, for instance, status codes in HTTP (protocol-level error codes). This does not work if error reporting has to cover multiple protocols, formats, and platforms. In such cases, the ERROR REPORT pattern is eligible.

	Pattern: ERROR REPORT
Problem	How can an API provider inform its clients about communication and processing faults? How can this information be made independent of the underlying communication technologies and platforms (for example, protocol-level headers representing status codes)?
Solution	Reply with error codes in response messages that indicate and classify the faults in a simple, machine-readable way. In addition, add textual descriptions of the errors for the API client stakeholders, including developers and/or end users such as administrators.

The decision is illustrated in Figure 3.20. The main decision drivers to introduce any kind of error reporting are the help in fixing defects and the increased robustness and reliability that this promises. Error reporting leads to better maintainability and evolvability. Detailed explanations of errors reduce the effort to locate the root cause of a defect; consequently, the Error Report pattern often is more effective than simple error codes. The target audiences of fault information include developers and operators, but also help desk and other supporting personnel. Thus, Error Reports should be designed to reach high expressiveness and achieve meeting the target audience's expectations. Error Reports are usually designed to score well with regard to interoperability and portability, compared to simple error codes. However, rather elaborate error messages can reveal information that is problematic with regard to security, as disclosing more information about system internals opens up attack vectors. An Error Report requires more work if internationalization is required because the more detailed information contained in the Error Report has to be translated.

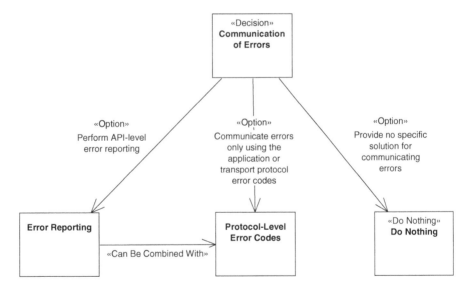

Figure 3.20 *Communicate errors decision*

Sample decision outcome. The API designers at Lakeside Mutual decided as follows:

In the context of all BACKEND INTEGRATION *APIs,*

facing the need to operate reliably even in case of failures,

the API designers at Lakeside Mutual decided to use the ERROR REPORT *pattern*

to achieve that clients can use the reported error information to decide on their reactions,

accepting that the reports have to be prepared and processed and that response message size will increase.

Explicit Context Representation

In some messages, in addition to ordinary data, context information has to be exchanged between client and provider. Examples of context information are location and other API user information, the preferences forming a WISH LIST, or security information such as login credentials used for authentication, authorization, and billing (for instance, including an API KEY).

To promote protocol independence and a platform-independent design, there is an alternative to the default use of standard headers and header extension capabilities of the networking protocol: each message can be enhanced with a CONTEXT REPRESENTATION in the message body. Figure 3.21 shows the decision between the default choice ("do nothing") and the alternative, pattern-based solution. Here, "do nothing" means either that no context information is sent at all or that the context information is sent as part of the protocol header and not made explicit in the message payload.

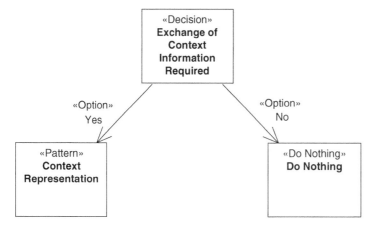

Figure 3.21 CONTEXT REPRESENTATION *decision*

Decision: *Context representation*

Is the exchange of explicit context information adequate?

This choice decides for or against the Context Representation pattern.

	Pattern: Context Representation
Problem	How can API consumers and providers exchange context information without relying on any particular remoting protocols? How can identity information and quality properties in a request be made visible to related subsequent ones in conversations?
Solution	Combine and group all Metadata Elements that carry the desired information into a custom representation element in request and/or response messages. Do not transport this single Context Representation in protocol headers, but place it in the message payload. Separate global from local context in a conversation by structuring the Context Representation accordingly. Position and mark the consolidated Context Representation element so that it is easy to find and distinguish from other Data Elements.

Interoperability and technical modifiability can be enhanced if context information is transported outside of protocol-level headers. Otherwise, it becomes difficult to ensure that context information exchange can pass each kind of intermediary, such as "Proxies" [Gamma 1995] and "API Gateways" [Richardson 2016] in a distributed system. When protocols are upgraded, the availability and semantics of predefined protocol headers may change. In addition, Context Representation helps to cope with the diversity of protocols to be supported in many distributed applications, which in turn can help to improve evolvability and lessen dependencies on technologies. The pattern can increase developer productivity:

Using protocol headers is convenient and makes it possible to leverage protocol-specific frameworks, middleware, and infrastructure (such as load balancers and caches) but delegates control to the protocol designers and implementers. By contrast, a custom approach maximizes control but causes development and test effort.

To achieve end-to-end security, tokens and digital signatures have to be transported across multiple nodes. Such security credentials are a type of control metadata that the consumer and provider have to exchange directly; involving intermediaries and protocol endpoints would break the desired end-to-end security. Similarly, logging and auditing information is critical context data that should be transported end to end without any interference from intermediaries.

Sample decision outcome. The API designers at Lakeside Mutual decided as follows:

In the context of its Backend Integration *APIs,*

having to cross technology boundaries to satisfy end-to-end quality of service needs,

the API designers at Lakeside Mutual decided to introduce an explicit Context Representation

to achieve that client can find all metadata in one place,

accepting that the underlying network might not have access to the context data in the payload.

This decision narrative covered the theme API quality governance; the next set of decisions aims at improving certain qualities, such as performance.

Deciding for API Quality Improvements

The previous section dealt with quality governance and management; in this section, we investigate quality improvements. We start with pagination and then investigate other ways to avoid unnecessary data transfer and how to handle referenced data in messages.

Pagination

Sometimes complex representation elements can contain large amounts of data that is repetitive in nature (for instance, record sets). If only a subset of this information at a time is required at the client, it might be better to send the information in small chunks rather than in one large transmission. For example, consider thousands of records being contained in the data, but a client displaying the information pagewise with 20 records per page; user input is required to advance to the next page. Displaying only the current page and maybe prefetching one or two pages in either stepping direction might be far more efficient in terms of performance and bandwidth use than downloading all data records before even starting to display the data.

The starting point is that API designers have decided to apply either PARAMETER TREE or PARAMETER FOREST. Both patterns are used to represent complex data records. In such cases, the designers should think about the following decision (illustrated in Figure 3.22):

Figure 3.22 *PAGINATION decision*

Decision: *Pagination decisions*

Does a data structure to be transmitted to API clients contain a large number of data records with the same structure? If yes: For the task of the API client, are only a few data records required?

If both conditions apply, the PAGINATION pattern is eligible.

	Pattern: PAGINATION
Problem	How can an API provider deliver large sequences of structured data without overwhelming clients?
Solution	Divide large response data sets into manageable and easy-to-transmit chunks (also known as pages). Send one chunk of partial results per response message, and inform the client about the total and/or remaining number of chunks. Provide optional filtering capabilities to allow clients to request a particular selection of results. For extra convenience, include a reference to the next chunk/page from the current one.

Figure 3.23 shows the pattern relations of PAGINATION.

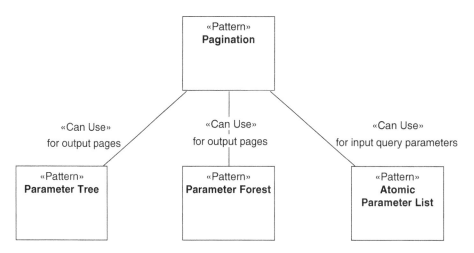

Figure 3.23 *PAGINATION dependencies*

The pattern has the following relations to the patterns presented earlier:

• An ATOMIC PARAMETER LIST is usually used for its request message containing the query parameters.

- A PARAMETER TREE or a PARAMETER FOREST is usually used for the data structuring in its response messages.

In addition to index-and page-based Pagination, the pattern has three variants:

- *Offset-Based Pagination:* Compared to simple pages, an offset specified by the API client enables more flexibility in controlling the number of requested results or changes in the page size.
- *Cursor-Based Pagination:* This variant does not rely on the index of an element but instead on a cursor that the API client can control.
- *Time-Based Pagination:* This variant is similar to *Cursor-Based Pagination* but uses timestamps instead of cursors to request chunks.

There are several key decision drivers when applying PAGINATION. The structure of data elements or of the additional data that have to be sent with the message needs to be repetitive in nature (contain data records, that is). The variability of the data should be considered: Are all data elements identically structured? How often do data definitions change?

PAGINATION aims to substantially improve resource consumption and performance by sending only the data needed at the moment as fast as possible to the API client. A single large response message might be inefficient to exchange and process.

In this context, data set size and data access profile (derived from the user wants and needs), especially the number of data records required to be available to an API client (immediately and over time), have to be considered. Especially when returning data for human consumption, not all data may be needed immediately.

Also related to resource consumption, the memory available for a request (on both API provider and API client sides) as well as the capacity of the network have to be considered. Network and endpoint processing capabilities should be used efficiently, but all results should be transferred and processed accurately and consistently.

Common text-based message exchange formats (for instance, expressively tagged XML or JSON) incur high parsing costs and transfer data size due to verbosity and overhead of the textual representations of the data. Some of this overhead can be significantly reduced by using binary formats such as Apache Avro or Protocol Buffers. However, many of these formats require dedicated serialization/deserialization libraries, which may not be available in all consumer environments, for example, API clients in Web browsers. The pattern is particularly eligible in such cases.

Underlying network transports, such as IP networking, transport data in packets, which leads to nonlinear transfer times with data size. For example, 1500 bytes fit into a single IP packet transmitted over Ethernet [Hornig 1984]. As soon as the data is one byte longer, two separate packets have to be transmitted and reassembled on the receiver side.

From a security standpoint, retrieving and encoding large data sets can incur high effort and cost on the provider side and can thus open up an attack vector for a denial-of-service attack. Moreover, transferring large data sets across a network can lead to interruptions because networks are not guaranteed to be reliable, especially cellular networks.

Finally, compared to using the PARAMETER TREE and PARAMETER FOREST patterns without PAGINATION, the pattern is substantially more complex to understand and thus can be less convenient to developers and generally requires more experience.

Sample decision outcome. The API designers at Lakeside Mutual decided as follows:

In the context of the retrieval operations in the Customer Core MASTER DATA HOLDER,

facing the need to balance the number of requests/responses and message sizes,

the API designers at Lakeside Mutual decided to use the cursor-based variant of the PAGINATION *pattern*

to achieve slicing of large data sets in responses,

accepting that these request-response pairs have to be coordinated, which requires control metadata.

Other Means of Avoiding Unnecessary Data Transfer

Sometimes unnecessary data is transferred when API operations are called. We already learned about PAGINATION as an option to reduce response message sizes. Four more patterns address such situations.

Most API quality aspects discussed earlier can be decided for broader groups of API and client combinations (such as all clients who have freemium API access). In contrast, the decisions about patterns in this section must be made per operation, as only an analysis of the individual information needs of the clients of a particular operation can indicate whether or not the data transfer can be reduced.

API providers often serve many different clients. It can be hard to design API operations that provide exactly the data required by all these clients. Some of them might use only a subset of the data offered by the operations; other clients might expect more data. The information need might not be predictable before runtime. A possible way to solve this problem is to let the client inform the provider at runtime about its data fetching preferences. A simple option to do this is to let the client send a list of its desires.

Pattern: WISH LIST

Problem	How can an API client inform the API provider at runtime about the data it is interested in?
Solution	As an API client, provide a WISH LIST in the request that enumerates all desired data elements of the requested resource. As an API provider, deliver only those data elements in the response message that are enumerated in the Wish List ("response shaping").

A simple list of wishes is not always easy to specify, for example, if a client wants to request only certain fractions of deeply nested or repetitive parameter structures. An alternative solution that works better for complex parameters is to let the client send a template (or mock object) expressing the wishes as examples in its request.

Pattern: WISH TEMPLATE

Problem	How can an API client inform the API provider about nested data that it is interested in? How can such preferences be expressed flexibly and dynamically?
Solution	Add one or more additional parameters to the request message that mirror the hierarchical structure of the parameters in the corresponding response message. Make these parameters optional or use Boolean as their types so that their values indicate whether or not a parameter should be included.

While WISH LISTS are typically specified as ATOMIC PARAMETER LISTS and lead to a reply based on a PARAMETER TREE, WISH TEMPLATE typically performs the specification of the wish in a mock PARAMETER TREE whose structure is also used for the response.

Let us consider another situation in which an analysis of the usage of the operations of an API provider shows that some clients keep requesting the same server-side data. The requested data changes much less frequently than the client's send requests. In such cases, we can avoid unnecessary data transfer by using a Conditional Request.

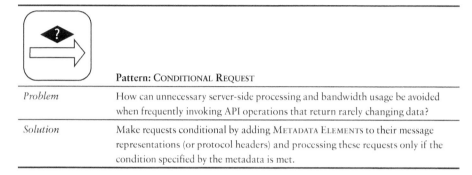

Pattern: Conditional Request

Problem	How can unnecessary server-side processing and bandwidth usage be avoided when frequently invoking API operations that return rarely changing data?
Solution	Make requests conditional by adding Metadata Elements to their message representations (or protocol headers) and processing these requests only if the condition specified by the metadata is met.

For example, the provider could supply a *fingerprint* for each resource accessed, which the client can then include in a subsequent request to indicate which "version" of the resource it already has cached locally so that only newer versions are sent.

In other situations, an analysis of the usage of the already-deployed API might reveal that clients are issuing many similar requests and that individual responses are returned for one or more of these calls. These batches of requests may have a negative impact on scalability and throughput. In such situations, the Request Bundle pattern is eligible.

Pattern: Request Bundle

Problem	How can the number of requests and responses be reduced to increase communication efficiency?
Solution	Define a Request Bundle as a data container that assembles multiple independent requests in a single request message. Add metadata such as identifiers of individual requests and bundle element counter.

Figure 3.24 summarizes the decision on how to avoid unnecessary data transfer.

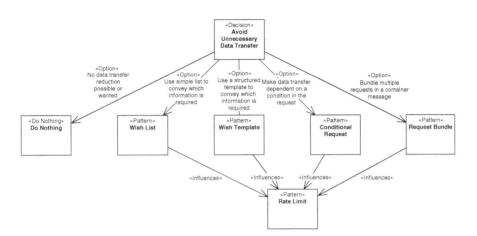

Figure 3.24 *Avoid unnecessary data transfer decision*

For many operations, no data transfer reduction is possible or wanted for the target operation(s). Alternatively, unnecessary data transfer can be avoided through one of the two patterns WISH LIST and WISH TEMPLATE, which both inform the provider about required data at runtime. Other alternatives are CONDITIONAL REQUEST to avoid repeated responses to the same requests and REQUEST BUNDLE to aggregate multiple requests in a single message.

The combination of CONDITIONAL REQUEST with either WISH LIST or WISH TEMPLATE is a rather useful choice to indicate which subset of resources is requested in case the condition evaluation states that the resource should be sent again. REQUEST BUNDLE can in principle be combined with each of the prior alternatives CONDITIONAL REQUEST or either WISH LIST or WISH TEMPLATE. However, a combination of two or even three of the patterns increases the complexity of the API design and programming substantially for rather little gains, as all four patterns influence a similar set of desired qualities positively. Figure 3.25 shows the possible pattern combinations.

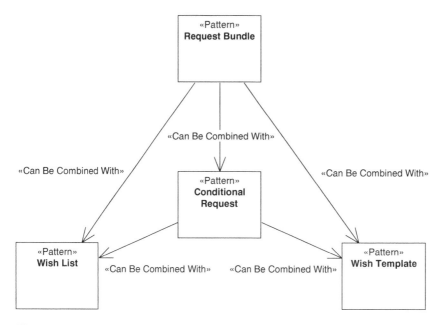

Figure 3.25 *Avoid unnecessary data transfer: Pattern combinations*

The main decision driver for this decision concerns the individual information needs of clients, which have to be analyzed in order to find out which of the patterns (and maybe even which combinations) are applicable and promise to have enough benefits. Consider situations where data transfer over the network is perceived as a potential bottleneck. In such cases, data parsimony can further drive the decision. Data parsimony is an important general design principle in distributed systems, and the four patterns can help to enhance parsimonious ways of data transmission.

Selecting any of the four patterns usually has a positive influence on the RATE LIMIT and on bandwidth use, as less data is transferred. This likely will also improve the performance, as transferring all data elements to all clients all the time, even to clients that have only a limited or minimal information need, wastes resources (including response time, throughput, and processing time).

Security can be a driver *not* to apply the patterns WISH LIST and WISH TEMPLATE. Enabling clients to provide options regarding which data to receive may unwittingly expose sensitive data to unexpected requests or generally open up additional attack vectors. For instance, sending long data element lists or using invalid attribute names might be used to introduce an API-specific form of denial-of-service attack. Data that is not transferred cannot be stolen and cannot be tampered with. Finally, complicating the API—as all four patterns do—increases the complexity of API client programming. The currently trending GraphQL technology can be seen as an extreme form of declarative WISH TEMPLATE. In addition, special invocation cases introduced by the patterns require more testing and maintenance efforts.

> **Sample decision outcome.** How does the Lakeside Mutual APIs provide a suited message granularity and call frequency? The architects and designers chose patterns as follows:
>
> *In the context of the Customer Management frontend for staff and agent use cases,*
>
> *having to deal with large amounts of customer records,*
>
> *the API designers at Lakeside Mutual selected the* WISH LIST *pattern and did not pick any other pattern from this section*
>
> *so that response messages are small,*
>
> *accepting that the wishes have to be prepared on the client side and processed on the provider side, and that additional metadata is required.*

Closely related to the decisions about message size optimization is the decision about inlining or splitting structured data (complex data with multifaceted relations between its parts, that is). We investigate two alternative patterns tackling this design issue next.

Handling Referenced Data in Messages

Not every DATA ELEMENT in a message can be represented as a plain data record, as some data records contain references to other data records. An important question is how these local data references should be reflected in the API; answers to it determine the API granularity and its coupling characteristics.

> **Decision:** *Handling of referenced data*
>
> How should referenced data in data records be represented in the API?

There are two major options for this decision, shown in Figure 3.26.

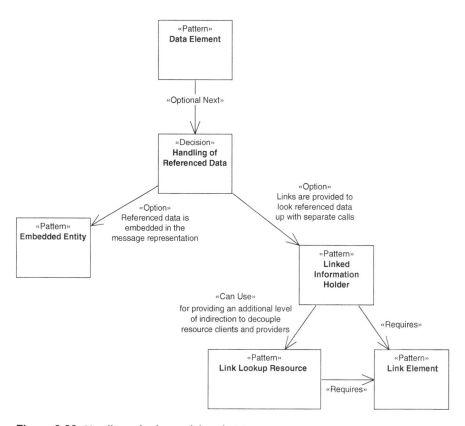

Figure 3.26 *Handling of referenced data decision*

One option to address this problem is to embed the data of the referenced data record in the DATA ELEMENT to be sent over the wire.

	Pattern: EMBEDDED ENTITY
Problem	How can one avoid sending multiple messages when their receivers require insights about multiple related information elements?
Solution	For any data relationship that the client wants to follow, embed a DATA ELEMENT in the request or response message that contains the data of the target end of the relationship. Place this EMBEDDED ENTITY inside the representation of the source of the relationship.

The alternative is to make the referenced data accessible remotely and point at it, introducing a Link Element to the message:

	Pattern: Linked Information Holder
Problem	How can messages be kept small even when an API deals with multiple information elements that reference each other?
Solution	Add a Link Element to messages that pertain to multiple related information elements. Let this Link Element reference another API endpoint that represents the linked element.

Figure 3.26 illustrates that this pattern can use a Link Lookup Resource for providing an additional level of indirection to decouple resource clients and providers. Both Linked Information Holder and Link Lookup Resource require the use of Link Elements.

It is possible to combine the two patterns, for instance, when using a top-level Embedded Entity that itself uses Linked Information Holders for (some of) its referenced data records.

As decision drivers, performance and scalability often play a major role. Both message size and the number of calls required to perform an integration should be low, but these two desires stand in conflict with each other.

Modifiability and flexibility have to be considered as well: information elements contained in structured self-contained data might be hard to change because any local updates have to be coordinated and synchronized with updates to related data structures and the API operations that send and receive them. Structured data that contains references to external resources usually is even harder to change than self-contained data as there are more consequences and (external) dependencies for clients.

Embedded Entity data sometimes gets stored for a while, whereas links always refer to the latest updates in the data. Thus, accessing data when it is needed via links is positive for data quality, data freshness, and data consistency. In terms of data privacy, a relationship source and target might have different protection needs—for example, a person and the credit card information belonging to this person. This has to be considered, for instance, before embedding the credit card information in a message requesting the person's data.

Sample decision outcome. Does Lakeside Mutual prefer many small or few large messages? They decided as follows:

In the context of the customer self-service channel,

facing the need to expose the customer aggregate that contains two entities (and works with two database tables), the API designers at Lakeside Mutual decided to use the EMBEDDED ENTITY *pattern*

and neglected LINKED INFORMATION HOLDER

so that all related data is transmitted in a single request,

accepting that the address data is transferred although not needed in some use cases.

The patterns API KEY, CONTEXT REPRESENTATION, and ERROR REPORT are used mainly in the elaboration (or Define) phase, which is covered in Chapter 6, "Design Request and Response Message Representations." Chapter 7, "Refine Message Design for Quality," then covers the construction (or Design) phase, containing the patterns CONDITIONAL REQUEST, REQUEST BUNDLE, WISH LIST, WISH TEMPLATE, EMBEDDED ENTITY, and LINKED INFORMATION HOLDER. Finally, the PRICING PLAN, RATE LIMIT, and SERVICE LEVEL AGREEMENT patterns are covered in Chapter 9, as they mainly concern the transition phase of an API.

This completes the coverage of decisions and pattern options about API quality (in this book). Next, we identify decisions required and patterns available to organize API evolution.

Decisions about API Evolution

To be successful, APIs should expose stable contracts serving as a baseline for building applications on top of them; developer expectations and delivery guarantees have to be balanced. APIs must be maintained, and they have to *evolve* while fixing bugs and adding features. The evolution of an API requires that API providers and clients, who usually follow different life cycles [Murer 2010], establish rules and policies to ensure that (1) the provider can improve and extend the API and its implementation, and (2) the client can keep functioning with no or few required changes for as long as possible. Modifying an API might lead to client-breaking changes. However, breaking changes should be minimized, as they cause migration efforts for a potentially large (and sometimes unknown) number of clients. If required changes cause API version upgrades, these changes and upgrades have to be managed and communicated well to reduce the associated risk and cost.

API providers and clients have to balance different, conflicting concerns in order to follow their own life cycles; a certain amount of autonomy is required to avoid tight coupling between them. In response to this conflict, the patterns presented here jointly support API owners, designers, and users who seek to answer the following question:

What are the governing rules balancing stability and compatibility with maintainability and extensibility during API evolution?

As illustrated in Figure 3.27, API evolution centers around three decisions. The first is whether the API supports some explicitly defined version identification scheme, and if so, how version information is exchanged. The second decision is on when and how new versions of an API should be introduced and old versions are decommissioned. It offers three alternative strategies as decision options. Finally, it can be decided whether or not any of the four strategies is augmented with an additional experimental preview. All those decisions are typically made at the *API* level.

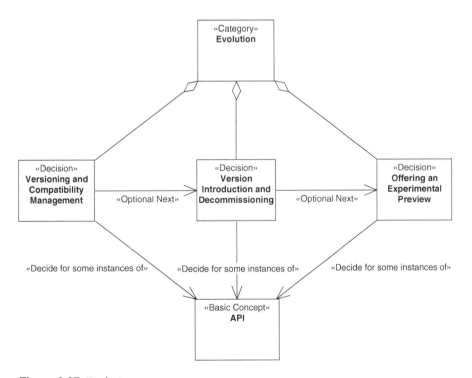

Figure 3.27 *Evolution category*

Versioning and Compatibility Management

An important early decision regarding API evolution is how versioning should be supported. In rare cases, even not versioning at all might be an option—consider, for instance, proof-of-concept, experimental preview, or hobby projects.

> **Decision:** *Versioning and compatibility management*
>
> Should API versioning and compatibility management be supported? How should it be supported?

Figure 3.28 illustrates the typical options for this decision. First, it has to be decided whether an explicit version identification and transmission scheme is used. The pattern Version Identifier covers this option. Next, Semantic Versioning describes the use of a structured Version Identifier that separates breaking from non-breaking changes.

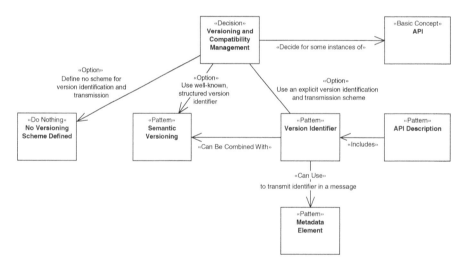

Figure 3.28 *Versioning and compatibility management decision*

Version Identifier defines how explicit version numbers are transmitted in APIs in order to indicate the API version. The related decision asks whether such an explicit versioning and version transmission scheme should be introduced. Important qualities that one can achieve by applying the pattern are accuracy and exactness of identification. When an API uses it, its clients can rely on the syntax and semantics defined in the specified API version; the message exchanges are interoperable as long as the Version Identifier stays the same. This way, client-side impact is minimized: the client can safely assume that "breaking changes" will only be introduced in subsequent versions. Furthermore, API providers want to avoid accidentally breaking compatibility: if a Version Identifier is part of the message, recipients can reject a message with an unknown version number. Finally, explicit versioning makes it easier for API providers to manage their APIs, as it provides traceability of API versions in use: API providers can monitor how many and which clients depend on a particular API version.

	Pattern: Version Identifier
Problem	How can an API provider indicate its current capabilities as well as the existence of possibly incompatible changes to clients in order to prevent malfunctioning of clients due to undiscovered interpretation errors?
Solution	Introduce an explicit version indicator. Include this Version Identifier in the API Description and in the exchanged messages. To do the latter, add a Metadata Element to the endpoint address, the protocol header, or the message payload.

Version Identifiers are typically specified in the API Description. In general, all patterns in this category are closely related to the API Description. They can be used to initially specify the API version and provide a mechanism to not only define syntactical structure (the technical API contract) but also cover organizational matters such as ownership, support, and evolution strategies.

There are many possible ways to include Version Identifiers in messages. A simple, technology-independent way is to define a Metadata Element as a special place in the message body to hold the Version Identifier; this special place can be part of a dedicated Context Representation. Protocol headers and endpoint addresses such as URLs are possible alternatives.

While there are many conventions that can be followed, Version Identifier is often used in conjunction with Semantic Versioning. The Semantic Versioning pattern describes a way in which compound version numbers can be defined, expressing backward compatibility and the impact of functional changes via major, minor, and patch versions.

Version Identifiers should be accurate and exact. Breaking changes will require changes to the clients; thus, they are closely linked to considerations about the client-side impact of software evolution steps. To make it impossible to accidentally break backward compatibility, recipients should be able to reject a message based on unknown version numbers. Finally, it should be considered that Version Identifiers can help to establish traceability of API versions in use.

	Pattern: Semantic Versioning	
Problem	How can stakeholders compare API versions to detect immediately whether they are compatible?	
Solution	Introduce a hierarchical three-number versioning scheme $x.y.z$, which allows API providers to denote different levels of changes in a compound identifier. The three numbers are usually called major, minor, and patch versions.	

In Semantic Versioning only minimal effort to detect version incompatibility is required, especially for clients, and more clarity of change impact can be achieved by just looking at the parts of the Version Identifier. A well-known Semantic Versioning scheme, such as the hierarchical three-number versioning scheme, can help to achieve a clear separation of changes with different levels of impact and compatibility. This brings clarity with regard to the evolution timeline of the API. In addition, the change impact caused by the release of a new API version should be clear to the API client and provider developers.

API providers must be careful not to support too many API versions at the same time, and a fine-grained versioning scheme can tempt them to do just that. The manageability of API versions and related governance effort for the API provider are important: more APIs, parallel API versions, and extended guarantees made to clients mean more API management and governance effort.

Sample decision outcome. The API product manager at Lakeside Mutual decided as follows:

In the context of the offer quotation features in the policy management API,

facing the need to integrate third-party developers and satisfy auditing requirements,

the API designers at Lakeside Mutual decided to combine the Version Identifier *pattern and the* Semantic Versioning *pattern to achieve that breaking changes are spotted as soon as possible and maintenance is eased,*

accepting that metadata has to be transmitted and API descriptions require updates as versions evolve.

Strategies for Commissioning and Decommissioning

Many API providers are eager to bring new versions to production quickly. However, they often overlook the importance of the ability to decommission old versions in order not to be overwhelmed with maintenance effort and resulting cost.

If new API versions are developed and deployed in production, different strategies for introducing the new versions and decommissioning old ones exist. This section covers the following decision:

Decision: *Version introduction and decommissioning*

When and how should new versions of an API be introduced and old versions be decommissioned?

Figure 3.29 illustrates the typical choices for this decision. The patterns explained in this section are alternative options, providing different strategies to introduce and decommission versions.

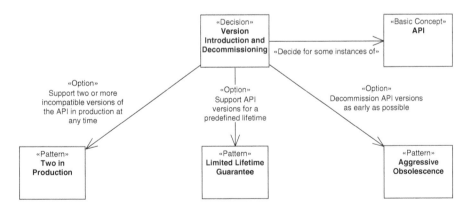

Figure 3.29 *Version introduction and decommissioning decision*

The first option is to give a Limited Lifetime Guarantee, which establishes a fixed time range for the lifetime of an API version after its initial release.

Pattern: LIMITED LIFETIME GUARANTEE	
Problem	How can a provider let clients know for how long they can rely on the published version of an API?
Solution	As an API provider, guarantee to not break the published API for a fixed timeframe. Label each API version with an expiration date.

Applying this pattern means that a limited number of API versions are kept in production. The goal is to guarantee that API changes do not lead to undetected backward-compatibility problems between clients and the provider, especially with regard to their semantics. It does so through a compromise: changes to the client caused by API changes are minimized as multiple versions are supported, and clients can stay on the last version for a defined time. But the pattern also limits the number of API versions supported by API providers, thereby minimizing the maintenance effort for supporting clients relying on these API versions. Thus, the pattern guarantees that API changes do not lead to undetected backward-compatibility problems between clients and the provider.

LIMITED LIFETIME GUARANTEE achieves this combination of force impacts through a concrete date in the lifetime guarantee that helps to make client-side changes caused by API changes more plannable. It also limits the maintenance effort to support old clients that API providers have to plan for.

The AGGRESSIVE OBSOLESCENCE pattern can be used for phasing out existing features as early as possible.

Pattern: AGGRESSIVE OBSOLESCENCE	
Problem	How can API providers reduce the effort for maintaining an entire API or its parts (such as endpoints, operations, or message representations) with guaranteed service quality levels?
Solution	Announce a decommissioning date to be set as early as possible for the entire API or its obsolete parts. Declare the obsolete API parts to be still available but no longer recommended to be used so that clients have just enough time to upgrade to a newer or alternative version before the API parts they depend on disappear. Remove the deprecated API parts and the support for it as soon as the deadline has passed.

Compared to all other options in this decision, Aggressive Obsolescence radically minimizes the maintenance effort for the API provider. Virtually no support for old clients must be provided. However, for clients that do not follow the same life cycle as the provider, this pattern forces changes to clients in a given time span as a consequence of the API changes. As this might not always be possible, clients might break. This pattern acknowledges or respects the power dynamics between API provider and client, but here the API provider is the "strong" partner in the relationship and can dictate when changes will happen. This often has to be viewed in the light of commercial goals and constraints of the API provider. For example, if revenues from the API are small and many clients have to be supported, the API provider might not be able to sustain other lifetime guarantees.

The Two in Production pattern defines a rather strict strategy of how many incompatible versions should be kept active at the same time.

Pattern: Two in Production

Problem	How can a provider gradually update an API without breaking existing clients but also without having to maintain a large number of API versions in production?
Solution	Deploy and support two versions of an API endpoint and its operations that provide variations of the same functionality but do not have to be compatible with each other. Update and decommission the versions in a rolling, overlapping fashion.

When releasing a new API version, the oldest one that still runs in production is retired (which is the second last one by default). As a variant, more than two versions—for instance, three—can be supported. In such cases, the pattern variant "N in Production" is chosen. To maintain the character and benefits of this pattern, however, it is crucial that the number N remains small.

Two in Production allows the API provider and the client to follow different life cycles so that a provider can roll out a new API version without breaking clients using the previous API version. Two in Production's impact on forces resolution is similar to that of Limited Lifetime Guarantee. The difference is that two (or in the general case, N) version are supported in parallel, which brings a sound compromise to the goal conflicts between clients and provider. As an additional benefit for providers, the pattern enables the ability to roll back to an old API version if a new version is not accepted by clients due to bugs, poor performance, or a dissatisfying developer experience.

Finally, to ease the design of new APIs, gain experience, and gather feedback, the EXPERIMENTAL PREVIEW pattern can be applied to indicate that no API availability and support guarantees are given, but the API can be used opportunistically with the objective to gather feedback (provider) and learn early (client).

Decision: *Using an experimental preview*

Should a new version of an API or a new API have an experimental preview?

Figure 3.30 illustrates the rather straightforward decision of allowing or disallowing an EXPERIMENTAL PREVIEW.

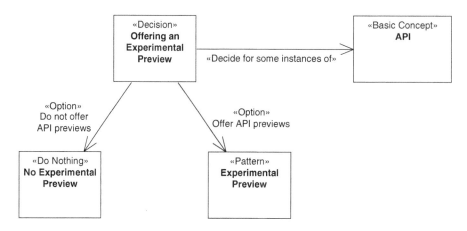

Figure 3.30 *Using an additional experimental preview decision*

This pattern can be applied to support innovations and new features. Such showcasing raises the awareness of a new API (version), facilitates feedback, and gives the customers time to decide whether to use the new API and initiate development projects.

An EXPERIMENTAL PREVIEW is an alternative to one or more official versions. It is eligible when API providers do not want to manage and support many API versions in order to focus their efforts.

Consumers want to learn early about new APIs or API versions so that they can plan ahead, build innovative products, and influence the API design. With regard to planning, clients especially want stable APIs in order to minimize change effort.

	Pattern: EXPERIMENTAL PREVIEW
Problem	How can providers make the introduction of a new API (version) less risky for their clients and obtain early adopter feedback without having to freeze the API design prematurely?
Solution	Provide access to an API on a best-effort base without making any commitments about the functionality offered, stability, and longevity. Clearly and explicitly articulate this lack of API maturity to manage client expectations.

This pattern can be seen as an additional consideration to the strategies in the version introduction and decommissioning strategies decision presented earlier, as the EXPERIMENTAL PREVIEW can be offered instead of a full-fledged additional version. That is, the decision about an additional experimental preview can be taken as a follow-on when a decision on versioning and decommissioning strategies has been made already. In addition, in any of the other strategies or even without any such strategy in place, EXPERIMENTAL PREVIEW can be used as well, such as to support experimenting with the API and gathering early feedback. For instance, an EXPERIMENTAL PREVIEW can be used in the initial phase of a new version introduced in the context of TWO IN PRODUCTION, which then, once it has matured enough, transits to become one of the two supported versions in production.

Sample decision outcome. The API product owner at Lakeside Mutual decided as follows:

In the context of the offer quotation API in the policy management backend,

facing the need to support multiple API clients with different release cycles,

the API designers at Lakeside Mutual decided both for the TWO IN PRODUCTION *pattern and the* EXPERIMENTAL PREVIEW *pattern*

to achieve that clients have a choice and gain time to migrate when breaking changes arise (and can play with upcoming features),

accepting that two versions have to be operated and supported simultaneously.

The patterns on API evolution are covered in Chapter 8, "Evolve APIs". They mainly concern the transition phase (and later phases) of an API.

Interlude: Quality and Evolution Patterns in the Lakeside Mutual Case

The Lakeside Mutual developers applied many of the quality patterns in the various services. To serve multiple clients with different information needs, WISH LISTS are introduced so that clients can retrieve exactly the data they need. For example, a client might need postal codes and birthdays of customers for a statistical survey, but not the full address:

```
curl -X GET --header 'Authorization: Bearer b318ad736c6c844b'\
http://localhost:8080/customers/gktlipwhjr?\
fields=customerId,birthday,postalCode
```

The returned response now contains only the requested fields (see the WISH LIST pattern in Chapter 7, "Refine Message Design for Quality," for the full example):

```
{
  "customerId": "gktlipwhjr",
  "birthday": "1989-12-31T23:00:00.000+0000",
  "postalCode": "8640"
}
```

All operations are guarded by API KEYS, which are represented by the `Authorization` header in the preceding command. In the Customer Core service, several requests can be combined into one as a REQUEST BUNDLE. Failures are communicated with ERROR REPORTS. In the following call, an `invalid-customer-id` is used:

```
curl -X GET --header 'Authorization: Bearer b318ad736c6c844b'\
http://localhost:8080/customers/invalid-customer-id
```

An ERROR REPORT informs the client that this customer was not found:

```
{
  "timestamp": "2022-02-17T11:03:58.517+00:00",
  "status": 404,
  "error": "Not Found",
  "path": "/customer/invalid-customer-id"
}
```

For more examples of API Keys and Error Reports, please refer to the pattern texts in Chapter 6.

Many response messages contain either Embedded Entity or Linked Information Holders. For example, in the Policy Management backend, the `CustomerDto` contains a nested representation of all customer policies. However, many clients may not be interested in the policies when they access the customer resource. To avoid sending large messages containing lots of data that is not processed on the client side, a Linked Information Holder is used that refers to a separate endpoint returning the customer policies:

```
curl -X GET http://localhost:8090/customers/rgpp0wkpec
{
  "customerId": "rgpp0wkpec",
  ...
  "_links": {
    ...
    "policies": {
      "href": "/customers/rgpp0wkpec/policies"
    }
  }
}
```

Policies can then be requested separately:

```
curl -X GET http://localhost:8090/customers/rgpp0wkpec/policies
[ {
  "policyId": "fvo5pkqerr",
  "customer": "rgpp0wkpec",
  "creationDate": "2022-02-04T11:14:49.717+00:00",
  "policyPeriod": {
    "startDate": "2018-02-04T23:00:00.000+00:00",
    "endDate": "2018-02-09T23:00:00.000+00:00"
  },
  "policyType": "Health Insurance",
  "deductible": {
    "amount": 1500.00,
    "currency": "CHF"
  },
  ...
```

Enforcing the decisions for Version Identifier, Semantic Versioning, Experimental Preview, and Two in Production, the API owners, architects, and developers at Lakeside Mutual might add identifiers such as `v1.0` to the URIs and use the release management capabilities of their source code repository and collaboration platform. The versioning and life-cycle management decisions are not shown in the code snippets in this interlude.

Assuming that git is the chosen version-control system providing the source code repositories, there could be two production branches and an experimental one. Each of these branches could feed a different continuous integration and continuous delivery/continuous deployment (CI/CD) pipeline ending with a deployment (for test or production, respectively).

More details on the implementation of Lakeside Mutual can be found in Appendix B, "Implementation of the Lakeside Mutual Case." Note that not all decisions from this chapter are fully implemented; the case study implementation continues to evolve.[3]

Summary

In this chapter, we identified pattern-related architectural decisions required during API design and evolution, covering the following topics:

- Selection of foundation patterns characterizing the visibility (public, community, solution-internal) and type of APIs (frontend vs. backend integration)

- Selecting endpoint roles and operation responsibilities that differ in their nature (activity vs. data orientation) and impact on provider-side state (read and/or write access)

- Choosing structure-related patterns that describe the individual message elements syntactically (flat and nested parameters) and semantically (element stereotypes such as data, metadata, identifier, and link element)

- Deciding about API quality governance and management (for instance, Service Level Agreements)

- API quality patterns to improve performance and rightsize messages including Pagination and Wish List

---

3. Are the Lakeside Mutual developers somewhat disconnected from the architects and the product owner of this sample case?

- Agreeing on suitable API lifetimes and approaches to versioning during API evolution

- Documenting API contracts and descriptions minimally or elaborately, including technical and commercial aspects such as billing

Each of our 44 patterns appears as an option (or alternative) in the architectural decision questions presented; its pros and cons with regard to design forces constitute the decision criteria. We used the Lakeside Mutual case study to provide exemplary decision outcomes, captured as why-statements.

This completes the introductory Part 1 of our book; the reference Part 2 contains the pattern texts and a pattern language overview.

Part 2

====

The Patterns

This part of the book presents our catalog of patterns for API design and evolution. Complementary to Chapter 3, "API Decision Narratives," in Part 1, it does not have to be read page by page but serves as a reference.

The catalog is organized along the four phases of the Align-Define-Design-Refine (ADDR) process introduced in *Principles of Web API Design: Delivering Value with APIs and Microservices* [Higginbotham 2021]:

- In the early stages, the API scope is derived from and *aligned* with client goals and other requirements, as, for instance, articulated in user stories or job stories. We briefly summarize the related *foundation* patterns that are eligible in this phase.

- Still at an early stage of the API design, endpoints and their operations are *defined* on a rather high level of abstraction and elaboration. Our *responsibility* patterns come into play in this phase.

- Next, technical details and technology bindings are *designed*. This is where our message *structure* and API *quality* patterns have their place.

- Finally, the API designs and their implementations are continuously *refined* during API *evolution*. Additional quality patterns can also be applied in this step, often in the form of API refactoring (to patterns).

The progress with the API design is continuously (and incrementally) *documented* throughout the design and evolution steps. Appendix A, "Endpoint Identification and Pattern Selection Guides" explains how the four ADDR phases and its seven steps (for instance, "Model API profiles") and our patterns relate to each other.

The chapter structure of this part comes from these considerations. Each chapter targets at least one role in our target audience:

- Chapter 4, **"Pattern Language Introduction,"** provides a pattern language overview and introduces foundation and basic structure patterns that serve as building blocks of the patterns in the subsequent chapters.

- Chapter 5, **"Define Endpoint Types and Operations,"** discusses endpoint roles and operation responsibilities, taking a conceptual architecture view on API design and evolution.

- Chapter 6, **"Design Request and Response Message Representations,"** is about request and response message structures, targeting integration architects and developers.

- Chapter 7, **"Refine Message Design for Quality,"** presents patterns that improve message structures with respect to certain qualities. This chapter also targets architects and developers.

- Chapter 8, **"Evolve APIs,"** discusses API evolution and life-cycle management. The API product manager comes in as an additional targeted role.

- Chapter 9, **"Document and Communicate API Contracts,"** covers API documentation and commercial aspects. It is relevant for all roles, API product managers in particular.

Let's get started with the pattern overview and orientation.

Chapter 4

Pattern Language Introduction

In Part 1, we learned that remote APIs have become an important feature of modern distributed software systems. APIs provide integration interfaces exposing remote system functionality to end-user applications such as mobile clients, Web applications, and third-party systems. Not only end-user applications consume and rely on APIs—distributed backend systems and microservices within those systems require APIs to be able to work with each other as well.

Lakeside Mutual, a fictitious insurance company, and its microservices-based applications provided us with an example case. We saw that API design and evolution involve many recurring design issues to resolve conflicting requirements and find appropriate trade-offs. Decision models for groups of related issues presented options and criteria to guide us through the required design work. Patterns appeared as alternative options in these decisions.

This chapter takes the next step. It starts with a pattern language overview and then proposes navigation paths through the language. It also introduces a first set of basic scoping and structuring patterns. Having read this chapter, you will be able to explain the scope of our pattern language (in terms of topics covered and architectural concerns) and find patterns you are interested in (for instance, by project phase). You will also be able to characterize the API under construction by its visibility and integration type by way of foundation patterns and know about the basic structure patterns that constitute the syntactic building blocks of request and response messages (and many of the other patterns in our language).

Positioning and Scope

According to our domain model, established in Chapter 1, "Application Programming Interface (API) Fundamentals," API clients and providers exchange request and response messages to call operations in API endpoints. Many of our patterns focus on the payload *content* of such messages that contain one or more representation elements, possibly nested. *Enterprise Integration Patterns* [Hohpe 2003] offers three alternative patterns about this message content: "Document Message," "Command Message," and "Event Message." In messaging systems, such messages travel from the sending endpoint to the receiving endpoint over communication "Channels." These Channels may be offered by queue-based messaging systems but also come as HTTP connections or other use integration technologies, such as GraphQL and gRPC. Protocol capabilities and configuration, as well as message size and content structure, influence the quality properties of an API and its implementation. In this messaging context, APIs can be seen as "Service Activators" [Hohpe 2003]—viewed from the communication channels, they serve as "Adapters" [Gamma 1995] for the application services available in the API implementation.

In our pattern language, we look into the command, document, and event messages in terms of their inner structures. We also investigate the roles played by representation elements, operations, and API endpoints—irrespective of the communication protocols used. We discuss how to group messages into endpoints to achieve suitable API granularity and coupling, how to document APIs, and how to manage the evolution of API endpoints and their parts.

We are particularly interested in message payloads that are exchanged as JSON objects—for instance, via HTTP GET, POST, and PUT—and in message queues offered by cloud providers or messaging systems (such as ActiveMQ or RabbitMQ). JSON is a popular message exchange format in Web APIs; our patterns work equally well when XML documents or other text structures are exchanged. They can even be applied to define the content of messages with binary encodings.

Figure 4.1 visualizes the scope of our patterns in a Web API example. An HTTP GET, shown as a curl command, asks for information about a single customer, `rgpp0wkpec`, of Lakeside Mutual (the case introduced in Chapter 2, "Lakeside Mutual Case Study").

The exemplary response message is nested: the customer information contains not only the birthday but also a log of address changes in the form of a `moveHistory`. Indicated by the JSON array notation `[...]`, a collection of relocation moves could be returned (in the example, the array contains only one move destination). Each move destination is characterized by three strings, `"city"`, `"postalCode"`, `"street-Address"`, wrapped in the JSON object notation `{...}` in the figure. This two-level structure raises an important, recurring API design issue:

Should complex data whose parts have containment or other domain-level relations be embedded in message representations, or should links be provided to look up this data with separate calls to other operations in the same (or other) API endpoints?

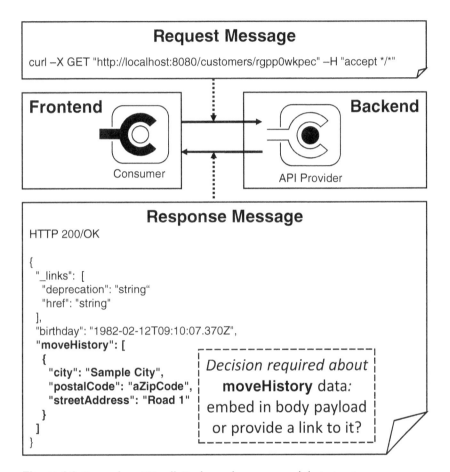

Figure 4.1 *Exemplary API call: Exchanged messages and their structure*

Two of our patterns offer alternative answers to this question: Embedded Entity (shown in Figure 4.1) and Linked Information Holder. Embedded Entity injects nested data representations into the payload, whereas a Linked Information Holder places hyperlinks in the payload. In the latter case, the client has to follow these hyperlinks to obtain the referenced data in subsequent requests to the endpoint location found in the links. The chosen combination of these two patterns has a strong impact on the API quality. For instance, message size and number of interactions influence both performance and changeability. Both patterns are valid choices, depending on network and endpoint capabilities, information needs and data access profiles of clients, backend location of the source data, and so on. These criteria, therefore, are pattern selection and adoption forces. We will come back to these patterns and their forces in Chapter 7, "Refine Message Design for Quality."

Patterns: Why and How?

Patterns can help resolve API design issues, presenting proven solutions to problems recurring in a particular context (here, API design and evolution). Patterns are platform-independent by definition, thus avoiding concept, technology, and vendor lock-in. They form a common language for a domain. Adequate pattern usage can make the designs that adopt them easier to understand, port, and evolve.

Each pattern text can be seen as a small, specialized, standalone article. These texts are structured according to a common template:

- *When and Why to Apply* establishes the context and preconditions for pattern eligibility, followed by a problem statement that specifies a design issue to be resolved. Different forces on the design explain why the problem is hard to solve. Architectural decision drivers and conflicting quality attributes are often referenced here; a nonsolution may also be pointed out.

- The *How It Works* section presents a conceptual, generalized solution to the design question from the problem statement that describes how the solution works and which variants (if any) we observed in practice.

- The *Example* section shows how the solution can be implemented in a concrete application context, for instance, when working with a particular technology set such as HTTP and JSON.

- The *Discussion* section explains to what extent the solution resolves the pattern forces; it may also include additional pros and cons and identify alternative solutions.

- The *Related Patterns* section points to the next patterns that become eligible and interesting once a particular one has been applied.

- Finally, additional pointers and references are given under *More Information*.

Coming back to our two exemplary patterns, LINKED INFORMATION HOLDER and EMBEDDED ENTITY are documented in this format in Chapter 7.

Note that using a pattern does not dictate a particular implementation but leaves a lot of flexibility for its project-context-specific adoption. In fact, patterns should never be followed blindly but should be seen as a tool or guide. A product- or project-specific design can satisfy its concrete, actual requirements only if it knows them (which is hard for a generalized artifact such as a pattern).

Navigating through the Patterns

When we decided how to organize our patterns, we looked at two other books for inspiration: *Enterprise Integration Patterns* [Hohpe 2003] is organized by the life cycle of messages traveling through a distributed system, from creation and sending to routing, transforming, and receiving. *Patterns of Enterprise Application Architecture* [Fowler 2002] uses logical layers as a chapter and topic breakdown, progressing from domain layer to persistence layer and presentation layer.

Regrettably, neither layers nor life cycles alone seemed to work well for the API domain. Hence, we could not decide on one best way to organize but offer multiple ones to guide you through the patterns: architectural scope (as defined by the API domain model from Chapter 1), topic categories, and refinement phases.[1]

Structural Organization: Find Patterns by Scope

Most of our patterns focus on API building blocks at different levels of abstraction and detail; some concern the API as a whole and its documentation, both technical and commercial. The resulting architectural scopes are API as a whole, endpoint, operation, and message. We introduced these basic concepts in the API domain model in Chapter 1. Figure 4.2 calls out patterns for these five scopes.

---

1. This "ask for one, get three" tactic is an exception to our general rule, "if in doubt, leave it out" [Zimmermann 2021b], fortunately only on the meta-level. Hopefully, standards committees and API designers stick to this rule better than we do ;-).

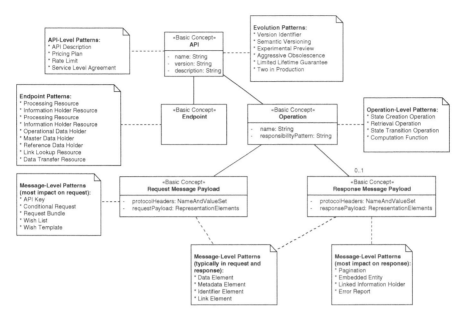

Figure 4.2 *Patterns by domain model element and architectural scope*

Patterns such as API DESCRIPTION and SERVICE LEVEL AGREEMENT concern the API as a whole. Others, such as PROCESSING RESOURCE and DATA TRANSFER RESOURCE, operate on single endpoints. Many patterns deal with operation or message design; some of these primarily target request messages (API KEY, WISH LIST), and others are more focused on response messages (PAGINATION, ERROR REPORT). Element stereotypes may appear both in requests and responses (IDENTIFIER ELEMENT, METADATA ELEMENT).

Call to action: When being confronted with an API design task, ask yourself which of these scopes you are about to deal with and refer to Figure 4.2 to find patterns of interest for this task.

Theme Categorization: Search for Topics

We grouped the patterns into five categories. Each category answers several related topical questions:

- **Foundation patterns:** Which types of systems and components are integrated? From where should an API be accessible? How should it be documented?

- **Responsibility patterns:** What is the architectural role played by each API endpoint? What are the operation responsibilities? How do these roles and responsibilities impact service decomposition and API granularity?

- **Structure patterns:** What is an adequate number of representation elements for request and response messages? How should these elements be structured? How can they be grouped and annotated?

- **Quality patterns:** How can an API provider achieve a certain level of design time and runtime qualities while using its resources in a cost-effective way? How can the API quality trade-offs be communicated and accounted for?

- **Evolution patterns:** How can life-cycle management concerns such as support periods and versioning be dealt with? How can backward compatibility be promoted and unavoidable breaking changes be communicated?

These theme categories organize the decision models in Chapter 3, "API Decision Narratives," and the Web site supporting this book.[2] Figure 4.3 groups the patterns by book chapter. The theme categories and Chapters 4 to 8 correspond with each other but for only two exceptions: API Description from the foundation category and three patterns related to quality management (Rate Limit, Pricing Plan, Service Level Agreement) are factored out into a separate Chapter 9, "Document and Communicate API Contracts." The patterns API Key, Error Report, and Context Representation are related to quality but appear in Chapter 6, "Design Request and Response Message Representations," due to their role of special-purpose representations. The cheat sheet in Appendix A follows the same structure.

> *Call to action:* Think about an API design issue you were confronted with recently. Does it fit in any of the preceding categories? Do any of the questions and pattern names suggest that the pattern might be able to resolve the issue? If so, you may want to go to the respective chapter and pattern right now (and return here later). If you need more information, you can consult the cheat sheet in Appendix A.

---

2. https://api-patterns.org

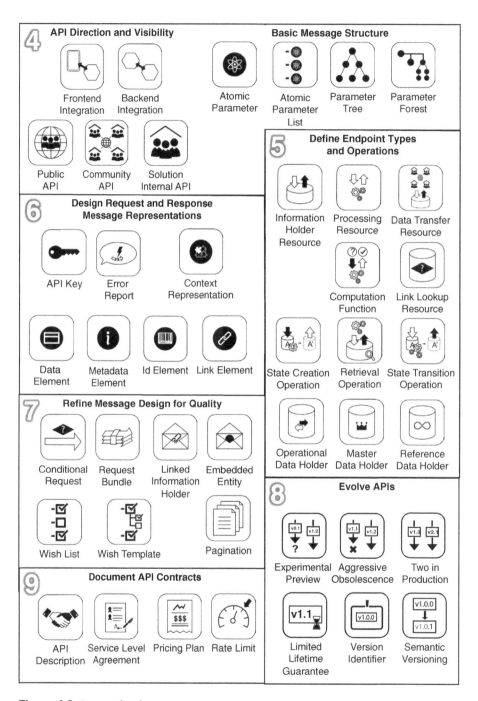

Figure 4.3 *Patterns by chapter*

Time Dimension: Follow Design Refinement Phases

Roughly following the "Unified Process" [Kruchten 2000], an API design evolves from project/product inception to design elaboration, implementation construction iterations, and project/product transition. Table 4.1 categorizes patterns by process phases; note that some patterns can be applied in multiple phases.

Table 4.1 *Patterns by Phase*

Phase	Category	Patterns
Inception	Foundation	Public API, Community API, Solution-Internal API
		Backend Integration, Frontend Integration
		API Description
Elaboration	Responsibility	Information Holder Resource, Processing Resource
		Master Data Holder, Operational Data Holder, Reference Data Holder
		Data Transfer Resource, Link Lookup Resource
	Quality	API Key, Context Representation, Error Report
Construction	Structure	Atomic Parameter, Atomic Parameter List, Parameter Tree, Parameter Forest
		Data Element, Id Element, Link Element, Metadata Element
	Responsibility	State Creation Operation, State Transition Operation
		Retrieval Operation, Computation Function
	Quality	Pagination
		Wish List, Wish Template
		Embedded Entity, Linked Information Holder
		Conditional Request, Request Bundle
Transition	Foundation	API Description
	Quality	Service Level Agreement, Pricing Plan, Rate Limit
	Evolution	Semantic Versioning, Version Identifier
		Aggressive Obsolescence, Experimental Preview
		Limited Lifetime Guarantee, Two in Production

APIs endpoints are identified and characterized by their roles in the overall system/architecture at the early stages (inception). Next, operations are drafted with their request and response message structure conceptualized and designed initially (elaboration). Quality improvements follow (construction). An approach to versioning and a support/lifetime strategy is specified for APIs when they go live (transition); updates are possible later on.

While Table 4.1 has an order from top to bottom (as all tables do), it can be walked through multiple times, even within a single two-week sprint. We do not propose a waterfall model here; it is perfectly fine to go back and forth, for instance when applying agile project organization practices. In other words, each sprint may contain inception, elaboration, construction, and transition tasks (and apply related patterns).

You might be wondering how the Align-Define-Design-Refine (ADDR) phases (see introduction to Part 2) relate to the phases in the Unified Process and Table 4.1. Our take is: Align corresponds to inception, the Define activities happen during elaboration. Design work stretches from elaboration to construction iterations; construction and transition (and later evolution and maintenance phases) provide opportunities to Refine the design continuously.

Call to action: Which phase is your current API design effort in? Do the listed patterns suggest being eligible for consideration in your design? You may want to revisit Table 4.1 each time your design reaches a certain milestone or each time you pick an API-related story from the product backlog at the start of a sprint.

How to Navigate: The Map to MAP

You can use the three navigation aids structure from this section—structure/scope, theme category/chapter, and time/phase—to explore the language for your immediate needs if you are not yet ready to read Part 2 page by page. Having picked one or more entry points, you can then follow the "Related Patterns" pointers provided in each pattern to move on; you can also return to one of the three organizers (scope, topic, phase). Having studied a few patterns, you may want to check out the Lakeside Mutual case study or the real-world pattern stories in Chapter 10, "Real-World Pattern Stories," to return to the big picture and learn how individual patterns can be combined.

The following section introduces basic API foundation and message structure patterns eligible during the Align phase of ADDR, with Chapters 5 to 9 covering the remaining phases Define, Design, and Refine as well as additional topics.

Foundations: API Visibility and Integration Types

The patterns presented in this section are rather simplistic terms of design forces and their resolution, but they serve as building blocks for the subsequent, more advanced patterns. Therefore, we present them here in a simplified form: Context and Problem, Solution, and Details. Feel free to proceed to Chapter 5, "Define Endpoint Types and Operations," and return here as needed.

The foundation patterns deal with the two strategic decisions:

- Which types of systems, subsystems, and components are integrated?
- From where should an API be accessible?

Answering these two questions helps to scope and characterize an API and its purpose: FRONTEND INTEGRATION and BACKEND INTEGRATION are two types of directions (or purpose and architectural position) of APIs. PUBLIC API, COMMUNITY API, and SOLUTION-INTERNAL API define API visibility. Figure 4.4 provides a pattern map for these five patterns.

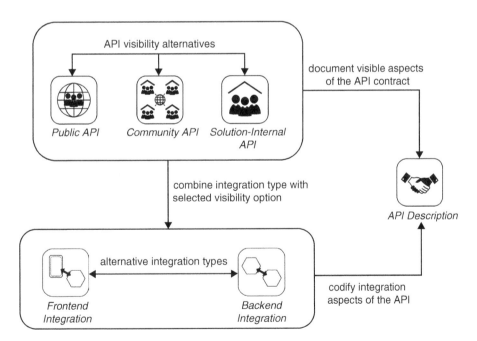

Figure 4.4 *Pattern map for foundation patterns*

Note that the API DESCRIPTION pattern is covered in Chapter 9.

Pattern:
FRONTEND INTEGRATION

In Chapter 1, we motivated the emergence of mobile apps and cloud-native applications as one reason why APIs matter so much. They provide mobile apps and Web clients of cloud applications with data and access to provider-side processing capabilities.

How can client-side end-user interfaces that are physically separated from server-side business logic and data storage be populated and updated with computing results, result sets from searches in data sources, and detailed information about data entities? How can application frontends invoke activities in a backend or upload data to it?

Let the backend of a distributed application expose its services to one or more application frontends via a message-based remote FRONTEND INTEGRATION API.

The application frontends serving end users may be internal ones or be part of external systems. FRONTEND INTEGRATION APIs are consumed by API clients in these types of application frontends. Figure 4.5 positions the FRONTEND INTEGRATION pattern in its context.

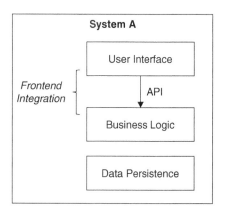

Figure 4.5 *FRONTEND INTEGRATION: An API connects a remote user interface with backend logic and data*

The Business Logic Layer [Fowler 2002] in the backend is a natural entry point. Sometimes the user interface is also split up between client and server. In such cases, the API might reside on the user interface level as well.

Details

Decide whether the API is a PUBLIC API, a COMMUNITY API, or a SOLUTION-INTERNAL API. Compose the request and, optionally, response messages of the API operations from one or more ATOMIC PARAMETERS and PARAMETER TREES (see later sections for explanations of these patterns).

Realize the selected API endpoint candidates with the help of the role and responsibility patterns (Chapter 5), the message structure patterns (Chapter 6), and the quality patterns (Chapters 6 and 7). Consciously decide if and how to version the integration API; consider one or more of our evolution patterns (Chapter 8, "Evolve APIs") when doing so. Document the API contract and the terms and conditions of its use in an API DESCRIPTION and supplemental artifacts (Chapter 9).

A message-based remote FRONTEND INTEGRATION API is often realized as an HTTP resource API.[3] Other remoting technologies, such as gRPC [gRPC], transferred over HTTP/2 [Belshe 2015], or Web Sockets [Melnikov 2011], can also be used. GraphQL has become popular recently, promising to avoid under- and overfetching.[4]

FRONTEND INTEGRATION APIs either have a general purpose that fits all clients or specialize in providing different "Backends For Frontends" [Newman 2015] per type of client or user interface technology.

Pattern:
BACKEND INTEGRATION

In Chapter 1, we discussed that cloud-native applications and microservices-based systems require APIs to both connect and separate their parts. APIs also play a key role in software ecosystems. More generally speaking, any backend system may benefit from and rely on remote APIs when requiring information from or desiring activity in other systems.

---

3. HTTP resource APIs use the uniform interface of the REST style and invoke HTTP methods such as POST, GET, PUT, PATCH, and DELETE on URIs. If they adhere to additional constraints of REST, such as using hyperlinks to transfer state, they may also be called RESTful HTTP APIs.

4. GraphQL can be seen as a large-scale framework realization of our WISH TEMPLATE pattern from Chapter 7.

▼

How can distributed applications and their parts, which have been built independently and are deployed separately, exchange data and trigger mutual activity while preserving system-internal conceptual integrity without introducing undesired coupling?

Integrate the backend of a distributed application with one or more other backends (of the same or other distributed applications) by exposing its services via a message-based remote BACKEND INTEGRATION API.

▲

Such BACKEND INTEGRATION APIs are never directly used by frontend clients of the distributed application but are consumed by other backends exclusively.

Figure 4.6 positions the pattern in the first of its two application contexts, business-to-business (or system-to-system) integration.

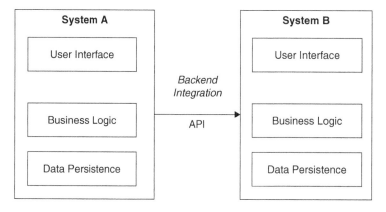

Figure 4.6 BACKEND INTEGRATION sketch 1: System-to-system message exchange

Figure 4.7 illustrates the second usage context of the pattern, application-internal decomposition of business logic into service components exposing a SOLUTION-INTERNAL API.

The entry to the business logic layer is a suitable location for a BACKEND INTEGRATION API. Access control, authorization enforcement, system transaction management, and business rule evaluation typically are already located here. In some data-centric scenarios not requiring much logic, it may make sense to integrate on the data persistence layer instead (this is not shown in Figure 4.7).

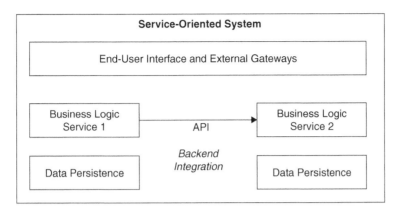

Figure 4.7 *BACKEND INTEGRATION sketch 2: Microservices communicating via SOLUTION-INTERNAL API*

Details

Decide on the visibility of the integration API: the options are PUBLIC API, COMMUNITY API, and SOLUTION-INTERNAL API. Compose the request and, optionally, response messages of the API operations from one or more ATOMIC PARAMETERS, possibly nested in PARAMETER TREES (discussed further under "Basic Structure Patterns"). Define the roles of the API endpoints in the BACKEND INTEGRATION and the responsibilities of their operation (Chapter 5). Design the messages in detail with element stereotypes and quality improvement patterns (Chapters 6 and 7). Consciously decide if and how to version the integration API over its lifetime (Chapter 8) when doing so. Create an API DESCRIPTION and supplemental information (Chapter 9).

Apply a systematic approach to application landscape planning (systems of systems design). Consider strategic domain-driven design (DDD) [Vernon 2013] as a light approach to enterprise architecture management ("software city planning"). To decompose a single system into services, apply cutting criteria derived from functional requirements and domain model [Kapferer 2021, Gysel 2016] and operational requirements such as scaling needs and developmental concerns such as independent changeability [Zimmermann 2017]. Also, consider cloud cost and workload patterns [Fehling 2014].

To promote interoperability, choose a mature remoting technology that supports standard messaging protocols and established message exchange formats. In addition to those listed as options to realize FRONTEND INTEGRATION, asynchronous, queue-based messaging is often used in BACKEND INTEGRATIONS (especially those integrating separate systems); see discussion in Chapter 1 for rationale and examples.

Pattern:
PUBLIC API

APIs exposed to the World Wide Web do not aim to limit their target audience and accessibility but often control access to them with API KEYS.

▼

How can an API be made available to an unlimited and/or unknown number of API clients outside the organization that are globally, nationally, and/or regionally distributed?

Expose the API on the public Internet along with a detailed API DESCRIPTION that describes both functional and nonfunctional properties of the API.

▲

Figure 4.8 sketches the PUBLIC API pattern in an exemplary scenario.

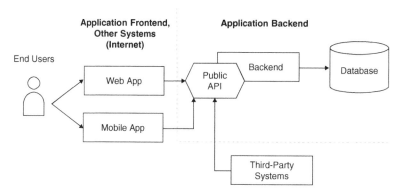

Figure 4.8 *API visibilities:* PUBLIC *API in context*

Details

Specify the API endpoints, operations, message representations, quality-of-service guarantees, and life-cycle support model. Continue this integration design by choosing responsibility patterns and choosing one or more evolution patterns (from Chapters 5 and 8). For instance, mark the API as a PROCESSING RESOURCE, introduce VERSION IDENTIFIERS, and apply SEMANTIC VERSIONING.

Use API KEYS (Chapter 7) or other security means to control access to the API. Harden the API from a security and reliability perspective, and also invest in the quality of API DESCRIPTION and support procedures (Chapter 9). From an API economy point of view, define a PRICING PLAN and implement billing/subscription management. Consider introducing RATE LIMITS for free plans. Document API usage terms and conditions, for instance, in a SERVICE LEVEL AGREEMENT, and let API consumers agree to them as a prerequisite to using the API. Cover fair use and indemnification in these terms and conditions.[5] These patterns are covered in Chapter 9.

Pattern:
COMMUNITY API

Some APIs are shared by clients in different organizations and might be deployed in and accessible via networks available only to community members.

How can the visibility of and the access to an API be restricted to a closed user group that does not work for a single organizational unit but for multiple legal entities (such as companies, nonprofit/nongovernment organizations, and governments)?

Deploy the API and its implementation resources securely in an access-restricted location so that only the desired user group has access to it—for instance, in an extranet. Share the API DESCRIPTION only with the restricted target audience.

Figure 4.9 sketches the COMMUNITY API pattern in its architectural context.

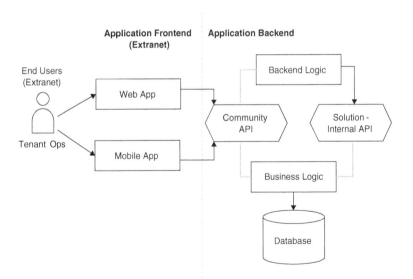

Figure 4.9 *API visibilities: COMMUNITY API in context*

---

5. Being legally binding artifacts, terms and conditions documents and SERVICE LEVEL AGREEMENTS of PUB-LIC APIs should be written or at least reviewed and approved by professionals specializing in legal matters.

Details

Specify the API in terms of its endpoints, operations, message representations, quality of service guarantees, and life-cycle model. Refer to the solution details of Public API for more comprehensive (equally valid) hints and related patterns.

Harden the API from a security and reliability perspective, and invest in the quality of API Description and support procedures (including community-managed member support). Appoint a communitywide API owner and seek shared funding.

This pattern combines elements from its sibling visibility patterns Public API and Solution-Internal API (and can be seen as a hybrid of these two patterns). For instance, it may define a community-specific pricing model (in an approach similar to that for a Public API), but also may consider colocation of API endpoints and their implementations (as many Solution-Internal APIs do).

 Pattern:
Solution-Internal API

Some APIs structure applications into components, for instance, services/microservices or program-internal modules. In such cases, API clients and their providers often run in the same data center or even on the same physical or virtual compute node.

▼

How can access to and usage of an API be limited to an application, for instance, components in the same or another logical layer and/or physical tier?

Decompose the application logically into components. Let these components expose local or remote APIs. Offer these APIs only to system-internal communication partners such as other services in the application backend.

▲

Figure 4.10 sketches two instances of the Solution-Internal API pattern, supporting an application frontend and another backend component, with sample API clients and backend implementation.

Details

A collection of related Solution-Internal APIs sometimes is referred to as *Platform API*. For instance, all Web APIs exposed in a single cloud provider offering (or collections of such offerings) qualify as platform APIs; examples include APIs in Amazon Web Services storage offerings and in Cloud Foundry. The same holds for all Solution-Internal APIs within a software product such as a message-oriented middleware; the endpoint and management APIs in ActiveMQ and RabbitMQ may serve as examples of such platform APIs.

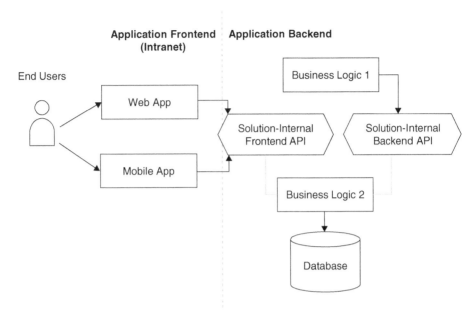

Figure 4.10 *API visibilities:* SOLUTION-INTERNAL *API*

Note that independent *deployability* does not have to imply independent *deployment*. A modular monolith [Mendonça 2021], for instance, uses plain messages exchanging data transfer objects via local APIs; such a modular monolith can be turned into a microservices-based system more easily than an object-oriented "instance jungle" with tight couplings between the objects at runtime caused by call-by-reference between remote methods and distributed garbage collection.

Designing and deploying SOLUTION-INTERNAL APIs for BACKEND INTEGRATION to improve the coupling characteristics of applications and their parts is a complex undertaking; both the first wave of service-oriented architectures in the 2000s and the microservices trend that gained momentum since 2014 target this part of the design space. Many books and articles exist, including some in this series [Vernon 2021]. We come back to the topic in Chapter 5.

Foundation Patterns Summary

This concludes our coverage of five foundation patterns in this chapter. Chapter 3 features these patterns as decisions required and problem-solution pairs.

Note that FRONTEND INTEGRATION is sometimes called *vertical* integration, while BACKEND INTEGRATION is called *horizontal* integration. The notion originates from a rather common visualization of distributed systems (and their layers and tiers) that places frontends at the top of figures/model diagrams and backends at the bottom; if several systems are displayed, this is done along the x-axis of the figure. Note that a left-to-right organization of such figures also is seen frequently.

You might be wondering why we call out the integration type and API visibility in pattern form; aren't all these APIs just APIs with endpoints, operations, and messages? They are. However, practical experience suggests that the business contexts and requirements for the two integration types are different; therefore, APIs serving frontend and backend fulfill other purposes and are designed differently. For instance, the protocol choice might differ in the two cases: HTTP often is a natural (or the only) choice in Frontend Integration, while message queuing is attractive in Backend Integration. The request and response message structures may vary too in terms of their breadth and depth. An API that does both either makes design compromises or has to offer optional features, which tends to complicate its usage. Similar concerns apply to API visibility; for instance, a Public API often has more advanced security requirements and stability needs than an internal one; the error reporting has to consider that API clients and providers might not even know each other (which is less likely for Solution-Internal APIs).

Next, we look at the building blocks of request and response messages, abstracting from the data definition concepts in exchange formats such as JSON.

Basic Structure Patterns

API contracts describe the unique address of one or more API endpoints (such as an HTTP resource URI), their operations (such as supported HTTP verbs or the name of a SOAP Web service operation), plus the structures of the request and response messages of each operation. The data structures defining these messages are an essential part of the API contract; the domain model in Chapter 1 features them as *representation elements*. Figure 4.1 presented exemplary request and response messages at the start of this chapter.

Design questions about these data structures (representation elements) arise:

- What is an adequate number of representation elements for request and response messages?
- How should these elements be structured and grouped?

For instance, these design issues affect the resource URI (including path parameters), query, cookie, header parameters, and message content (also called *message body*) when HTTP is the message exchange protocol. GET and DELETE requests usually do not contain bodies, but responses to such requests do. HTTP POSTs, PUTs, and PATCHes often contain both request and response bodies but may also define one or more path, query, header, and cookie parameters. In a WSDL/SOAP context, we can interpret this design issue as how the SOAP message parts should be organized and which data types should be used to define the corresponding XML schema elements. gRPC Protocol Buffers and GraphQL provide similar concepts to specify messages, with similar granularity decisions required.

The four patterns in this section answer the two questions differently. An ATOMIC PARAMETER describes plain data such as texts and numbers, and an ATOMIC PARAMETER LIST groups several such elementary parameters. PARAMETER TREES provide nesting (of atoms and other trees), and a PARAMETER FOREST groups multiple such tree parameters at the top level of a message. The pattern map in Figure 4.11 shows these four patterns with their relations to each other.

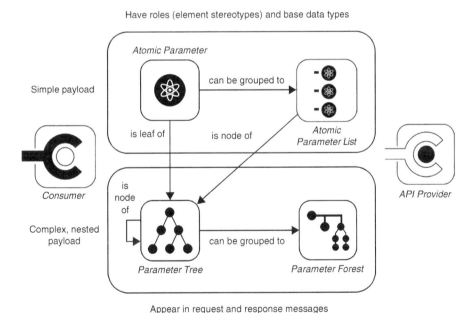

Figure 4.11 *Patterns to structure messages and their representation elements*

Pattern:
ATOMIC PARAMETER

Known from programming languages, basic types are the simplest unit of transmission in message exchanges between API clients and API providers (of all visibilities and integration types introduced earlier in this section).

How can simple, unstructured data (such as a number, a string, a Boolean value, or a block of binary data) be exchanged between API client and API provider?

Define a single parameter or body element. Pick a basic type from the type system of the chosen message exchange format for it. If justified by receiver-side usage, identify this ATOMIC PARAMETER with a name. Document name (if present), type, cardinality, and optionality in the API DESCRIPTION.

Decide whether the atom is single- or set-valued. Describe the meaning of the transported values, at least informally, including, for instance, a unit of measure. Consider specifying a value range to constrain the type of the ATOMIC PARAMETER. Make this value-range information explicit—statically in the schema definition language for the chosen message exchange format (for example, JSON Schema, Protocol Buffers, GraphQL Schema Language, or XML Schema) and/or dynamically in runtime metadata.

Figure 4.12 visualizes a single-valued string parameter as a single instance of the pattern appearing in a request message.

Figure 4.12 *ATOMIC PARAMETER pattern: Single scalar (of basic type)*

In the Lakeside Mutual sample case, ATOMIC PARAMETERS can be found in all API operations, for instance, those dealing with services concerning customer information. The first example is single-valued:

```
"city":Data<string>
```

The notation of this example is Microservice Domain-Specific Language (MDSL; see Appendix C for an introduction). In the API of the Customer Core application at Lakeside Mutual, such parameters can be used to retrieve the city of a customer:

```
curl -X GET --header 'Authorization: Bearer b318ad736c6c844b' \
http://localhost:8110/customers/gktlipwhjr?fields=city
{
  "customers": [{
    "city": "St. Gallen",
    "_links": {
      "self": {
        "href": "/customers/gktlipwhjr?fields=city"
      },
      "address.change": {
        "href": "/customers/gktlipwhjr/address"
      }
    }
  }],
  ...
}
```

Note that `city` is not the only ATOMIC PARAMETER in the example. The customer identifier `gktlipwhjr` in the path of the URI also qualifies as such.

Atomic parameters may come as collections of basic types, which is expressed by making the atom set-valued *, as shown in the following MDSL example:

```
"streetAddress":D<string>*
```

A JSON instance of the preceding definition is

```
{ "streetAddress": [ "sampleStreetName1", "sampleStreetName2"]}
```

ATOMIC PARAMETERS appear in all operation definitions and in their schema components. Appendix B presents an OpenAPI specification from the Lakeside Mutual case.

Details

Expressive names from the domain that the API belongs to make the API understandable for client developers and nontechnical stakeholders. Each atom might have an exactly-one cardinality but also be optional (zero-or-one cardinality), set-valued (at-least-one), or both (zero-or-more). Binary data might have to be encoded, for instance, in Base64 [Josefsson 2006].

Note that the texts and numbers that travel in ATOMIC PARAMETERS may actually be structured internally, for instance, if a string has to match a certain regular expression or is a collection of identically structured entries (such as the lines in the CSV format). However, this structure is not something the API provider and the API client deal with during serialization and deserialization. Preparing and processing valid data remains a responsibility of the application containing the API client and the API implementation on the provider side. The API DESCRIPTION may define certain value range and validation rules, but typically, the enforcement of these rules is not part of the interoperability contract but is an implementation-level task (as explained earlier). Note that this "tunneling" approach is sometimes perceived as an antipattern because it bypasses serialization/deserialization tools and middleware; this approach might appear to be convenient, but it introduces technical risk and, possibly, security threats.

ATOMIC PARAMETERS often play certain roles within a request or response message. Chapter 6 highlights four such roles in the section on "Element Stereotypes": domain DATA ELEMENT, METADATA ELEMENT, ID ELEMENT, and LINK ELEMENT.

 ## Pattern:
ATOMIC PARAMETER LIST

Sometimes, a single ATOMIC PARAMETER is not expressive enough. Two or more such ATOMIC PARAMETERS might have strong semantic ties, or the content of a request or response message might need several parts that are worth distinguishing from an API client, API provider, or intermediary point of view.

How can multiple related ATOMIC PARAMETERS be combined in a representation element so that each of them stays simple, but their relatedness becomes explicit in the API DESCRIPTION and the runtime message exchanges?

Group two or more simple, unstructured data elements in a single cohesive representation element to define an ATOMIC PARAMETER LIST that contains multiple ATOMIC PARAMETERS. Identify its items by position (index) or by a string-valued key. Identify the ATOMIC PARAMETER LIST as a whole with its own name as well if that is needed to process it in the receiver. Specify how many elements are required and permitted to appear.

The ATOMIC PARAMETER LIST as a whole, but also its elements, can be optional or set-valued. These properties should be expressed as cardinalities in the API DESCRIPTION.

Figure 4.13 sketches an application of the pattern in a request message. The data transfer representation in the figure has three ATOMIC PARAMETER entries.

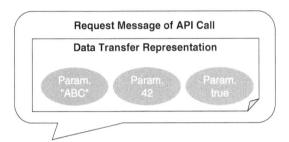

Figure 4.13 *ATOMIC PARAMETER LIST pattern: Grouped atoms*

In the Lakeside Mutual case, an ATOMIC PARAMETER LIST may represent customer addresses (MDSL notation):

```
data type AddressRecord (
  "streetAddress":D<string>*,
  "postalCode":D<int>?,
  "city":D<string>
)
```

The `streetAddress` is set-valued, indicated by the asterisk `*`. The `postalCode` is marked as optional in this example, indicated by the question mark `?`.

A JSON representation of sample data adhering to this definition is

```
{
  "street": ["sampleStreetName"],
  "postalCode": "42",
  "city": "sampleCityName"
}
```

Revisiting the Customer Core example from the ATOMIC PARAMETER, it might be required to specify multiple fields in the request. In that case, a single `fields=city,postalCode` parameter, which is an ATOMIC PARAMETER LIST, allows the API client to indicate that it wants the provider to include certain (but not all) fields in the response:

```
curl -X GET --header 'Authorization: Bearer b318ad736c6c844b' \
http://localhost:8110/customers/gktlipwhjr?\
fields=city,postalCode
```

The client does not identify the individual fields by a key but by position in the GET request. The provider iterates through the list to decide whether or not to include a field in the response. This, in fact, is the essence of an API quality pattern called WISH LIST (presented in Chapter 7).

Details

Design advice for single ATOMIC PARAMETERS is applicable here too; for instance, the parameters should be named in a meaningful and consistent way; the chosen names should be part of the domain vocabulary. The order of the atoms in the list should be logical and express the proximity of the elements to improve human readability. The API DESCRIPTION should provide representative examples for the permitted combinations (instances of valid lists, that is).

Some platforms do not allow the communication participants to send multiple scalars in a particular message type. For instance, many programming languages allow only one return value or object in a response message; the default mappings from these languages to JSON and XML schema follow this convention (for example, JAX-RS and JAX-WS in Java). The pattern cannot be used in that case; a PARAMETER TREE has the required expressivity.

 Pattern:
PARAMETER TREE

Listing basic representation elements in a flat ATOMIC PARAMETER LIST that by definition contains only plain ATOMIC PARAMETERS often is not sufficient, for instance, when publishing rich domain data such as an order that contains order items or products that are sold to many customers (that in turn buy many products).

▼

How can containment relationships be expressed when defining complex representation elements and exchanging such related elements at runtime?

Define a PARAMETER TREE as a hierarchical structure with a dedicated root node that has one or more child nodes. Each child node may be a single ATOMIC PARAMETER, an ATOMIC PARAMETER LIST, or another PARAMETER TREE, identified locally by a name and/or by position. Each node might have an exactly-one cardinality but also a zero-or-one cardinality, an at-least-one cardinality, or a zero-or-more cardinality.

▲

Note that the pattern is defined recursively to yield the desired nested structures. In HTTP APIs, nested JSON objects provide the tree structure expressed by this pattern; set-valued tree nodes can be represented with JSON arrays containing JSON objects corresponding to the nodes.

Figure 4.14 illustrates the pattern conceptually.

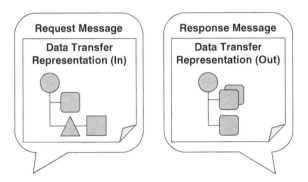

Figure 4.14 *Parameter Tree pattern: Two versus one nesting level*

In the Lakeside Mutual case, Parameter Trees can be found in several API operations that deal with customer and contract data. Picking up the example in Figure 4.1 at the beginning of this chapter, an example of a two-level nesting is as follows (note that the `AddressRecord` in the example has already been defined as an Atomic Parameter List above):

```
data type MoveHistory {
  "from":AddressRecord, "to":AddressRecord, "when":D<string>
}
data type CustomerWithAddressAndMoveHistory {
  "customerId":ID<int>,
  "addressRecords":AddressRecord+, // one or more
  "moveHistory":MoveHistory*      // type reference, collection
}
```

This MDSL data definition `CustomerWithAddressAndMoveHistory` might produce the following JSON object-array structure at runtime:

```
{
  "customerId": "111",
  "addressRecords": [{
    "street": "somewhere1",
    "postalCode": "42",
    "city": "somewhere2"
  }],
```

```
"moveHistory": [{
  "from": {
    "street": "somewhere3",
    "postalCode": "44",
    "city": "somewhere4"
  },
  "to": {
    "street": "somewhere1",
    "postalCode": "42",
    "city": "somewhere2"
  },
  "when": "2022/01/01"
}]
}
```

The MDSL Web site[6] provides more examples.

Details

If the structure of the domain model element(s) represented as parameters is hierarchical or associative (with 1:1 relations such as customer overview and details or *n:m* relations such as customers buying products), then using PARAMETER TREE is a natural choice that is beneficial for understandability compared to other options, such as representing the complex structure in a flattened list. If additional data (such as security information) has to be transmitted with the message, the hierarchical nature of a PARAMETER TREE can set the additional data structurally apart from the domain parameters and is thus well suited for this use case (CONTEXT REPRESENTATION, Chapter 6).

PARAMETER TREES are more complex to process than atoms, and bandwidth may be wasted during message transfer if they contain unnecessary elements or an excessive number of nesting levels. But if the structure that needs to be transferred is a deep hierarchy, they typically are more efficient both in processing and bandwidth use than sending multiple messages with simpler structures. PARAMETER TREES introduce the risk that sometimes unnecessary information and/or more structure(s) information is shared between API client and provider, for instance, when the optionality of information is not defined explicitly. This might not be optimal with regard to format autonomy as a facet of loose coupling.

Note the recursive definition of the pattern. When applying the pattern, for instance, when defining a JSON schema for the body of an HTTP POST request, making use of such recursive definitions might be elegant (and sometimes cannot be avoided); choices and optionality of nodes give tree construction processors a chance

---

6. https://microservice-api-patterns.github.io/MDSL-Specification/datacontract

to terminate. However, even when doing so, such recursive definitions might also lead to large message payloads that stress tools and runtime serializers such as Jackson (or even crash them).

 ## Pattern:
PARAMETER FOREST

Just as ATOMIC PARAMETERS may form ATOMIC PARAMETER LISTS, PARAMETER TREES can also be assembled into groups. This is useful only at the top level of a request or response message header or payload.

How can multiple PARAMETER TREES be exposed as a request or response payload of an API operation?

Define a PARAMETER FOREST comprising two or more PARAMETER TREES. Locate the forest members by position or name.

Figure 4.15 illustrates the pattern.

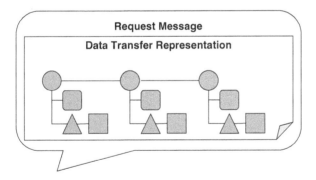

Figure 4.15 *PARAMETER FOREST pattern*

The PARAMETER TREES in the forest are accessed by position or name; in contrast to trees that may contain other trees, PARAMETER FORESTS may not contain other forests.

```
data type CustomerProductForest [
  "customers": { "customer":CustomerWithAddressAndMoveHistory }*,
  "products": { "product":ID<string> }
]
```

The JSON rendering of this specification looks very similar to that of a tree of the same structure:

```
{
  "customers": [{
    "customer": {
      "customerId": "42",
      "addressRecords": [{
        "street": "someText",
        "zipCode": "42",
        "city": "someText"
      }],
      "moveHistory": []
    }}],
  "products": [{ "product": "someText" }]
}
```

However, a Java interface of the service unveils the slight difference in the operation signature:

```
public interface CustomerInformationHolder {
    boolean uploadSingleParameter(
        CustomerProductForest newData);
    boolean uploadMultipleParameters(
        List<Customer> newCustomer, List<String> newProducts);
}
```

The `uploadSingleParameter` method uses a single class `CustomerProduct-Forest` as its input (containing customer and product trees), while `uploadMul-tipleParameters` works with two parameters, of type `List<Customer>` and `List<String>`. Note that the latter can easily be refactored into the former.

Details

This pattern represents the special case of two or more nested top-level parameters (or message body elements). In most technology mappings of the pattern, it is semantically equivalent to a PARAMETER TREE with the forest members as the first nesting level (see the JSON example presented earlier).

In HTTP resource APIs, the collection of query, path, cookie parameters, and body jointly can be seen as such a forest (and is one of the reasons we have this pattern).

A PARAMETER FOREST can be turned into a PARAMETER TREE by introducing an "artificial" root node; similarly, ATOMIC PARAMETER LISTS and flat PARAMETER TREES are equivalent. Therefore, recursive PARAMETER TREES and ATOMIC PARAMETER as leaf nodes would suffice to represent arbitrarily complex data structures. One might wonder about the merit of having four distinct patterns rather than two. We decided to present four design options as patterns to be able to model the intricacies of various technologies such as HTTP, WSDL/SOAP, gRPC, and so on—without hiding their conceptual differences and without losing generality.

Basic Structure Patterns Summary

The data part of the API contract, established by the structures of request and response message payload, directly contributes to (or harms) the developer experience. Qualities such as interoperability and maintainability are at stake. Chapter 1 provides a deeper discussion of these and many more desired qualities (and related design challenges).

The use of the patterns results in platform-independent schema definitions that correspond to JSON schema (as used in OpenAPI), Protocol Buffer specifications, or GraphQL Schema Language (see Table 4.2).

Table 4.2 *Basic Structure Patterns and Their Known Uses*

Theme	Pattern	JSON	XML, XML Schema	Protocol Buffers	GraphQL
Plain data	ATOMIC PARAMETER (single-valued)	Basic/primitive types	Simple types	Scalar value types	Scalar types
Map/ record	ATOMIC PARAMETER LIST	Object {...}, not including other objects	Sequence of size 1, referencing built-in or custom types	Nested types	`input` and `type` definitions
Nesting	PARAMETER TREE	Object including other objects {...{...}...}	Complex types	Message referencing other messages	`input` and `type` definitions referencing others
Group of nested elements	PARAMETER FOREST	Top-level array of objects	Can be modeled in WSDL (but not used in practice)	n/a	n/a
Collection	Variant of other patterns (atoms, trees)	Array [...]	`maxOccurs= "unbounded"`	`repeated` flag	Array [...]

Flat Parameter Trees and Atomic Parameter Lists can be mapped to path parameters or the query string of a URI, for instance, via "deepObject" serialization [OpenAPI 2022]. This gets more difficult or might even be impossible for deeply nested trees; according to the OpenAPI Specification, the "behavior for nested objects and arrays is undefined."

All four types of basic structure elements can be used and combined to create Metadata Elements, Id Elements, and Link Elements as variations of general-purpose Data Elements (patterns from Chapter 6). Embedded Entities often come as Parameter Trees, and Linked Information Holders use Atomic Parameter Lists to define the link target (Chapter 7). A Version Identifier often is an Atomic Parameter (Chapter 8).

Optionally, data provenance information can be provided in the API Description. Such information might include the entities, people, and processes involved in producing the representation elements; the data origins; and where the data moves over time. Note that such information may increase coupling because the message receiver might start interpreting and depending on it, making the API harder to change. The element stereotypes in Chapter 6 describe how to add this and other semantic information to the representation elements: Metadata Element, Id Element, and Link Element.

Chapter 3 covers the four basic structure patterns presented in this section with their problem-solution pairs.

Summary

In this chapter, we established the scope of our pattern language, introduced its organization, and discussed possible navigation paths. We also introduced five foundation and four basic structure patterns not covered in depth later in the book.

The patterns capture proven solutions to design problems commonly encountered when specifying, implementing, and maintaining message-based APIs. To ease navigation, the patterns are grouped by life-cycle phase, scope, and category of design concern. Each pattern in the following chapters is described following a common template, progressing from context and problem to solution and example to discussion and related patterns.

The basic building blocks of our pattern language were introduced in this chapter, starting from PUBLIC API for FRONTEND INTEGRATION to COMMUNITY API and SOLUTION-INTERNAL API for FRONTEND INTEGRATION and BACKEND INTEGRATION to flat and nested message structures including ATOMIC PARAMETERS and PARAMETER TREES.

Once it has been decided which type of API to build and where to expose it, endpoints and their operations can be identified. Assigning endpoint roles and operation responsibilities helps with that, which is the topic of Chapter 5. The message and data contract design continues in Chapter 6. LINKED INFORMATION HOLDER and EMBEDDED ENTITY are two more of the 44 patterns in this book. They served as examples at the start of this chapter, and we return to them in Chapter 7.

Chapter 5

Define Endpoint Types and Operations

API design affects not only the structure of request and response messages, which we covered in Chapter 4, "Pattern Language Introduction." It is equally—or even more—important to position the API endpoints and their operations within the architecture of the distributed system under construction (the terms *endpoints* and *operations* were introduced in the API domain model in Chapter 1, "Application Programming Interface (API) Fundamentals"). If positioning is done without careful thought, in a hurry, or not at all, the resulting API provider implementation is at risk for being hard to scale and maintain when inconsistencies degrade conceptual integrity; API client developers might find it difficult to learn and utilize the resulting mishmash APIs.

The architectural patterns in this chapter play a central role in our pattern language. Their purpose is to connect high-level endpoint identification activities with detailed design of operations and message representations. We employ a role- and responsibility-driven approach for this transition. Knowing about the technical roles of API endpoints and the state management responsibilities of their operations allows API designers to justify more detailed decisions later and also helps with runtime API management (for instance, infrastructure capacity planning).

This chapter corresponds to the Define phase of the Align-Define-Design-Refine (ADDR) process outlined in the introduction to Part 2 of the book. You do not have to be familiar with ADDR to be able to apply its patterns.

Introduction to API Roles and Responsibilities

Business-level ideation activities often produce collections of *candidate API endpoints*. Such initial, tentative design artifacts typically start from API design goals expressed as user stories (of various forms), event storming output, or collaboration scenarios [Zimmermann 2021b]. When the API realization starts, these interface candidates have to be defined in more detail. API designers seek an appropriate balance between architectural concerns such as granularity of the services exposed by the API (small and specific vs. large and universal) and degree of coupling between clients and API provider implementations (as low as possible, as high as needed).

The requirements for API design are diverse. As explained previously, goals derived from the business-level activities are a primary source of input, but not the only one; for instance, external governance rules and constraints imposed by existing backend systems have to be taken into account as well. Consequently, the architectural roles of APIs in applications and service ecosystems differ widely. Sometimes, API clients just want to inform the provider about an incident or hand over some data; sometimes, they look for provider-side data to continue their processing. When responding to client requests, providers may simply return a data element already available—or may perform rather complex processing steps (including calls to other APIs). Some of the provider-side processing, whether simple or complex, may change the provider state, some might leave this state untouched. Calls to API operations may or may not be part of complex interaction scenarios and conversations. For instance, long-running business processes such as online shopping and insurance claims management involve complex interactions between multiple parties.

The granularity of the operations varies greatly. Small API operations are easy to write, but there might be many, which have to be composed with their invocations being coordinated over time; few large API operations may be self-contained and autonomous, but they can be difficult to configure, test, and evolve. The runtime operations management of many small units also differs from that of a few big ones; there is a flexibility versus efficiency trade-off.

API designers have to decide how to give operations a business meaning (this, for instance, is a principle in service-oriented architectures [Zimmermann 2017]). They also have to decide if and how to manage state; an operation might simply return a calculated response but might also have a permanent mutational effect on the provider-side data stores.

In response to these challenges, the patterns in this chapter deal with endpoint and operation semantics in API design and usage. They carve out the architectural role of API endpoints (emphasis on data or activity?) and the responsibilities of operations (read and/or write behavior?).

Challenges and Desired Qualities

The design of endpoints and operations, expressed in the API contract, directly influences the developer experience in terms of function, stability, ease of use, and clarity.

- **Accuracy:** Calling an API rather than implementing its features oneself requires a certain amount of trust that the called operation will deliver correct results reliably; in this context, accuracy means the functional correctness of the API implementation with regard to its contract. Such accuracy certainly helps building trust. Mission-critical functionality deserves particular attention. The more important the correct functioning of a business process and its activities is, the more effort should be spent on their design, development, and operations. Preconditions, invariants, and postconditions of operations in the API contract communicate what clients and providers expect from each other in terms of request and response message content.

- **Distribution of control and autonomy:** The more work is distributed, the more parallel processing and specialization become possible. However, distribution of responsibilities and shared ownership of business process instances require coordination and consensus between API client and provider; integrity guarantees have to be defined, and consistent activity termination must be designed. The smaller and more autonomous an endpoint is, the easier it becomes to rewrite it; however, many small units often have a lot of dependencies among each other, making an isolated rewrite activity risky; think about the specification of pre- and postconditions, end-to-end testing, and compliance management.

- **Scalability, performance, and availability:** Mission-critical APIs and their operations typically have demanding SERVICE LEVEL AGREEMENTS that go along with the API DESCRIPTION. Two examples of mission-critical components are day trading algorithms at a stock exchange and order processing and billing in an online shop. A 24/7 availability requirement is an example of a highly demanding, often unrealistic quality target. Business processes with many concurrent instances, implemented in a distributed fashion involving a large number of API clients and involving multiple calls to operations, can only be as good as their weakest component in this regard. API clients expect the response times for their operations calls to stay in the same order of magnitude when the number of clients and requests increases. Otherwise, they will start to question the reliability of the API.

  Assessing the consequences of failure or unavailability is an analysis and design task in software engineering but also a business leadership and risk management activity. An API design exposing business processes and their activities can ease the recovery from failures but also make it more difficult. For example, APIs might provide compensating operations that undo work done by previous calls to the same API; however, a lack of architectural clarity and request coordination might also lead to inconsistent application state within API clients and providers.

- **Manageability:** While one can design for runtime qualities such as performance, scalability, and availability, only running the system will tell whether API design and implementation are adequate. Monitoring the API and its exposed services is instrumental in determining its adequacy and what can be done to resolve mismatches between stated requirements and observed performance, scalability, and availability. Monitoring supports management disciplines such as fault, configuration, accounting, performance, and security management.

- **Consistency and atomicity:** Business activities should have an all-or-nothing semantics; once their execution is complete, the API provider finds itself in a consistent state. However, the execution of the business activity may fail, or clients may choose to explicitly abort or *compensate* it (here, compensation refers to an application-level undo or other follow-up operation that resets the provider-side application state to a valid state).

- **Idempotence:** Idempotence is another property that influences or even steers the API design. An API operation is idempotent if multiple calls to it (with the same input) return the same output and, for stateful operations, have the same effect on the API state. Idempotence helps deal with communication errors by allowing simple message retransmission.

- **Auditability:** Compliance with the business process model is ensured by audit checks performed by risk management groups in enterprises. All APIs that expose functionality that is subject to be audited must support such audits and implement related *controls* so that it is possible to monitor business activities execution with logs that cannot be tampered with. Satisfying audit requirements is a design concern but also influences service management at runtime significantly. The article "Compliance by Design—Bridging the Chasm between Auditors and IT Architects," for instance, introduces "Completeness, Accuracy, Validity, Restricted Access (CAVR)" compliance controls and suggests how to realize such controls, for instance in service-oriented architectures [Julisch 2011].

Patterns in this Chapter

Resolving the preceding design challenges is a complex undertaking; many design tactics and patterns exist. Many of those have already been published (for instance, in the books that we list in the preface). Here, we present patterns that carve out important architectural characteristics of API endpoints and operations; doing so simplifies and streamlines the application of these other tactics and patterns.

Some of the architectural questions an API design has to answer concern the input to operations:

What can and should the API provider expect from the clients? For instance, what are its preconditions regarding data validity and integrity? Does an operation invocation imply state transfer?

The output produced by API implementations when processing calls to operations also requires attention:

What are the operation postconditions? What can the API client in turn expect from the provider when it sends input that meets the preconditions? Does a request update the provider state?

In an online shopping example, for instance, the order status might be updated and can be obtained in subsequent API calls, with the order confirmation containing all (and only) the purchased products.

Different types of APIs deal with these concerns differently. A key decision is whether the endpoint should have activity- or data-oriented semantics. Hence, we introduce two *endpoint roles* in this chapter. These types of endpoints correspond to architectural roles as follows:

- The pattern Processing Resource can help to realize activity-oriented API endpoints.

- Data-oriented API endpoints are represented by Information Holder Resources.

The section "Endpoint Roles" covers Processing Resource and Information Holder Resource. Specialized types of Information Holder Resources exist. For instance, Data Transfer Resource supports integration-oriented APIs, and Link Lookup Resource has a directory role. Operational Data Holders, Master Data Holders, and Reference Data Holders differ concerning the characteristics of data they expose in terms of data lifetime, relatedness, and mutability.

The four *operation responsibilities* found in these types of endpoints are Computation Function, Retrieval Operation, State Creation Operation, and State Transition Operation. These types are covered in the section "Operation Responsibilities." They differ in terms of client commitment (preconditions in API contract) and expectation (postconditions), as well as their impact on provider-side application state and processing complexity.

Figure 5.1 summarizes the patterns in this chapter.

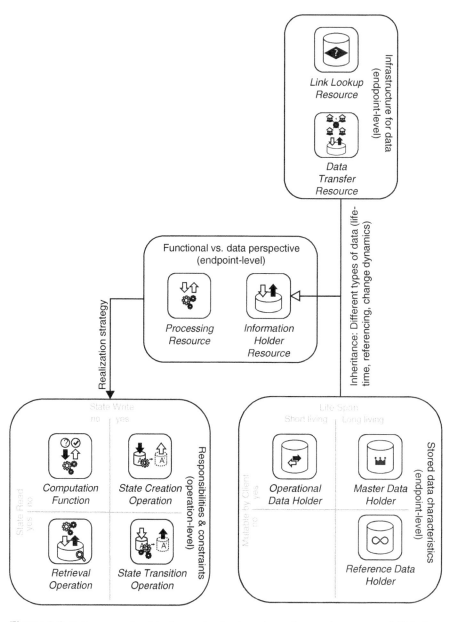

Figure 5.1 *Pattern map for this chapter (endpoint roles and operations responsibilities)*

Endpoint Roles (aka Service Granularity)

Refining the pattern map for this chapter, Figure 5.2 shows the patterns representing two general endpoint roles and five types of information holders.

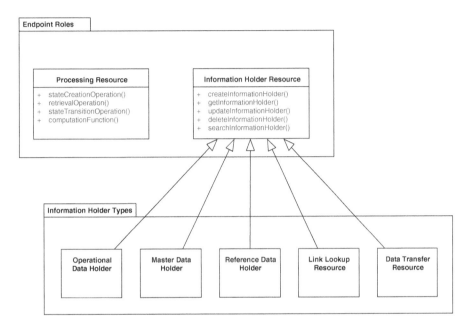

Figure 5.2 *Patterns distinguishing endpoint roles*

The two general endpoint roles are Processing Resource and Information Holder Resource. They may expose different types of operations that write, read, read-write, or only compute. There are five Information Holder Resource specializations, answering the following question differently:

How can data-oriented API endpoints be classified by data lifetime, link structure, and mutability characteristics?

Let us cover Processing Resource first, followed by Information Holder Resource and its five specializations.

Pattern:
PROCESSING RESOURCE

When and Why to Apply

The functional requirements for an application have been specified, for instance, in the form of user stories, use cases, and/or analysis-level business process models. An analysis of the functional requirements suggests that something has to be computed or a certain activity is required. This cannot or should not be done locally; remote FRONTEND INTEGRATION and/or BACKEND INTEGRATION APIs are required. A preliminary list of candidate API endpoints might have been collected already.

> How can an API provider allow its remote clients to trigger actions in it?

Such actions may be short-lived, standalone commands and computations (application-domain-specific ones or technical utilities) or long-running activities in a business process; they may or may not read and write provider-side state.

We can ask more specifically:

> How can clients ask an API endpoint to perform a function that represents a business capability or a technical utility? How can an API provider expose the capability of executing a command to its clients that computes some output from the client's input and, possibly, from the provider's own state?

When invoking provider-side processing upon request from remote clients, general design concerns are as follows:

- **Contract expressiveness and service granularity (and their impact on coupling):** Ambiguities in the invocation semantics harm interoperability and can lead to invalid processing results (which in turn might cause bad decisions to be made and consequently other harm). Hence, the meaning and side effects of the invoked action (such as a self-contained command or part of a conversation), including the representations of the exchanged messages, must be made clear in the API DESCRIPTION. The API DESCRIPTION must be clear in what endpoints and operations do and do not do; preconditions, invariants, and postconditions should be specified. State changes, idempotence, transactionality, event emission, and resource consumption in the API implementation should also be defined. Not all of these properties have to be disclosed to API clients, but they still must be described in the provider-internal API documentation.

API designers have to decide how much functionality each API endpoint and its operations should expose. Many simple interactions give the client a lot of control and can make the processing highly efficient, but they also introduce coordination effort and evolution challenges; few rich API capabilities can promote qualities such as consistency but may not suit each client and therefore may waste resources. The accuracy of the API Description matters as much as that of its implementation.

- **Learnability and manageability:** An excessive number of API endpoints and operations leads to orientation challenges for client programmers, testers, and API maintenance and evolution staff (which might or might not include the original developers); it becomes difficult to find and choose the ones appropriate for a particular use case. The more options available, the more explanations and decision-making support have to be given and maintained over time.

- **Semantic interoperability:** Syntactic interoperability is a technical concern for middleware, protocol, and format designers. The communication parties must also agree on the meaning and impact of the data exchanged before and after any operation is executed.

- **Response time:** Having invoked the remote action, the client may block until a result becomes available. The longer the client has to wait, the higher the chances that something will break (either on the provider side or in client applications). The network connection between the client and the API may time out sooner or later. An end user waiting for slow results may click refresh, thus putting additional load on an API provider serving the end-user application.

- **Security and privacy:** If a full audit log of all API invocations and resulting server-side processing has to be maintained (for instance, because of data privacy requirements), statelessness on the provider side is an illusion even if application state is not required from a functional requirement point of view. Personal sensitive information and/or otherwise classified information (for example, by governments or enterprises) might be contained in the request and response message representations. Furthermore, in many scenarios one has to ensure that only authorized clients can invoke certain actions (that is, commands, conversation parts); for instance, regular employees are usually not permitted to increase their own salary in the employee management systems integrated via Community APIs and implemented as microservices. Hence, the security architecture design has to take the requirements of processing-centric

API operations into account—for instance in its policy decision point (PDP) and policy enforcement point (PEP) design and when deciding between role-based access control (RBAC) and attribute-based access control (ABAC). The processing resource is the subject of API security design [Yalon 2019] but also is an opportunity to place PEPs into the overall control flow. The threat model and controls created by security consultants, risk managers, and auditors also must take processing-specific attacks into account, for instance denial-of-service (DoS) attacks [Julisch 2011].

• **Compatibility and evolvability:** The provider and the client should agree on the assumptions concerning the input/output representations as well as the semantics of the function to be performed. The client expectations should match what is offered by the provider. The request and response message structures may change over time. If, for instance, units of measure change or optional parameters are introduced, the client must have a chance to notice this and react to it (for instance, by developing an adapter or by evolving itself into a new version, possibly using a new version of an API operation). Ideally, new versions are forward and backward compatible with existing API clients.

These concerns conflict with each other. For instance, the richer and the more expressive a contract is, the more has to be learned, managed, and tested (with regard to interoperability). Finer-grained services might be easier to protect and evolve, but there will be many of them, which have to be integrated. This adds performance overhead and may raise consistency issues [Neri 2020].

A "Shared Database" [Hohpe 2003] that offers actions and commands in the form of stored procedures could be a valid integration approach (and is used in practice), but it creates a single point of failure, does not scale with a growing number of clients, and cannot be deployed or redeployed independently. Shared Databases containing business logic in stored procedures do not align well with service design principles such as single responsibility and loose coupling.

How It Works

Add a PROCESSING RESOURCE endpoint to the API exposing operations that bundle and wrap application-level activities or commands.

For the new endpoint, define one or more operations, each of which takes over a dedicated processing responsibility ("action required"). COMPUTATION FUNCTION, STATE CREATION OPERATION, and STATE TRANSITION OPERATION are common in activity-oriented PROCESSING RESOURCES. RETRIEVAL OPERATIONS mostly are limited to mere status/state checks here and are more commonly found in data-oriented INFORMATION HOLDER RESOURCES. For each of these operations, define a "Command Message" for the request. Add a "Document Message" for the response when realizing an operation as a "Request-Reply" message exchange [Hohpe 2003]. Make the endpoint remotely accessible for one or more API clients by providing a unique logical address (for instance, a Uniform Resource Identifier [URI] in HTTP APIs).

Figure 5.3 sketches this endpoint-operation design in a UML class diagram.

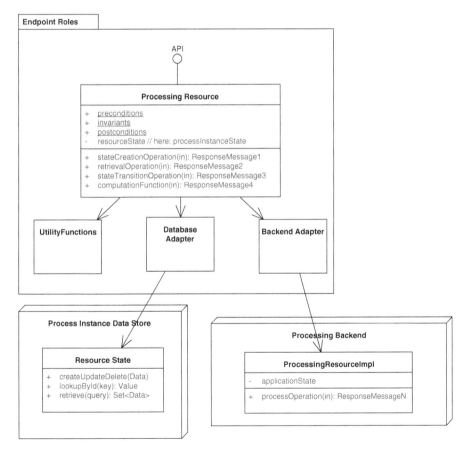

Figure 5.3 PROCESSING RESOURCES *represent activity-oriented API designs. Some operations in the endpoint access and change application state, others do not. Data is exposed only in request and response messages*

The request message should make the performed action explicit and allow the API endpoint to determine which processing logic to execute. These actions might represent a general-purpose or an application-domain-specific functional system capability (implemented within the API provider or residing in some backend and accessed via an outbound port/adapter) or a technical utility.

The request and response messages possibly can be structured according to any of the four structural representation patterns ATOMIC PARAMETER, ATOMIC PARAMETER LIST, PARAMETER TREE, and PARAMETER FOREST. The API DESCRIPTION has to document the syntax and semantics of the PROCESSING RESOURCE (including operation pre- and postconditions as well as invariants).

The PROCESSING RESOURCE can be a "Stateful Component" or a "Stateless Component" [Fehling 2014]. If invocations of its operations cause changes in the (shared) provider-side state, the approach to data management must be designed deliberately; required decisions include strict vs. weak/eventual consistency, optimistic vs. pessimistic locking, and so on. The data management policies should not be exposed in the API (which would make them visible to the API client), but open and close (or commit, rollback) system transactions be placed inside the API implementation, preferably at the operation boundary. Application-level compensating operations should be offered to handle things that cannot be undone easily by system transaction managers. For instance, an email that is sent in an API implementation cannot be taken back once it has left the mail server; a second mail, "Please ignore the previous mail," has to be sent instead [Zimmermann 2007; Richardson 2018].

Example

The Policy Management backend of the Lakeside Mutual case contains a stateful PROCESSING RESOURCE InsuranceQuoteRequestCoordinator that offers STATE TRANSITION OPERATIONS, which move an insurance quotation request through various stages. The resource is implemented as an HTTP resource API in Java and Spring Boot:

```
@RestController
@RequestMapping("/insurance-quote-requests")
public class InsuranceQuoteRequestCoordinator {

  @Operation(
    summary = "Updates the status of an existing " +
    "Insurance Quote Request")
  @PreAuthorize("isAuthenticated()")
  @PatchMapping(value = "/{id}")
  public ResponseEntity<InsuranceQuoteRequestDto>
    respondToInsuranceQuote(
```

```
        Authentication,
        @Parameter(description = "the insurance quote " +
          "request's unique id", required = true)
        @PathVariable Long id,
        @Parameter(description = "the response that " +
          "contains the customer's decision whether " +
          "to accept or reject an insurance quote",
           required = true)
        @Valid @RequestBody
        InsuranceQuoteResponseDto insuranceQuoteResponseDto) {
```

The Lakeside Mutual application services also contain RiskComputation-Service, a stateless PROCESSING RESOURCE that implements a single COMPUTATION FUNCTION called computeRiskFactor:

```
@RestController
@RequestMapping("/riskfactor")
public class RiskComputationService {
  @Operation(
    summary = "Computes the customer's risk factor.")
  @PostMapping(
    value = "/compute")
  public ResponseEntity<RiskFactorResponseDto>
    computeRiskFactor(
        @Parameter(description = "the request containing " +
          "relevant customer attributes (e.g., birthday)",
          required = true)
        @Valid @RequestBody
          RiskFactorRequestDto riskFactorRequest) {

        int age = getAge(riskFactorRequest.getBirthday());
        String postalCode = riskFactorRequest.getPostalCode();
        int riskFactor = computeRiskFactor(age, postalCode);
        return ResponseEntity.ok(
          new RiskFactorResponseDto(riskFactor));
    }
```

Discussion

Business activity- and process-orientation can reduce coupling and promote information hiding. However, instances of this pattern must make sure not to come across as remote procedure call (RPC) tunneled in a message-based API (and consequently be criticized because RPCs increase coupling, for instance, in the time and format autonomy dimensions). Many enterprise applications and information systems do have "business RPC" semantics, as they execute a business command or transaction from a user that must be triggered, performed, and terminated somehow. According to the original literature and subsequent collections of design advice [Allamaraju 2010], an HTTP resource does not have to model data (or only data), but can represent such business transactions, long-running ones in particular.[1] Note that "REST was never about CRUD" [Higginbotham 2018]. The evolution of PROCESSING RESOURCES is covered in Chapter 8.

A PROCESSING RESOURCE can be identified when applying a service identification technique such as *dynamic process analysis* or *event storming* [Pautasso 2017a]; this has a positive effect on the "business alignment" tenet in service-oriented architectures. One can define one instance of the pattern per backend integration need becoming evident in a use case or user story; if a single `execute` operation is included in a PROCESSING RESOURCE endpoint, it may accept self-describing action request messages and return self-contained result documents. All operations in the API have to be protected as mandated by the security requirements.

In many integration scenarios, activity- and process-orientation would have to be forced into the design, which makes it hard to explain and maintain (among other negative consequences). In such cases, INFORMATION HOLDER RESOURCE is a better choice. It is possible to define API endpoints that are both processing- and data-oriented (just like many classes in object-oriented programming combine storage and behavior). Even a mere PROCESSING RESOURCE may have to hold state (but will want to hide its structure from the API clients). Such joint use of PROCESSING RESOURCE and INFORMATION HOLDER RESOURCE is not recommended for microservices architectures due to the amount of coupling possibly introduced.

Different types of PROCESSING RESOURCES require different message exchange patterns, depending on (1) how long the processing will take and (2) whether the client must receive the result immediately to be able to continue its processing (otherwise, the result can be delivered later). Processing time may be difficult to estimate, as it depends on the complexity of the action to be executed, the amount of data sent by the client, and the load/resource availability of the provider. The Request-Reply pattern requires at least two messages that can be exchanged via one network connection, such as one HTTP request-response pair in an HTTP resource API. Alternatively, multiple technical connections can be used, for instance, by sending the command via an HTTP POST and polling for the result via HTTP GET.

---

1. Note that HTTP is a synchronous protocol as such; hence, asynchrony has to be added on the application level (or by using QoS headers or HTTP/2) [Pautasso 2018]. The DATA TRANSFER RESOURCE pattern describes such design.

Decomposing the PROCESSING RESOURCE to call operations in other API endpoints should be considered (it is rather common that no single existing or to-be-constructed system can satisfy all processing needs, due to either organizational or legacy system constraints). Most of the design difficulty lies in how to decompose a PROCESSING RESOURCE to a manageable granularity and set of expressive, learnable operations. The Stepwise Service Design activity in our *Design Practice Reference (DPR)* [Zimmermann 2021b] investigates this problem set.

Related Patterns

This pattern explains how to emphasize activity; its INFORMATION HOLDER RESOURCE sibling focuses on data orientation. PROCESSING RESOURCES may contain operations that differ in the way they deal with provider-side state (stateless services vs. stateful processors): STATE TRANSITION OPERATION, STATE CREATION OPERATION, COMPUTATION FUNCTION, and RETRIEVAL OPERATION.

PROCESSING RESOURCES are often exposed in COMMUNITY APIs, but also found in SOLUTION-INTERNAL APIs. Their operations are often protected with API KEYS and RATE LIMITS. A SERVICE LEVEL AGREEMENT that accompanies the technical API contract may govern their usage. To prevent technical parameters from creeping into the payload in request and response messages, such parameters can be isolated in a CONTEXT REPRESENTATION.

The three patterns "Command Message," "Document Message," and "Request-Reply" [Hohpe 2003] are used in combination when realizing this pattern. The "Command" pattern in [Gamma 1995] codifies a processing request and its invocation data as an object and as a message, respectively. PROCESSING RESOURCE can be seen as the remote API variant of the "Application Service" pattern in [Alur 2013]. Its provider-side implementations serve as "Service Activators" [Hohpe 2003].

Other patterns address manageability; see our evolution patterns in Chapter 8, "Evolve APIs," for design-time advice and remoting patterns books [Voelter 2004; Buschmann 2007] for runtime considerations.

More Information

PROCESSING RESOURCES correspond to "Interfacers" that provide and protect access to service providers in responsibility-driven design (RDD) [Wirfs-Brock 2002].

Chapter 6 in *SOA in Practice* [Josuttis 2007] is on service classification; it compares several taxonomies, including the one from *Enterprise SOA* [Krafzig 2004]. Some of the examples in the process services type/category in these SOA books qualify as known uses of this pattern. These two books include project examples and case studies from domains such as banking and telecommunications.

"Understanding RPC vs REST for HTTP APIs" [Sturgeon 2016a] talks about RPC and REST, but taking a closer look, it actually (also) is about deciding between PROCESSING RESOURCE and INFORMATION HOLDER RESOURCE.

The action resource topic area/category in the *API Stylebook* [Lauret 2017] provides a (meta) known use for this pattern. Its "undo" topic is also related because undo operations participate in application-level state management.

Pattern:
INFORMATION HOLDER RESOURCE

When and Why to Apply

A domain model, a conceptual entity-relationship diagram, or another form of glossary of key application concepts and their interconnections has been specified. The model contains entities that have an identity and a life cycle as well as attributes; entities cross reference each other.

From this analysis and design work, it has become apparent that structured data will have to be used in multiple places in the distributed system being designed; hence, the shared data structures have to be made accessible from multiple remote clients. It is not possible or is not easy to hide the shared data structures behind domain logic (that is, processing-oriented actions such as business activities and commands); the application under construction does not have a workflow or other processing nature.

How can domain data be exposed in an API, but its implementation still be hidden?

More specifically,

How can an API expose data entities so that API clients can access and/or modify these entities concurrently without compromising data integrity and quality?

- **Modeling approach and its impact on coupling:** Some software engineering and object-oriented analysis and design (OOAD) methods balance processing and structural aspects in their steps, artifacts, and techniques; some put a strong emphasis on either computing or data. Domain-driven design

(DDD) [Evans 2003; Vernon 2013], for instance, is an example of a balanced approach. Entity-relationship diagrams focus on data structure and relationships rather than behavior. If a data-centric modeling and API endpoint identification approach is chosen, there is a risk that many CRUD (create, read, update, delete) APIs operating on data are exposed, which can have a negative impact on data quality because every authorized client may manipulate the provider-side data rather arbitrarily. CRUD-oriented data abstractions in interfaces introduce operational and semantic coupling.

- **Quality attribute conflicts and trade-offs:** Design-time qualities such as simplicity and clarity; runtime qualities such as performance, availability, and scalability; as well as evolution-time qualities such as maintainability and flexibility often conflict with each other.

- **Security:** Cross-cutting concerns such as application security also make it difficult to deal with data in APIs. A decision to expose internal data through an API must consider the required data read/write access rights for clients. Personal sensitive information and/or information classified as confidential might be contained in the request and response message representations. Such information has to be protected. For example, the risk of the creation of fake orders, fraudulent claims, and so on, has to be assessed and security controls introduced to mitigate it [Julisch 2011].

- **Data freshness versus consistency:** Clients desire data obtained from APIs to be as up-to-date as possible, but effort is required to keep it consistent and current [Helland 2005]. Also, what are the consequences for clients if such data may become temporarily or permanently unavailable in the future?

- **Compliance with architectural design principles:** The API under construction might be part of a project that has already established a logical and a physical software architecture. It should also play nice with respect to organization-wide architectural decisions [Zdun 2018], for instance, those establishing architectural principles such as loose coupling, logical and physical data independence, or microservices tenets such as independent deployability. Such principles might include suggestive or normative guidance on whether and how data can be exposed in APIs; a number of pattern selection decisions are required, with those principles serving as decision drivers [Zimmermann 2009; Hohpe 2016]. Our patterns provide concrete alternatives and criteria for making such architectural decisions (as we discussed previously in Chapter 3).

One could think of hiding all data structures behind processing-oriented API operations and data transfer objects (DTOs) analogous to object-oriented programming (that is, local object-oriented APIs expose access methods and facades while keeping all individual data members private). Such an approach is feasible and promotes information hiding; however, it may limit the opportunities to deploy, scale, and replace remote components independently of each other because either many fine-grained, chatty API operations are required or data has to be stored redundantly. It also introduces an undesired extra level of indirection, for instance, when building data-intensive applications and integration solutions.

Another possibility would be to give direct access to the database so that consumers can see for themselves what data is available and directly read and even write it if allowed. The API in this case becomes a tunnel to the database, where consumers can send arbitrary queries and transactions through it; databases such as CouchDB provide such data-level APIs out-of-the-box. This solution completely removes the need to design and implement an API because the internal representation of the data is directly exposed to clients. Breaking basic information-hiding principles, however, it also results in a tightly coupled architecture where it will be impossible to ever touch the database schema without affecting every API client. Direct database access also introduces security threats.

How It Works

Add an INFORMATION HOLDER RESOURCE endpoint to the API, representing a data-oriented entity. Expose create, read, update, delete, and search operations in this endpoint to access and manipulate this entity.

In the API implementation, coordinate calls to these operations to protect the data entity.

Make the endpoint remotely accessible for one or more API clients by providing a unique logical address. Let each operation of the INFORMATION HOLDER RESOURCE have one and only one of the four operation responsibilities (covered in depth in the next section): STATE CREATION OPERATIONS create the entity that is represented by the INFORMATION HOLDER RESOURCE. RETRIEVAL OPERATIONS access and read an entity but do not update it. They may search for and return collections of such entities, possibly filtered. STATE TRANSITION OPERATIONS access existing entities and update them fully or partially; they may also delete them.

For each operation, design the request and, if needed, response message structures. For instance, represent entity relationships as LINK ELEMENTS. If basic reference data such as country codes or currency codes are looked up, the response message typically is an ATOMIC PARAMETER; if a rich, structured domain model entity is looked up, the response is more likely to contain a Parameter Tree that represents the data transfer representation (a term from the API domain model introduced in Chapter 1) of the looked-up information. Figure 5.4 sketches this solution.

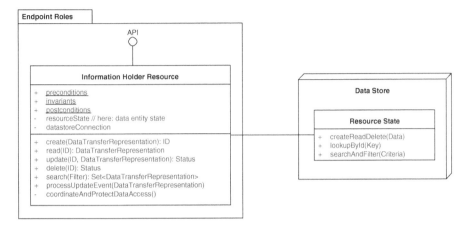

Figure 5.4 *Information Holder Resources model and expose general data-oriented API designs. This endpoint role groups information-access-oriented responsibilities. Its operations create, read, update, or delete the data held. Searching for data sets is also supported*

Define operation-level pre- and postconditions as well as invariants to protect the resource state. Decide whether the Information Holder Resource should be a "Stateful Component" or a "Stateless Component," as defined in [Fehling 2014]. In the latter case, there still is state (because the exposed data has to be held somewhere), but the entire state management is outsourced to a backend system. Define the quality characteristics of the new endpoint and its operation, covering transactionality, idempotence, access control, accountability, and consistency:

- Introduce access/modification control policies. API Keys are a simple way of identifying and authorizing clients, and more advanced security solutions are also available.

- Protect the concurrent data access by applying an optimistic or a pessimistic locking strategy from the database and concurrent programming communities. Design coordination policies.

- Implement consistency-preserving checks, which may support "Strict Consistency" or "Eventual Consistency" [Fehling 2014].

Five patterns in our language refine this general solution to data-oriented API endpoint modeling: OPERATIONAL DATA HOLDER, MASTER DATA HOLDER, REFERENCE DATA HOLDER, DATA TRANSFER RESOURCE, and LINK LOOKUP RESOURCE.

Example

The Customer Core microservice in the Lakeside Mutual sample exposes master data. The semantics and its operations (for example, `changeAddress(...)`) of this service are data- rather than action-oriented (the service is consumed by other microservices that realize the PROCESSING RESOURCE pattern). Hence, it exposes a `CustomerInformationHolder` endpoint, realized as an HTTP resource:

```
@RestController
@RequestMapping("/customers")
public class CustomerInformationHolder {
    @Operation(
        summary = "Change a customer's address.")
    @PutMapping(
        value = "/{customerId}/address")
    public ResponseEntity<AddressDto> changeAddress(
        @Parameter(
            description = "the customer's unique id",
            required = true)
        @PathVariable CustomerId,
        @Parameter(
            description = "the customer's new address",
            required = true)
        @Valid @RequestBody AddressDto requestDto) {
            [...]
    }

    @Operation(
        summary = "Get a specific set of customers.")
    @GetMapping(
        value = "/{ids}")
    public ResponseEntity<CustomersResponseDto>
      getCustomer(
        @Parameter(description =
            "a comma-separated list of customer ids",
            required = true)
        @PathVariable String ids,
        @Parameter(description =
            "a comma-separated list of the fields" +
```

```
        "that should be included in the response",
        required = false)
    @RequestParam(
        value = "fields", required = false,
        defaultValue = "")
    String fields) {
        [...]
    )
}
```

This `CustomerInformationHolder` endpoint exposes two operations, a read-write STATE TRANSITION OPERATION `changeAddress` (HTTP PUT) and a read-only RETRIEVAL OPERATIONS `getCustomer` (HTTP GET).

Discussion

INFORMATION HOLDER RESOURCES resolve their design forces as follows:

- **Modeling approach and its impact on coupling:** Introducing INFORMATION HOLDER RESOURCES often is the consequence of a data-centric approach to API modeling. Processing will typically shift to the consumer of the INFORMATION HOLDER RESOURCE. The INFORMATION HOLDER RESOURCE then is solely responsible for acting as a reliable source of linked data. The resource may serve as a relationship sink, source, or both.

  It depends on the scenario at hand and the project goals/product vision whether such an approach is adequate. While activity- or process-orientation is often preferred, it simply is not natural in a number of scenarios; examples include digital archives, IT infrastructure inventories, and server configuration repositories. Data-oriented analysis and design methods are well suited to identify INFORMATION HOLDER endpoints but sometimes go too far, for instance, when tackling system behavior and logic.[2]

- **Quality attribute conflicts and trade-offs:** Using an INFORMATION HOLDER RESOURCE requires carefully considering security, data protection, consistency, availability, and coupling implications. Any change to the INFORMATION HOLDER RESOURCE content, metadata, or representation formats must be controlled to avoid breaking consumers. Quality attribute trees can steer the pattern selection process.

---

2. One of the classic cognitive biases is that every construction problem looks like a nail if you know how to use a hammer (and have one at hand). Analysis and design methods are tools made for specific purposes.

- **Security:** Not all API clients may be authorized to access each INFORMATION HOLDER RESOURCE in the same way. API KEYS, client authentication, and ABAC/RBAC help protect each INFORMATION HOLDER RESOURCE.

- **Data freshness versus consistency:** Data consistency has to be preserved for concurrent access of multiple consumers. Likewise, clients must deal with the consequences of temporary outages, for instance, by introducing an appropriate caching and offline data replication and synchronization strategy. In practice, the decision between availability and consistency is not as binary and strict as the CAP theorem suggests, which is discussed by its original authors in a 12-year retrospective and outlook [Brewer 2012].

  If several fine-grained INFORMATION HOLDERS appear in an API, many calls to operations might be required to realize a user story, and data quality is hard to ensure (because it becomes a shared, distributed responsibility). Consider hiding several of them behind any type of PROCESSING RESOURCE.

- **Compliance with architectural design principles:** The introduction of INFORMATION HOLDER RESOURCE endpoints may break higher-order principles such as strict logical layering that forbids direct access to data entities from the presentation layer. It might be necessary to refactor the architecture [Zimmermann 2015]—or grant an explicit exception to the rule.

INFORMATION HOLDER RESOURCES have the reputation for increasing coupling and violating the information-hiding principle. A post in Michael Nygard's blog calls for a responsibility-based strategy for avoiding pure INFORMATION HOLDER RESOURCES, which he refers to as "entity service anti-pattern." The author recommends always evolving away from this pattern, because it creates high semantic and operational coupling, and rather "focus[ing] on behavior instead of data" (which we describe as PROCESSING RESOURCE) and "divid[ing] services by life cycle in a business process" [Nygard 2018b] (which we see as one of several service identification strategies). In our opinion, INFORMATION HOLDER RESOURCES do have their place both in service-oriented systems and in other API usage scenarios. However, any usage should be a conscious decision justified by the business and integration scenario at hand—because of the impact on coupling that is observed and criticized. For certain data, it might be better indeed not to expose it at the API level but hide it behind PROCESSING RESOURCES.

Related Patterns

"Information Holder" is a role stereotype in RDD [Wirfs-Brock 2002]. This general INFORMATION HOLDER RESOURCE pattern has several refinements that differ with regard to mutability, relationships, and instance lifetimes: OPERATIONAL DATA HOLDER, MASTER DATA HOLDER, and REFERENCE DATA HOLDER. The LINK LOOKUP RESOURCE pattern is another specialization; the lookup results may be other INFORMATION HOLDER RESOURCES. Finally, DATA TRANSFER RESOURCE holds temporary shared data owned by the clients. The PROCESSING RESOURCE pattern represents complementary semantics and therefore is an alternative to this pattern.

STATE CREATION OPERATIONS and RETRIEVAL OPERATIONS can typically be found in INFORMATION HOLDER RESOURCES, modeling CRUD semantics. Stateless COMPUTATION FUNCTIONS and read-write STATE TRANSITION OPERATIONS are also permitted in INFORMATION HOLDER RESOURCES but typically operate on a lower level of abstraction than those of PROCESSING RESOURCES.

Implementations of this pattern can be seen as the API pendant to the "Repository" pattern in DDD [Evans 2003], [Vernon 2013]. An INFORMATION HOLDER RESOURCE is often implemented with one or more "Entities" from DDD, possibly grouped into an "Aggregate." Note that no one-to-one correspondence between INFORMATION HOLDER RESOURCE and Entities should be assumed because the primary job of the tactical DDD patterns is to organize the business logic layer of a system, not a (remote) API "Service Layer" [Fowler 2002].

More Information

Chapter 8 in *Process-Driven SOA* is devoted to business object integration and dealing with data [Hentrich 2011]. "Data on the Outside versus Data on the Inside" by Pat Helland explains the differences between data management on the API and the API implementation level [Helland 2005].

"Understanding RPC vs REST for HTTP APIs" [Sturgeon 2016a] covers the differences between INFORMATION HOLDER RESOURCES and PROCESSING RESOURCES in the context of an RPC and REST comparison.

Various consistency management patterns exist. "Eventually Consistent" by Werner Vogels, the Amazon Web Services CTO, addresses this topic [Vogels 2009].

Pattern:
OPERATIONAL DATA HOLDER

When and Why to Apply

A domain model, an entity-relationship diagram, or a glossary of key business concepts and their interconnections has been specified; it has been decided to expose some of the data entities contained in these specifications in an API by way of INFORMATION HOLDER RESOURCE instances.

The data specification unveils that the entity lifetimes and/or update cycles differ significantly (for instance, from seconds, minutes, and hours to months, years, and decades) and that the frequently changing entities participate in relationships with slower-changing ones. For instance, fast-changing data may act mostly as link sources, while slow-changing data appears mostly as link targets.[3]

▼

How can an API support clients that want to create, read, update, and/or delete instances of domain entities that represent operational data that is rather short-lived, changes often during daily business operations, and has many outgoing relations?

▲

Several desired qualities are worth calling out, in addition to those applying to any kind of INFORMATION HOLDER RESOURCE.

- **Processing speed for content read and update operations:** Depending on the business context, API services dealing with operational data must be fast, with low response time for both reading and updating its current state.

- **Business agility and schema update flexibility:** Depending on the business context (for example, when performing A/B testing with parts of the live users), API endpoints dealing with operational data must also be easy to change, especially when the data definition or schema evolves.

- **Conceptual integrity and consistency of relationships:** The created and modified operational data must meet high accuracy and quality standards if it is business-critical. For instance, system and process assurance audits inspect financially relevant business objects such as invoices and payments in enterprise applications [Julisch 2011]. Operational data might be owned, controlled, and managed by external parties such as payment providers; it might have many outgoing relations to similar data and longer-lived, less frequently changing master data. Clients expect that the referred entities will be correctly accessible after the interaction with an operational data resource has successfully completed.

---

3. The context of this pattern is similar to that of its sibling pattern MASTER DATA HOLDER. It acknowledges and points out that the lifetimes and relationship structure of these two types of data differ (in German: *Stammdaten* vs. *Bewegungsdaten;* see [Ferstl 2006; White 2006]).

One could think of treating all data equally to promote solution simplicity, irrespective of its lifetime and relationship characteristics. However, such a unified approach might yield only a mediocre compromise that meets all of the preceding needs somehow but does not excel with regard to any of them. If, for instance, operational data is treated as master data, one might end up with an overengineered API with regard to consistency and reference management that also leaves room for improvement with regard to processing speed and change management.

How It Works

▼

Tag an Information Holder Resource as Operational Data Holder and add API operations to it that allow API clients to create, read, update, and delete its data often and fast.

▲

Optionally, expose additional operations to give the Operational Data Holder domain-specific responsibilities. For instance, a shopping basket might offer fee and tax computations, price update notifications, discounting, and other state-transitioning operations.

The request and response messages of such Operational Data Holders often take the form of Parameter Trees; however, the other types of request and response message structure can also be found in practice. One must be aware of relationships with master data and be cautious when including master data in requests to and responses from Operational Data Holders via Embedded Entity instances. It is often better to separate the two types in different endpoints and realize the cross references via Linked Information Holder instances.

Figure 5.5 sketches the solution. A System of Engagement is used to support everyday business and typically holds operational data; related master data can be found in a System of Record. The API implementation might also keep its own Data Stores in addition to integrating with such backend systems, which may hold both operational data and master data.

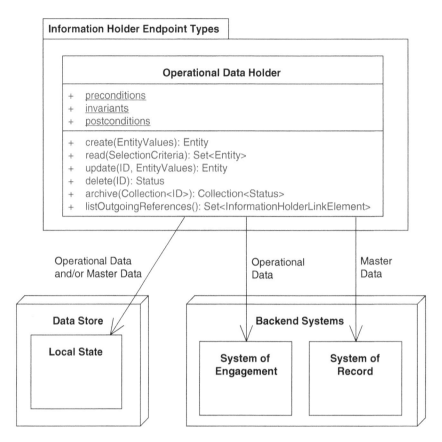

Figure 5.5 *OPERATIONAL DATA HOLDER: Operational data has a short to medium lifetime and may change a lot during daily business. It may reference master data and other operational data*

OPERATIONAL DATA HOLDERS accessed from multiple concurrent clients should provide transactional guarantees in terms of isolation and atomicity so that multiple clients may attempt to access the same data items at the same time while keeping its state consistent. If failures occur during the interaction with a specific client, the state of the OPERATIONAL DATA HOLDER should be reverted back to the last known consistent state. Likewise, update or creation requests being retried should be deduplicated when not idempotent. Closely related OPERATIONAL DATA HOLDERS should also be managed and evolved together to assure their clients that references across them will remain valid. The API should provide atomic update or delete operations across all related OPERATIONAL DATA HOLDERS.

Operational Data Holders are good candidates for *event sourcing* [Stettler 2019] whereby all state changes are logged, making it possible for API clients to access the entire history of state changes for the specific Operational Data Holder. This may increase the API complexity, as consumers may want to refer to or retrieve arbitrary snapshots from the past as opposed to simply querying the latest state.

Example

In an online shop, purchase orders and order items qualify as operational data; the ordered products and the customers placing an order meet the characteristics of master data. Hence, these domain concepts are typically modeled as different "Bounded Context" instances (in DDD) and exposed as separate services, as shown in Figure 5.6.

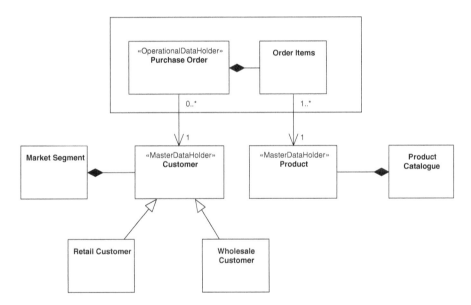

Figure 5.6 *Online shop example:* Operational Data Holder *(Purchase Order) and* Master Data Holders *(Customer, Product) and their relations*

Lakeside Mutual, our sample application from the insurance domain, manages operational data such as claims and risk assessments that are exposed as Web services and REST resources (see Figure 5.7).

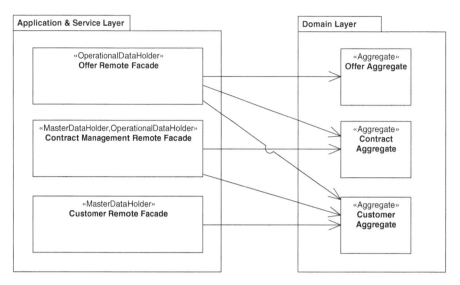

Figure 5.7 *Examples of combining OPERATIONAL DATA HOLDER and MASTER DATA HOLDER: Offers reference contracts and customers, contracts reference customers. In this example, the remote facades access multiple aggregates isolated from each other. The logical layer names come from [Evans 2003] and [Fowler 2002]*

Discussion

The pattern primarily serves as a "marker pattern" in API documentation, helping to make technical interfaces "business-aligned," which is one of the SOA principles and microservices tenets [Zimmermann 2017].

Sometimes even operational data is kept for a long time: in a world of big data analytics and business intelligence insights, operational data is often archived for analytical processing, such as in data marts, data warehouses, or semantic data lakes.

The fewer inbound dependencies an OPERATIONAL DATA HOLDER has, the easier to update it is. A limited lifetime of data and data definitions makes API evolution less challenging; for instance, backward compatibility and integrity management become less of an issue. It might even be possible to rewrite OPERATIONAL DATA HOLDERS rather than maintain older versions of them [Pautasso 2017a]. Relaxing their consistency properties from strict to eventual [Fehling 2014] can improve availability.

The consistency and availability management of OPERATIONAL DATA HOLDERS may prioritize the conflicting requirements differently than MASTER DATA HOLDERS (depending on the domain and scenario). Business agility, schema update flexibility, and processing speed are determined by the API implementation.

The distinction between master data and operational data is somewhat subjective and dependent on application context; data that is needed only temporarily in one application might be a core asset in another one. For instance, think about purchases in an online shop. While the shopper cares about the order only until it is delivered and paid for (unless there is a warranty case or the customer wants to return the good or repeat the same order in the future), the shop provider will probably keep all details forever to be able to analyze buying behavior over time (customer profiling, product recommendations, and targeted advertisement).

The Operational Data Holder pattern can help to satisfy regulatory requirements expressed as compliance controls. An example of such requirement and compliance control is "all purchase orders reference a customer that actually exists in a system of record and in the real world." Enforcing this rule prevents (or finds) cases of fraud [Julisch 2011].

Related Patterns

Longer-living information holders with many incoming references are described by the patterns Master Data Holder (mutable) and Reference Data Holder (immutable via the API). An alternative, less data- and more action-oriented pattern is Processing Resource. All operation responsibilities patterns, including State Creation Operation and State Transition Operation, can be used in Operational Data Holder endpoints.

Patterns from Chapters 4, 6, and 7 are applied when designing the request and response messages of the operations of the Operational Data Holder. Their suitability heavily depends on the actual data semantics. For instance, entering items into a shopping basket might expect a Parameter Tree and return a simple success flag as an Atomic Parameter. The checkout activity then might require multiple complex parameters (Parameter Forest) and return the order number and the expected delivery date in an Atomic Parameter List. The deletion of operational data can be triggered by sending a single Id Element and might return a simple success flag and/or Error Report representation. Pagination slices responses to requests for large amounts of operational data.

The "Data Type Channel" pattern in [Hohpe 2003] describes how to organize a messaging system by message semantics and syntax (such as query, price quote, or purchase order).

Operational Data Holders referencing other Operational Data Holders may choose to include this data in the form of an Embedded Entity. By contrast, references to Master Data Holders often are not included/embedded but externalized via Linked Information Holder references.

More Information

The notion of operational (or transactional) data has its roots in the database and information integration community and in business informatics (*Wirtschaftsinformatik*) [Ferstl 2006].

Pattern:
MASTER DATA HOLDER

When and Why to Apply

A domain model, an entity-relationship diagram, a glossary, or a similar dictionary of key application concepts has been specified; it has been decided to expose some of these data entities in an API by way of INFORMATION HOLDER RESOURCES.

The data specification unveils that the lifetimes and update cycles of these INFORMATION HOLDER RESOURCE endpoints differ significantly (for instance, from seconds, minutes, and hours to months, years, and decades). Long-living data typically has many incoming relationships, whereas shorter-living data often references long-living data. The data access profiles of these two types of data differ substantially.[4]

> How can I design an API that provides access to master data that lives for a long time, does not change frequently, and will be referenced from many clients?

In many application scenarios, data that is referenced in multiple places and lives long has high data quality and data protection needs.

- **Master data quality:** Master data should be accurate because it is used directly, indirectly, and/or implicitly in many places, from daily business to strategic decision making. If it is not stored and managed in a single place, uncoordinated updates, software bugs, and other unforeseen circumstances may lead to inconsistencies and other quality issues that are hard to detect. If it is stored centrally, access to it might be slow due to overhead caused by access contention and backend communication.

- **Master data protection:** Irrespective of its storage and management policy, master data must be well protected with suitable access controls and auditing

---

4. The context of this pattern is similar to that of its alternative pattern OPERATIONAL DATA HOLDER. It emphasizes that the lifetimes and relationship structure of these two types of data differ. Here we are interested in *master data*, often contrasted with *operational data*, also called *transactional data* (in German, *Stammdaten* vs. *Bewegungsdaten;* see Ferstl [2006], White [2006]).

policies, as it is an attractive target for attacks, and the consequences of data breaches can be severe.

- **Data under external control:** Master data may be owned and managed by dedicated systems, often purchased by (or developed in) a separate organizational unit. For instance, there is an application genre of *master data management systems* specializing in product or customer data. In practice, external hosting (strategic outsourcing) of these specialized master data management systems happens and complicates system integration because more stakeholders are involved in their evolution.

Data ownership and audit procedures differ from those of other types of data. Master data collections are assets with a monetary value appearing in the balance sheets of enterprises. Therefore, their definitions and interfaces often are hard to influence and change; due to external influences on its life cycle, master data may evolve at a different speed than operational data that references it.

One could think of treating all entities/resources equally to promote solution simplicity, irrespective of their lifetime and relationship patterns. However, such an approach runs the risk of not satisfactorily addressing the concerns of stakeholders, such as security auditors, data owners, and data stewards. Hosting providers and, last but not least, the real-world correspondents of the data (for instance, customers and internal system users) are other key stakeholders of master data whose interests might not be fulfilled satisfactorily by such an approach.

How It Works

Mark an INFORMATION HOLDER RESOURCE to be a dedicated MASTER DATA HOLDER endpoint that bundles master data access and manipulation operations in such a way that the data consistency is preserved and references are managed adequately. Treat delete operations as special forms of updates.

Optionally, offer other life-cycle events or state transitions in this MASTER DATA HOLDER endpoint. Also optionally, expose additional operations to give the MASTER DATA HOLDER domain-specific responsibilities. For instance, an archive might offer time-oriented retrieval, bulk creations, and purge operations.

A MASTER DATA HOLDER is a special type of INFORMATION HOLDER RESOURCE. It typically offers operations to look up information that is referenced elsewhere. A MASTER DATA HOLDER also offers operations to manipulate the data via the API (unlike a REFERENCE DATA HOLDER). It must meet the security and compliance requirements for this type of data.

Figure 5.8 shows its specific design elements.

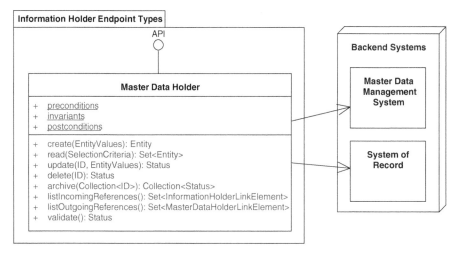

Figure 5.8 *MASTER DATA HOLDER. Master data lives long and is frequently referenced by other master data and by operational data. It therefore faces specific quality and consistency requirements*

The request and response messages of MASTER DATA HOLDERS often take the form of PARAMETER TREES. However, more atomic types of request and response message structure can also be found in practice. Master data *creation* operations typically receive a simple to medium complex PARAMETER TREE because master data might be complex but is often created in one go, for instance, when being entered completely by a user in a form (such as an account creation form). They usually return an ATOMIC PARAMETER or an ATOMIC PARAMETER LIST to report the ID ELEMENT or LINK ELEMENT that identifies the master data entity uniquely/globally and reports whether or not the creation request was successful (for instance, using the ERROR REPORT pattern). Reasons for failure can be duplicate keys, violations of business rules and other invariants, or internal server-side processing errors (for instance, temporary unavailability of backend systems).

A master data *update* may come in two forms:

1. *Coarse-grained* full update operation that replaces most or all attributes in a master data entity such as customer or product. This form corresponds to the HTTP PUT verb.

2. *Fine-grained* partial update operation that updates only one or a few of the attributes in a master data entity, for instance, the address of a customer (but not its name) or the price of a product (but not its supplier and taxation rules). In HTTP, the verb PATCH has such semantics.

Read access to master data is often performed via RETRIEVAL OPERATIONS that offer parameterized search-and-filter query capabilities (possibly expressed declaratively).

Deletion might not be desired. If supported, *delete* operations on master data sometimes are complicated to implement due to legal compliance requirements. There is a risk of breaking a large number of incoming references when removing master data entirely. Hence, master data often is not deleted at all but is set into an immutable state "archived" in which updates are no longer possible. This also allows keeping audit trails and historic data manipulation journals; master data changes are often mission-critical and thus must be nonrepudiable. If deletion is indeed necessary (and this can be a regulatory requirement), the data may actually be hidden from (some or all) consumers but still preserved in an invisible state (unless yet another regulatory requirement forbids this).

In an HTTP resource API, the address (URI) of a MASTER DATA HOLDER resource can be widely shared among clients referencing it, which can access it via HTTP GET (a read-only method that supports caching). The creation and update calls make use of POST, PUT, and PATCH methods, respectively [Allamaraju 2010].

Please note that the discussion of the words *create, read, update,* and *delete* in the context of this pattern should not indicate that CRUD-based API designs are the intended or only possible solution for realizing the pattern. Such designs quickly lead to chatty APIs with bad performance and scalability properties, and lead to unwanted coupling and complexity. Beware of such API designs! Instead, follow an incremental approach during resource identification that aims to first identify well-scoped interface elements such as Aggregate roots in DDD, business capabilities, or business processes. Even larger formations, such as Bounded Contexts, may serve as starting points. In infrequent cases, domain Entities can also be considered to supply endpoint candidates. This inevitably will lead to MASTER DATA HOLDER designs that are semantically richer and more meaningful—and with a more positive impact on the mentioned qualities. In DDD terms, we aim for a rich and deep domain model, as opposed to an anemic domain model [Fowler 2003]; this should be reflected in the API design. In many scenarios, it makes sense to identify and call out master data (as well as operational data) in the domain models so that later design decisions can use this information.

Example

Lakeside Mutual, our sample application from the insurance domain, features master data such as customers and contracts that are exposed as Web services and REST resources, thus applying the MASTER DATA HOLDER pattern. Figure 5.9 illustrates two of these resources as remote facades.

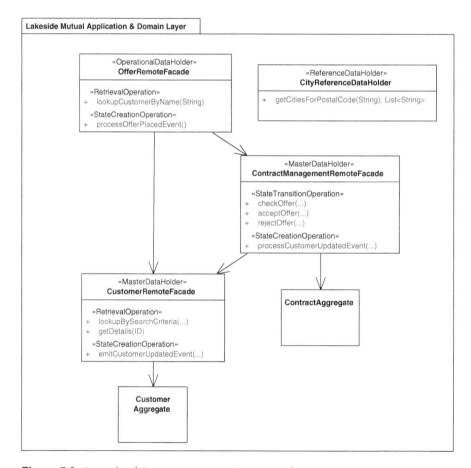

Figure 5.9 *Example of OPERATIONAL DATA HOLDER and MASTER DATA HOLDER interplay. Operational data references master data, but not vice versa. An application of the REFERENCE DATA HOLDER pattern is also shown*

In this example, the remote facades (offer, contract, customer) access each other and two domain-layer aggregates in the API implementation.

Discussion

Tagging an API endpoint as a Master Data Holder can help achieve the required focus on data quality and data protection.

Master data by definition has many inbound dependencies and might also have outbound ones. Since such data is often under external control, tagging an API endpoint as Master Data Holder also helps to control and limit where such external dependency is introduced. This way, there will be only one API providing fresh access to a specific master data source in a consistent way.

Master data often is a valuable company asset that is key to success in the market (it might even turn a company into an acquisition target). Hence, when exposed as part of the API, it is particularly important to plan its future evolution in a roadmap that respects backward compatibility, considers digital preservation, and protects the data from theft and tampering.

Related Patterns

The Master Data Holder pattern has two alternatives: Reference Data Holder (with data that is immutable via the API) and Operational Data Holder (exposing shorter-lived data with less incoming references).

More Information

The notion of master data versus operational data comes from literature in the database community (more specifically, information integration) and in business informatics (*Wirtschaftsinformatik* in German) [Ferstl 2006]. It plays an important role in online analytical processing (OLAP), data warehouses, and business intelligence (BI) efforts [Kimball 2002].

 Pattern:
Reference Data Holder

When and Why to Apply

A requirements specification unveils that some data is referenced in most if not all system parts, but it changes only very rarely (if ever); these changes are administrative in nature and are not caused by API clients operating during everyday business. Such data is called *reference data*. It comes in many forms, including country codes, zip codes, geolocations, currency codes, and units of measurement. Reference data often is represented by enumerations of string literals or numeric value ranges.

The data transfer representations in the request and response messages of API operations may either contain or point at reference data to satisfy the information needs of a message receiver.

How should data that is referenced in many places, lives long, and is immutable for clients be treated in API endpoints?

How can such reference data be used in requests to and responses from PROCESSING RESOURCES or INFORMATION HOLDER RESOURCES?

Two desired qualities are worth calling out (in addition to those applying to any kind of INFORMATION HOLDER RESOURCE).

- **Do not repeat yourself (DRY):** Because reference data rarely changes (if ever), there is a temptation to simply hardcode it within the API clients or, if using a cache, retrieve it once and then store a local copy forever. Such designs work well in the short run and might not cause any immanent problems—until the data and its definitions have to change.[5] Because the DRY principle is violated, the change will impact every client, and if clients are out of reach, it may not be possible to update them.

- **Performance versus consistency trade-off for read access:** Because reference data rarely changes (if at all), it may pay off to introduce a cache to reduce round-trip access response time and reduce traffic if it is referenced and read a lot. Such replication tactics have to be designed carefully so that they function as desired and do not make the end-to-end system overly complex and hard to maintain. For instance, caches should not grow too big, and replication has to be able to tolerate network partitions (outages). If the reference data does change (on schema or on content level), updates have to be applied consistently. Two examples are new zip codes introduced in a country and the transition from local currencies to the Euro (EUR) in many European countries.

---

5. For instance, it was sufficient to use two digits for calendar years through 1999.

One could treat static and immutable reference data just like dynamic data that is both read and written. This works fine in many scenarios but misses opportunities to optimize the read access, for instance, via data replication in content delivery networks (CDNs) and might lead to unnecessary duplication of storing and computing efforts.

How It Works

▼

Provide a special type of Information Holder Resource endpoint, a Reference Data Holder, as a single point of reference for the static, immutable data. Provide read operations but no create, update, or delete operations in this endpoint.

▲

Update the reference data elsewhere if required, by directly changing back-end assets or through a separate management API. Refer to the Reference Data Holder endpoint via Linked Information Holders.

The Reference Data Holder may allow clients to retrieve the entire reference data set so that they can keep a local copy that can be accessed multiple times. They may want to filter its content before doing so (for instance, to implement some auto-completion feature in an input form in a user interface). It is also possible to look up individual entries of the reference data only (for instance, for validation purposes). For example, a currency list can be copy-pasted all over the place (as it never changes), or it can be retrieved and cached from the Reference Data Holder API, as described here. Such API can provide a complete enumeration of the list (to initialize and refresh the cache) or feature the ability to project/select the content (for instance, a list of European currency names), or allow clients to check whether some value is present in the list for client-side validation ("Does this currency exist?").

Figure 5.10 sketches the solution.

The request and response messages of Reference Data Holders often take the form of Atomic Parameters or Atomic Parameter Lists, for instance, when the reference data is unstructured and merely enumerates certain flat values.

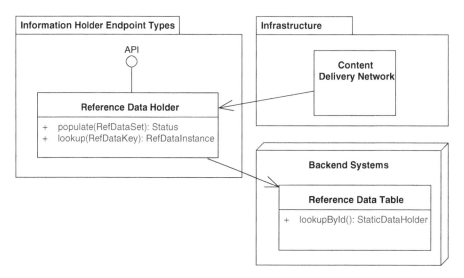

Figure 5.10 *REFERENCE DATA HOLDER. Reference data lives long but cannot be changed via the API. It is referenced often and in many places*

Reference data lives long but hardly ever changes; it is referenced often and in many places. Hence, the operations of REFERENCE DATA HOLDERS may offer direct access to a reference data table. Such lookups can map a short identifier (such as a provider-internal surrogate key) to a more expressive, human-readable identifier and/or entire data set.

The pattern does not prescribe any type of implementation; for instance, a relational database might come across as an overengineered solution when managing a list of currencies; a file-based key-value store or indexed sequential access method (ISAM) files might be sufficient. Key-value stores such as a Redis or a document-oriented NoSQL database such as CouchDB or MongoDB may also be considered.

Example

Figure 5.11 shows an instance of the pattern that allows API clients to look up zip codes based on addresses, or vice versa.

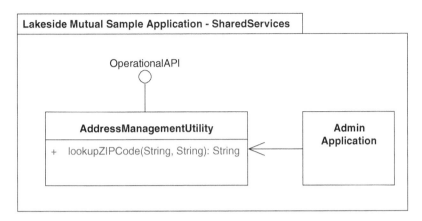

Figure 5.11 *REFERENCE DATA HOLDER: Zip code lookup*

Discussion

The most common usage scenario for this pattern is the lookup of simple text data whose value ranges meet certain constraints (for example, country codes, currency codes, or tax rates).

Explicit REFERENCE DATA HOLDERS avoid unnecessary repetition. The purpose of a REFERENCE DATA HOLDER is to give a central point of reference for helping disseminate the data while keeping control over it. Read performance can be optimized; immutable data can be replicated rather easily (no risk of inconsistencies as long as it never changes).

Dedicated REFERENCE DATA HOLDERS have to be developed, documented, managed, and maintained. This effort will still be less than that required to upgrade all clients if such reference data gets hardcoded in them.

- **DRY:** Clients no longer have to implement reference management on their own, at the expense of introducing a dependency on a remote API. This positive effect can be viewed as a form of data normalization, as known from database design and information management.

- **Performance versus consistency trade-off for read access:** The pattern hides the actual data behind the API and therefore allows the API provider to introduce proxies, caches, and read-only replicas behind the scenes. The only effect that is visible to the API clients is an improvement (if done right) in terms of quality properties such as response times and availability, possibly expressed in the SERVICE LEVEL AGREEMENT that accompanies the functional API contract.

A standalone REFERENCE DATA HOLDER sometimes turns out to cause more work and complexity than it adds value (in terms of data normalization and performance improvements). In such cases, one can consider merging the reference data with an already existing, more complex, and somewhat more dynamic MASTER DATA HOLDER endpoint in the API by way of an API *refactoring* [Stocker 2021a].

Related Patterns

The MASTER DATA HOLDER pattern is an alternative to REFERENCE DATA HOLDER. It also represents long-living data, which still is mutable. OPERATIONAL DATA HOLDERS represent more ephemeral data.

The section "Message Granularity" in Chapter 7, "Refine Message Design for Quality," features two related patterns, EMBEDDED ENTITY and LINKED INFORMATION HOLDER. Simple static data is often embedded (which eliminates the need for a dedicated REFERENCE DATA HOLDER) but can also be linked (with the link pointing at a REFERENCE DATA HOLDER).

More Information

"Data on the Outside versus Data on the Inside" introduces reference data in the broad sense of the word [Helland 2005]. Wikipedia provides links to inventories/directories of reference data [Wikipedia 2022b].

 Pattern:
LINK LOOKUP RESOURCE

When and Why to Apply

The message representations in request and response messages of an API operation have been designed to meet the information needs of the message receivers. To do so, these messages may contain references to other API endpoints (such as INFORMATION HOLDER RESOURCES and/or PROCESSING RESOURCES) in the form of LINK ELEMENTS. Sometimes it is not desirable to expose such endpoint addresses to all clients directly because this adds coupling and harms location and reference autonomy.

> How can message representations refer to other, possibly many and frequently changing, API endpoints and operations without binding the message recipient to the actual addresses of these endpoints?

Following are two reasons to avoid an address coupling between communication participants:

- API providers want to be able to change the destinations of links freely when evolving their APIs while workload grows and requirements change.
- API clients do not want to have to change code and configuration (for example, application startup procedures) when the naming and structuring conventions for links change on the provider side.

The following design challenges also have to be addressed:

- **Coupling between clients and endpoints:** If clients use the address of an endpoint to reference it directly, a tight link is created between these parties. The client references can break for many reasons, such as if the endpoint address changes or the endpoint is down temporarily.
- **Dynamic endpoint references:** API designs often bind references to endpoints at design or deployment time, for instance, hardcoding references in the clients (while more sophisticated binding schemes exist as well). Sometimes this is not flexible enough; dynamic changes to endpoint references at runtime are required. Two examples are endpoints that are taken offline for maintenance and load balancers working with a dynamic number of endpoints. Another usage scenario involves intermediaries and redirecting helpers that help overcome formatting differences after new API versions have been introduced.
- **Centralization versus decentralization:** Providing exactly one INFORMATION HOLDER RESOURCE per data element in the Published Language that is referenced in requests and responses to other API endpoints via hardcoded addresses leads to highly decentralized solutions. Other API designs could centralize the registration and binding of endpoint addresses instead. Any centralized solution is likely to receive more traffic than a partially autonomous, distributed one; decentralized ones are easy to build but might become hard to maintain and evolve.
- **Message sizes, number of calls, resource use:** An alternative solution to consider for any form of references used in clients is to avoid them, following the EMBEDDED ENTITY pattern. However, this increases message sizes. Any solutions for managing references to endpoints in clients generally cause additional API calls. All these considerations influence the resource use in terms of provider-side processing resources and network bandwidth.

- **Dealing with broken links:** Clients following references will assume these references point at the right existing API endpoints. If such references no longer work because an API endpoint has been moved, existing clients that do not know about this may fail (as they are no longer able to connect to the API) or, even worse, run the risk of receiving out-of-date information from a previous endpoint version.

- **Number of endpoints and API complexity:** The coupling problem could be avoided by having a specific endpoint only for getting the address of another endpoint. But in the extreme case that all endpoints require such functionality, this tactic would double the number of endpoints, which would make API maintenance more difficult and increase the API complexity.

A simple approach could be to add lookup operations, which are special types of RETRIEVAL OPERATIONS that return LINK ELEMENTS to already existing endpoints. This solution is workable but compromises cohesion within the endpoints.

How It Works

Introduce a special type of INFORMATION HOLDER RESOURCE endpoint, a dedicated LINK LOOKUP RESOURCE that exposes special RETRIEVAL OPERATION operations. These operations return single instances or collections of LINK ELEMENTS that represent the current addresses of the referenced API endpoints.

These LINK ELEMENTS may point at action-oriented PROCESSING RESOURCES as well as data-oriented INFORMATION HOLDER RESOURCES endpoints (or any of its refinements dealing with operational data, master data, reference data, or serving as a shared data exchange space).

The most basic LINK LOOKUP RESOURCE uses a single ATOMIC PARAMETER for the request message to identify the lookup target by its primary key, such as a plain/ flat but globally unique ID ELEMENT . Such unique identifiers are also used to create API KEYS. On the next level of client convenience, an ATOMIC PARAMETER LIST can be used if multiple lookup options and query parameters exist (this way, the lookup mode can/has to be specified by the client). The LINK LOOKUP RESOURCE returns global, network-accessible references to the held information (each taking the form of a LINK ELEMENT, possibly amended with METADATA ELEMENTS that disclose the link type).

If the network addresses of instances of the different types of INFORMATION HOLDER RESOURCE are returned, the client can access these resources subsequently to obtain attributes, relationship information, and so on. Figure 5.12 sketches this solution.

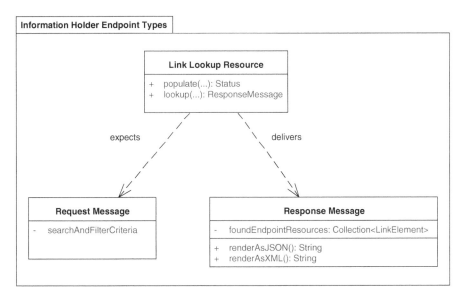

Figure 5.12 *A LINK LOOKUP RESOURCE is an API endpoint that merely holds information about other ones*

The link information may come in different forms. Many notations have been proposed to represent hyperlinks in messages, including JSON-LD [W3C 2019], HAL [Kelly 2016], WS-Addressing (XML) [W3C 2004].

Variant   When the LINK ELEMENTS point at PROCESSING RESOURCES rather than INFORMATION HOLDER RESOURCES, a variant of this pattern is constituted: *Hypertext as the Engine of Application State (HATEOAS)* is one of the defining characteristics of truly RESTful Web APIs, according to the definitions of the REST style [Webber 2010; Erl 2013]. Note that the links in HATEOAS are also referred to as *hypermedia controls*.

The addresses of a few root endpoints (also called *home resources*) are published (that is, communicated to prospective API clients); the addresses of related services can then be found in each response. The clients parse the responses to discover the URIs of resources to be called subsequently. If a PROCESSING RESOURCE is referenced this way, the control flow and application state management become dynamic and highly decentralized; the operation-level pattern STATE TRANSITION OPERATION covers this REST principle in detail. RESTful INFORMATION HOLDER RESOURCES may support the slicing or partitioning of large, complex data.

Example

In the Lakeside Mutual sample case, two operations to find INFORMATION HOLDER RESOURCES that represent customers can be specified as follows (notation: MDSL, introduced in Appendix C):

```
API description LinkLookupResourceExample

data type URI D<string> // protocol, domain, path, parameters

endpoint type LinkLookupResourceInterface // sketch
 exposes
  operation lookupInformationHolderByLogicalName
    expecting payload
      <<Identifier_Element>> "name": ID
    delivering payload
      <<Link_Element>> "endpointAddress": URI

  operation lookupInformationHolderByCriteria
    expecting payload {
      "filter": P // placeholder parameter P
    }
    delivering payload {
      <<Link_Element>> "uri": URI* // 0..m cardinality
    }

API provider CustomerLookupResource
  offers LinkLookupResourceInterface
```

Discussion

A centralized LINK LOOKUP RESOURCE providing dynamic endpoint references decouples clients and providers in terms of location autonomy. The pattern promotes high cohesion within one endpoint, as the lookup responsibility is separated from the actual processing and information retrieval. As a negative consequence, a LINK LOOKUP RESOURCE causes extra calls and increases the number of endpoints. The pattern increases operational costs; the lookup resource must be kept current. Use of the pattern improves cohesion within endpoints (at the expense of adding additional, specialized ones).

The pattern has a negative impact on the number of calls clients are required to send unless caching is introduced to mitigate this effect and lookup calls are performed only after detecting broken links. The pattern can improve performance only if the overhead for looking up the INFORMATION HOLDER RESOURCE (or other provider-internal data storage) over an API operation boundary (so making two calls) does not exceed the savings achieved by leaner message payloads (of each operation).

If the combination of a LINKED INFORMATION HOLDER with a LINK LOOKUP RESOURCE turns out to add more overhead than performance and flexibility gains, the LINKED INFORMATION HOLDER can be changed to contain a direct link. If the direct linking still leads to overly chatty message exchanges (conversations) between API clients and API providers, the referenced data could be flattened as an instance of EMBEDDED ENTITY.

The added indirection can help to change the system runtime environment more freely. Systems that include direct URIs might be harder to change as server names change. The REST principle of HATEOAS solves this problem for the actual resource names; only hardcoded client-side links are problematic (unless HTTP redirections are introduced). Microservices middleware such as API gateways can be used as well; however, such usage adds complexity to the overall architecture as well as additional runtime dependencies. Using hypermedia to advance the application state is one of the defining constraints of the REST style. One has to decide whether the hypermedia should refer to the resources responsible for provider-side processing (of any endpoint type) directly or whether a level of indirection should be introduced to further decouple clients and endpoints (this pattern).

Related Patterns

Instances of this pattern can return links to any of the endpoint types/roles, often to INFORMATION HOLDER RESOURCES. The pattern uses RETRIEVAL OPERATIONS. For instance, RETRIEVAL OPERATION instances may return ID ELEMENTS pointing at INFORMATION HOLDER RESOURCES indirectly (that in turn return the data); the LINK LOOKUP RESOURCE turns the ID ELEMENT into a LINK ELEMENT.

Infrastructure-level service discovery can be used alternatively. For instance, patterns such as "Service Registry," "Client-Side Discovery," and "Self Registration" have been captured by [Richardson 2018].

This pattern is an API-specific version/refinement of the more general "Lookup" pattern described in [Kircher 2004] and [Voelter 2004]. At a more abstract level, the pattern also is a specialization of the Repository pattern described in [Evans 2003], effectively acting as a meta-repository.

More Information

SOA books cover related concepts such as service repositories and registries. In RDD terms, a LINK LOOKUP RESOURCE acts as a "Structurer" [Wirfs-Brock 2002].

If multiple results of the same type are returned, the LINK LOOKUP RESOURCE turns into a "Collection Resource." Collection Resources can be seen as a RESTful HTTP pendant of this pattern, adding add and remove support. Recipe 2.3 in the *RESTful Web Services Cookbook* [Allamaraju 2010] features them; Chapter 14 of that book discusses discovery. Collections use links to enumerate their content and allow clients to retrieve, update, or delete individual items. As shown in [Serbout 2021], APIs can feature read-only collections, appendable collections, as well as mutable collections.

Pattern:
DATA TRANSFER RESOURCE

When and Why to Apply

Two or more communication participants want to exchange data. The number of exchange participants might vary over time, and their existence might be known to each other only partially. They might not always be active at the same time. For instance, additional participants may want to access the same data after it has already been shared by its originator.

Participants may also be interested in accessing only the latest version of the shared information and do not need to observe every change applied to it. Communication participants may be constrained in the networking and integration technologies they are permitted to use.

How can two or more communication participants exchange data without knowing each other, without being available at the same time, and even if the data has already been sent before its recipients became known?

- **Coupling (time dimension):** Communication participants may not be able to communicate synchronously (that is, at the same time), as their availability and connectivity profiles may differ and change over time. The more communication participants want to exchange data, the more unlikely it is that all will be ready to send and receive messages at the same time.

- **Coupling (location dimension):** The location of communication participants may be unknown to the other participants. It might not be possible to address all participants directly due to asymmetric network connectivity, making it difficult, for example, for senders to know how to reach the recipients of the data exchange that are hidden behind a Network Address Translation (NAT) table or a firewall.

- **Communication constraints:** Some communication participants may be unable to talk to each other directly. For instance, clients in the client/server architectural style by definition are not capable of accepting incoming connections. Also, some communication participants may not be allowed to install any software required for communication beyond a basic HTTP client library locally (for example, a messaging middleware). In such cases, indirect communication is the only possibility.

- **Reliability:** Networks cannot be assumed to be reliable, and clients are not always active at the same time. Hence, any distributed data exchanges must be designed to be able to cope with temporary network partitions and system outages.

- **Scalability:** The number of recipients may not be known at the time the data is sent. This number could also become very large and increase access requests in unexpected ways. This, in turn, may harm throughput and response times. Scaling up the amount of data can be an issue: the amount of data to be exchanged may grow unboundedly and beyond the capacity limits of individual messages (as defined by the communication and integration protocols used).

- **Storage space efficiency:** The data to be exchanged has to be stored somewhere along its way, and sufficient storage space must be available. The amount of data to be shared must be known, as there may be limits on how much data can be transferred or stored due to bandwidth constraints.

- **Latency:** Direct communication tends to be faster than indirect communication via relays or intermediaries.

- **Ownership management:** Ownership of the exchanged information has to be established to achieve explicit control over its availability life cycle. The initial owner is the participant sharing the data; however, there may be different parties responsible for cleanup: the original sender (interested in maximizing the reach of the shared data), the intended recipient (who may or not want to read it multiple times), or the host of the transfer resource (who must keep storage costs in check).

One could think of using publish-subscribe mechanisms, as offered by message-oriented middleware (MOM) such as ActiveMQ, Apache Kafka, or Rabbit MQ, but then the clients would have to run their own local messaging system endpoint to receive and process incoming messages. MOM needs to be installed and operated, which adds to the overall systems management effort [Hohpe 2003].

How It Works

Introduce a DATA TRANSFER RESOURCE as a shared storage endpoint accessible from two or more API clients. Provide this specialized INFORMATION HOLDER RESOURCE with a globally unique network address so that two or more clients can use it as a shared data exchange space. Add at least one STATE CREATION OPERATION and one RETRIEVAL OPERATION to it so that data can be placed in the shared space and also fetched from it.

Share the address of the transfer resource with the clients. Decide on data ownership and its transfer; prefer client ownership over provider ownership here.

Multiple applications (API clients) can use the shared DATA TRANSFER RESOURCE as a medium to exchange information that is originally created by one of them and then transferred to the shared resource. Once the information has been published in the shared resource, any additional client that knows the URI of the shared resource and is authorized to do so may retrieve it, update it, add to it, and delete it (when the data is no longer useful for any client application). Figure 5.13 sketches this solution.

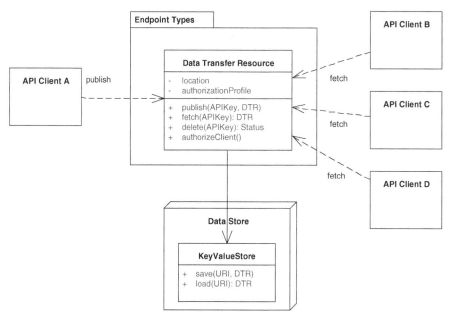

Figure 5.13 DATA TRANSFER RESOURCE. A DATA TRANSFER RESOURCE endpoint holds temporary data to decouple two or more API clients sharing this data. The pattern instance provides a data exchange space between these clients. Data ownership remains with the application clients

The shared Data Transfer Resource establishes a blackboard between its clients, providing them with an asynchronous, virtual data flow channel to mediate all their interactions. As a result, clients can exchange data without having to connect directly to each other, or (perhaps even more important) without having to address each other directly and without being up and running at the same time. Hence, it decouples them in time (they do not have to be available at the same time) and makes their location irrelevant—as long as they all can reach the shared Data Transfer Resource.

How do clients negotiate the URI for the shared resource? Clients may need to agree in advance about the shared resource address, or they may dynamically discover it using a dedicated Link Lookup Resource. Also, it is possible that the first client sets the URI while publishing the original content and informs the others about it via some other communication channel, or, again, by registering the address with a Link Lookup Resource, whose identity has been agreed upon in advance by all clients.

HTTP Support for the Pattern   From an implementation perspective, this solution is directly supported in HTTP, whereby Client A first performs a PUT request to publish the information on the shared resource, uniquely identified by a URI, and then Client B performs a GET request to fetch it from the shared resource. Note that the information published on the shared resource does not disappear as long as no clients perform an explicit DELETE request. Client A publishing the information to the shared resource can do so reliably, as the HTTP PUT request is idempotent. Likewise, if the subsequent GET request fails, Client B may simply retry it to be able to read the shared information eventually. Figure 5.14 illustrates the HTTP realization of the pattern.

Clients cannot know whether other clients have retrieved the information from the shared resource. To address this limitation, the shared resource can track access traffic and offer additional metadata about the delivery status so that it is possible to inquire whether and how many times the information has been fetched after it has been published. Such Metadata Elements exposed by Retrieval Operations may also help with the garbage collection of shared resources that are no longer in use.

Variants   Access patterns and resource lifetimes may differ, which suggests the following variants of this pattern:

1. *Relay Resource:* There are two clients only, one that writes and one that reads. Data ownership is shifted from the writer to the reader. Figure 5.15 illustrates this variant.

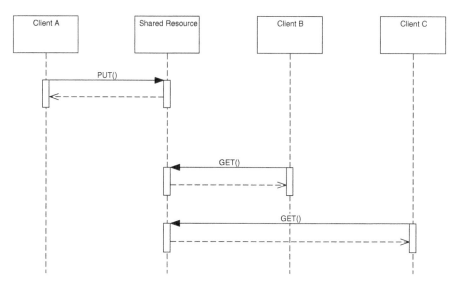

Figure 5.14 *DATA TRANSFER RESOURCE (HTTP realization)*

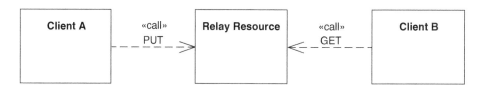

Figure 5.15 *RELAY RESOURCE*

2. *Published Resource:* One client writes as before, but then a very large, unpre-dictable number of clients read it at different times (maybe years later), as shown in Figure 5.16. The original writer determines how long the shared resource remains publicly available to its multiple readers. Routing patterns such as "Recipient List" can be supported this way [Hohpe 2003]; streaming middleware may realize this variant.

3. *Conversation Resource:* Many clients read, write, and eventually delete the shared resource (Figure 5.17). Any participant owns the transfer resource (and can therefore both update and delete it).

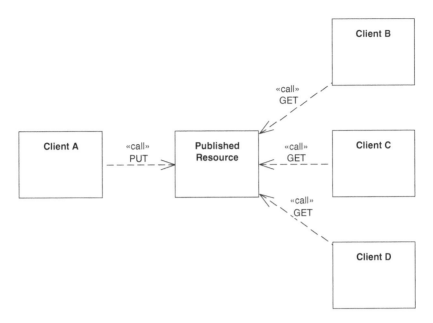

Figure 5.16 *Published Resource*

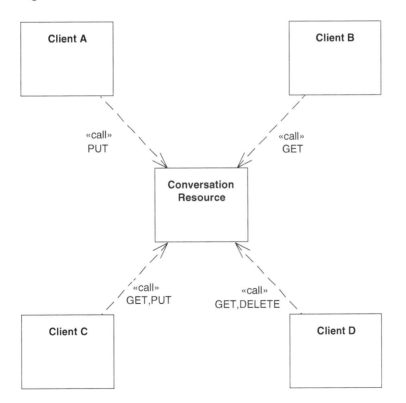

Figure 5.17 *Conversation Resource*

Example

The example in Figure 5.18 instantiates the pattern for an integration interface in the Lakeside Mutual sample case. The Claim Reception System Of Engagement is the data source, and a Claim Transfer Resource decouples the two data sinks Claim Processing System Of Records and Fraud Detection Archive from it.

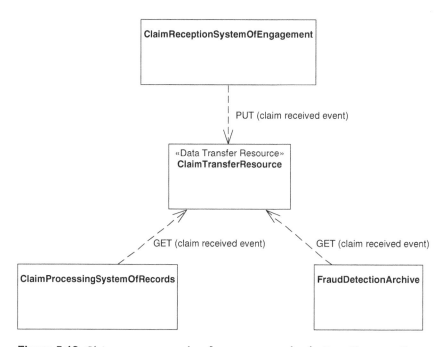

Figure 5.18 *Claims management data flow as an example of a DATA TRANSFER RESOURCE*

Discussion

The pattern combines the benefits of messaging and shared data repositories: flexibility of data flow and asynchrony [Pautasso 2018]. Let us go through the forces and pattern properties one by one (in the context of HTTP and Web APIs).

- **Coupling (time and location dimensions):** Asynchronous and indirect communication are supported.

- **Communication constraints:** Clients that cannot directly connect use the transfer resource as a shared blackboard. Clients sometimes cannot directly talk to each other for these reasons:

a) They are clients and therefore are not supposed to receive any incoming requests.

b) They are running behind a firewall/NAT that allows only outgoing connections.

c) They are running inside a Web browser, which only allows sending HTTP requests to and receiving responses from a Web server.

d) They are not running at the same time.

If direct connectivity is impossible, then an indirect route may still work. The shared DATA TRANSFER RESOURCE provides such an intermediary element and can serve as a joint storage space, which is reachable from both clients and remains available even when some of the clients temporarily disappear.

- **Reliability:** When using messaging systems, the connection from the client to the middleware can be a local one (the messaging system broker process then takes care of the remote messaging, guaranteeing message delivery). Such "programming without a call stack" is conceptually harder and more error prone than blocking remote procedure invocations, but it is also more powerful when done properly [Hohpe 2003]. When applying the DATA TRANSFER RESOURCE pattern, the client-to-resource connection always is a remote one. Moreover, HTTP cannot guarantee message delivery. However, the idempotence of the PUT and GET methods in HTTP can mitigate the problem because the sending clients can retry calls to the DATA TRANSFER RESOURCE until the upload or download succeeds. When using such idempotent HTTP methods to access the shared resource, neither the middleware nor the receiver has to detect and remove duplicate messages.

- **Scalability:** The amount of data that can be stored on a Web resource is bound by the capacity of the data storage/file system that underlies the Web server. The amount of data that can be transferred to and from the Web resource within one standard HTTP request/response is virtually unlimited according to the protocol and therefore constrained only by the underlying middleware implementations and hardware capacity. The same constraints also apply for the number of clients.

- **Storage space efficiency:** The DATA TRANSFER RESOURCE provider has to allocate sufficient space.

- **Latency:** Indirect communication requires two hops between participants, which, however, do not have to be available at the same time. In this pattern, the ability to transfer data across large periods and multiple participants takes priority over the performance of the individual transfer.

• **Ownership management:** Depending on the pattern variant, data ownership—the right but also the obligation to ensure the validity of the shared resource content and to clean it up eventually—can stay with the source, be shared among all parties aware of its URI, or be transferred to the DATA TRANSFER RESOURCE. The latter option is adequate if the source originally publishing the data is not expected to be present until all recipients have had a chance to read it.

Once a DATA TRANSFER RESOURCE has been introduced, additional design issues arise:

• **Access control:** Depending on the type of information being exchanged, clients reading from the resource trust that the resource was initialized by the right sources. Therefore, in some scenarios, only authorized clients may be allowed to read from or write to the shared resource. Access may be controlled with an API KEY or more advanced security solutions.

• **(Lack of) coordination:** Clients may read from and write to the shared resource at any time, even multiple times. There is little coordination between writers and readers beyond being able to detect empty (or noninitialized) resources.

• **Optimistic locking:** Multiple clients writing at the same time may run into conflicts, which should be reported as an error and trigger a systems management activity to reconcile.

• **Polling:** Some clients cannot receive notifications when the shared resource state is changed, and they must resort to polling to be able to fetch the most recent version.

• **Garbage collection:** The DATA TRANSFER RESOURCE cannot know whether any client that has completed reading will be the last one; hence, there is a risk of leaking data unless it is explicitly removed. Housekeeping is required: purging DATA TRANSFER RESOURCES that have outlived their usefulness avoids waste of storage resources.

Related Patterns

The pattern differs from other types of INFORMATION HOLDER RESOURCES with respect to data access and storage ownership. The DATA TRANSFER RESOURCE acts both as a data source and a data sink. The DATA TRANSFER RESOURCE exclusively owns and controls its own data store; the only way to access its content is via the published API of the DATA TRANSFER RESOURCE. Instances of other INFORMATION HOLDER RESOURCE types often work with data that is accessed and possibly even owned by other parties (such as backend systems and their non-API clients). A LINK LOOKUP RESOURCE can be seen as a DATA TRANSFER RESOURCE that holds a special type of data, namely addresses (or LINK ELEMENTS).

Patterns for asynchronous messaging are described in *Enterprise Integration Patterns* [Hohpe 2003]. Some of these patterns are closely related to DATA TRANSFER RESOURCE. A DATA TRANSFER RESOURCE can be seen as a Web-based realization of a "Message Channel," supporting message routing and transformation, as well as several message consumption options ("Competing Consumers" and "Idempotent Receiver"). Queue-based messaging and Web-based software connectors (as described by this DATA TRANSFER RESOURCE pattern) can be seen as two different but related integration styles; these styles are compared in "The Web as a Software Connector" [Pautasso 2018].

"Blackboard" is a POSA 1 pattern [Buschmann 1996], intended to be eligible in a different context but similar in its solution sketch. *Remoting Patterns* [Voelter 2004] describes the remoting style "Shared Repository"; our DATA TRANSFER RESOURCE can be seen as the API for a Web-flavored shared repository.

More Information

"Interfacer" is a role stereotype in RDD that describes a related but more generic programming-level concept [Wirfs-Brock 2002].

Operation Responsibilities

An API endpoint exposes one or more operations in its contract. These operations show some recurring patterns in the way they work with provider-side state. The four operations responsibility patterns are COMPUTATION FUNCTION, STATE CREATION OPERATION, RETRIEVAL OPERATION, and STATE TRANSITION OPERATION. Figure 5.19 gives an overview of these patterns, including their variants.

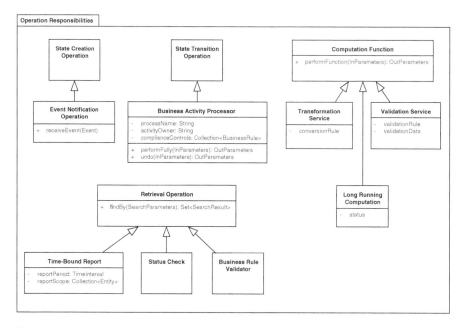

Figure 5.19 *Patterns distinguishing operation responsibilities*

Note that we call state-preserving API responsibilities *functions* (as they just get some self-contained work done on behalf of a client) and state-changing responsibilities *operations* (as they become active because the client hands in some data, which is then processed and stored; it can be retrieved as well).

Pattern:
STATE CREATION OPERATION

When and Why to Apply

An API endpoint has been introduced. The API client has expressed its API wants and needs, for instance, in the form of user stories and/or given-when-then clauses [Fowler 2013]; quality requirements have been elicited as well.

The API client(s) would like to inform the API provider about new client-side incidents without being interested in detailed information about further server-side processing (if any).

The client might want to instruct the API provider to initiate a long-running business transaction (like an order management and fulfillment process) or report the completion of a client-side batch job (like the bulk reinitialization of a product catalog). Such requests cause data to be added to the provider-internal state.

An immediate response can be returned, which might just be a simple "got it" acknowledgment.

▼
How can an API provider allow its clients to report that something has happened that the provider needs to know about, for instance, to trigger instant or later processing?
▲

- **Coupling trade-offs (accuracy and expressiveness versus information parsimony):** To ease processing on the provider side, the incoming incident report should be self-contained so that it is independent of other reports. To streamline report construction on the client-side, save transport capacities, and hide implementation details, it should contain only the bare minimum of information the API provider is interested in.

- **Timing considerations:** The client-side occurrence of an incident may differ from the moment it is reported and the time when the incident report finally reaches the provider. It may not be possible to determine the sequencing/serialization of incidents happening on different clients.[6]

- **Consistency effects:** Sometimes the provider-side state cannot be read, or should be read as little as possible, when calls to an API arrive. In such cases, it becomes more difficult to validate that the provider-side processing caused by incoming requests does not break invariants and other consistency properties.

- **Reliability considerations:** Reports cannot always be processed in the same order in which they were produced and sent. Sometimes reports get lost or the same report is transmitted and received multiple times. It would be nice to acknowledge that the report causing state to be created has been processed properly.

One could simply add yet another API operation to an endpoint without making its state read-write profile explicit. If this is done, the specific integration needs and concerns described previously still have to be described in the API documentation and usage examples; there is a risk of making implicit assumptions that get forgotten over time. Such an informal, ad hoc approach to API design and documentation can cause undesired extra efforts for client developers and API maintainers when they find out that their assumptions about effects on state and operation pre- and postconditions no longer hold. Furthermore, cohesion within the endpoint might be

---

6. Time synchronization is a general theoretical limitation and challenge in any distributed system; logical clocks have been invented for that reason.

harmed. Load balancing becomes more complicated if stateful operations and stateless operations appear in the same endpoint. Operations staff must guess where and how to deploy the endpoint implementation (for instance, in certain cloud environments and container managers).

How It Works

Add a STATE CREATION OPERATION sco: in -> (out,S') that has a write-only nature to the API endpoint, which may be a PROCESSING RESOURCE or an INFORMATION HOLDER RESOURCE.

Let such a STATE CREATION OPERATION represent a single business incident that does not mandate a business-level reaction from the provider-side endpoint; it may simply store the data or perform further processing in the API implementation or an underlying backend. Let the client receive a mere "got it" acknowledgment or identifier (for instance, to be able to inquire about the state in the future and to resend the incident report in case of transmission problems).

Such operations might have to read some state, for instance, to check for duplicate keys in existing data before creation, but their main purpose should be state creation. This intent is sketched in Figure 5.20.

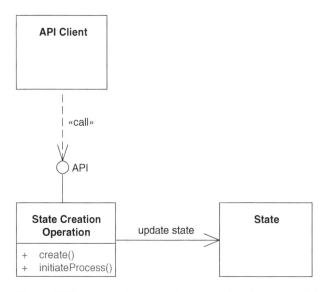

Figure 5.20 *A STATE CREATION OPERATION has the responsibility to write to provider-side storage but cannot read from it*

Describe the abstract and the concrete syntax as well as the semantics of the incident report (the incoming state creation messages, that is) and the acknowledging response (if any) in the API Description. Express the operation behavior in pre- and postconditions.

State Creation Operations may or may not have fire-and-forget semantics. In the latter case, give each state item caused by calls to instances of this pattern a unique id (for duplicate detection and removal). Include a timestamp to capture the time when the reported incident happened (according to the client-side clock).

Unless you write to an append-only event store, perform the required write/insert operation in its own system transaction whose boundaries match that of the API operation (but are not visible to the API client). Let the processing of the State Creation Operation appear to be idempotent.

The request messages accepted by a State Creation Operation contain the full data set that is required to describe the incident that has happened, often in the form of a Parameter Tree, possibly including Metadata Elements that annotate other Data Elements. The response message typically contains only a basic and simple "report received" element, for instance, an Atomic Parameter containing an explicit acknowledgment flag (of Boolean type). Sometimes, an Atomic Parameter List combining an error code with an error message is used, thus forming an Error Report.

Variant   A popular variant of this pattern is *Event Notification Operation,* notifying the endpoint about an external event without assuming any visible provider-side activity and thus realizing event sourcing [Fowler 2006]. Event Notification Operations can report that data has been created, updated (fully or partially), or deleted elsewhere. Past tense is often used to name events (for example, "customer entity created"). Unlike in most implementations of stateful processing, the incoming event is only stored as-is, but the provider-side application state is not updated instantly. If the most recent state is required later on, all stored events (or all events up to a certain point in time when snapshots are taken) are rather replayed and the application state is calculated in the API implementation. This makes the event reporting fast, at the expense of slowing down the later state lookup. An additional benefit of event sourcing is that time-based queries can be performed, as the entire data manipulation history is available in the event journal. Modern event-based systems such as Apache Kafka support such replays in their event journals and distributed transaction logs.

Events can either contain absolute new values that form *full reports* or, as *delta reports,* communicate the changes since the previous event (identified by a "Correlation Identifier" [Hohpe 2003] or indirectly by timestamp and entity identifier).

Event Notification Operations and event sourcing can form the base of event-driven architectures (EDAs). Other pattern languages provide advice for EDA design [Richardson 2016].

A second variant of this pattern is a *Bulk Report*. The client combines multiple related incident events into one report and sends this report as a REQUEST BUNDLE. The bundle entries may all pertain to the same entity or may refer to different ones, for instance, when creating a snapshot or an audit log from the individual events in the Bulk Report or when passing a journal of events that occurred in a certain period on to a data warehouse or data lake.

Examples

In the online shopping scenario, messages such as "new product XYZ created" sent from a product management system or "customer has checked out order 123" from an online shop qualify as examples.

Figure 5.21 gives an example in the Lakeside Mutual case. The events received by the STATE CREATION OPERATION report that a particular customer has been contacted, for instance by a sales agent.

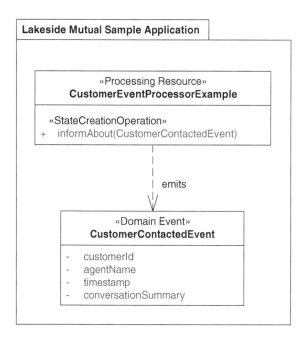

Figure 5.21 *Example of a STATE CREATION OPERATION: EVENT NOTIFICATION OPERATION*

Discussion

Loose coupling is promoted because client and provider do not share any application state; the API client merely informs the provider about incidents on its side. Provider-side consistency checks might be difficult to implement because state reads are supposed to be avoided in STATE CREATION OPERATIONS (for instance, if scaling APIs and their endpoints up and out is desired). Hence, consistency cannot always be fully ensured when operations are defined as write-only (for instance, how should events reporting contradictory information be dealt with?). Time management remains a difficult design task for the same reason. Reliability might suffer if no acknowledgment or state identifier is returned; if it is returned, the API client has to make sure to interpret it correctly (for instance, to avoid unnecessary or premature resending of messages).

Exposing write-only API operations with business semantics that report external events is a key principle of EDAs; we discussed it in the context of the Event Notification Operation variant. In replication scenarios, events represent state changes that have to be propagated among the replicas.

The pattern leaves some room for interpretation when implementing it:

- What should be done with arriving reports: should they be simply stored locally, processed further, or passed on? Does provider-side state have to be accessed, even if it is not desired, for instance, to check the uniqueness of keys?

- Does the report processing change the behavior of future calls to other operations in the same endpoint?

- Is operation invocation idempotent? Events can get lost, for instance, in the case of unreliable network connections or temporary server outages, and might be transmitted multiple times if the client attempts to resend unacknowledged ones. How is consistency ensured in such situations? Strict and eventual consistency are two of the options here [Fehling 2014].

STATE CREATION OPERATIONS are sometimes exposed in PUBLIC APIs; if this is done, they must be protected, for instance, with an API KEY and RATE LIMITS.

This pattern covers scenarios in which an API client notifies a known API provider about an incident. An API provider notifying its clients via callbacks and publish-subscribe mechanisms is another approach covered in other pattern languages and middleware/distributed systems books [Hohpe 2003; Voelter 2004; Hanmer 2007].

Related Patterns

The endpoint role patterns PROCESSING RESOURCE and INFORMATION HOLDER RESOURCE typically contain at least one STATE CREATION OPERATION (unless they are mere compute resources or view providers). Other operation responsibilities are STATE TRANSITION OPERATION, COMPUTATION FUNCTION, and RETRIEVAL OPERATION. A STATE TRANSITION OPERATION usually identifies a provider-side state element in its request message (for instance, an order id or a serial number of a staff member); STATE CREATION OPERATIONS do not have to do this (but might).

"Event-Driven Consumer" and "Service Activator" [Hohpe 2003] describe how to trigger message reception and operation invocation asynchronously (all four operation responsibilities can be combined with these patterns). Chapter 10 in *Process-Driven SOA* features patterns for integrating events into process-driven SOAs [Hentrich 2011].

"The Domain Event" pattern in DDD [Vernon 2013] can help identify STATE CREATION OPERATIONS, specifically but not limited to the Event Notification Operation variant.

More Information

Instances of this pattern may trigger long-running and therefore stateful *conversations* [Hohpe 2007; Pautasso 2016]. The STATE TRANSITION OPERATION pattern covers this usage scenario.

Martin Fowler describes "Command Query Responsibility Segregation" (CQRS) [Fowler 2011] and event sourcing [Fowler 2006]. The Context Mapper DSL and tools support DDD and event modeling, model refactoring, as well as diagram and service contract generation [Kapferer 2021].

DPR features a seven-step service design method to carve out API endpoints and their operations [Zimmermann 2021b].

 Pattern:
RETRIEVAL OPERATION

When and Why to Apply

A PROCESSING RESOURCE or INFORMATION HOLDER RESOURCE endpoint has been identified as required; functional and quality requirements for it have been specified. The operations of these resources do not yet cover all required capabilities—the API consumer(s) also demand read-only access to data, possibly large amounts of repetitive data in particular. This data can be expected to be structured differently than in the domain model of the underlying API implementation; for instance, it might pertain to a particular time period or domain concept (like a product category or customer profile group). The information need arises either ad hoc or regularly, for instance, at the end of a certain period (such as week, month, quarter, or year).

▼

> How can information available from a remote party (the API provider, that is) be retrieved to satisfy an information need of an end user or to allow further client-side processing?

▲

Processing data in context turns it into information, interpreting it in context creates knowledge. Related design issues are as follows:

- How can data model differences be overcome, and how can data be aggregated and combined with information from other sources?

- How can clients influence the scope and the selection criteria for the retrieval results?

- How can the timeframe for reports be specified?

Veracity, Variety, Velocity, and Volume: Data comes in many forms, and client interest in it varies in terms of volume, required accuracy, and processing speed. The variability dimensions include frequency, breadth, and depth of data access. Data production on the provider side and its usage on the client side also change over time.

Workload Management: Data processing takes time, especially if the data volume is big and the processing power is limited. Should clients download entire databases so that they can process their content at will locally? Should some of the processing be performed on the provider-side instead so that the results can be shared and retrieved by multiple clients?

Networking Efficiency versus Data Parsimony (Message Sizes):   The smaller messages are, the more messages have to be exchanged to reach a particular goal. Few large messages cause less network traffic but make the individual request and response messages harder to prepare and process in the conversation participants.

It is hard to imagine a distributed system that does not require some kind of retrieval and query capability. One could replicate all data to its users "behind the scenes" periodically, but such an approach has major deficiencies with regard to consistency, manageability, and data freshness, not to mention the coupling of all clients to the fully replicated, read-only database schema.

How It Works

Add a read-only operation `ro:  (in,S)  -> out` to an API endpoint, which often is an INFORMATION HOLDER RESOURCE, to request a result report that contains a machine-readable representation of the requested information. Add search, filter, and formatting capabilities to the operation signature.

Access the provider-side state in read-only mode. Make sure that the pattern implementation does not change application/session state (except for access logs and other infrastructure-level data), as shown in Figure 5.22. Document this behavior in the API DESCRIPTION.

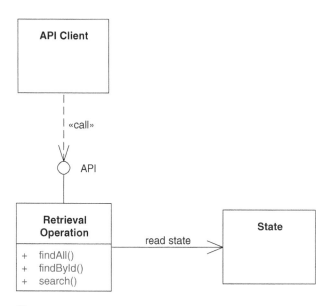

Figure 5.22 *A RETRIEVAL OPERATION reads from but does not write to provider-side storage. Searching (and filtering) may be supported*

For simple retrievals, one can use an ATOMIC PARAMETER LIST to define the query parameters for the report and return the report as a PARAMETER TREE or PARA-METER FOREST. In more complex scenarios, a more expressive query language (such as GraphQL [GraphQL 2021] with its hierarchical call resolvers or SPARQL [W3C 2013], used for big data lakes) can be introduced; the query then describes the desired output declaratively (for instance, as an expression formulated in the query language); it can travel as an ATOMIC PARAMETER string. Such an expressive, highly declarative approach supports the "variety" V (one of the four Vs introduced earlier).

Adding support for PAGINATION is common and advised if result collections are large (the "volume" V of the four big data Vs). Clients can shape and streamline the responses when providing instances of WISH LIST or WISH TEMPLATE in their retrieval requests.

Access control might be required to steer what API client are permitted to ask for. Data access settings (including transaction boundaries and isolation level) may have to be configured in the operation implementation.

Examples

In an online shopping example, an analytic RETRIEVAL OPERATION is "show all orders customer ABC has placed in the last 12 months."

In the Lakeside Mutual case, we can define multiple operations to find customers and retrieve information about them as illustrated in Figure 5.23. The `allData` parameter is a primitive yes/no WISH LIST. When set to `true`, an EMBEDDED ENTITY containing all customer data is included in the response; when `false`, a LINKED INFORMATION HOLDER pointing at this data is returned instead.

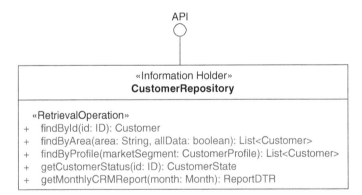

Figure 5.23 *Examples of RETRIEVAL OPERATIONS: Search, filter, direct access*

In the Lakeside Mutual implementation, we find many Web-based retrieval operations (HTTP GETs), which can be called with `curl` on the command line. An example is `listClaims`:

```
curl -X GET http://localhost:8080/claims?limit=10&offset=0
```

The command arrives at this API endpoint operation (Java Spring):

```
@GET
public ClaimsDTO listClaims(
  @QueryParam("limit") @DefaultValue("3") Integer limit,
  @QueryParam("offset")@DefaultValue("0") Integer offset,
  @QueryParam("orderBy") String orderBy
) {
  List<ClaimDTO> result = [...]
  return new ClaimsDTO(
    limit, offset, claims.getSize(), orderBy, result);
}
```

Variants   Several variants of this pattern exist, for instance, *Status Check* (also known as Progress Inquiry, Polling Operation), *Time-Bound Report,* and *Business Rule Validator.*

A Status Check has rather simple in and out parameters (for example, two ATOMIC PARAMETER instances): an id (for instance, a process or activity identifier) is passed in and a numeric status code or a state name (defined in an enumeration type) is returned.

A Time-Bound Report typically specifies the time interval(s) as an additional query parameter (or set of parameters); its responses then contain one PARAMETER TREE per interval.

A Business Rule Validator is similar to the *Validation Service* variant of a COMPUTATION FUNCTION. However, it does not validate data that is passed on but retrieves this data from the provider-side application state. A list of identifiers of entities already present in the API implementation (validation target) might be included in the request. One example of a Business Rule Validator is a check whether the provider will be able to process this business object in the current state of the conversation with the client. Such a validator can be invoked prior to a call to a STATE TRANSITION OPERATION that primarily works on the business object that is passed in. The validation may also include provider-side application state into the checking process. In an online shopping example, "check whether all order items point to existing products that are currently in stock" is an example of such a validator. This Business Rule Validator helps catch errors early, which can reduce workload.

Discussion

With respect to workload management, RETRIEVAL OPERATIONS can scale out by replicating data. This is simplified by their read-only nature. RETRIEVAL OPERATIONS may also become a performance bottleneck, for instance, if user information needs and query capabilities do not match and many complex calculations are required to match information demand and supply. Network efficiency is at risk.

Pagination is commonly used to address the "volume" aspect and to reduce message sizes. The "velocity" aspect cannot be easily supported with standard request-reply retrievals; the introduction of streaming APIs and stream processing (which is out of our scope here) can be considered instead.

From a security point of view, the request message often has low to medium data protection needs in case of aggregated data retrieval; however, the request may contain secure credentials to authorize access to sensitive information and has to avoid DoS attacks. The response message protection requirements might be more advanced, as returned data reports might contain business performance data or sensitive personal information.[7]

Retrieval Operation instances are commonly exposed in Public APIs, such as those of open data [Wikipedia 2022h] and open government data scenarios. If this is done, they often are protected with an API Key and Rate Limits.

Time-Bound Report services can use denormalized data replicas and apply the extract-transform-load staging commonly used in data warehouses. Such services are common in Community APIs and Solution-Internal APIs, for example, those supporting data analytics solutions.

Related Patterns

The endpoint pattern Processing Resource and all types of Information Holder Resources may expose Retrieval Operations. The Pagination pattern is often applied in Retrieval Operations.

If query responses are not self-explanatory, Metadata Elements can be introduced to reduce the risk of misinterpretations on the consumer side.

The sibling patterns are State Transition Operation, State Creation Operation, and Computation Function. A State Creation Operation pushes data from the client to the API provider, whereas a Retrieval Operation pulls data; Computation Function and State Transition Operation can support both unidirectional data flows and bidirectional ones.

More Information

Chapter 8 in the *RESTful Web Services Cookbook* [Allamaraju 2010] discusses queries (in the context of HTTP APIs). There is a large body of literature on database design and information integration, including data warehouses [Kimball 2002].

---

7. OWASP has published an API Security Top 10 [Yalon 2019] that any API should respect, especially those dealing with sensitive and/or classified data.

Implementing Domain-Driven Design [Vernon 2013] talks about Query Models in Chapter 4 in the section on CQRS. Endpoints that expose only Retrieval Operations form the Query Model in CQRS.

Pattern:
State Transition Operation

When and Why to Apply
A Processing Resource or an Information Holder Resource exists in an API. Its functionality should be decomposed into multiple activities and entity-related operations, whose execution state should be visible in the API so that clients can advance it.

▼

How can a client initiate a processing action that causes the provider-side application state to change?

▲

For instance, functionality that is part of a longer-running business process might call for incremental updates of entities and coordination of application state transitions to move process instances from initiation to termination in a decentralized, stepwise fashion. The process behavior and interaction dynamics might have been specified in a use case model and/or set of related user stories. An analysis-level business process model or entity-centric state machine might have been specified as well.

▼

How can API clients and API providers share the responsibilities required to execute and control business processes and their activities in a distributed approach to business process management?

▲

In this process management context, *frontend* business process management (BPM) and BPM *services* can be distinguished:

- How can API clients ask an API provider to take over certain functions that represent business activities of varying granularities, from atomic activities to subprocesses to entire processes, but still own the process state?

- How can API clients initiate, control, and follow the asynchronous execution of remote business processes (including subprocesses and activities) exposed and owned by an API provider?

The process instances and the state ownership can lie with the API client (frontend BPM) or the API provider (BPM services), or they can be shared responsibilities.

A canonical example process from the insurance domain is claim processing, with activities such as initial validation of a received claim form, fraud check, additional customer correspondence, accept/reject decision, payment/settlement, and archiving. Instances of this process can live for days to months or even years. Process instance state has to be managed; some parts of the processing can run in parallel, whereas others have to be executed one by one sequentially. When dealing with such complex domain semantics, the control and data flow depends on a number of factors. Multiple systems and services may be involved along the way, each exposing one or more APIs. Other services and application frontends may act as API clients.

The following forces have to be resolved when representing business processes and their activities as API operations or, more generally speaking, when updating provider-side application state: service granularity; consistency; dependencies on state changes being made beforehand, which may collide with other state changes; workload management; and networking efficiency versus data parsimony. Time management and reliability also qualify as forces of this pattern; these design concerns are discussed in the pattern STATE CREATION OPERATION.

- **Service granularity:** Large business services may contain complex and rich state information, updated only in a few transitions, while smaller ones may be simple but chatty in terms of their state transitions. It is not clear per se whether an entire business process, its subprocesses, or its individual activities should be exposed as operations of a PROCESSING RESOURCE. The data-oriented services provided by INFORMATION HOLDER RESOURCES also come in different granularities, from simple attribute lookups to complex queries and from single-attribute updates to bulk uploads of rich, comprehensive data sets.

- **Consistency and auditability:** Process instances are often subject to audit; depending on the current process instance state, certain activities must not be performed. Some activities have to be completed in a certain time window because they require resources that have to be reserved and then allocated. When things go wrong, some activities might have to be undone to bring the process instance and backend resources (such as business objects and database entities) back into a consistent state.

- **Dependencies on state changes being made beforehand:** State-changing API operations may collide with state changes already initiated by other system parts. Examples of such conflicting changes are system transactions triggered by other API clients, by external events in downstream systems, or by provider-internal batch jobs. Coordination and conflict resolution might be required.

- **Workload management:** Some processing actions and business process activities may be computationally or memory intensive, run for a long time, or require interactions with other systems. High workload may affect the scalability of the provider and make it difficult to manage.

- **Networking efficiency versus data parsimony:** One can reduce the message size (or the weight of the message payload) and only send the difference with regard to a previous state (an incremental approach). This tactic makes messages smaller; another option is to always send complete and consistent information, which leads to larger messages. The number of messages exchanged can be reduced by combining multiple updates into a single message.

One could decide to ban provider-side application state entirely. This is only realistic in trivial application scenarios such as pocket calculators (not requiring any storage) or simple translation services (working with static data). One could also decide to expose stateless operations and transfer state to and from the endpoint every time. The "Client Session State" pattern [Fowler 2002] describes the pros and cons of this approach (and the REST principle of "hypertext as the engine of application state" promotes it). It scales well but may introduce security threats with non-trusted clients and, if state is large, cause bandwidth problems. Client programming, testing, and maintenance become more flexible but also more complex and riskier. Auditability suffers; for instance, it is not clear how to guarantee that all execution flows are valid. In our order cancellation example, a valid flow would be "order goods → pay → deliver → return goods → receive refund," whereas "order goods → deliver → refund" is an invalid, possibly fraudulent sequence.

How It Works

Introduce an operation in an API endpoint that combines client input and current state to trigger a provider-side state change `sto: (in,S) -> (out,S')`. Model the valid state transitions within the endpoint, which may be a PROCESSING RESOURCE or an INFORMATION HOLDER RESOURCE, and check the validity of incoming change requests and business activity requests at runtime.

Pair a "Command Message" with a "Document Message" [Hohpe 2003] to describe the input and the desired action/activity and receive an acknowledgment or result. In a business-process-like context, such as claims processing or order management, a STATE TRANSITION OPERATION may realize a single business activity in a process or even wrap the complete execution of an entire process instance on the provider side.

The basic principle is shown in Figure 5.24. The update() and replace() operations are entity-centric and primarily found in data-centric INFORMATION HOLDER RESOURCES; processActivity() operations are at home in action-oriented PROCESS-ING RESOURCES. Calls to such STATE TRANSITION OPERATIONS trigger one or more instances of the "Business Transaction" pattern described in *Patterns of Enterprise Application Architecture* [Fowler 2002]. When multiple STATE TRANSITION OPERA-TIONS are offered by a PROCESSING RESOURCE, the API hands out explicit control to the internal processing states so that the client may cancel the execution, track its progress, and influence its outcome.

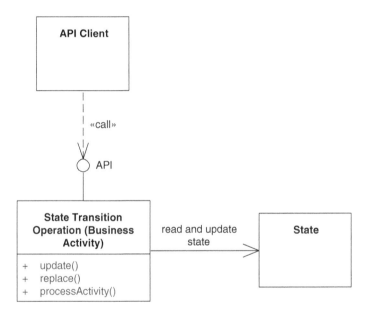

Figure 5.24 *STATE TRANSITION OPERATIONS are stateful, both reading and writing provider-side storage*

There are two quite different types of update, *full overwrite* (or state replacement) and *partial change* (or incremental update). Full overwrites often can be processed without accessing the current state and then can be seen as instances of STATE CREATION OPERATIONS. Incremental change typically requires read access to state (as described in this pattern). *Upsert* (update + insert) is a special case combining both themes: attempting to replace a nonexisting entity results in creating a new one (with the identifier provided in the request message) [Higginbotham 2019]. With HTTP-based APIs, full overwrite is typically exposed with the PUT method, while partial change can be achieved with PATCH.

From a message representation structure point of view, the request and response messages of STATE TRANSITION OPERATION instances can be fine-grained (in the simplest case, a single ATOMIC PARAMETER) as well as coarse-grained (nested PARAMETER TREES). Their request message representations vary greatly in their complexity.

Many STATE TRANSITION OPERATIONS are transactional internally. Operation execution should be governed and protected by a transaction boundary that is identical to the API operation boundary. While this should not be visible to the client on the technical level, it is okay to disclose it in the API documentation due to the consequences for composition. The transaction can either be a *system transaction* following the atomicity, consistency, isolation, and durability (ACID) paradigm [Zimmermann 2007] or a saga [Richardson 2018], roughly corresponding to compensation-based business transactions [Wikipedia 2022g]. If ACID is not an option, the BASE principles or try-cancel-confirm (TCC) [Pardon 2011] can be considered; a conscious decision between strict and eventual consistency [Fehling 2014] is required, and a locking strategy also has to be decided upon. The transaction boundaries have to be chosen consciously; long-running business transactions usually do not fit into a single database transaction with ACID properties.

The processing of the STATE TRANSITION OPERATION should appear to be idempotent, for instance, by preferring absolute updates over incremental ones. For example, "set value of x to y" is easier to process with consistent results than is "increase value of x by y," which could lead to data corruption if the action request gets duplicated/resent. "Idempotent Receiver" in *Enterprise Integration Patterns* [Hohpe 2003] provides further advice.

It should be considered to add compliance controls and other security means such as ABAC, for instance, based on an API KEY or a stronger authentication token, to the entire API endpoint or individual STATE TRANSITION OPERATIONS. This may degrade performance caused by extra computations and data transfers.

Variant   A *Business Activity Processor* is a variant of this pattern that can support frontend BPM scenarios and realize BPM services as well (Figure 5.25). Note that we use the term activity in a general sense here; activities might be rather fine-grained and participate in larger processes (for example, accept or reject claim or proceed to checkout in our sample scenarios) but might also be rather coarse grained (for instance, process claim or shop online).

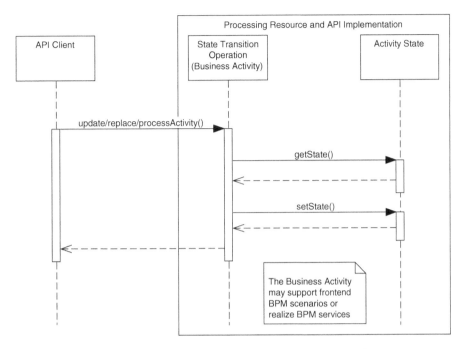

Figure 5.25 *STATE TRANSITION OPERATION in a PROCESSING RESOURCE (here: Business Activity Processor variant)*

Single activities can be responsible for any of the following fine-grained *action primitives* providing process control: prepare, start, suspend/resume, complete, fail, cancel, undo, restart, and cleanup. Given an asynchronous nature of the business activity execution and, in the frontend BPM case, client-side process ownership, it should also be possible to receive the following *events* via STATE TRANSITION OPERATIONS: activity finished, failed, or aborted; and state transition occurred.

Figure 5.26 assembles the action primitives and states into a generic state machine modeling the behavior of PROCESSING RESOURCES and their STATE TRANSITION OPERATIONS in the Business Activity Processor variant. Depending on the complexity of their behavior, instances of INFORMATION HOLDER RESOURCES can also be specified, implemented, tested, and documented this way.

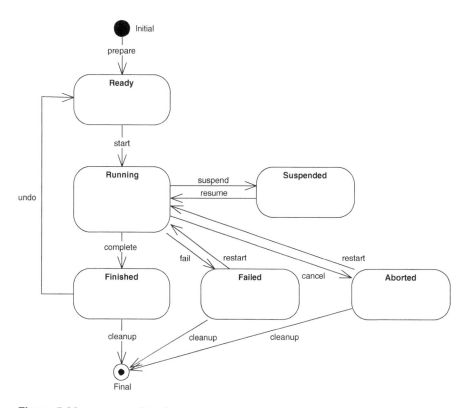

Figure 5.26 *A state machine featuring common action primitives as transitions*

Domain-specific API endpoints and their STATE TRANSITION OPERATIONS should refine and customize this generic state machine for their particular business scenario and API use cases; each required primitive becomes one API operation (or an option of a coarser-grained operation, selected by an ID ELEMENT parameter in the request message representation). API implementation, pre- and postconditions in the API documentation and test cases then can be organized according to the resulting API-specific state machine, which should be documented in the API DESCRIPTION.

The semantics of the states and state transitions in Figure 5.26 are as follows:

- **Prepare (or initialize):** This primitive allows clients to prepare the execution of a state-changing activity by transferring the input prior to the actual activity, for instance, for validation purposes. Depending on the complexity of such information, an initialization may involve a single call or a more complex conversation. Once all information has been provided, the activity is "Ready" to start and an activity identifier is assigned. This primitive can be seen as an instance of the sibling pattern State Creation Operation.

- **Start:** This primitive allows clients to explicitly start the execution of an activity, which has been initialized and is ready to start. The state of the activity becomes "Running."

- **Suspend/resume:** These two primitives allow clients to pause and later continue the execution of a running activity. Suspending a running activity may free execution resources within the API endpoint.

- **Complete:** This primitive transitions the activity state from "Running" to "Finished" to indicate that the activity ended successfully.

- **Fail:** This activity transitions the state from "Running" to "Failed," possibly explained in an Error Report.

- **Cancel:** This primitive allows clients to interrupt the execution of the activity and "Abort" it in case they are no longer interested in its results.

- **Undo:** This primitive allows compensating the actions performed by the activity, effectively reverting the state of the API endpoint back to its original one, before the activity was started. It may not always be possible to do so, especially when activities provoke side effects that impact the outside of the API provider. An example is an email that is sent and cannot be recalled. Note that we assume compensation can be done within the undo transition. In some cases, it may require to set up a separate activity (with its own state machine).

- **Restart:** This primitive allows clients to retry the execution of a failed or aborted activity. The activity state goes back to "Running".

- **Cleanup:** This primitive removes any state associated with finished, failed, or aborted activities. The activity identifier is no longer valid and the activity state transitions to "Final."

In frontend BPM, API clients own the process instance state. They may inform the API provider about the following two types of events (when exposing BPM services, such event notifications may travel in the other direction, from the service provider to its clients):

- **Activity finished, failed, or aborted:** Once the execution of the activity completes, affected parties should be notified of its successful or failed completion so that they can retrieve its output. This may happen via a call to a State

CREATION OPERATION pattern (in its Event Notification Operation variant). It may also be realized differently, for instance, via server-sent events or callbacks.

- **State transition occurred:** For monitoring and tracking the progress of the activity, affected parties might want to learn about the current state of an activity and changes to it; they want to be notified when a state transition occurs. Realization options for this type of event, that follow a push model, include event streaming, server-sent events, and callbacks. Following a pull model, state lookups can be realized as instances of the RETRIEVAL OPERATION pattern.

Multiple STATE TRANSITION OPERATIONS, often located in the same API endpoint, can be composed to cover subprocesses or entire business processes. It has to be decided consciously where to compose: frontend BPM often uses a Web frontend as API client; BPM services yield composite PROCESSING RESOURCES exposing rather coarse-grained STATE TRANSITION OPERATIONS, effectively realizing the "Process Manager" pattern from [Hohpe 2003]. Other options are to (1) introduce an API Gateway [Richardson 2018] as a single integration and choreography coordination point or (2) choreograph services in a fully decentralized fashion via peer-to-peer calls and/or event transmission.

Executing these activities, STATE TRANSITION OPERATIONS change the business activity state in the API endpoint; the complexity of their pre- and postconditions as well as invariants varies, depending on the business and integration scenario at hand. Medium to high complexities of these rules are common in many application domains and scenarios. This behavior must be specified in the API DESCRIPTION; the transition primitives and state transitions should be made explicit in it.

When realizing the pattern and its Business Activity Processor variant in HTTP, suitable verbs (POST, PUT, PATCH, or DELETE) should be picked from the uniform REST interface options. Process instance and activity identifiers typically appear in the URI as an ID ELEMENT. This makes it easy to retrieve status information via HTTP GET. Each action primitive can be supported by a separate STATE TRANSITION OPERATION; alternatively, the primitive can be provided as an input parameter to a more general process management operation. In HTTP resource APIs, process identifier and primitive name often are transported as path parameters; the same holds for the activity identifier. LINK ELEMENTS and URIs then advance the activity state and inform affected parties about subsequent and alternative activities, compensation opportunities, and so on.

Example

The activity "proceed to checkout and pay" in an online shop illustrates the pattern in an order management process. "Add item to shopping basket" is an activity in the "product catalog browsing" subprocess. These operations do change provider-side state, they do convey business semantics, and they do have nontrivial pre- and post-conditions as well as invariants (for instance, "do not deliver the goods and invoice the customer before the customer has checked out and confirmed the order"). Some of these might be long running too, thus requiring fine-grained activity status control and transfer.

The following example from the Lakeside Mutual case, shown in Figure 5.27, illustrates the two extremes of activity granularity. Offers are created in a single-step operation; claims are managed step by step, causing incremental state transitions on the provider side. Some of the primitives from Figure 5.26 can be assigned to STATE TRANSITION OPERATIONS in the example; for instance, createClaim() corresponds to the start primitive, and closeClaim() completes the business activity of claim checking. The fraud check might be long running, which indicates that the API should support the suspend and resume primitives in the corresponding STATE TRANSITION OPERATIONS of the PROCESSING RESOURCE for claims management.

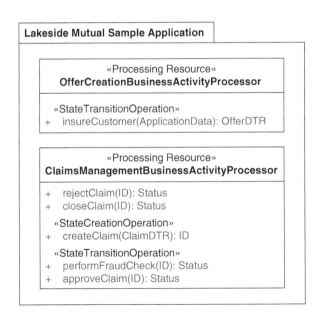

Figure 5.27 *Two examples of STATE TRANSITION OPERATIONS: Coarse-grained BPM service and fine-grained frontend BPM process execution*

Discussion

The design forces are resolved as follows:

- **Service granularity:** PROCESSING RESOURCES and their STATE TRANSITION OPERATIONS can accommodate both smaller and larger "service cuts" [Gysel 2016] and therefore promote agility and flexibility. INFORMATION HOLDER RESOURCES come in different sizes too. The impact of the endpoint sizing decisions on coupling and other qualities was discussed previously in these two patterns. The fact that such states are explicitly modeled as part of the API DESCRIPTION makes it possible to track them in the first place.

- **Consistency and auditability:** STATE TRANSITION OPERATIONS can and must handle business and system transaction management internally in the API implementation; the chosen design options, discussed previously, and their realization determine whether the pattern instance is able to resolve these forces and meet its requirements. Similarly, API implementation-internal logging and monitoring support auditability.

- **Dependencies on state changes made beforehand:** State changes may collide with each other. The API providers should check the validity of a requested state transition, and clients should expect that their state transition requests might be denied due to their out-of-date assumptions about the current state.

- **Workload management:** Stateful STATE TRANSITION OPERATIONS cannot scale easily, and endpoints featuring such operations cannot be relocated to other compute nodes (hosting servers) seamlessly. This is particularly relevant when deploying to clouds because cloud features such as elasticity and autoscaling can be leveraged only if the deployed application is designed for them. Managing process instance state is delicate by design; its intricacies do not necessarily suggest that it is easy to feel at home in a cloud.[8]

- **Networking efficiency versus data parsimony:** A RESTful API design of frontend BPM and BPM services can use state transfers from clients to providers and resource designs to come up with a suitable balance between expressiveness and efficiency. The choice between incremental updates (small, nonidempotent messages) or replacement updates (larger but idempotent messages) influences the message sizes and exchange frequency.

Idempotence is good for fault resiliency and scalability, as mentioned earlier. While the concept is easy to understand in textbooks and basic examples, it is often not clear how to achieve idempotence in more complex real-world scenarios—nor

---

8. Serverless cloud functions, for instance, seem to be better suited for other usage scenarios.

is it an easy task. For instance, a recommendation to send a "new value is n" message rather than "value of x has increased by one" is easy to give and take, but the picture gets more complex in advanced business scenarios such as order management and payment processing in which multiple related implementation-level entities are modified by a single API call. The concept is covered in depth in *Cloud Computing Patterns* [Fehling 2014] and *Enterprise Integration Patterns* [Hohpe 2003].

When State Transition Operations are exposed in Public APIs or Community APIs, they typically must be protected against security threats. For instance, some actions and activities may require authorization so that only certain authenticated clients can trigger state transitions; furthermore, the validity of state transitions might depend on the message content as well. A deeper discussion of security requirements and designs responding to them is out of scope here.

Performance and scalability are primarily driven by the technical complexity of the API operation. The amount of backend processing required in API implementations, concurrent access to shared data, and the resulting IT infrastructure workload (remote connections, computations, disk I/O, CPU energy consumption) differ widely in practice. From a reliability point of view, single points of failure should be avoided, and a centralized approach to process management in the API implementation may turn into one.

Related Patterns

The pattern differs from its siblings as follows: A Computation Function does not touch the provider-side application state (read or write) at all; a State Creation Operation only writes to it (in append mode). Instances of Retrieval Operation read but do not write to it; State Transition Operation instances both read and write the provider-side state. Retrieval Operation pulls information from the provider; State Creation Operations push updates to the provider. State Transition Operations may push and/or pull. A State Transition Operation may refer to a provider-side state element in its request message (for instance, an order id or a serial number of a staff member); State Creation Operations usually do not do this (except for technical reasons such as preventing usage of duplicate keys or updating audit logs). They often return Id Elements for later access.

State Transition Operations can be seen to trigger and/or realize "Business Transactions" [Fowler 2002]. Instances of this pattern may participate in long-running and therefore stateful conversations [Hohpe 2007]. If this is done, context information necessary for logging and debugging often has to be propagated—for instance, by introducing an explicit Context Representation. State Transition Operations can use and go along with one or more of the RESTful conversation patterns from "A Pattern Language for RESTful Conversations" [Pautasso 2016].

For instance, one may want to consider factoring out the state management and the computation parts of a process activity into separate services. Conversation patterns or choreographies and/or orchestrations may then define the valid combinations and execution sequences of these services.

STATE TRANSITION OPERATIONS are often exposed in COMMUNITY APIs; Chapter 10, "Real-World Pattern Stories," features such a case in depth. Services-based systems expose such operations in SOLUTION-INTERNAL APIs as well. An API KEY typically protects external access to operations that write to the provider-side state, and a SERVICE LEVEL AGREEMENT may govern their usage.

More Information
There is a large body of literature on BPM(N) and workflow management that introduces concepts and technologies to implement stateful service components in general and STATE TRANSITION OPERATIONS in particular (for instance, [Leymann 2000; Leymann 2002; Bellido 2013; Gambi 2013]).

In RDD [Wirfs-Brock 2002], STATE TRANSITION OPERATIONS correspond to "Coordinators" and "Controllers" that are encapsulated as "Service Providers" made accessible remotely with the help of an "Interfacer." Michael Nygard suggests many patterns and recipes that improve reliability in *Release It!* [Nygard 2018a].

The seven-step service design method in DPR suggests calling out endpoint roles and operation responsibilities such as STATE TRANSITION OPERATION when preparing candidate endpoint lists and refining them [Zimmermann 2021b].

Pattern:
COMPUTATION FUNCTION

When and Why to Apply
The requirements for an application indicate that something has to be calculated. The result of this calculation exclusively depends on its input. While the input is available in the same place that requires the result, the calculation should not be run there—for instance, for cost, efficiency, workload, trust, or expertise reasons.

An API client, for example, might want to ask the API endpoint provider whether some data meets certain conditions or might want to convert it from one format to another.

▼

How can a client invoke side-effect-free remote processing on the provider side to have a result calculated from its input?

▲

- **Reproducibility and trust:** Outsourcing work to a remote party causes a loss of control, which makes it harder to guarantee that the results are valid. Can the client trust the provider to perform the calculation correctly? Is it always available when needed, and is there a chance that it might be withdrawn in the future? Local calls can be logged and reproduced rather easily. While this is possible over remote connections too, more coordination is required, and an additional type of failure may happen when debugging and reproducing remote executions.[9]

- **Performance:** Local calls within a program are fast. Remote calls between system parts incur delays due to network latency, message serialization and deserialization, as well as the time required to transfer the input and output data, which depends on the message sizes and the available network bandwidth.

- **Workload management:** Some computations might require many resources, such as CPU time and main memory (RAM), which may be insufficient on the client side. Some calculations may run for a long time due to their computational complexity or the large amount of input to be processed. This may affect the scalability of the provider and its ability to meet the SERVICE LEVEL AGREEMENT.

One could perform the required calculation locally, but this might require processing large amounts of data, which in turn might slow down clients that lack the necessary CPU/RAM capacity. Eventually, such a nondistributed approach leads to a monolithic architecture, which will require reinstalling clients every time the calculation has to be updated.

How It Works

▼

Introduce an API operation cf with cf: in -> out to the API endpoint, which often is a PROCESSING RESOURCE. Let this COMPUTATION FUNCTION validate the received request message, perform the desired function cf, and return its result in the response.

▲

---

9. These observations hold when shifting calculations from a client to an API provider in a PROCESSING RESOURCE but also when outsourcing data management to an INFORMATION HOLDER RESOURCE.

A COMPUTATION FUNCTION neither accesses nor changes the server-side application state, as shown in Figure 5.28.

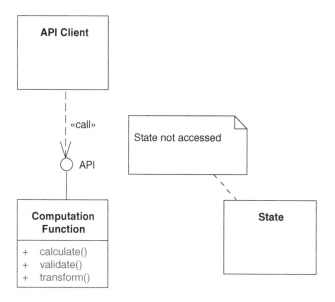

Figure 5.28 *A COMPUTATION FUNCTION is stateless, neither reading nor writing to provider-side storage*

Design request and response message structures that fit the purpose of the COMPUTATION FUNCTION. Include the COMPUTATION FUNCTION in the API DESCRIPTION (in the context of the endpoint it is added to). Define at least one explicit precondition that references the elements in the request message and one or more postconditions that specify what the response message contains. Explain how this data should be interpreted.

There is no need to introduce transaction management in the API implementation because a mere COMPUTATION FUNCTION is stateless by definition.

Variants   The general, rather simple COMPUTATION FUNCTION pattern has several variants, *Transformation Service* and *Validation Service* as well as *Long Running Computation* (which is more challenging technically than the general case). Each variant requires different request/response message representations.

A Transformation Service implements one or more of the message translation patterns from *Enterprise Integration Patterns* [Hohpe 2003] in a network-accessible form. A Transformation Service does not change the meaning of the data that it processed, but alters its representation. It might convert from one representation structure to another format (for example, customer record schemas used in two different subsystems) or from one notation to another (for example, XML to JSON, JSON to CSV). Transformation Services typically accept and return Parameter Trees of varying complexity.

Validation Service is also known as (Pre-)Condition Checker. To deal with potentially incorrect input, the API provider should always validate it before processing it and make it explicit in its contract that the input may be rejected. It may be useful for clients to be able to test their input validity explicitly and independently from the invocation of the function for processing it. The API thus breaks down into a pair of two operations, a Validation Service and another Computation Function:

1. An operation to validate the input without performing the computation

2. An operation to perform the computation (which may fail due to invalid input unless this input has been validated before)

The Validation Service solves the following problem:

How can an API provider check the correctness/accuracy of incoming data transfer representations (parameters) and provider-side resources (and their state)?

The solution to this problem is to introduce an API operation that receives a Data Element of any structure and complexity and returns an Atomic Parameter (for example, a Boolean value or integer) that represents the validation result. The validation primarily pertains to the payload of the request. If the API implementation consults the current internal state during the validation, the Validation Service becomes a variant of a Retrieval Operation (for instance, to look up certain values and calculation rules), as shown in Figure 5.29.

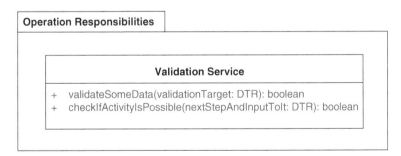

Figure 5.29 *Validation Service variant: Arbitrary request data, Boolean response (DTR: data transfer representation)*

Two exemplary requests are "Is this a valid insurance claim?" and "Will you be able to accept this purchase order?" invoked prior to a call to a State Transition Operation in our sample scenarios. In case of such "pre-activity validation," the parameter types can be complex (depending on the activity to be prevalidated); the response might contain suggestions on how to correct any errors that were reported.

There are many other types of conditions and items worth validating, ranging from classifications and categorizations such as `isValidOrder(orderDTR)` and status checks such as `isOrderClosed(orderId)` to complex compliance checks such as `has4EyesPrinicipleBeenApplied(...)`. Such validations typically return rather simple results (such as a success indicator and possibly some additional explanations); they are stateless and operate on the received request data exclusively, which makes them easy to scale and move from one deployment node to another.

The third variant is Long Running Computation. A simple function operation may be sufficient under the following assumptions:

- The input representation is expected to be correct.

- The expected function execution time is short.

- The server has enough CPU processing capacity for the expected peak workload.

However, sometimes the processing will take a noticeable amount of time, and sometimes it cannot be assured that the processing time of a computation will be short enough (for instance, due to unpredictable workload or resource availability on the API provider side or due to varying sizes of input data sent by the client). In such cases, clients should be provided some form of asynchronous, nonblocking invocation of a processing function. A more refined design is needed for such Long Running Computations, which may receive invalid input and may require investing a significant amount of CPU time to execute.

There are different ways of implementing this pattern variant:

1. *Call over asynchronous messaging.* The client sends its input via a request message queue, and the API provider puts the output on a response message queue [Hohpe 2003].

2. *Call followed by callback.* The input is sent via a first call, and the result is sent via a callback, which assumes that clients support callbacks [Voelter 2004].

3. *Long-running request.* The input is posted, and a LINK ELEMENT informs where the progress can be polled via RETRIEVAL OPERATIONS. Eventually, the result is published at its own INFORMATION HOLDER RESOURCE—there is an optional but useful opportunity to use the link to cancel the request and clean up the result when no longer needed (such stateful request processing is further detailed in the Business Activity Processor variant of the STATE TRANSITION OPERATION pattern). This implementation option is often chosen in Web APIs [Pautasso 2016].

Examples

A simple, rather self-explanatory example of a Transformation Service is shown in Figure 5.30.

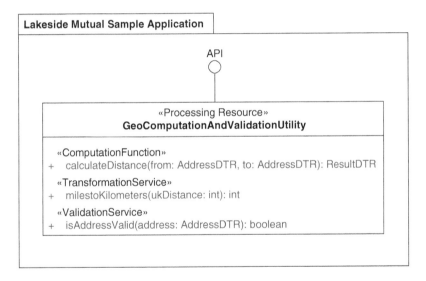

Figure 5.30 *A PROCESSING RESOURCE providing Transformation Services*

An operation to find out about the health of a service is called *heartbeat*. Such a test message is an example of a simple command exposed remotely within a PROCESSING RESOURCE endpoint (see Figure 5.31).

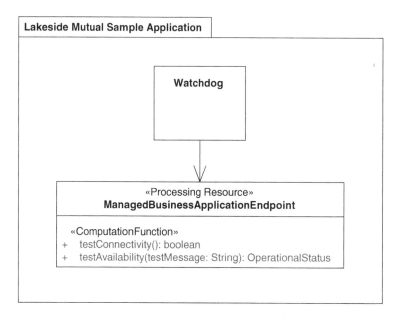

Figure 5.31 *Examples of Validation Services: Health check operations*

"I am alive" operations, sometimes called "application-level ping," accept and respond to test messages. They are often added to mission-critical API implementations as part of a systems management strategy (here, fault and performance management). Its pre- and postconditions are simple; its API contract is sketched in the preceding UML snippet.

Neither system transactions nor business-level compensation (undo) are required in these simple examples of the pattern and its variants.

Discussion

Reproducibility and trust suffer because an external dependency is introduced that cannot be controlled by the client; it has to trust the provider that multiple subsequent calls will be answered coherently. The decision to outsource functionality must be compliant with legislation and inhouse policies, for instance, those about data protection and software licensing.

Performance is negatively impacted due to the network latency. Message sizes might increase because stateless servers cannot retrieve any intermediate results from their own data stores. Still, it may also occur that for the given computation, the performance penalty due to the network may be compensated by the faster computation time on the provider side and thus make it worthwhile to offload the computation from the client. If exposing a transformation or validation operation as a remote service is too costly, a local library-based API is a cheaper alternative.

Caching makes sense only under certain conditions. More than one client has to request the same computation over the same input, and the result has to be deterministic. Furthermore, the provider must have enough storage capacity. Only then may it be worthwhile to invest in caching results so that they can be shared across multiple clients.

From a security point of view, the protection needs of the request and response messages depend on the sensitivity of the message content. For example, the response message of a Validation Service might have low protection needs if the result alone is hard to interpret without its invocation context. DoS attacks are a threat for all remote API operations; suitable countermeasures and risk management are required.

Workload management is simplified because stateless operations can be moved freely. By definition, implementations of the pattern do not change application state on the provider side (possibly except for access logs and temporary or permanent storage of validation results, if/as needed to meet security requirements such as non-repudiation). They are therefore easy to scale and move, which makes them eligible to cloud deployments.

Maintenance of the COMPUTATION FUNCTION implementation is separated from client updates, as long as the COMPUTATION FUNCTION interface does not change. If the API implementation is deployed to a cloud, the cost of renting the cloud service offering has to be taken into account.

If the computation is resource-intense (CPU, RAM), algorithm and distribution design might have to be rethought to avoid bottlenecks and single points of failure. The conversation pattern "Long-Running Request" [Pautasso 2016] covers this topic. While not directly observable in the functional API contract, this is critical for the API design because it may affect the ability to meet the SERVICE LEVEL AGREEMENT for the API. CPU and RAM workload also affect the components implementing the API; it becomes more challenging to scale the function implementation. Caching computation results and computing some results before they are even requested (anticipating what clients want based on what they requested previously) are two performance and workload management tactics eligible here.

Related Patterns

The "Service" pattern in DDD covers similar semantics (but is broader and targets the business logic layer of an application). It can help identify Computation Function candidates during endpoint identification [Vernon 2013].

Serverless computing lambdas, deployed to public clouds such as AWS or Azure, may be seen as COMPUTATION FUNCTIONS unless they are backed by cloud storage offerings, which makes them stateful.

More Information

Service types are a topic covered by SOA literature from the early 2000s, such as *Enterprise SOA* [Krafzig 2004] and *SOA in Practice* [Josuttis 2007]. While the service type taxonomies in these books are more focused on the overall architecture, some of the basic services and utility services have responsibilities that do not require read or write access to provider/server state and therefore qualify as instances of this pattern and its variants.

The design-by-contract approach in the object-oriented programming method and language Eiffel [Meyer 1997] includes validation into the codification of business commands and domain methods and automates pre- and postcondition checking. This program-internal approach can be seen as an alternative to external Validation Services (but also as a rather advanced known use of it).

A lot of online resources on serverless computing exist. One starting point is Jeremy Daly's Web site and blog Serverless [Daly 2021].

Summary

This chapter presented patterns that address API architectural concerns. We specified endpoint roles and operation responsibilities in the early steps of an API design such as those in the Define phase of the ADDR process.

The roles and responsibilities help clarify the architectural significance of these API design elements and serve as input to the following phases. Chapter 3, "API Decision Narratives," covered the questions, options, and criteria eligible when designing endpoints and operations in a role- and responsibility-driven way; complementary to that discussion, this chapter provided the full pattern texts.

Following the pattern template introduced in Chapter 4, we covered data-oriented API endpoint roles:

- One specific kind of INFORMATION HOLDER RESOURCE is DATA TRANSFER RESOURCE, eligible when multiple clients want to share information without becoming coupled with each other directly.

- Other kinds that differ in terms of their lifetime, relations, and changeability are MASTER DATA HOLDER, OPERATIONAL DATA HOLDER, and REFERENCE DATA HOLDER. Master data is changeable, lives long, and has many incoming references. Operational data is short-lived and can be changed by clients as well. Reference data also lives long and is immutable.

- A LINK LOOKUP RESOURCE can decouple API clients and API provider further (in terms of endpoint references in request and response message payload).

We modeled activity-oriented API endpoints as stateless or stateful PROCESSING RESOURCES. A Business Activity Processor is an important variant of PROCESSING RESOURCE, supporting two scenarios, frontend BPM and BPM services.

The runtime concerns of INFORMATION HOLDER RESOURCES and PROCESSING RESOURCES are different, and the architectural significance of a mere lookup often is different from that of a data transfer. Such considerations provide good reasons to call out these endpoint roles and the operation responsibilities and possibly to separate them by introducing multiple endpoints. These role-driven endpoints are designed and then operated differently at runtime. For instance, a dedicated MASTER DATA HOLDER management policy regarding data retention and protection might differ from the data management rules employed for PROCESSING RESOURCES that work with transient, short-lived data only.

We used the following role stereotypes from RDD [Wirfs-Brock 2002]: information holder (for data-oriented endpoints) and controller/coordinator (as roles taken by our PROCESSING RESOURCE pattern). Both endpoint patterns also qualify as interfacer and service provider.

Data-oriented holder resources and activity-oriented processors also have different characteristics in terms of their semantics, structure, quality, and evolution. For example, while an API may offer access to several individual data stores separately, clients may want to perform activities touching multiple backend/implementation resources in a single request. The API may therefore include a dedicated PROCESSING RESOURCE, playing the role of an RDD controller operating on top of (and/or processing data from) multiple, fine-grained INFORMATION HOLDER RESOURCES.[10]

We defined four types of operation responsibilities for endpoint resources. The four operation responsibilities differ in the way they read and write provider-side application state, as shown in Table 5.1.

Table 5.1 *Operation Impact on State by Responsibility Pattern*

	No Read	Read
No Write	COMPUTATION FUNCTION	RETRIEVAL OPERATION
Write	STATE CREATION OPERATION	STATE TRANSITION OPERATION

---

10. The *RESTful Web Services Cookbook* mentions such controller resources explicitly [Allamaraju 2010].

The patterns in this section compare to each other as follows:

- Just like a RETRIEVAL OPERATION, a COMPUTATION FUNCTION does not change the application state (but delivers nontrivial data to the client); it receives all required input from the client, whereas a RETRIEVAL OPERATION consults provider-side application state (in read-only mode).

- Both STATE CREATION OPERATIONS instances and COMPUTATION FUNCTIONS receive all required data from the client; a STATE CREATION OPERATION changes the provider-side application state (write access), whereas a COMPUTATION FUNCTION preserves it (no access).

- A STATE TRANSITION OPERATION also returns nontrivial data (like RETRIEVAL OPERATION and COMPUTATION FUNCTION), but it also changes the provider-side application state. Input comes from the client but also from the provider-side application state (read-write access).

Many COMPUTATION FUNCTIONS and STATE CREATION OPERATIONS can be designed to be idempotent. This also holds for most instances of RETRIEVAL OPERATIONS; some of these may be more difficult to make idempotent (for example, those using advanced caches or an implementation of the PAGINATION pattern using "Server Session State" [Fowler 2002]; note that this usually is not recommended for this reason). Some types of STATE TRANSITION OPERATIONS cause inherent state changes, for instance, when calls to the operations contribute to managing business process instances; idempotence is not always achievable in such cases. For instance, starting an activity is not idempotent if every start request may initiate a separate concurrent activity instance. Canceling a particular started activity instance, by contrast, is idempotent.

All operations, whether they realize any of the patterns presented in this chapter or not, communicate via request and response messages whose structure often is a PARAMETER TREE (a pattern from Chapter 4). The header and payload content of these messages can be designed—and then progressively improved to achieve certain qualities—with the help of the patterns in Chapters 6 and 7. Endpoints and entire APIs are usually versioned, and clients expect a lifetime and support guarantee for them (as discussed in Chapter 8). These guarantees and the versioning policy may differ by endpoint role; for instance, instances of the MASTER DATA HOLDER pattern live longer and change less frequently than OPERATIONAL DATA HOLDER instances (not only in terms of content and state, but also in terms of API and data definitions).

The roles and responsibilities of endpoints and their operations should be documented. They impact the business aspects of APIs (patterns in Chapter 9, "Document and Communicate API Contracts"): the API DESCRIPTION should specify when an API can be called and what the client can expect to be returned (assuming that a response is sent).

Software Systems Architecture: Working with Stakeholders Using Viewpoints and Perspectives [Rozanski 2005] has an information viewpoint. "Data on the Outside versus Data on the Inside" [Helland 2005] explains design forces and constraints for data exposed in APIs and application-internal data. While not specific to APIs and service-oriented systems, *Release It!* captures a number of patterns that promote stability (including reliability and manageability). Examples include "Circuit Breaker" and "Bulkhead" [Nygard 2018a]. *Site Reliability Engineering* [Beyer 2016] reports how Google runs production systems.

Next up are the responsibilities of message representations elements—and their structure (Chapter 6, "Design Request and Response Message Representations").

Chapter 6

Design Request and Response Message Representations

Having defined API endpoints and their operations in the previous chapter, we now look into the request and response messages that the API clients and providers exchange. These messages are a key part of the API contract; they bring or break interoperability. Large and rich messages might be very informative, but they also add runtime overhead; small and terse messages might be efficient to transport, but they might not be understood easily and may cause clients to emit follow-up requests to fully satisfy their information needs.

We start with a discussion of related design challenges and then introduce patterns responding to these challenges. The patterns are presented in two sections, "Element Stereotypes" and "Special-Purpose Representations."

This chapter corresponds to the Design phase of the Align-Define-Design-Refine (ADDR) process that we reviewed at the beginning of Part 2.

Introduction to Message Representation Design

API clients and providers exchange messages, usually represented in textual formats such as JSON or XML. According to our domain model introduced in Chapter 1, "Application Programming Interface (API) Fundamentals," these messages contain content representations that may be rather complex. The basic structure patterns introduced in Chapter 4, "Pattern Language Introduction"—ATOMIC PARAMETER, PARAMETER TREE, ATOMIC PARAMETER LIST, and PARAMETER FOREST—help define the names, types, and nesting of these request and response message elements. In addition to the payload (or body) of the messages, most communication protocols offer other ways to transport data. For example, HTTP allows transmitting key-value pairs as headers but also as path, query, and cookie parameters.

One might think that knowing about these different ways to exchange information is sufficient to design request and response messages. But if we look closer, we can detect recurring usage patterns in the message representation elements, leading to the following questions:

What are the meanings of the message elements? Can these meanings be stereotyped?

Which responsibilities within conversations do certain message elements have? Which quality goals do they help satisfy?

The patterns in this chapter answer these questions by first inspecting individual elements and then looking at composite representations for specific usage scenarios.

Challenges When Designing Message Representations

Two overarching themes for the patterns in this chapter are *message size* and *conversation verbosity* because these factors determine the resource consumption in API endpoint, network, and clients. Security, as a cross-cutting concern, is also influenced. The following architectural decision drivers also have to be taken into account:

- *Interoperability* on protocol and message content (format) level, as influenced by the communication platforms and the programming languages used by consumer and provider implementation (for example, during parameter marshaling and unmarshaling).

- *Latency* from API consumer/client point of view, for instance, determined by the network infrastructure (its bandwidth and the latency of the underlying hardware in particular) and endpoint processing effort for marshaling/unmarshaling the payload and delivering it to the API implementation.

- *Throughput* and *scalability* are primarily API provider concerns; response times should not degrade even if provider-side load grows because more clients use it (or existing clients cause more load).

- *Maintainability,* especially extensibility of existing messages, and the ability to deploy and evolve API clients and providers independently of each other. Modifiability is an important sub-concern of maintainability (for example, backward compatibility to promote parallel development and deployment flexibility).

- *Developer convenience and experience* on both the consumer and the provider sides, defined in terms of function, stability, ease of use, and clarity (including learning and programming effort). The wants and needs of these two sides often conflict. For instance, a data structure that is easy to create and populate might be difficult to read; a compact format that is light in transfer might be difficult to document, prepare, understand, and parse.

For some of these concerns, their impact on representations appearing in APIs is obvious; for others, the relationship will become clear as we proceed through this chapter. We cover detailed forces in the individual pattern texts that follow.

Patterns in this Chapter

DATA ELEMENTS are the fundamental building blocks of any client-provider communication, representing domain model concepts in request and response messages. By exposing the Published Language of the API [Evans 2003] through an explicit schema, provider-internal data definitions are not unveiled, and communication participants can be decoupled as much as possible.

Some of these DATA ELEMENTS have special missions because certain communicating participants appreciate or require additional information that is not part of the core domain model. This is the purpose of METADATA ELEMENTS. Frequently used types of METADATA ELEMENTS are *control metadata, provenance metadata*, and *aggregated metadata*.

Questions of identity arise in different parts of the API: endpoints, operations, and elements inside messages may require identification to prevent misunderstandings between decoupled clients and providers. ID ELEMENTS can be used to distinguish communication participants and API parts from each other. ID ELEMENTS can be globally unique or be valid within a certain constrained context. When they are network accessible, ID ELEMENTS turn into LINK ELEMENTS. LINK ELEMENTS often come in the form of Web-style hyperlinks, for instance, when working with HTTP resource APIs.

Many API providers want to identify the communication participants from which they receive messages. Such identity information helps determine whether a message originates from a registered, valid customer or some unknown client. A simple approach is to instruct clients to include an API KEY in each request message that the provider evaluates to identify and authenticate the client.

Combinations of basic DATA ELEMENTS result in more complex structures. One such example is an ERROR REPORT, a common message structure comprising DATA ELEMENTS, METADATA ELEMENTS, and ID ELEMENTS to report communication and processing faults. ERROR REPORTS state what happened when and where but also have to make sure not to disclose provider-side implementation details.

Context information is often transmitted in application- or transport-protocol-specific places. Sometimes it is useful to assemble a Context Representation out of Metadata Elements that can be placed in the message payload. Such representations may contain Id Elements, for instance, to correlate requests and responses or subsequent requests.

Figure 6.1 shows the patterns in the chapter and their relations.

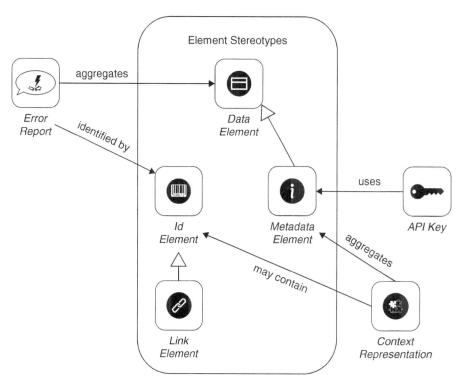

Figure 6.1 *Pattern map for this chapter: Element stereotypes and their relations to other patterns*

Element Stereotypes

The four patterns expressing data responsibilities are Data Element, Metadata Element, Id Element, and Link Element. These element stereotypes give meaning to the parts of request and response message representations.

Pattern:
DATA ELEMENT

When and Why to Apply

API endpoints and their operations have been identified on a high level of abstraction and refinement. For instance, in forward engineering, the key domain concepts to be exposed and their relationships have been elicited. In the context of system evolution and modernization, it has been decided to open up a system or provide a view on the content of a database or backend system via API endpoints and their operations.

An API "goals canvas" [Lauret 2019], an API "action plan" [Sturgeon 2016b], or another type of candidate endpoint list [Zimmermann 2021b] has been created; the operation signatures have been defined at least tentatively. The request and response message design is not yet finalized, however.

> How can domain- and application-level information be exchanged between API clients and API providers without exposing provider-internal data definitions in the API?

The exchanged data may or may not be involved in reading and writing the provider-side application state and data in the API implementation. Such relations should not be visible to the client.

> How can API client and API provider implementation be decoupled from a data management point of view?

In addition to the desire to promote loose coupling, the following competing forces concern whether data elements should be hidden behind the interface or be exposed (partially or fully):

* **Rich functionality versus ease of processing and performance:** The more data and behavior is modeled and exposed in an API and its underlying domain model, the more data processing options for the communication participants arise. However, it also becomes increasingly complex to read and write to instances of the domain model elements accurately and consistently. Interoperability is at risk, and the API documentation effort increases. Remote object references and procedure invocation stubs might be convenient to program against and be supported in tools, but they quickly make the communication stateful. Statefulness, in turn, violates SOA principles and microservices tenets.

- **Security and data privacy versus ease of configuration:** Letting a communication partner know many details about an application and its data introduces security threats such as the risk that data is tampered with. Extra data protection, on the other hand, can cause configuration and processing effort. Security-related information might have to travel with request and response payload and therefore becomes part of the technical part of the API DESCRIPTION.

- **Maintainability versus flexibility:** The data contract and its implementations should be flexible to accommodate continuously changing requirements; however, any new feature and change to an existing feature has to be analyzed with respect to compatibility issues and, if implemented, be maintained in the future (if clients still use it). To satisfy the information needs of different clients, API operations sometimes offer different data representations in a customizable way. The customization means must be designed, implemented, documented, and taught. All possible combinations must be tested and supported as the API evolves. Hence, the provided flexibility means may increase maintenance efforts.[1]

One could send plain, unstructured strings to be interpreted by the consumer, but in many domains, such an ad hoc approach to API design is not adequate. For instance, when integrating enterprise applications, it couples API client and provider tightly and may harm performance and auditability.

One could use object-based remoting concepts such as Common Object Request Broker Architecture (CORBA) or Java RMI (Remote Method Invocation), but remoting paradigms based on distributed objects have been reported to lead to integration solutions being difficult to test, operate, and maintain in the long term [Hohpe 2003].[2]

How It Works

▼

Define a dedicated vocabulary of DATA ELEMENTS for request and response messages that wraps and/or maps the relevant parts of the data in the business logic of an API implementation.

▲

In domain-driven design (DDD) terms, such a dedicated vocabulary is called *Published Language* [Evans 2003]. It shields the DDD Aggregates, Entities, and Value Objects in the domain layer. With respect to the concepts in our domain model, introduced in Chapter 1, DATA ELEMENTS describe a general role for the message representation elements (also known as parameters).

---

1. Also see discussions about SEMANTIC VERSIONING, API DESCRIPTION (including technical service contracts), WISH LIST, and SERVICE LEVEL AGREEMENT in Chapters 7, 8, and 9.

2. Distributed objects and other forms of remote references are core concepts in the integration style "Remote Procedure Invocation" [Hohpe 2003].

The DATA ELEMENT can be flat, unstructured ATOMIC PARAMETERS or ATOMIC PARAMETER LISTS. Basic DATA ELEMENTS may form the leaves of PARAMETER TREES; more complex ones often contain an ID ELEMENT and feature a number of domain-specific attributes as additional structured or unstructured values. Single or multiple instances of these data elements that jointly comprise the application state may be exposed; if multiple instances are managed and transferred jointly, they form an element *collection* [Allamaraju 2010; Serbout 2021], also known as element set.

Explicit schema definitions for the message representation elements should be defined (and shared with the API clients) in the API DESCRIPTION.[3] Open, tool-supported formats such as JSON or XML are commonly used in these *data contracts*. Exemplary instances should be provided of data that pass the schema validation. The schema can promote strong typing and validation but also be rather generic and only weakly typed. Key-value lists are often used in generic interfaces `<ID, key1, value1, key 2, value 2, ... keyn, valuen>`.

Figure 6.2 sketches two types of DATA ELEMENTS with exemplary attributes, placed in message representations. One is typed, one is generic.

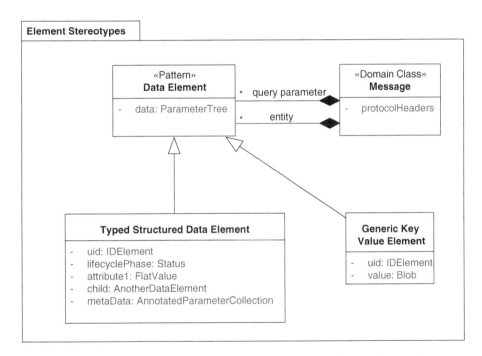

Figure 6.2 *DATA ELEMENTS can either be generic or typed, providing supplemental information optionally*

---

3. According to our API domain model from Chapter 1, these data transfer representations (DTRs) are wire-level equivalents of program-level data transfer objects (DTOs) described by [Daigneau 2011] and [Fowler 2002].

The attributes of DATA ELEMENTS can be role-stereotyped, for instance, into "descriptive attributes," "time-dependent attributes," "life cycle state attributes," and "operational state attributes," according to Rebecca Wirfs-Brock in her presentation "Cultivating Your Design Heuristics" [Wirfs-Brock 2019, p. 39].

To support nesting and structuring of entities in the API operations, for instance, following a relationship from an order to the purchased product and the buying customer in an online shop, an EMBEDDED ENTITY can be included. Alternatively, a LINKED INFORMATION HOLDER might reference a separate API endpoint. An EMBEDDED ENTITY contains one or more nested DATA ELEMENTS, while a LINKED INFORMATION HOLDER contains navigable LINK ELEMENTS that point at API endpoints that provide information about relationship target(s) such as INFORMATION HOLDER RESOURCES.

Variants   Two variants of this pattern are worth calling out. An *Entity Element* is a DATA ELEMENT that contains an identifier hinting at an object life cycle in the implementation of the Published Language of the API (hence, our terminology here is in line with the "Entity" pattern in [Evans 2003]).

A *Query Parameter* is a DATA ELEMENT that does not represent one or more entities owned and managed by the API implementation. Instead, it represents an expression that can be used to select a subset of such entities when exposing a RETRIEVAL OPERATION in an endpoint, for instance, an INFORMATION HOLDER RESOURCE.

Example
The following excerpt from the solution-internal API of a customer relationship management (CRM) system features strongly typed DATA ELEMENTS: a structured one, name, and a flat, textual one, phoneNumber (contract notation: Microservice Domain-Specific Language (MDSL), introduced in Appendix C):

```
data type Customer {
  "customerId": ID,
    "name": ("first":D<string>, "last":D<string>),
    "phoneNumber":D<string>
}


endpoint type CustomerRelationshipManagementService
  exposes
      operation getCustomer
        expecting payload "customerId": ID
        delivering payload Customer
```

Customer is a PARAMETER TREE that combines the two data elements. The example also features an ATOMIC PARAMETER and ID ELEMENT: customerId. Note that these data representations might have been specified in a domain model first; that said, the domain model elements used for the API implementation should not be exposed directly without wrapping and/or mapping them; loose coupling of the client, interface, and implementation is desired.

Discussion

A rich, deeply structured Published Language is expressive but also hard to secure and maintain; a simple one can be taught and understood easily but may not be able to represent the domain specifics adequately. This set of trade-offs makes API design hard; answering the data contract granularity question is nontrivial.

Reasonable compromises regarding these conflicting forces require an iterative and incremental approach to pattern selection and adoption; best practices on DDD in service design have been published and should be considered [Vernon 2013]; Appendix A summarizes some of these and adds our own insights. The use of many domain-driven DATA ELEMENTS makes APIs expressive so that clients can find and use what they need easily.

Security and data privacy can be improved by exposing as few DATA ELEMENTS as possible. Lean interfaces also promote maintainability and ease of configuration (that is, flexibility on the provider side). "Less is more" and "if in doubt, leave it out" are rules of thumb when defining secure data contracts in APIs. The "less is more" philosophy may limit expressiveness, but it promotes understandability. The entity data must be included in any security analysis and design activities, such as threat modeling, security and compliance by design, penetration testing, and compliance audits [Julisch 2011]. This is an essential point because sensitive information may be leaked otherwise.

Using the same DATA ELEMENT structures across an entire API or a set of in-house services allows for easier composition of the services. *Enterprise Integration Patterns* calls such an approach a "Canonical Data Model" but advises to handle it with care [Hohpe 2003]. One can consider microformats [Microformats 2022] in such a standardization effort.

If many related/nested DATA ELEMENTS are defined, some of which are optional, processing becomes complicated; performance and testability are impaired. While client-side flexibility is high initially, things get difficult when the rich API starts to change over time.

Organizational patterns (and antipatterns), such as the "not invented here" syndrome and "fiefdoms" or "power games," often lead to overengineered, unnecessarily complex abstractions. Simply exposing such abstractions via a new API (without putting "Anti-Corruption Layers" [Evans 2003] in place that hide complexity) is bound to fail in the long run. Project schedules and budgets are at risk in such cases.

Related Patterns

A Data Element can contain instances of the "Value Object" pattern in DDD [Evans 2003] in transit; DDD "Entity" is represented as a variant of our pattern. That said, one should be aware that instances of DDD patterns should not be translated into API designs one-to-one. While an Anti-Corruption Layer can protect the downstream participant in a relation (here, API client), the upstream (here, API provider) should design its Published Language in such a way that undesired coupling is minimized [Vernon 2013].

It might make sense to have different representations for the same entity depending on the context it is used in. For example, a customer is a widespread business concept modeled as an entity in many domain models; typically, many of its attributes are relevant only in certain use cases (for example, account information for the payment domain). In that case, a Wish List can let clients decide what information they want. In HTTP resource APIs, content negotiation and custom media types provide flexible realization options for multipurpose representations. The "Media Type Negotiation" pattern in *Service Design Patterns* is related [Daigneau 2011].

Core J2EE Patterns [Alur 2013] presents a "Data Transfer Object" pattern for use within an application boundary (for example, data transfer between tiers). *Patterns of Enterprise Application Architecture* [Fowler 2002] touches on many aspects of remote API design, such as Remote Facades and DTOs. Similarly, Eric Evans touches on functional API aspects in DDD patterns such as "Bounded Contexts" and "Aggregates" [Evans 2003]. Instances of these patterns contain multiple entities; hence, they can be used to assemble Data Elements into coarser-grained units.

The general data modeling patterns in [Hay 1996] cover data representations but focus on data storage and presentation rather than data transport (therefore, the discussed forces differ from ours). Domain-specific modeling archetypes for enterprise information systems also can be found in the literature [Arlow 2004].

The "Cloud Adoption Patterns" Web site [Brown 2021] has a process pattern called "Identify Entities and Aggregates."

More Information

Chapter 3 in the *RESTful Web Services Cookbook* gives representation design advice in the context of HTTP; for instance, recipe 3.4 discusses how to choose a representation format and a media type (with Atom being one of the options) [Allamaraju 2010].

Design Practice Reference features DDD and related agile practices eligible in API and data contract design [Zimmermann 2021b].

Context Mapper clarifies the relationships between strategic DDD patterns in its domain-specific language (DSL) and tools [Kapferer 2021].

Pattern:
METADATA ELEMENT

When and Why to Apply

The request and response message representations of an API operation have been defined using one or more of the basic structure patterns ATOMIC PARAMETER, ATOMIC PARAMETER LIST, PARAMETER TREE, and PARAMETER FOREST. To process these representations accurately and efficiently, message receivers require their name and type, but also appreciate more information about their meaning and content.

> How can messages be enriched with additional information so that receivers can interpret the message content correctly without having to hardcode assumptions about the data semantics?

In addition to the quality concerns discussed at the beginning of this chapter, the impact on interoperability, coupling, and ease of use versus runtime efficiency have to be considered.

- **Interoperability:** If data travels with corresponding type, version, and author information, the receiver can use this extra information to resolve syntactic and semantic ambiguities. For example, one representation element might contain a monetary value, and an extra element might specify the currency of this value. The fact that an optional element is not present or that a mandatory element is not set to a meaningful value can also be indicated by extra information.

- **Coupling:** If runtime data is accompanied by additional explanatory data, it becomes easier to interpret and process; the shared knowledge between consumer and provider is made explicit and shifted from the design-time API contract to the runtime message content; this may add to the coupling of the communication parties but may also decrease it. Low coupling eases long-term maintenance.

- **Ease of use versus runtime efficiency:** Extra representation elements in the payload may help the message recipient to understand the message content and process it efficiently. However, such elements increase the message size; they require processing and transport capacity and have an inherent complexity. The API test cases have to cover its creation and usage. A client that hardcodes assumptions about data semantics (including their meaning and any restrictions that might apply) be easier to write, but it will be harder to maintain over time as requirements change and the API evolves.

The extra data that explains other data can be provided solely in the API DESCRIPTION. Such static and explicit metadata documentation often is sufficient; however, it limits the ability of the message receiver to make metadata-based decisions dynamically at runtime.

A second API endpoint could be introduced to inquire about metadata separately. However, such an approach bloats the API and introduces additional documentation/training, testing, and maintenance effort.

How It Works

Introduce one or more METADATA ELEMENTS to explain and enhance the other representation elements that appear in request and response messages. Populate the values of the METADATA ELEMENTS thoroughly and consistently; use them to steer interoperable, efficient message consumption and processing.

Metadata and metadata modeling are mature and well-established concepts in many fields in computer science, for example, databases and programming languages under terms such as *runtime type information, reflection,* and *introspection.* In the real world, book libraries and document archives apply it extensively.

Many instances of this pattern are simple and scalar ATOMIC PARAMETERS with a name and a type (such as Boolean, integer, or string), but metadata can also be aggregated and composed into PARAMETER TREE hierarchies. A flexible but somewhat error-prone solution is to represent METADATA ELEMENTS as pairs of key-value strings that are then parsed and typecasted at the message recipient.

Figure 6.3 shows the pattern in context. METADATA ELEMENTS become part of the API DESCRIPTION. They have to be kept current while an API evolves, both on the specification (schema) level and on the content (instance) level. The metadata currentness (or freshness) should be specified to balance usefulness for the client with effort to compute and keep up to date. Some metadata, such as the original creator of a document, might be immutable. For some metadata, for example, list counters, it might make sense to define an expiration date. Interoperability might suffer otherwise, and semantic mismatches might remain undetected.

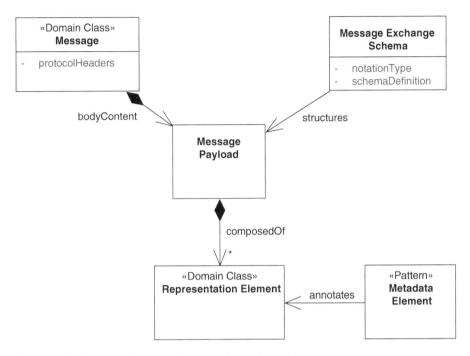

Figure 6.3 *Usage of METADATA ELEMENTS (data about data) in context*

Variants   Three variants of this pattern exist, representing particular types and usage of metadata we observed in APIs:

- *Control Metadata Elements* such as identifiers, flags, filters, hypermedia controls, links, security information (including API KEYS, access control lists, role credentials, checksums, and message digests) steer the processing. Query parameters can be seen as a special case of control metadata when driving the behavior of the query engine on the provider side. Control metadata often comes in the form of Boolean, strings, or numeric parameters.

- *Aggregated Metadata Elements* provide semantic analyses or summaries of other representation elements. Calculations such as counters of PAGINATION units qualify as instances of this variant. Statistical information about entity elements in the Published Language, such as insurance claims by customer or product sales per quarter, also qualifies as aggregated metadata.

- *Provenance Metadata Elements* unveil the origin of data. In our context of API design, examples include owner, message/request IDs, creation date and other timestamps, location information, version numbers, and other context information.

These variants are visualized in Figure 6.4. Other forms of METADATA ELEMENTS exist (covered later).

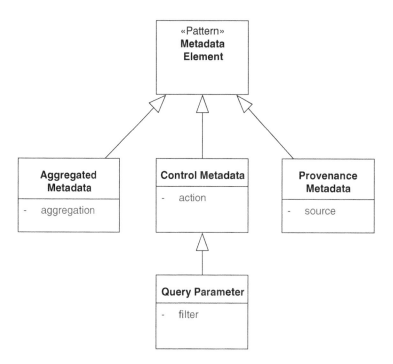

Figure 6.4 *METADATA ELEMENT variants*

Each METADATA ELEMENT can realize more than one of the variants. For instance, a region code might give provenance information but also be used to control data processing. Such data might act as a filter in a digital rights management scenario or be used in "Context-Based Routers" in enterprise application integration [Hohpe 2003].

In information management, three main types of metadata are used to describe any type of resource (such as a book or multimedia content) [Zeng 2015]: Descriptive metadata has purposes such as discovery and identification; it can include elements such as title, abstract, author, and keywords. Structural metadata indicates how compound information elements are put together, for example, how pages (or sections) are ordered to form chapters. Administrative metadata provides information to help manage a resource, such as when and how it was created, what its file type and other technical properties are, and who can access it. Two common subsets of administrative data are rights management metadata, including intellectual property rights, and preservation metadata, which contains information used to archive a resource.

Example

The following example from the Lakeside Mutual case study shows all three metadata types: provenance (`Content-Type`, `Date`), control (the API Key `b318ad-736c6c844b` in the header), and aggregated metadata (`size`).

```
curl -X GET --header 'Authorization: Bearer b318ad736c6c844b' \
--verbose http://localhost:8110/customers\?limit\=1
> GET /customers?limit=1 HTTP/1.1
> Host: localhost:8110
> User-Agent: curl/7.77.0
> Accept: */*
> Authorization: Bearer b318ad736c6c844b
>
< HTTP/1.1 200
< ETag: "0fcf9424c411d523774dc45cc974190ff"
< X-Content-Type-Options: nosniff
< X-XSS-Protection: 1; mode=block
< Content-Type: application/hal+json
< Content-Length: 877
< Date: Fri, 19 Nov 2021 15:10:41 GMT
<
{
  "filter": "",
  "limit": 1,
  "offset": 0,
  "size": 50,
  "customers": [ {
    ...
  } ],
  "_links": {
    "self": {
      "href": "/customers?filter=&limit=1&offset=0"
    },
    "next": {
      "href": "/customers?filter=&limit=1&offset=1"
    }
  }
}
```

Most Metadata Elements are Atomic Parameters in this example. The JSON object `_links` forms a simple Parameter Tree that bundles two Atomic Parameters serving as Link Elements.

Discussion

Accuracy usually improves when the pattern is applied (assuming a correct and consistent implementation). Coupling decreases on the data level but is still there on the metadata level. Ease of use can be achieved.

Processing efficiency may suffer due to the increased message sizes. Maintainability, security, and interoperability may improve but also suffer depending on the amount, structure, and meaning of the metadata. Excessive use of such METADATA ELEMENTS risks bloating an interface and making it more challenging to maintain and evolve (for example, in terms of SEMANTIC VERSIONING).

Defined, populated, exchanged, and interpreted wisely, METADATA ELEMENTS can streamline receiver-side processing (by avoiding unnecessary work), improve computation results and their display (by steering/guiding the application frontend and the human user), and contribute to an end-to-end security model that protects the communication participants from external and internal threats. Security metadata may serve as input to encryption/decryption algorithms, support integrity checks, and so on.

Metadata can reside and be defined in several of the logical layers defined in *Patterns of Enterprise Application Architecture* [Fowler 2002]. PAGINATION, for instance, is a presentation layer or service layer concern; the business logic layer of the provider-side API implementation does not care about it. The same holds for caching of previous responses. Access/access control type of metadata typically also is created and used on the presentation or service layer. Data provenance and validity information such as video/audio owners and intellectual property rights in media streaming APIs and certain types of control metadata belong to the business logic layer. Query statistics and aggregations, on the other hand, can be seen as data access layer (or persistence layer) information. If lower-layer metadata is already present, API designs must decide whether to pass this metadata on or to convert and wrap it (tradeoff: effort versus coupling).

The client should depend on metadata only when it is necessary to satisfy mandatory functional and nonfunctional requirements. In all other cases, the available metadata should be treated as an optional convenience feature to make API usage more efficient; the API and its clients should still function if the metadata is not present. For example, control metadata such as PAGINATION links and related page counts will make the client depend on it once introduced. Some aggregation metadata, such as the size of embedded entity collections, can be calculated on the message receiver side rather than on the provider side alternatively.

An alternative to adding metadata to request or response messages is to foresee a dedicated operation returning metadata about a particular API element. In such a design, an ID ELEMENT or LINK ELEMENT identifies the data that is supplemented with metadata; the dedicated operation takes the form of a RETRIEVAL OPERATION. An even more advanced approach is to define dedicated *Metadata Information Holders* as special types of MASTER DATA HOLDER (or REFERENCE DATA HOLDER if immutable), possibly referenced indirectly via LINK LOOKUP RESOURCES.

ETags in HTTP messages, defined in RFC 7232 [Fielding 2014a] can be seen as control and provenance metadata; expiration dates of one-time-only passwords qualify as metadata too. The CONDITIONAL REQUEST pattern explains and elaborates on ETags in Chapter 7, "Refine Message Design for Quality."

Related Patterns

A METADATA ELEMENT is a specialization of the more abstract concept of a DATA ELEMENT; not all metadata affects business logic and domain model in the API implementation (as explained earlier). ID ELEMENTS sometimes are accompanied by additional METADATA ELEMENTS (for instance, to classify the identifier/link or to define an expiration time). Metadata often comes in the syntactic form of ATOMIC PARAMETERS. Several related instances of the pattern can be transported as ATOMIC PARAMETER LISTS or be included in PARAMETER TREES.

The PAGINATION pattern relies on metadata to inform the client about the current, previous, and next result pages; the total amount of pages/results; and so on. Hypermedia controls such as typed link relations contain metadata as well (as explained later in the LINK ELEMENT pattern).

A "Context Object" to which "Interceptors" can add their information is presented in several pattern languages, including *Remoting Patterns* [Voelter 2004]. Our CONTEXT REPRESENTATION pattern suggests defining an API-wide, technology-independent standard location and structure for metadata in general and control metadata in particular.

The "Format Indicator" and "Message Expiration" information, both introduced in *Enterprise Integration Patterns* [Hohpe 2003], rely on metadata. The same holds for control and provenance information such as "message id" and "message date" in messaging APIs such as Jakarta Messaging (formerly JMS). Other enterprise integration patterns, for instance, "Correlation Identifier" and "Routing Slip," can be seen as special METADATA ELEMENTS. A Correlation Identifier holds control metadata primarily but also shares provenance metadata (because it identifies a previous request message). The same holds for "Return Address" (because it points at an endpoint or channel). "Message Filters," "Message Selectors," and "Aggregators" often operate on control and provenance metadata.

More Information

For a general introduction to types of metadata and eligible standards, refer to the following sources:

- The Wikipedia page on metadata [Wikipedia 2022c]; Wikipedia also lists numerous metadata standards focusing on certain areas, for instance, document identification (DOIs) and security assertions (SAML) [Wikipedia 2022d].

- *Understanding Metadata: What Is Metadata, and What Is It For?* [Riley 2017].

- Dublin Core [DCMI 2020] is a widely adopted metadata standard for networked resources such as books or digital multimedia content.

The information management literature covers metadata in depth. Two examples are "A Gentle Introduction to Metadata" [Good 2002] and *Introduction to Metadata* [Baca 2016]. Murtha Baca distinguishes fives types of metadata [Baca 2016]:

- Administrative: metadata used in managing and administering collections and information resources

- Descriptive: metadata used to identify, authenticate, and describe collections and related trusted information resources

- Preservation: metadata related to the preservation management of collections and information resources

- Technical: metadata related to how a system functions or metadata behaves

- Use: metadata related to the level and type of use of collections and information resources

These metadata types are also summarized in the tutorial Metadata Basics [Zeng 2015].

Our Control Metadata Element variant corresponds to the technical type, and use information often comes as Aggregate Metadata Element. Provenance Metadata Elements often have an administrative, descriptive, or preservation nature.

The *Zalando RESTful API and Event Scheme Guidelines* [Zalando 2021] point out the importance of OpenAPI metadata. A blog post by Steve Klabnik covers metadata in resource representations [Klabnik 2011].

Pattern:
ID ELEMENT

When and Why to Apply

A domain model representing the core concepts of an application, software-intensive system, or software ecosystem has been designed and implemented. Remote access to the domain model implementation is under construction (for instance, as HTTP resources, Web service operations, or gRPC service methods). Architectural principles such as loose coupling, independent deployability, and isolation (of system parts and data) might have been established.

The domain model consists of multiple related elements that have different life cycles and semantics. Its currently chosen decomposition into remotely accessible API endpoints (for instance, exposed by a set of microservices) suggests that these related entities should be split up into several API endpoints and operations (for instance, HTTP resources exposing uniform POST-GET-PUT-PATCH-DELETE interfaces, Web service port types with operations, or gRPC services and methods). API clients want to be able to follow the relationships within and across API boundaries to satisfy their information and integration needs. To do so, both design-time artifacts and runtime instances of such artifacts have to be pointed at without ambiguities or mistakes in names.

> How can API elements be distinguished from each other at design time and at runtime?

API elements requiring identification include endpoints, operations, and representation elements in request and response messages. They may or may not have been designed with DDD:

> When applying domain-driven design, how can elements of the Published Language be identified?

The following nonfunctional requirements have to be satisfied when addressing these identification problems:

- **Effort versus stability:** In many APIs, plain character strings are used as logical names. Such *local identifiers* are easy to create but may become ambiguous when used outside their original context (for instance, when clients work with multiple APIs). They might have to be changed in that case. On the contrary, *global* *identifiers* are designed to last longer but require some address space coordination and maintenance. In both cases, the namespace should be designed with care and purpose. Changing requirements might make it necessary to rename elements, and API versions might become incompatible with prior versions. In such cases, certain names may no longer be unique and may therefore cause conflicts.

- **Readability for machines and humans:** Humans who work with identifiers include developers, system administrators, and system and process assurance auditors. Long, logically structured, and/or self-explanatory names are more accessible for humans than are short, encrypted, and/or encoded ones. However, humans often do not want to read identifiers in their entirety; for instance, the primary audience for query parameters and session identifiers is the API implementation and supporting infrastructure, not an end user of a Web application.

- **Security (confidentiality):** In many application contexts, it should be impossible, or at least extremely hard, to guess instance identifiers; however, the effort to create unique identifiers that cannot be spoofed must be justified. Testers, support staff, and other stakeholders of an API DESCRIPTION may want to be able to understand, and possibly even memorize, identifiers even if they qualify as sensitive information that has to be protected.

One could always embed all related payload data as EMBEDDED ENTITIES, thus avoiding the need to introduce identifiers referencing information that is not included. But this simple solution wastes processing and communication resources if information is transferred that receivers do not require. The construction of a complex, partially redundant payload can also be error-prone.

How It Works

Introduce a special type of Data Element, a unique ID ELEMENT, to identify API endpoints, operations, and message representation elements that have to be distinguished from each other. Use these ID ELEMENTS consistently throughout API description and implementation. Decide whether an ID ELEMENT is globally unique or valid only within the context of a particular API.

Decide on the naming scheme to be used in the API, and document it in the API DESCRIPTION. Following are popular approaches to unique identification:

- Numeric universally unique identifiers (UUIDs) [Leach 2005] supply ID ELEMENTS in many distributed systems. Often, 128-bit integers serve as UUIDs.

Many standard libraries of programming languages can generate them. In some sources, UUIDs are also called *globally unique identifiers (GUIDs)*.

- Some cloud providers generate *human-readable strings* to identify service instances uniquely (discussed shortly); such an approach is also feasible for ID ELEMENTS appearing in request and response messages.

- The use of *surrogate key* identifiers assigned by lower layers in the overall architecture (for example, operating system, database, or messaging system) is another approach. Primary keys assigned by databases fall in this category.

Instances of the ID ELEMENT pattern often travel as ATOMIC PARAMETERS; they may also become entries in ATOMIC PARAMETER LISTS or leaves of PARAMETER TREES. The API DESCRIPTION specifies the scope of the ID ELEMENT (locally vs. globally unique?) and the lifetime of the uniqueness guarantee. Figure 6.5 shows that ID ELEMENTS are special types of DATA ELEMENTS. URIs and URNs as two types of human-readable strings appear in the figure.

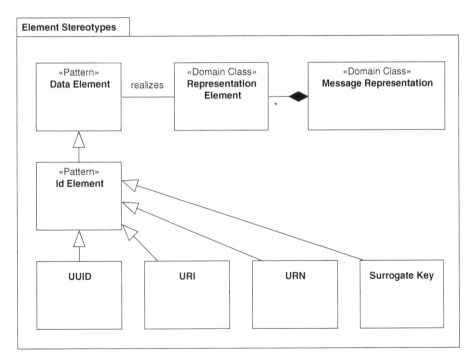

Figure 6.5 *ID ELEMENTS come in different forms: UUID, URI, URN, Surrogate Key*

Note that identifiers can be made both human- and machine-readable. If identifiers have to be entered by users at times, choose a scheme that creates short names that are easy to pronounce. For instance, see the names for applications created by the cloud provider Heroku; an example is `peaceful-reaches-47689`). Otherwise, go with numeric UUIDs. The blog site Medium, for instance, uses hybrid URIs as page identifiers; an example of a story URI is `https://medium.com/olzzio/seven-microservices-tenets-e97d6b0990a4`.

If mandated by the security requirements, make sure that any exposed ID ELEMENT—no matter whether it is a UUID, a human-readable string, or a surrogate key coming from the API implementation—is random and unpredictable and that access to the identified elements is protected by an appropriate authorization mechanism, as recommended by OWASP to prevent broken object-level authorization [Yalon 2019].

URIs are globally unique, for instance, but can be reassigned over time (and then link to unexpected targets, for instance, when used by older clients or when working with restored backup data). Sometimes, Unified Resource Names (URNs) are preferred over URIs, using a hierarchical `prefix:firstname:lastname` syntax according to RFC 2141 [Moats 1997]:

```
<URN> ::= "urn:" <NID> ":" <NSS>
```

`<NID>` is the namespace identifier, and `<NSS>` is the namespace-specific string. Examples of URNs can be found on its Wikipedia page [Wikipedia 2022e].

Example

PAGINATION cursors in the Twitter REST API [Twitter 2022] use ID ELEMENTS, for instance, `next_cursor`:

```
{
    "data": [...],
    "next_cursor": "c-3yvu1pzhd3i7",
    "request": {...}
}
```

The API implementation added an autogenerated identifier for the `next_cursor` in this HTTP response snippet. This identifier must be guaranteed to be unique at least until the user session expires. Also, the association between this identifier and the next cursor position for this user session must be stored so that the correct content is returned when the user requests the `next_cursor` with this identifier via HTTP GET. This example also shows that the scope of the identifier can be bound not only by space but also by time.

Discussion

ID ELEMENTS such as UUIDs and URNs provide a good balance between being short and easy to process but also expressive enough to identify members of a large entity population and guarantee secure and reliable uniqueness in distributed systems (if constructed and managed correctly). The implementation of the ID generation algorithm determines how accurate they are.

Local identifiers are straightforward to create. Plain string identifiers are easy for humans to process and compare, for example, when debugging. UUIDs are hard to remember and process manually but still are easier to handle than hashed or generated content such as access tokens that may be hundreds of characters long. Using plain and primitive string literals as identifiers is usually not future-proof; systems and system integrations come, change, and go over time. The less expressive names are, the more likely it is that similar or identical names are used elsewhere.

A simplistic approach would be to use auto-incrementing numbers such as `sid001`, `sid002`, and so on. But there are several problems with this. Besides leaking information, it is unnecessarily hard to keep these numbers unique in distributed settings (which introduce security threats, discussed later).

Ideally, all identifiers of a certain kind spread across a distributed system should share the same structure or naming scheme; end-to-end monitoring and event correlation during root cause analyses in incident management are simplified this way. Still, sometimes it is preferable (or unavoidable) to switch the scheme for different entities (for instance, when legacy system constraints come into play). This is an instance of a common conflict: flexibility versus simplicity.

UUIDs alone may not be suitable in all cases. UUID generation is implementation-dependent and varies between libraries and programming languages. Although they usually are 128-bits long (according to RFC 4122), some implementations follow a somewhat predictable pattern, making it possible for brute force attackers to guess them. It depends on the project context and requirements whether such "guessability" is a problem. ID ELEMENTS must be included in any security analysis and design activities such as threat modeling, security and compliance by design, penetration testing, and compliance audits [Julisch 2011].

When multiple systems and components are integrated to realize the API, it is hard to guarantee the uniqueness of surrogate keys from lower logical layers (such as the database implementation) that become API-level ID ELEMENTS. Security concerns also arise. Furthermore, the database keys of the corresponding entities are not allowed to change in this case, even when recovering the database from a backup. Implementation-level surrogate keys couple every consumer tightly to the database.

Related Patterns

An ID ELEMENT can travel as an ATOMIC PARAMETER and be contained in PARAMETER TREES. API KEYS and VERSION IDENTIFIERS can be seen as particular kinds of identifiers. MASTER DATA HOLDERS often require robust identification schemes because of their longevity; OPERATIONAL DATA HOLDERS typically are identified uniquely as well. The data elements returned by REFERENCE DATA HOLDERS may serve as ID ELEMENTS, for instance, zip codes identifying cities (or parts of them). LINK LOOKUP RESOURCES may expect ID ELEMENTS in requests and deliver LINK ELEMENTS in responses; DATA TRANSFER RESOURCES use locally or globally unique ID ELEMENTS to define the transfer units or storage locations; examples of such design can be found in cloud storage offerings such as AWS Simple Storage Service (S3) with its URI-identified buckets.

Local identifiers are not sufficient to implement REST fully (up to maturity level 3). If plain or structured global identifiers turn out to be insufficient, one can switch to using absolute URIs, as described in the LINK ELEMENT pattern. LINK ELEMENTS make remote reference to API elements not only globally unique but also network accessible; they often are used to realize LINKED INFORMATION HOLDERS.

A "Correlation Identifier" and a "Return Address" and the keys used in the "Claim Check" and the "Format Identifier" patterns [Hohpe 2003] are related patterns. Creating unique identifiers is also required when applying these patterns (that have a different usage context).

More Information

"Quick Guide to GUIDs" [GUID 2022] provides a deeper discussion of GUIDs, including their pros and cons.

The distributed systems literature discusses general naming, identification, and addressing approaches (for instance, [Tanenbaum 2007]). RFC 4122 [Leach 2005] describes the basic algorithm for random number generation. XML namespaces and Java package names are hierarchal, globally unique identification concepts [Zimmermann 2003].

Pattern:
LINK ELEMENT

When and Why to Apply

A domain model consists of multiple related elements with varying life cycles and semantics. The currently chosen wrapping and mapping of this model in the API suggests that these related entities should be exposed separately.

API clients want to follow element relationships and call additional API operations to satisfy their overall information and integration needs. Following a relationship, for instance, can define the next processing step offered by a PRO-CESSING RESOURCE or provide more details about the content of an INFORMATION HOLDER RESOURCE that appears in a collection or an overview report. The address where this next processing step can be invoked must be specified somewhere; a mere ID ELEMENT is not sufficient.[4]

How can API endpoints and operations be referenced in request and response message payloads so that they can be called remotely?

More specifically:

How can globally unique, network-accessible pointers to API endpoints and their operations be included in request and response messages? How can these pointers be used to allow clients to drive provider-side state transitions and operation invocation sequencing?

The requirements here are similar to those for the sibling pattern ID ELEMENT; endpoint and operation identification should be unique, easy to create and read, stable, and secure. The remoting context of this pattern makes it necessary to deal with broken links and network failures.

One could use simple ID ELEMENTS to identify related remote resources/entities, but additional processing is required to turn these identifiers into network addresses on the Web. ID ELEMENTS are managed in the context of the API endpoint implementation that assigns them. For local ID ELEMENTS to be used as pointers to other API endpoints, they would have to be combined with the unique network address of the endpoint.

How It Works

Include a special type of ID ELEMENT, a LINK ELEMENT, to request or response messages. Let these LINK ELEMENTS act as human- and machine-readable, network-accessible pointers to other endpoints and operations. Optionally, let additional METADATA ELEMENTS annotate and explain the nature of the relationship.

---

4. Such pointers are required to implement the REST principle of Hypertext as the Engine of Application State (HATEOAS) [Allamaraju 2010] with "Hypermedia Controls" [Webber 2010; Amundsen 2011]. PAGINATION of query response results delivered by RETRIEVAL OPERATIONS requires such control links too.

When realizing HTTP resource APIs on REST maturity level 3, add metadata as needed to support hypermedia controls, for instance, the HTTP verb and MIME type that is supported (and expected) by the link target resource.

The instances of the LINK ELEMENT pattern may travel as ATOMIC PARAMETERS; they may also become entries in ATOMIC PARAMETER LISTS or leaves of PARAMETER TREES. Figure 6.6 illustrates the solution on a conceptual level, featuring HTTP URI as a prominent technology-level installment.

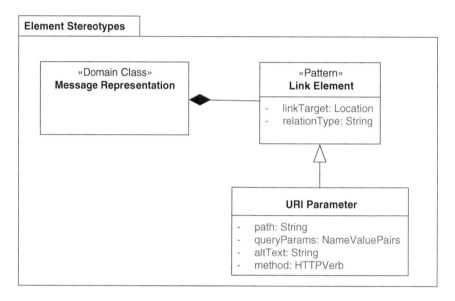

Figure 6.6 *LINK ELEMENT solution*

The links should contain not only an address (such as a URL in RESTful HTTP) but also information about the semantics and consequences of following the link in a subsequent API call:

- Does the LINK ELEMENTS indicate a next possible or required processing step, for instance, in a long-running business process?
- Does it allow undoing and/or compensating a previous action?
- Does the link point at the next slice of a result set (such as a page in PAGINATION)?
- Does the link provide access to detailed information about a particular item?
- Or does it allow to switch to "something completely different"?[5]

---

5. https://en.wikipedia.org/wiki/And_Now_for_Something_Completely_Different.

Answering the preceding questions, semantic *link types* typically include the following:

1. *Next:* Next processing step when an incremental service type (for example, a PROCESSING RESOURCE) is used.

2. *Undo:* Undo or compensation operation in the current context.

3. *More:* The address to retrieve more results. This can also be seen as making a horizontal move in result data.

4. *Details:* Further information about the link source. Following this link performs a vertical move in the data.

Some link types have been registered and therefore standardized somewhat. See, for instance, the Internet Assigned Numbers Authority's collection of link relation types [IANA 2020] and *Design and Build Great Web APIs: Robust, Reliable, and Resilient* by Mike Amundsen [Amundsen 2020].

Application-Level Profile Semantics (ALPS) [Amundsen 2021] can be used to define Web links. Siren [Swiber 2017], another hypermedia specification for representing entities, implements the pattern in JSON. Here is the example given in the Siren repository:

```
{
   "links":[
      {
         "rel":[
            "self"
         ],
         "href":"http://api.x.io/orders/42"
      }
   ]
}
```

When using WSDL/SOAP, WS-Addressing [W3C 2004] can be used to define links; when using XML and not JSON, XLink [W3C 2010] is a solution alternative on the platform-specific level.

Example

A paginated response from the Lakeside Mutual Customer Core API that contains many LINK ELEMENTS is shown in the following listing:

```
curl -X GET --header 'Authorization: Bearer b318ad736c6c844b' \
http://localhost:8110/customers\?limit\=1
{
  "filter": "",
  "limit": 1,
  "offset": 0,
  "size": 50,
  "customers": [{
    ...
    "_links": {
      "self": {
        "href": "/customers/bunlo9vk5f"
      },
      "address.change": {
        "href": "/customers/bunlo9vk5f/address"
      }
    }
  }],
  "_links": {
    "self": {
      "href": "/customers?filter=&limit=1&offset=0"
    },
    "next": {
      "href": "/customers?filter=&limit=1&offset=1"
    }
  }
}
```

The `self` link in `customers` can be used to get more information about the customer with the ID `bunlo9vk5f`, the `address.change` affords a way to change the customer address, and the `self` and `next` links at the end point at the current and next pagination chunk with offsets 0 and 1 respectively.

Discussion

LINK ELEMENTS such as URIs are accurate. When structured nicely, URIs are human- and machine-readable; complex URI schemas are hard to maintain. A solution- or organization-wide URI scheme can promote consistency and ease of use. Using standardized link types such as those defined by IANA improves maintainability, as does structuring LINK ELEMENTS according to the "Web Linking" RFC 8288 [Nottingham 2017]. Using URIs exclusively for resource identification is a REST principle. Global addressability is achieved with decentralized naming.

The pattern solves the "global, timeless, and absolute" identification problem at the cost of a more complicated client-side programming model (which in turn is very flexible). Designing stable, secure URIs is nontrivial from a risk and effort point of view. LINK ELEMENTS such as URIs introduce security threats, therefore the URIs must be included in the security design and testing efforts to ensure that invalid URIs do not crash the server or become entry doors for attackers.

The REST style as such does not distinguish between an ID ELEMENT and a LINK ELEMENT. This has advantages (supposed ease of use and guaranteed addressability), but also drawbacks (it is hard to change URLs). Once URIs have been used in LINK ELEMENTS, it becomes very risky and costly to change the URI scheme (the LINK LOOKUP RESOURCE pattern and HTTP redirects may come to the rescue). Humans browsing the Web can derive link information from the currently displayed HTML page and their intuition about the provided service (or consult the service documentation); API client programs and their developers cannot do this as easily.

Knowing the LINK ELEMENT is not enough to interact with a remote endpoint (such as a resource in RESTful HTTP or a SOAP operation); in addition, details about the endpoint are required to communicate successfully (for example, in RESTful HTTP, the HTTP verb, the request parameters, and the structure of the response body). To ease the communication of the additional details, these details should be defined in the API DESCRIPTION of the service linked to by the LINK ELEMENT and/or included in METADATA ELEMENTS at runtime.

Related Patterns

ID ELEMENT is a related pattern, providing uniqueness of local references to API elements. ID ELEMENTS do not contain network-accessible and therefore globally unique addresses. ID ELEMENTS typically also do not contain semantic type information, as we suggest including in LINK ELEMENTS. Both LINK ELEMENTS and ID ELEMENTS can be accompanied by METADATA ELEMENTS.

LINK ELEMENTS are often used to realize PAGINATION. They can also organize hypermedia-driven state transfers. Either locally valid ID ELEMENTS or full, globally valid LINK ELEMENTS might be returned by STATE CREATION OPERATIONS and STATE TRANSITION OPERATIONS. Using LINK ELEMENTS can be beneficial (or imperative) when realizing distributed business processes as an orchestrated set of STATE TRANSITION OPERATIONS exposed by one or more PROCESSING RESOURCES (such advanced use was discussed as frontend BPM and BPM services in Chapter 5, "Define Endpoint Types and Operations").

"Linked Service" [Daigneau 2011] captures a related concept, the target of the LINK ELEMENT. *A Pattern Language for RESTful Conversations* [Pautasso 2016] features related patterns for RESTful integration such as "Client-side Navigation following Hyperlinks," "Long Running Request," and "Resource Collection Traversal."

More Information

"Designing & Implementing Hypermedia APIs" [Amundsen 2013], a QCon presentation, is a good starting point for investigation. Many examples can be found in the GitHub repositories of the API Academy [API Academy 2022].

Chapter 5 in the *RESTful Web Services Cookbook* presents eight recipes for "Web Linking" [Allamaraju 2010]. For instance, Section 5.4 discusses how to assign link relation types. Chapter 4 in the same book advises on how to design URIs. Also see Chapter 12 of *Build APIs You Won't Hate* [Sturgeon 2016b] for LINK ELEMENTS in HTTP resource APIs on maturity level 3.

The ALPS specification also deals with link representations. It is described, for instance, in *Design and Build Great Web APIs* [Amundsen 2020]. RFC 6906 is about the "profile" link relation type" [Wilde 2013]. Another draft RFC, called *JSON Hypertext Application Language,* suggests a media type for link relations. The REST Level 3 Web site [Bishop 2021] suggests profiles and patterns to realize HTTP LINK ELEMENTS.

Libraries and notations that implement the concept include HAL, Hydra [Lanthaler 2021], JSON-LD, Collection+JSON, and Siren; see Kai Tödter's presentation, "RESTful Hypermedia APIs" [Tödter 2018], and Kevin Sookocheff's blog post for an overview [Sookocheff 2014].

Special-Purpose Representations

Some element stereotypes are so prevalent in APIs and/or so multifaceted that they warrant their own pattern. One example is the API KEY, which is a mere atomic METADATA ELEMENT from a message representation perspective; however, its application in the security context adds unique forces that must be addressed. Both ERROR REPORT and CONTEXT REPRESENTATION comprise one or more representation elements. Another common trait of the three patterns in this section is a focus on API quality (continued and intensified in the next chapter).

You might be wondering why we touch on security considerations in a chapter on message representation design. We do not aim to provide a complete picture, but we feature API KEYS because they are widely known and used in various APIs. Security is a broad and important topic, and usually, more sophisticated security designs than mere API KEYS are required. We provide pointers to related information in the summary section that ends this chapter.

Pattern:
API KEY

When and Why to Apply

An API provider offers services to subscribed, registered participants only. One or more clients have signed up that want to use the services. These clients have to be identified, for instance, to enforce a RATE LIMIT or to implement a PRICING PLAN.

▼

How can an API provider identify and authenticate clients and their requests?

▲

When identifying and authenticating clients on the API provider side, many questions arise:

- How can client programs identify themselves at an API endpoint without having to store and transmit user account credentials?

- How can the identity of an API client program be made independent of the client's organization and program users?

- How can varying levels of API authentication, depending on security criticality, be implemented?

Conflicts between security requirements and other qualities exist:

- How can clients be identified and authenticated at an API endpoint while still keeping the API easy to use for clients?

- How can endpoints be secured while minimizing performance impacts?

For example, the Twitter API offers an API endpoint to update the user status—which means sending a tweet. Only identified and authenticated users should be able to do that, and only for their own accounts.

- **Establishing basic security:** An API serving subscribed clients has to associate incoming requests with the corresponding client. Not all API endpoints and operations have the same security requirements, though. For instance, an API provider might just want to enforce a RATE LIMIT, which requires some kind of identification but does not justify the introduction of high-fidelity security features.

- **Access control:** Let customers control which API clients can access the service. Not all API clients might need the same permissions, so it should be possible to manage these in a fine-grained way.

- **Avoiding the need to store or transmit user account credentials:** An API client could simply send the credentials (for example, a user identifier and password) for its user account with each request (for example, via basic HTTP authentication).[6] However, these credentials are used not only for the API but also for account management, for example, to change the payment details. Sending these sensitive credentials through a nonencrypted channel or storing the credentials on a server as part of the API configuration introduces a significant security risk. A successful attack is much more severe if the attacker also gains access to the client's account and, as a consequence, to billing records or other user-related information.

- **Decoupling clients from their organization:** External attacks can be a major threat. Using the customer's account credentials as an API security means would also give internal staff (such as system administrators and API developers) full account access, which is not needed. A solution should allow distinguishing between the personnel who administrate and pay for an account from the development and operations teams that configure the client programs.

- **Security versus ease of use:** An API provider wants to make it easy for its customers to access its service and get up to speed quickly. Forcing a complex and possibly onerous authentication scheme (for example, SAML,[7] which provides powerful authentication functionality) on its clients might discourage them from using the API. Finding the right balance highly depends on the security requirements of the API.

- **Performance:** Securing an API can have an impact on the performance of the infrastructure—encrypting requests requires computing, and the date volumes increase with any additional payload transmitted for authentication and authorization purposes.

A rich portfolio of application-level security solutions addressing confidentiality, integrity, and availability (CIA) requirements is available. However, for a free and public API their management overhead and performance impact might not be

---

6. Basic HTTP Authentication, described in RFC 7617 [Reschke 2015], is an "authentication scheme, which transmits credentials as user-id/password pairs, encoded using Base64."

7. SAML, the Security Assertion Markup Language [OASIS 2005], is an OASIS standard for parties to exchange authentication and authorization information. One application of SAML is implementing single sign-on.

economically feasible. For a SOLUTION-INTERNAL API or a COMMUNITY API, security could be implemented at the network level with a virtual private network (VPN) or a two-way Secure Sockets Layer (SSL). This approach complicates application-level usage scenarios such as enforcing RATE LIMITS.

How It Works

As an API provider, assign each client a unique token—the API KEY—that the client can present to the API endpoint for identification purposes.

Encode the API KEY as an ATOMIC PARAMETER, that is, a single plain string. This interoperable representation makes it easy to send the key in the request header, in the request body, or as part of a URL query string.[8] Because of its small size, including it in every request causes only minimal overhead. Figure 6.7 shows an example of a request to a protected API that includes the API KEY `b318ad736c6c844b` in the `Authorization` header of HTTP.

Figure 6.7 *API KEY example: HTTP GET with Bearer authentication*

Before implementing a custom solution, check whether your framework, or a third-party extension, already offers support for working with API KEYS. Make sure to put automated integration or end-to-end tests into place to ensure that endpoints are accessible only with a valid API KEY.

---

8. For security reasons, sending a key in a URL query string is not recommended and should be used only as a last resort. Query strings often show up in log files or analytics tools, compromising the security of the API KEY.

As the API provider, make sure that the generated API KEYS are unique and hard to guess. This can be achieved by using a serial number (to guarantee uniqueness) padded by random data and signed and/or encrypted with a private key (to prevent guessing). Alternatively, base the key on a UUID [Leach 2005]. UUIDs are easier to use in a distributed setting because there is no serial number to be synchronized across systems. However, UUIDs are not necessarily randomized;[9] hence, they also require further obfuscation just like in the serial number scheme.

An API KEY can also be combined with an additional secret key to ensure the integrity of requests. The secret key is shared between the client and the server but never transmitted in API requests. The client uses this key to create a signature hash of the request and sends the hash along with the API KEY. The provider can identify the client with the provided API KEY, calculate the same signature hash using the shared secret key, and compare the two. This ensures that the request was not tampered with. For instance, Amazon uses such asymmetric cryptography to secure access to its Elastic Compute Cloud.

Example

The following call to a PROCESSING RESOURCE in the Cloud Convert API initiates the conversion of a .docx file from Microsoft Word into PDF. The client creates a new conversion process by informing the provider of the desired input and output format in a STATE CREATION OPERATION. These formats are passed as two ATOMIC PARAMETERS in the body of the request; the input file then has to be provided by a second call to a STATE TRANSITION OPERATION in the same API:

```
curl -X POST https://api.cloudconvert.com/process \
--header 'Authorization: Bearer gqmbwwB74tToo4YOPEsev5' \
--header 'Content-Type: application/json' \
--data '
{
    "inputformat": "docx",
    "outputformat": "pdf"
}'
```

For billing purposes, the client identifies itself by passing the API KEY gqmbw-wB74tToo4YOPEsev5 in the Authorization header of the request, according to the HTTP/1.1 Authentication RFC 7235 specification [Fielding 2014b]. HTTP

---

9. Version 1 UUIDs are a combination of timestamp and hardware addresses. The "Security Considerations" section in RFC 4122 [Leach 2005] warns: "Do not assume that UUIDs are hard to guess; they should not be used as security capabilities (identifiers whose mere possession grants access), for example."

supports various types of authentication; here the RFC 6750 [Jones 2012] `Bearer` type is used. The API provider can thus identify the client and charge their account. The response contains an ID ELEMENT to represent the specific process, which can then be used to retrieve the converted file.

Discussion

An API KEY is a lightweight alternative to a full-fledged authentication protocol and balances basic security requirements with the desire to minimize management and communication overhead.

Having the API KEY as a shared secret between the API endpoint and the client, the endpoint can identify the client making the call and use this information to further authenticate and authorize the client. Using a separate API KEY instead of the customer's account credentials decouples different customer roles, such as administration, business management, and API usage, from each other. This makes it possible to let the customer create and manage multiple API KEYS, for example, to be used in different client implementations or locations, with varying permissions associated with them. In the case of a security break or leak, they can also be revoked and a new one generated independently of the client account. A provider might also give clients the option to use multiple API KEYS with different permissions or provide analytics (for example, the number of API calls performed) and RATE LIMITS per API KEY. Because the API KEY is small, it can be included in each request without impacting performance much.

The API KEY is a shared secret, and because it is transported with each request, it should be used only over a secure connection such as HTTPS. If this is not possible, additional security measures (VPN, public-key cryptography) have to be used to protect it and to satisfy the overall security requirements (such as confidentiality and nonrepudiation). Configuring and using secure protocols and other security measures has a certain configuration management and performance overhead.

An API KEY is just a simple identifier that cannot be used to transport additional data or metadata elements such as an expiration time or authorization tokens.

Even when combined with a secret key, API KEYS might be insufficient or impractical as the sole means of authentication and authorization. API KEYS are also not meant to authenticate and authorize users of the application. Consider the case where three parties are involved in a conversation: the user, the service provider, and a third party that wants to interact with the service provider on behalf of the user. For example, a user might want to allow a mobile app to store its data on the user's Dropbox account. In this case, API KEYS cannot be used if the user does not want to share them with the third party. One should consider using OAuth 2.0 [Hardt 2012] and OpenID Connect [OpenID 2021] instead in this (and many other) scenarios.

More secure alternatives to API KEYS are full-fledged authentication or authorization protocols, where authorization protocols include authentication functionality.

Kerberos [Neuman 2005] is an authentication protocol that is often used inside a network to provide single sign-on. Combined with Lightweight Directory Access Protocol (LDAP) [Sermersheim 2006], it can also provide authorization. LDAP itself offers authorization as well as authentication capabilities. Other examples of point-to-point authentication protocols are Challenge-Handshake Authentication Protocol (CHAP) [Simpson 1996] and Extensible Authentication Protocol (EAP) [Vollbrecht 2004]. We come back to this discussion in the chapter summary.

Related Patterns

Many Web servers use session identifiers [Fowler 2002] to maintain and track user sessions across multiple requests; the concept is similar to that of API KEYS. In contrast to API KEYS, session identifiers are used for only a single session and then discarded.

Security Patterns [Schumacher 2006] provides solutions satisfying security requirements such as CIA and discusses their strengths and weaknesses in detail. Access control mechanisms such as role-based access control (RBAC) and attribute-based access control (ABAC) can complement API KEYS and other approaches to authentication. These access control practices require one of the described authentication mechanisms to be in place.

More Information

The OWASP API Security Project [Yalon 2019] and "REST Security Cheat Sheet" [OWASP 2021] should be consulted when securing HTTP resource APIs. The cheat sheet contains a section on API KEYS and contains other valuable information on security as well.

Chapter 15 in *Principles of Web API Design* addresses ways to protect APIs [Higginbotham 2021]. Chapter 12 of the *RESTful Web Services Cookbook* [Allamaraju 2010] is dedicated to security and presents six related recipes. "A Pattern Language for RESTful Conversations" [Pautasso 2016] covers two related patterns of alternative authentication mechanism in a RESTful context, "Basic Resource Authentication" and "Form-Based Resource Authentication."

 Pattern:
ERROR REPORT

When and Why to Apply

Communication participants have to reliably manage unexpected situations at runtime. For instance, a client has called an API, but the API provider is not able to process this request successfully. The failure could be caused by incorrect request data, invalid application state, missing access rights, or numerous other problems that could be the fault of the client, the provider and its backend implementation, or the underlying communications infrastructure (including the network and intermediaries).

▼

How can an API provider inform its clients about communication and processing faults? How can this information be made independent of the underlying communication technologies and platforms (for example, protocol-level headers representing status codes)?

▲

- **Expressiveness and target audience expectations:** The target audience of fault information includes developers and operators as well as help desk and other supporting personnel (in addition to middleware, tools, and application programs). Elaborate error messages suggest better maintainability and evolvability; the more they explain, the more helpful they can be when fixing defects because they reduce the effort for finding root causes of failures. However, error messages should not assume any consumer-side context or usage scenario or technology skills due to the diversity of the target audience. They have to find a balance between expressiveness and compactness (brevity); chatty explanations that contain unfamiliar jargon might confuse some recipients and cause a "too long; didn't read" reaction.

- **Robustness and reliability:** Main decision drivers when introducing any kind of error reporting and handling come from the desire to increase robustness and reliability. Error reports must cover many different cases, including errors that occur during error handling and reporting. They should help manage the system and help fix defects.

- **Security and performance:** Error codes or messages should be expressive and meaningful to their consumers, but they must not unveil any provider-side implementation details for security and data privacy reasons.[10] Provoking errors can be used for denial-of-service-attacks. API providers have to keep track of their performance budgets when reporting errors, security being one reason. Provider-side logging and monitoring also have performance (and storage) costs attached.

- **Interoperability and portability:** When reporting errors, the means of the underlying technology should be taken into account. For example, when using HTTP, a suitable response status code allows others (for example, monitoring tools) to make sense of the error. However, to avoid unnecessarily tight

---

10. When did you last see a SQL exception with full server-side stack trace in a Web page?

couplings, it should not be the sole means of communicating errors. Protocol, format, and platform/technology autonomy as facets of loose coupling [Fehling 2014] should be preserved.

- **Internationalization:** Most developers are used to English error messages; if such messages reach end users and administrators, they have to be translated to achieve natural language support (NLS) and to support internationalization.

How It Works

Reply with error codes in response messages that indicate and classify the faults in a simple, machine-readable way. In addition, add textual descriptions of the errors for the API client stakeholders, including developers and/or human users such as administrators.

The ERROR REPORT information takes the structure of an ATOMIC PARAMETER LIST, a two-tuple comprising an error code (which may take the form of an ID ELEMENT) and a textual description. The error codes can be the same as those of the protocol or transport layer, such as HTTP 4xx status codes.

The ERROR REPORT can also contain a correlating ID ELEMENT that allows the provider to analyze a failed request internally; the CONTEXT REPRESENTATION pattern realizes such design in a platform-neutral way. Timestamps are another common information element in ERROR REPORTS too.

Figure 6.8 illustrates the solution building blocks.

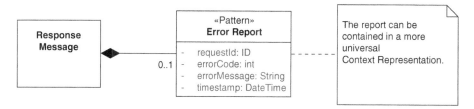

Figure 6.8 *ERROR REPORT pattern, providing machine- and human-readable information, including provenance metadata*

Example

Customers logging in to their Lakeside Mutual accounts have to provide their username and password:

```
curl -i -X POST \
  --header 'Content-Type: application/json' \
  --data '{"username":"xyz","password":"wrong"}' \
  http://localhost:8080/auth
```

If the credentials are not correct, an HTTP 401 error is returned along with a more detailed response rendered as a JSON object, both assembled by the Spring framework in this example (the status code is repeated and explained with two texts):

```
HTTP/1.1 401
Content-Type: application/json;charset=UTF-8
Date: Wed, 20 Jun 2018 08:25:10 GMT

{
  "timestamp": "2018-06-20T08:25:10.212+0000",
  "status": 401,
  "error": "Unauthorized",
  "message": "Access Denied",
  "path": "/auth"
}
```

Similarly, consider the client does not specify the content type of the request body:

```
curl -i -X POST --data '{"username":"xyz","password":"wrong"}' \
  http://localhost:8080/auth
```

Then the provider will answer with an appropriate error message (again using the Spring defaults):

```
HTTP/1.1 415
EHDate: Wed, 20 Jun 2018 08:29:09 GMT

{
  "timestamp": "2018-06-20T08:29:09.452+0000",
  "status": 415,
  "error": "Unsupported Media Type",
  "message": "Content type
      'application/x-www-form-urlencoded;
      charset=UTF-8' not supported",
  "path": "/auth"
}
```

The `message` tells the developer that the (default) content type of `application/x-www-form-urlencoded` is not supported by this endpoint. The Spring framework allows customizing the default error reporting.

Discussion

An ERROR REPORT that contains a code allows the API consumer to handle the error programmatically and to present a human-readable message to the end user. By including a textual error message, the error can be explained in more detail than with a protocol- or transport-level code. An elaborate ERROR REPORT response can also contain hints to solve the problem that led to the error, following the conventions from first aid/emergency (911) calls: what happened to whom, where, and when.

Compared to a simple numeric error code, a detailed textual message is at a higher risk to expose provider-side implementation details or other sensitive data accidentally. For example, when informing about a failed login attempt, such a message should not reveal whether the used user ID (for example, an email) actually maps to an account or not, in order to make brute force attacks harder. The textual error message might also have to be internationalized if it can reach a human user.

Explicit error reporting leads to better maintainability and evolvability, and the more it explains errors and thus reduces the effort in the task of finding the cause of a defect, the more effective it is; thus, the ERROR REPORT pattern is more effective in this regard than simple protocol-level error codes. ERROR REPORT also has better interoperability and portability properties, as it promotes protocol, format, and platform autonomy. However, the more elaborate error messages can reveal information that is sensitive with regard to security; such revealing of detailed information about system internals opens up attack vectors.

Transport-level codes can still be used in addition to the payload ERROR REPORTS that aim at becoming independent of the transport protocol. Payload ERROR REPORTS can describe a finer-grained set of errors than possible with a predefined set of transport-level error categories; reporting communication problems with transport-level codes and application/endpoint processing problems in the payload is in line with the general separation of concerns principle.

If the API is capable of responding with an internationalized message, it might be tempting to leave out the error code. But this forces any nonhuman consumer to parse the error message to find out what went wrong; therefore, an error report should always include error codes that are easily machine-readable. Furthermore, this ensures that the client developer can change messages presented to human users.

When reporting errors that occurred when processing a REQUEST BUNDLE, it is desirable to report the error status or success both per entry in the bundle and for the entire bundle. Different options exist; for instance, the error report for an entire request batch can be combined with an associative array of individual error reports that are accessible via a request ID.

Related Patterns

An ERROR REPORT can be part of the CONTEXT REPRESENTATION in response messages. It may contain METADATA ELEMENTS, for instance, those that inform about next possible steps (to work around the reported problem or to correct it).

The "Remoting Error" pattern [Voelter 2004] contains a generalized and more low-level notion of this pattern, focused on the viewpoint of distributed system middleware.

Error reporting is an important building block in making API implementations robust and resilient. Many more patterns are required for a full solution, for instance, "Circuit Breakers," first described in [Nygard 2018a]. The systems management category [Hohpe 2003] contains related patterns such as "Dead Letter Channel."

More Information

See Chapter 4 of *Build APIs You Won't Hate* [Sturgeon 2016b] for detailed coverage of error reporting in the context of RESTful HTTP.

Production readiness in general is covered in *Production-Ready Microservices: Building Standardized Systems across an Engineering Organization* [Fowler 2016].

Pattern:
CONTEXT REPRESENTATION

When and Why to Apply

An API endpoint and its operations have been defined. Context information has to be exchanged between API client and provider. Examples of such context information are client location and other API user profile data, the preferences forming a WISH LIST, or quality-of-service (QoS) controls such as credentials used to authenticate, authorize, and bill clients. Such credentials may be API KEYS or JSON Web Token (JWT) claims.

How can API consumers and providers exchange context information without relying on any particular remoting protocols?

Important examples of remoting protocols are application protocols such as HTTP or transport protocols such as TCP. In the context of this pattern, we assume that a concrete protocol has not been selected yet, but it is already clear that some QoS guarantees have to be delivered.

Interactions between API client and API provider might be part of conversations and consist of multiple related operation calls. API providers can also act as API clients that consume services provided by other APIs (in their implementations) to create operation invocation sequences. Some parts of the context information might be local to single operations; others might be shared and handed over from operation invocation to operation invocation in such conversations.

▼

How can identity information and quality properties in a request be made visible to related subsequent requests in conversations?

▲

- **Interoperability and modifiability:** Requests may cross multiple compute nodes and travel over different communication protocols on the way from client to provider; the same is true for responses on the way back. It is difficult to ensure that control information exchanged between consumer and provider is able to pass each kind of intermediary (including gateways and service buses) in a distributed system successfully but remains unmodified when the underlying protocol switches. The existence and semantics of predefined protocol headers may change as protocols evolve. Modifiability as a maintainability concern has a business domain and a platform technology facet; here, we are interested in upgradability in particular. A decision about centralization or decentralization of context information may have an impact on this quality.

- **Dependency on evolving protocols:** The history of distributed systems and software engineering suggests that protocols and formats keep changing (with a few notable exceptions such as TCP). For example, lightweight messaging protocols such as MQTT can be found in addition to HTTP in Internet-of-Things scenarios. Using protocol-specific headers gives the API client and provider developers maximum control over what happens during transport and saves them from having to implement the QoS property transport and usage themselves. However, this choice also introduces an extra dependency with associated learning effort. In case a protocol is replaced by another as the API evolves, extra maintenance effort is required to port the API implementation.

To promote protocol independence and a platform-independent design, the default headers and header extension capabilities available in the underlying communication protocol sometimes should not be used.

- **Developer productivity (control versus convenience):** Not all API clients and providers have the same integration requirements, and not all of their programmers can be expected to be protocol, networking, or remote communication experts.[11] Hence, a control versus convenience trade-off exists when it comes to defining and transporting QoS information and other forms of control metadata: using protocol headers is convenient and makes it possible to leverage protocol-specific frameworks, middleware, and infrastructure (such as load balancers and caches), but it delegates control to the protocol designers and implementers. A custom approach maximizes control but causes development and test effort.

- **Diversity of clients and their requirements:** When different clients use the services of an API for varying use cases, possibly under other circumstances and at different times, some generalization takes place, and points of variability are introduced. In such settings, application- and infrastructure-level context information about the client may be required to route and process requests in client-specific ways, log activities systematically for offline analysis, or propagate security credentials. For example, banking regulations may allow storing and accessing customer data only in the customer's country. Multinational banks then have to make sure to protect the data accordingly. This can be achieved by putting the client's country in the context and routing all requests accordingly to the correct national customer management system instance.

- **End-to-end security (across services and protocols):** To achieve end-to-end security, tokens and digital signatures must be transported across multiple nodes. Such security credentials are a typical type of metadata that the consumer and provider have to exchange directly; intermediaries and protocol endpoints would break the desired end-to-end security.

- **Logging and auditing on business domain level (across invocations):** A business transaction identifier is typically generated when a user request arrives at the first point of contact in a larger distributed system such as a multi-tier enterprise application. This ID ELEMENT is then included in all requests to backend systems, which yields a full audit trace of user requests. For instance, an API Design Guide from Cisco introduces a custom HTTP header called `TrackingID` for this purpose [Cisco Systems 2015]. This works well if HTTP is used for all message exchanges, but what happens to the `TrackingID` if protocols are switched as we move down an invocation hierarchy?

---

11. Despite the notion of "full stack developers," which is often mentioned today.

How It Works

Combine and group all METADATA ELEMENTS that carry the desired information into a custom representation element in request and/or response messages. Do not transport this single CONTEXT REPRESENTATION in protocol headers, but place it in the message payload.

Separate global from local context in a conversation by structuring the Context Representation accordingly. Position and mark the consolidated CONTEXT REPRESENTATION element so that it is easy to find and distinguish from other DATA ELEMENTS.

The pattern can be realized by defining a PARAMETER TREE to encapsulate META-DATA ELEMENTS that comprise the custom CONTEXT REPRESENTATION. Figure 6.9 shows a solution sketch in UML. The resulting PARAMETER TREE structure typically is of low to medium complexity (in terms of nesting level and element cardinalities). While PARAMETER TREES are a common choice, a simple ATOMIC PARAMETER LIST can be used alternatively if the requirements only ask for numbers or enumerations (for instance, keyword classifiers or product codes in the context of a shop API).

Examples of the included METADATA ELEMENTS are priority classifiers, session identifiers, correlation identifiers, as well as logical clock values and timers used, for instance, for coordination and correlation purposes (in both request and response messages). Location data, locale, client version, operating system requirements (and so on) also qualify as context information about requests.

One should use the same structure and location across all operations in an API to make the CONTEXT REPRESENTATIONS easy to locate, understand, and process. If the context information differs substantially across operations in an endpoint, an abstraction-refinement hierarchy may model commonalities and variabilities; optional fields and default values may be used as well (which adds development and test effort).

Variants   In some settings, context information is processed only locally by the API provider implementation; other context information is passed on to backend systems (with the API provider taking a client role). Some context information may be relevant only for the current call, while other context information is used to coordinate subsequent calls to the same API endpoint.

Hence, two variants of this pattern exist: *Global Context Representations* (in conversations) and *Local Context Representations*. API designers are usually concerned about reducing the chattiness of their APIs. However, multiple operations still have to be called in certain scenarios. This can happen in the form of nesting calls.

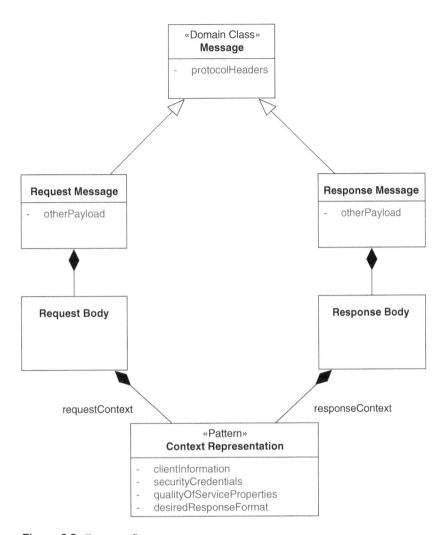

Figure 6.9 *CONTEXT REPRESENTATION*

For instance, a microservice might be invoked that calls another service, which possibly calls yet another one. A deep hierarchy makes it difficult to achieve end-to-end reliability, understandability, and performance—especially when the calls are synchronous. In other scenarios, services may have to be called in a particular order, for instance, to realize complex business processes or login procedures (such as fetching an authorization token before a business operation can be called). In both cases, it is necessary to carry context information over to the following API calls. For example, a user credential (or token) might have to be passed on after its creation.

The business process identifier (ID) or the original transaction might have to be delegated to services deeper in the call hierarchy to guarantee correct request authorization. Tracing and logging throughout a conversation benefits from such context handover.

Figure 6.10 visualizes operation call nesting.

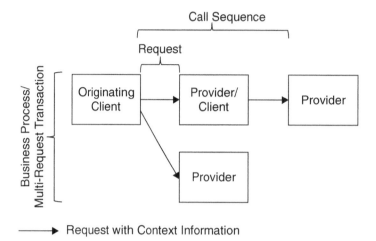

Figure 6.10 *An API provider also acting as API client, requiring context information*

When sharing context information as desired, a context can comprise different scopes. Information in the context can be classified as local or global. The *local* context contains information valid only to this request. This can be message IDs, usernames, time-to-live of this message, and so on. The *global* context contains information that is valid for longer than a single request, for example, in the context of nested operation calls or within a long-running business process. As mentioned earlier, authentication tokens that are delegated across multiple calls, global transactions, or business process identifiers are examples of context information typically found in a global context. Figure 6.11 illustrates.

This division into local (operation/message-level, that is) and global contexts shared among distributed communication participants is beneficial for reasoning about the stakeholders and lifetime of the context information. The global context is often handled via application-level intermediaries (for instance, API gateways validating, transforming, and/or routing requests) because it is standardized, and the handling of the information is repetitive. Libraries and framework components (such as annotation processors in application servers) can process it alternatively. By contrast, information in the local context is processed by libraries or frameworks at the API implementation level (for instance, server-side support for HTTP and container frameworks such as Spring). The message payload is then analyzed and processed in the API provider implementation.

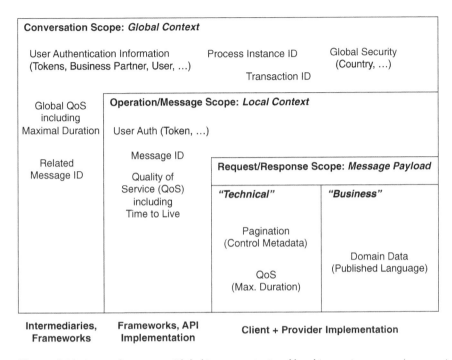

Figure 6.11 *Scopes for context: Global (conversation) and local (operation, request/response)*

Example

The following service contract sketch introduces a custom CONTEXT REPRESENTA-
TION called `RequestContext` in the payload of the request message of the
`getCustomerAttributes` operation. It is decorated with the stereotype
`<<Context_Representation>>` and therefore easily recognizable in the request
payload. The API contract notation used in the example is Microservice
Domain-Specific Language (MDSL). An MDSL primer and reference is presented in
Appendix C:

```
API description ContextRepresentationExample

data type KeyValuePair P // not specified further
data type CustomerDTO P // not specified further

data type RequestContext {
    "apiKey":ID<string>,
    "sessionId":D<int>?,
    "qosPropertiesThatShouldNotGoToProtocolHeader":KeyValuePair*}

endpoint type CustomerInformationHolderService
  exposes
```

```
operation getCustomerAttributes
  expecting payload {
   <<Context_Representation>> {
       "requestContextSharedByAllOperations": RequestContext,
       <<Wish_List>>"desiredCustomerAttributes":ID<string>+
   },
   <<Data_Element>> "searchParameters":D<string>*
  }
  delivering payload {
   <<Context_Representation>> {
       <<Metadata_Element>> {
         "billingInfo": D<int>,
         "moreAnalytics":D},
       <<Error_Report>> {
         "errorCode":D<int>,
         "errorMessage":D<string>}
   }, {
   <<Pagination>> {
     "thisPageContent":CustomerDTO*,
     "previousPage":ID?,
     "nextPage":ID?}
   }
  }
```

The RequestContext contains an API Key as well as a sessionId Id Element (to be created by the provider upon successful authentication). Additional freeform headers can be added in the key-value part of it. The response payload of get-CustomerAttributes contains a second use of the pattern. Note that the example also features three additional patterns: Wish List, Error Report, and Pagination.

When the MDSL contract is transformed into OpenAPI, the preceding example can be rendered as YAML, like this:

```
openapi: 3.0.1
info:
  title: ContextRepresentationExample
  version: "1.0"
servers: []
tags:
- name: CustomerInformationHolderService
  externalDocs:
    description: The role of this endpoint is not specified.
    url: ""
```

```
paths:
  /CustomerInformationHolderService:
    post:
      tags:
      - CustomerInformationHolderService
      summary: POST
      description: POST
      operationId: getCustomerAttributes
      requestBody:
        content:
          application/json:
            schema:
              type: object
              properties:
                anonymous1:
                  type: object
                  properties:
                    requestContextSharedByAllOperations:
                      $ref:'#/components/schemas/RequestContext'
                    desiredCustomerAttributes:
                      minItems: 1
                      type: array
                      items:
                        type: string
                searchParameters:
                  type: array
                  items:
                    type: string
      responses:
        "200":
          description: getCustomerAttributes successful
            execution
          content:
            application/json:
              schema:
                type: object
                properties:
                  anonymous2:
                    type: object
                    properties:
                      anonymous3:
                        type: object
                        properties:
```

```
                           billingInfo:
                             type: integer
                             format: int32
                           moreAnalytics:
                             type: string
                     anonymous4:
                       type: object
                       properties:
                         errorCode:
                           type: integer
                           format: int32
                         errorMessage:
                           type: string
                 anonymous5:
                   type: object
                   properties:
                     anonymous6:
                       type: object
                       properties:
                         thisPageContent:
                           type: array
                           items:
                             $ref: "#/components\
                                       /schemas/CustomerDTO"
                         previousPage:
                           type: string
                           format: uuid
                           nullable: true
                         nextPage:
                           type: string
                           format: uuid
                           nullable: true
components:
  schemas:
    KeyValuePair:
      type: object
    CustomerDTO:
      type: object
    RequestContext:
      type: object
      properties:
        apiKey:
          type: string
```

```
      sessionId:
        type: integer
        format: int32
        nullable: true
      qosPropertiesThatShouldNotGoToProtocolHeader:
        type: array
        items:
          $ref: '#/components/schemas/KeyValuePair'
```

The MDSL specification is much shorter than the OpenAPI one generated from it.

Discussion

Use of this pattern not only promotes context Metadata Elements from protocol headers into payloads but does so in a non-scattered way. The information in the Context Representation may deal with runtime QoS such as priority classifiers; control metadata and provenance metadata often are included in Context Representations appearing in request messages. Exchanging aggregated metadata such as result counts in responses is also possible but is less common.

By representing control information and other metadata in a common form as part of the payload, API client and provider can be isolated/abstracted from changes in the underlying protocol or technology used (for instance, if different protocols such as plain HTTP, AMQP, WebSockets, or gRPC are used). A dependency on a single protocol header format (and protocol support for it) is avoided. A single request traveling through a gateway or proxy could be switched from one protocol to another and therefore lose or modify its original protocol header information along the way. For example, the gRPC-Gateway project [gRPC-Gateway 2022] generates a reverse-proxy server that translates a RESTful JSON API into gRPC; HTTP headers are mapped to gRPC request headers by the proxy. Regardless of such a protocol switch, header information in the payload stays the same and reaches the client.

The introduction of a shared/standardized Context Representation pays off if the information needs of clients and consumers are similar or identical across the entire endpoint or API. If an API is served by only a single transport protocol, an explicit, custom Context Representation leads to one-time-only design and also processing effort; it might be easier to stay with the native, protocol-level way of transmitting the context (such as HTTP headers). Protocol purists may perceive the introduction of custom headers in the payload as an antipattern that indicates a lack of understanding of the protocol and its capabilities. This discussion comes down to the relative priorities of conformance with technical recommendations versus control of one's API destiny.

A potential downside of explicit CONTEXT REPRESENTATIONS is redundancy, for instance of status codes, in the protocol and the payload. One might have to deal with accidental or deliberate differences. For example, what should a Web client do if it receives a message with HTTP status "200 OK," but a failure is indicated as part of the payload? What about the opposite case, HTTP indicating a failure but the payload stating that the request was processed correctly? Merely including header information such as an HTTP status code verbatim in the payload does not provide any abstraction of the underlying protocol. Additional effort is required to map this information to a platform-independent form that is meaningful on the application level. For instance, a "404" code will be understandable for all Web developers but does not mean anything to Jakarta Messaging (formerly called JMS) experts. A textual message "service endpoint unavailable," however, makes sense both for HTTP resources and for message queue usage. Also note that the underlying transport protocol might rely on the presence of some headers. Including such header information in the payload and thus transporting it twice again leads to redundancy and increased message size. This may harm performance and can lead to inconsistencies. If possible, such duplication should be avoided.

Regarding programmer productivity, it is not clear whether programmers are more productive (in the short and the long term) when delegating context information to the protocol or when implementing a CONTEXT REPRESENTATION themselves. Most of the effort lies in gathering the required information and putting it somewhere (on the sender side), then locating and processing it (on the receiver side). Assuming that the protocol libraries provide a proper local API, the development effort can be expected not to differ much. Some protocols may not support all required QoS headers; in that case, developers have to implement these features in the API if they cannot select protocols that do.

Separation of concerns and cohesiveness (assembling all context information in one place) can be conflicting forces; the related design decisions should be driven by answers to the following questions: Who produces and who consumes the context information, and when does this happen? How often will the data definitions change over time? How large is the data? What are its protection needs?

Related Patterns

This pattern is often combined with other patterns; for instance, the data requests expressed in a WISH LIST can be part of CONTEXT REPRESENTATIONS (but do not necessarily have to be). Similarly, an ERROR REPORT can find its place in response message contexts. REQUEST BUNDLES might require two types of CONTEXT REPRESENTATION, one on the container level and one for each individual request or response element. For instance, both individual ERROR REPORTS and an aggregated bundle-level report might make sense when one or more individual responses in a REQUEST BUNDLES fail. A VERSION IDENTIFIER can be transported in the CONTEXT REPRESENTATION as well.

While the "Front Door" pattern [Schumacher 2006] is applied frequently to introduce reverse proxies, API providers and clients might not want all headers to go through the security procedures provided by such proxies; Context Representation can be applied in such cases. An "API Gateway" [Richardson 2016] or proxy could act as an intermediary and modify the original request(s) and response(s), but this makes the overall architecture more complex and more challenging to manage and evolve. While this approach might be convenient, it also means giving up control (or having less control, but an extra dependency).

A similar pattern appears in several other pattern languages. For instance, the "Context Object" [Alur 2013] solves the problem of protocol-independent storage of state and system information in a Java programming context (rather than in a remoting context). The "Invocation Context" pattern [Voelter 2004] describes a solution for bundling contextual information in an extensible invocation context of a distributed invocation.

An Invocation Context is transferred between a client and remote object with every remote invocation. The "Envelope Wrapper" pattern [Hohpe 2003] solves a similar problem, making certain parts of a message visible to the messaging infrastructure responsible for a particular leg. Systems management patterns such as "Wire Tap" [Hohpe 2003] can be used to implement the required auditing and logging.

More Information

Chapter 3 in the *RESTful Web Services Cookbook* discusses an alternative approach based on *entity headers* (in the context of HTTP) in two of its recipes [Allamaraju 2010].

"On the Representation of Context" [Stalnaker 1996] gives an overview of context representation in linguistics.

The Metadata Element pattern provides more pointers to related patterns and other background information.

Summary

This chapter investigated the structure and meaning of representation elements in request and response messages. Element stereotypes distinguish data from metadata, identifiers, and links; some representation elements have special and common purposes.

We concentrated on the data contract as represented by Data Elements. Most data that an API contract exposes comes from the API implementation (for example, instances of domain model entities). As data about data, Metadata Elements provide supplemental information such as origin traces, statistics, or usage hints. Another specialization of DATA ELEMENT is ID ELEMENT. ID ELEMENTS provide the glue code necessary to address, distinguish, and interconnect API parts (such as endpoints, operations, or representation elements). ID ELEMENTS do not contain network-accessible addresses and typically do not contain semantic type information; if this information is required, the LINK ELEMENT pattern is eligible. All types of DATA ELEMENTS might come as ATOMIC PARAMETERS but can also be grouped as ATOMIC PARAMETER LISTS or assembled within PARAMETER TREES. Read and write access to INFORMATION HOLDER RESOURCES endpoints naturally requires DATA ELEMENTS; the in and out parameters of PROCESSING RESOURCES do so as well. METADATA ELEMENTS might explain the semantics of these resources or ease their usage on the client side. All these structural considerations and DATA ELEMENT properties should be defined in the API contract and explained in the API DESCRIPTION.

We also covered three special-purpose representation elements. API KEYS can be used whenever clients must be identified, for example, to enforce a RATE LIMIT or PRICING PLAN (see Chapter 8, "Evolve APIs"). A CONTEXT REPRESENTATION contains and bundles multiple METADATA ELEMENTS and/or ID ELEMENTS for the particular purpose of sharing context information via the payload. An ERROR REPORT can find its place in a CONTEXT REPRESENTATION, for instance, when reporting errors caused by a REQUEST BUNDLE (because the required summary-details structure is difficult to model in protocol-level headers or status codes). The REQUEST BUNDLE pattern is covered in Chapter 7.

Many complements and alternatives to API KEYS exist, as security is a challenging, multifaceted topic. For instance, OAuth 2.0 [Hardt 2012] is an industry-standard protocol for authorization that is also the foundation for secure authentication through OpenID Connect [OpenID 2021]. For FRONTEND INTEGRATION, a common choice is JWT, as defined by RFC 7519 [Jones 2015]. JWT defines a simple message format for access tokens. The access tokens are created and cryptographically signed by the API provider. Providers can verify the authenticity of such a token and use it to identify clients. Unlike API KEYS, JWTs may contain a payload, according to the specification. The provider can store additional information in this payload for the client to read that an attacker cannot change without breaking the signature.

Another example of a full-fledged authentication or authorization protocol is Kerberos [Neuman 2005], which is often used inside a network to provide single sign-on (authentication). In combination with LDAP [Sermersheim 2006], it can also provide authorization. LDAP itself also offers authentication features, so LDAP can be used as authentication and/or authorization protocol. Examples of point-to-point authentication protocols are CHAP [Simpson 1996] and EAP [Vollbrecht 2004]. SAML [OASIS 2005] is another alternative, which can, for instance, be used in BACKEND INTEGRATION to secure the communication between the APIs of backend systems. These alternatives offer better security but also come with a much higher implementation and runtime complexity.

Advanced API Security [Siriwardena 2014] provides a comprehensive discussion on securing APIs with OAuth 2.0, OpenID Connect, JWS, and JWE. Chapter 9 of *Build APIs You Won't Hate* [Sturgeon 2016b] discusses conceptual and technology alternatives and provides instructions on how to implement an OAuth 2.0 server. The OpenID Connect [OpenID 2021] specification deals with user identification on top of the OAuth 2.0 protocol. Chapter 15 in *Principles of Web API Design* [Higginbotham 2021] discusses ways to protect APIs.

All patterns in this chapter work with any textual message exchange format and exchange pattern. Our examples use the request-response message exchange pattern due to its widespread usage; the patterns are written in such a way that they are also eligible when choosing another message exchange pattern. While being particularly relevant when designing services-based systems, none of the presented patterns assumed any particular integration style or technology.

Next up, in Chapter 7, is advanced message structure design, targeting ways to improve certain qualities.

Chapter 7

Refine Message Design for Quality

This chapter covers seven patterns that address issues with API quality. Arguably, it would be hard to find any API designers and product owners who do not value qualities such as intuitive understandability, splendid performance, and seamless evolvability. That said, any quality improvement comes at a price—a literal cost such as extra development effort but also negative consequences such as an adverse impact on other qualities. This balancing act is caused by the fact that some of the desired qualities conflict with each other—just think about the almost classic performance versus security trade-offs.

We first establish why these issues are relevant in "Introduction to API Quality." The next section presents two patterns dealing with "Message Granularity." Three patterns for "Client-Driven Message Content" follow, and two patterns aim at "Message Exchange Optimization."

These patterns support the third and the fourth phases of the Align-Define-Design-Refine (ADDR) design process for APIs that we introduced at the start of Part 2.

Introduction to API Quality

Modern software systems are distributed systems: mobile and Web clients communicate with backend API services, often hosted by a single or even multiple cloud providers. Multiple backends also exchange information and trigger activities in each other. Independent of the technologies and protocols used, messages travel through one or several APIs in such systems. This places high demands on quality aspects of the API contract and its implementation: API clients expect any provided API to be reliable, responsive, and scalable.

API providers must balance conflicting concerns to guarantee a high service quality while ensuring cost-effectiveness. Hence, all patterns presented in this chapter help resolve the following overarching design issue:

How to achieve a certain level of quality of a published API while at the same time utilizing the available resources in a cost-effective way?

Performance and scalability concerns might not have a high priority when initially developing a new API, especially in agile development—if they arise at all. Usually, there is not enough information on how clients will use the API to make informed decisions. One could also just guess, but that would not be prudent and would violate principles such as making decisions in the most responsible moment [Wirfs-Brock 2011].

Challenges When Improving API Quality

The usage scenarios of API clients differ from each other. Changes that benefit some clients may negatively impact others. For example, a Web application that runs on a mobile device with an unreliable connection might prefer an API that offers just the data that is required to render the current page as quickly as possible. All data that is transmitted, processed, and then not used is a waste, squandering valuable battery time and other resources. Another client running as a backend service might periodically retrieve large amounts of data to generate elaborate reports. Having to do so in multiple client-server interactions introduces a risk of network failures; the reporting has to resume at some point or start from scratch when such failures occur. If the API has been designed with its request/response messages tailored to either use case, the API very likely is not ideally suited for the other one.

Taking a closer look, the following conflicts and design issues arise:

- **Message sizes versus number of requests:** Is it preferable to exchange several small messages or few larger ones? Is it acceptable that some clients might have to send multiple requests to obtain all the data required so that other clients do not have to receive data they do not use?

- **Information needs of individual clients:** Is it valuable and acceptable to prioritize the interests of some customers over those of others?

- **Network bandwidth usage versus computation efforts:** Should bandwidth be preserved at the expense of higher resource usage in API endpoints and their clients? Such resources include computation nodes and data storage.

- **Implementation complexity versus performance:** Are the gained bandwidth savings worth their negative consequences, for instance, a more complex implementation that is harder and more costly to maintain?

- **Statelessness versus performance:** Does it make sense to sacrifice client/provider statelessness to improve performance? Statelessness improves scalability.

- **Ease of use versus latency:** Is it worth speeding up the message exchanges even if doing so results in a harder-to-use API?

Note that the preceding list is nonexhaustive. The answers to these questions depend on the quality goals of the API stakeholders and additional concerns. The patterns in this chapter provide different options to choose from under a given set of requirements; adequate selections differ from API to API. Part 1 of this book provided a decision-oriented overview of these patterns in the "Deciding for API Quality Improvements" section of Chapter 3, "API Decision Narratives." In this chapter, we cover them in depth.

Patterns in This Chapter

The section "Message Granularity" contains two patterns: Embedded Entity and Linked Information Holder. Data Elements offered by API operations frequently reference other elements, for example, using hyperlinks. A client can follow these links to retrieve the additional data; this can become tedious and lead to a higher implementation effort and latency on the client side. Alternatively, clients can retrieve all data at once when providers directly embed the referenced data instead of just linking to it.

"Client-Driven Message Content" features three patterns. API operations sometimes return large sets of data elements (for example, posts on a social media site or products in an e-commerce shop). API clients may be interested in all of these data elements, but not necessarily all at once and not all the time. Pagination divides the data elements into chunks so that only a subset of the sequence is sent and received at once. Clients are no longer overwhelmed with data, and performance and resource usage improve. Providers may offer relatively rich data sets in their response messages. If the problem is that not all clients require all information all the time, then a Wish List allows these clients to request only the attributes in a response data set that they are interested in. Wish Template addresses the same problem but offers clients even more control over possibly nested response data structures. These patterns address concerns such as accuracy of the information, data parsimony, response times, and processing power required to answer a request.

Finally, the "Message Exchange Optimization" section features two patterns, Conditional Request and Request Bundle. The other patterns in this chapter offer several options to fine-tune message contents to avoid issuing too many requests or transmitting data that is not used; in contrast, CONDITIONAL REQUESTS avoid sending data that a client already has. While the number of messages exchanged stays the same, the API implementation can respond with a dedicated status code to inform the client that more recent data is not available. The number of requests sent and responses received can also impair the quality of an API. If clients have to issue many small requests and wait for individual responses, bundling them into a larger message can improve throughput and reduce the client-side implementation effort. The REQUEST BUNDLE pattern presents this design option.

Figure 7.1 provides an overview of the patterns in this chapter and shows their relations.

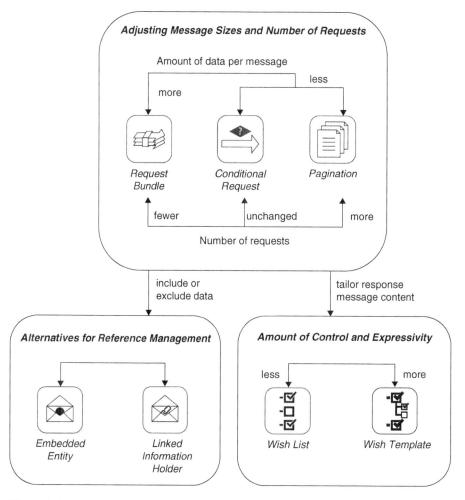

Figure 7.1 *Pattern map for this chapter (API quality)*

Message Granularity

Information elements in request and response message representations, concepts from our API domain model (see Chapter 1, "Application Programming Interface (API) Fundamentals"), often reference other ones to express containment, aggregation, or other relationships. For instance, operational data such as orders and shipments typically is associated with master data such as product and customer records. To expose such references when defining API endpoints and their operations, the two basic options are as follows:

1. EMBEDDED ENTITY: Embed the referenced data in a possibly nested DATA ELEMENT (introduced in Chapter 6, "Design Request and Response Message Representations") in the message representation.

2. LINKED INFORMATION HOLDER: Place a LINK ELEMENT (also Chapter 6) in the message representation to look up the referenced data via a separate API call to an INFORMATION HOLDER RESOURCE (Chapter 5, "Define Endpoint Types and Operations").

These message sizing and scoping options have an impact on the API quality:

- **Performance and scalability:** Both message size and number of calls required to cover an entire integration scenario should be kept low. Few messages that transport a lot of data take time to create and process; many small messages are easy to create but cause more work for the communications infrastructure and require receiver-side coordination.

- **Modifiability and flexibility:** Backward compatibility and extensibility are desired in any distributed system whose parts evolve independently of each other. Information elements contained in structured, self-contained representations might be hard to change because any local updates must be coordinated and synchronized with updates to the API operations that work with them and related data structures in the API implementation. Structured representations that contains references to external resources usually is even harder to change than self-contained data because clients have to be aware of such references so that they can follow them correctly.

- **Data quality:** Structured master data such as customer profiles or product details differs from simple unstructured reference data such as country and currency codes (Chapter 5 provides a categorization of domain data by lifetime and mutability). The more data is transported, the more governance is required to make this data useful. For instance, data ownership might differ for products and customers in an online shop, and the respective data owners usually have different requirements, for example, regarding data protection, data validation, and update frequency. Extra metadata and data management procedures might be required.

- **Data privacy:** In terms of data privacy classifications, the source and the target of data relationships might have different protection needs; an example is a customer record with contact address and credit card information. More fine-grained data retrieval facilitates the enforcement of appropriate controls and rules, lowering the risk of embedded restricted data accidentally slipping through.

- **Data freshness and consistency:** If data is retrieved by competing clients at different times, inconsistent snapshots of and views on data in these clients might materialize. Data references (links) may help clients to retrieve the most recent version of the referenced data. However, such references may break, as their targets may change or disappear after the link referring to it has been sent. By embedding all referenced data in the same message, API providers can deliver an internally consistent snapshot of the content, avoiding the risk of link targets becoming unavailable. Software engineering principles such as single responsibility may lead to challenges regarding data consistency and data integrity when taken to the extreme because data may get fragmented and scattered.

The two message granularity patterns, EMBEDDED ENTITY and LINKED INFORMATION HOLDER in this section address these issues in opposite ways. Combining them on a case-by-case basis leads to adequate message sizes, balancing the number of calls and the amount of data exchanged to meet diverse integration requirements.

Pattern:
EMBEDDED ENTITY

When and Why to Apply
The information required by a communication participant contains structured data. This data includes multiple elements that relate to each other in certain ways. For instance, master data such as a customer profile may *contain* other elements providing contact information including addresses and phone numbers, or a periodic business results report may *aggregate* source information such as monthly sales figures summarizing individual business transactions. API clients work with

several of the related information elements when creating request messages or processing response messages.

> How can one avoid exchanging multiple messages when their receivers require insights about multiple related information elements?

One could simply define one API endpoint for each basic information element (for instance, an entity defined in an application domain model). This endpoint is accessed whenever API clients require data from that information element, for example, when it is referenced from another one. But if API clients use such data in many situations, this solution causes many subsequent requests when references are followed. This could possibly make it necessary to coordinate request execution and introduce conversation state, which harms scalability and availability; distributed data also is more difficult than local data to keep consistent.

How It Works

> For any data relationship that the receiver wants to follow, embed a DATA ELEMENT in the request or response message that contains the data of the target end of the relationship. Place this EMBEDDED ENTITY inside the representation of the source of the relationship.

Analyze the outgoing relationships in the new DATA ELEMENT and consider embedding them in the message as well. Repeat this analysis until *transitive closure* is reached—that is, until all reachable elements have been either included or excluded (or circles are detected and processing stopped). Review each source-target relationship carefully to assess whether the target data is really needed on the receiver side in enough cases. A yes answer to this question warrants transmitting relationship information as EMBEDDED ENTITIES; otherwise, transmitting references to LINKED INFORMATION HOLDERS might be sufficient. For instance, if a purchase order has a *uses* relation to product master data and this master data is required to make sense of the purchase order, the purchase order representation in request or response messages should contain a copy of all relevant information stored in the product master data in an EMBEDDED ENTITY.

Figure 7.2 sketches the solution.

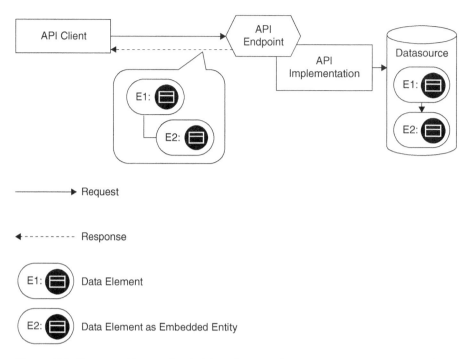

Figure 7.2 *EMBEDDED ENTITY: Single API endpoint and operation, returning structured message content that matches the structure of the source data in the API implementation to follow data relations*

Including an EMBEDDED ENTITY in a message leads to a PARAMETER TREE structure that contains the DATA ELEMENT representing the related data. Additional METADATA ELEMENTS in this tree may denote the relationship type and other supplemental information. There are several options for structuring the tree, corresponding to the contained DATA ELEMENT. It may be nested, for instance, when representing deep containment relationship hierarchies; it may be flat and simply list one or more ATOMIC PARAMETERS. When working with JSON in HTTP resource APIs, JSON objects (possibly including other JSON objects) realize these options. One-to-many relationships (such as a purchase order referring to its order items) cause the EMBEDDED ENTITY to be set-valued. JSON arrays can represent such sets. The options for representing many-to-many relationships are similar to those in the LINKED INFORMATION HOLDERS pattern; for instance, the PARAMETER TREE might contain dedicated nodes for the relationships. Some redundancy might be desired or tolerable, but it also may confuse consumers who expect normalized data. Bidirectional relationships require special attention. One of the directions can be used to create the EMBEDDED ENTITY hierarchy; if the opposite direction should also be made explicit in the message representation, a second instance of this pattern might be required, causing data duplication. In that case, it might be better to express the second relationship with embedded ID ELEMENTS or LINK ELEMENTS instead.

In any of these cases, the API DESCRIPTION has to explain the existence, structure, and meaning of the EMBEDDED ENTITY instances.

Example

Lakeside Mutual, our microservices sample application introduced in Chapter 2, "Lakeside Mutual Case Study," contains a service called Customer Core that aggregates several information items (here, entities and value objects from domain-driven design [DDD]) in its operation signatures. API clients such as the Customer Self-Service frontend can access this data via an HTTP resource API. This API contains several instances of the EMBEDDED ENTITY pattern. Applying the pattern, a response message might look as follows:[1]

```
curl -X GET http://localhost:8080/customers/gktlipwhjr
```

```
{
  "customer": {
    "id": "gktlipwhjr"
  },
  "customerProfile": {
    "firstname": "Robbie",
    "lastname": "Davenhall",
    "birthday": "1961-08-11T23:00:00.000+0000",
    "currentAddress": {
      "streetAddress": "1 Dunning Trail",
      "postalCode": "9511",
      "city": "Banga"
    },
    "email": "rdavenhall0@example.com",
    "phoneNumber": "491 103 8336",
    "moveHistory": [{
      "streetAddress": "15 Briar Crest Center",
      "postalCode": "",
      "city": "Aeteke"
    }]
  },
  "customerInteractionLog": {
    "contactHistory": [],
    "classification": "??"
  }
}
```

---

1. Note that the data shown is fictitious, generated by https://www.mockaroo.com.

The referenced information elements are all fully contained in the response message; examples are `customerProfile` and `customerInteractionLog`. No URI links to other resources appear. Note that the `customerProfile` entity actually embeds nested data in this exemplary data set (for example, `currentAddress` and `moveHistory`), while the `customerInteractionLog` does not (but is still included as an empty EMBEDDED ENTITY).

Discussion

Applying this pattern solves the problem of having to exchange multiple messages when receivers require multiple related information elements. An EMBEDDED ENTITY reduces the number of calls required: if the required information is included, the client does not have to create a follow-on request to obtain it. Embedding entities can lead to a reduction in the number of endpoints, because no dedicated endpoint to retrieve linked information is required. However, embedding entities leads to larger response messages, which usually take longer to transfer and consume more bandwidth. Care must also be taken to ensure that the included information does not have higher protection needs than the source and that no restricted data slips through.

It can be challenging to anticipate what information different message receivers (that is, API clients for response messages) require to perform their tasks. As a result, there is a tendency to include more data than most clients need. Such design can be found in many PUBLIC APIs serving many diverse and possibly unknown clients.

Traversing all relationships between information elements to include all possibly interesting data may require complex message representations and lead to large message sizes. It is unlikely and/or difficult to ensure that all recipients will require the same message content. Once included and exposed in an API DESCRIPTION, it is hard to remove an EMBEDDED ENTITY in a backward-compatible manner (as clients may have begun to rely on it).

If most or all of the data is actually used, sending many small messages might require more bandwidth than sending one large message (for instance, because protocol header metadata is sent with each small message). If the embedded entities change at different speeds, retransmitting them causes unnecessary overhead because messages with partially changed content can only be cached in their entirety. A fast-changing operational entity might refer to immutable master data, for instance.

The decision to use EMBEDDED ENTITY might depend on the number of message consumers and the homogeneity of their use cases. For example, if only one consumer with a specific use case is targeted, it is often good to embed all required data straight away. In contrast, different consumers or use cases might not work with the same data. In order to minimize message sizes, it might be advisable not to transfer all data. Both client and provider might be developed by the same organization—for example, when providing "Backends for Frontends" [Newman 2015]. Embedding entities can be a reasonable strategy to minimize the number of requests in that case. In such a setting, they simplify development by introducing a uniform regular structure.

Combinations of linking and embedding data often make sense, for instance, embedding all data immediately displayed in a user interface and linking the rest for retrieval upon demand. The linked data is then fetched only when the user scrolls or opens the corresponding user interface elements. Atlassian [Atlassian 2022] discusses such a hybrid approach: "Embedded related objects are typically limited in their fields to avoid such object graphs from becoming too deep and noisy. They often exclude their own nested objects in an attempt to strike a balance between performance and utility."

"API Gateways" [Richardson 2016] and messaging middleware [Hohpe 2003] can also help when dealing with different information needs. Gateways can either provide two alternative APIs that use the same backend interface and/or collect and aggregate information from different endpoints and operations (which makes them stateful). Messaging systems may provide transformation capabilities such as filters and enrichers.

Related Patterns

LINKED INFORMATION HOLDER describes the complementary, opposite solution for the reference management problem. One reason for switching to the LINKED INFORMATION HOLDER might be to mitigate performance problems, for instance, caused by slow or unreliable networks that make it difficult to transfer large messages. LINKED INFORMATION HOLDERS can help to improve the situation, as they allow caching each entity independently.

If reducing message size is the main design goal, a WISH LIST or, even more expressive, a WISH TEMPLATE can also be applied to minimize the data to be transferred by letting consumers dynamically describe which subset of the data they need. WISH LIST or WISH TEMPLATE can help to fine-tune the content in an EMBEDDED ENTITY.

OPERATIONAL DATA HOLDERS reference MASTER DATA HOLDERS by definition (either directly or indirectly); these references often are represented as LINKED INFORMATION HOLDERS. References between data holders of the same type are more likely to be included with the EMBEDDED ENTITY pattern. Both INFORMATION HOLDER RESOURCES and PROCESSING RESOURCES might deal with structured data that needs to be linked or embedded; in particular, RETRIEVAL OPERATIONS either embed or link related information.

More Information

Phil Sturgeon features this pattern as "Embedded Document (Nesting)" in [Sturgeon 2016b]. See Section 7.5 of *Build APIs You Won't Hate* for additional advice and examples.

Pattern:
LINKED INFORMATION HOLDER

When and Why to Apply

An API exposes structured data to meet the information needs of its clients. This data contains elements that relate to each other (for example, product master data may *contain* other information elements providing detailed information, or a performance report for a period of time may *aggregate* raw data such as individual measurements). API clients work with several of the related information elements when preparing request messages or processing response messages. Not all of this information is always useful for the clients in its entirety.[2]

> How can messages be kept small even when an API deals with multiple information elements that reference each other?

A rule of thumb for distributed system design states that exchanged messages should be small because large messages may overutilize the network and the endpoint processing resources. However, not all of what communication participants want to share with each other might fit into such small messages; for instance, they might want to follow many or all of the relationships within information elements. If relationship sources and targets are not combined into a single message, participants have to inform each other how to locate and access the individual pieces. This distributed information set has to be designed, implemented, and evolved; the resulting dependencies between the participants and the information they share have to be managed. For instance, insurance policies typically refer to customer and product master data; each of these related information elements might, in turn, consist of several parts (see Chapter 2 for deeper coverage of the data and domain entities in this example).

One option is to always (transitively) include all the related information elements of each transmitted element in request and response messages throughout the API, as described in the EMBEDDED ENTITY pattern. However, this approach can lead to large messages containing data not required by some clients and harm the performance of individual API calls. It couples the stakeholders of this data.

---

2. This pattern context is similar to that of EMBEDDED ENTITY but emphasizes the diversity of client wants and needs.

How It Works

Add a Link Element to messages that pertain to multiple related information elements. Let the resulting Linked Information Holder reference another API endpoint that exposes the linked element.

The referenced API endpoint often is an Information Holder Resource representing the linked information element. This element might be an entity from the domain model that is exposed by the API (possibly wrapped and mapped); it can also be the result of a computation in the API implementation.

Linked Information Holders might appear in request and response messages; the latter case is more common. Typically, a Parameter Tree is used in the representation structure, combining collections of Link Elements and, optionally, Metadata Elements explaining the link semantics; in simple cases, a set of Atomic Parameters or a single Atomic Parameter might suffice as link carriers.

Figure 7.3 illustrates the two-step conversation realizing the pattern.

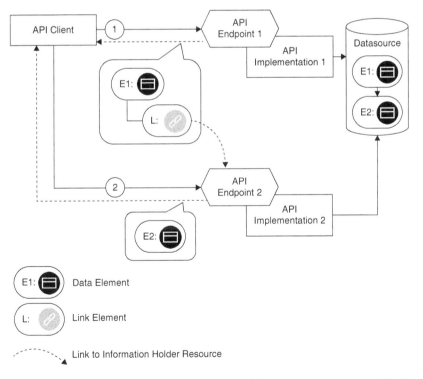

Figure 7.3 *Linked Information Holder: Two API endpoints are involved. The first response contains a link rather than data from the data source; the data is retrieved from it in a follow-on request to the second endpoint*

The LINK ELEMENT that constitutes the LINKED INFORMATION HOLDER provides location information, for instance, a URL (with domain/hostname and port number when using HTTP over TCP/IP). The LINK ELEMENT also has a local name to be able to identify it within the message representation (such as a JSON object). If more information about the relation should be sent to clients, this LINK ELEMENT can be annotated with details about the corresponding relationship, for instance, a META-DATA ELEMENT specifying its type and semantics. In any case, API clients and providers must agree on the meaning of the link relationships and be aware of coupling and side effects introduced. The existence and the meaning of the LINKED INFORMATION HOLDER, including cardinalities on both ends of the relation, has to be documented in the API DESCRIPTION.

One-to-many relationships can be modeled as collections, for instance, by transmitting multiple LINK ELEMENTS as ATOMIC PARAMETER LISTS. Many-to-many relationships (such as that between books and their readers in a library management system) can be modeled as two one-to-many relationships, with one collection linking the source data to the targets and a second one linking the target data to the sources (assuming that the message recipient wants to follow the relation in both directions). Such design may require the introduction of an additional API endpoint, a *relationship holder resource,* representing the relation rather than its source or target. This endpoint then exposes operations to retrieve all relationships with their sources and targets; it may also allow clients to find the other end of a relationship they already know about. Different types of LINK ELEMENTS identify these ends in messages sent to and from the relationship holder resource. Unlike in the EMBEDDED ENTITY pattern, circular dependencies in the data are less of an issue when working with LINKED INFORMATION HOLDERS (but still should be handled); the responsibility to avoid endless loops in the data processing shifts from the message sender to the recipient.

Example

Our Lakeside Mutual sample application for Customer Management utilizes a Customer Core service API that aggregates several information elements from the domain model of the application, in the form of entities and value objects from DDD. API clients can access this data through a Customer Information Holder, implemented as a REST controller in Spring Boot.

The Customer Information Holder, called customers, realizes the Information Holder Resource pattern. When applying Linked Information Holder for its customerProfile and its moveHistory a response message may look as follows:

```
curl -X GET http://localhost:8080/customers/gktlipwhjr

{
  "customer": {
    "id": "gktlipwhjr"
  },
  "links": [{
    "rel": "customerProfile",
    "href": "/customers/gktlipwhjr/profile"
  }, {
    "rel": "moveHistory",
    "href": "/customers/gktlipwhjr/moveHistory"
  }],
  "email": "rdavenhall0@example.com",
  "phoneNumber": "491 103 8336",
  "customerInteractionLog": {
    "contactHistory": [],
    "classification": "??"
  }
}
```

Both profile and moveHistory are implemented as sub-resources of the Customer Information Holder. The customerProfile can be retrieved by a subsequent GET request to the URI /customers/gktlipwhjr/profile. How does the client know that a GET request must be used? This information could have been included in a Metadata Element. In this example, the designers of the API decided not to include it. Instead, their API Description specifies that GET requests are used by default to retrieve information.

Discussion
Linking instead of embedding related data results in smaller messages and uses fewer resources in the communications infrastructure when exchanging individual messages. However, this has to be contrasted with the possibly higher resource use caused by the extra messages required to follow the links: Additional requests are required to dereference the linked information. Linking instead of embedding might demand more resources in the communications infrastructure. Additional Information Holder Resource endpoints have to be provided for the linked data, causing development and operations effort and cost, but allowing to enforce additional access restrictions.

When introducing Linked Information Holders into message representations, an implicit promise is made to the recipient that these links can be followed successfully. The provider might not be willing to keep such a promise infinitely. Even if a long lifetime of the linked endpoint is guaranteed, links still may break, for instance, when the data organization or deployment location changes. Clients should expect this and be able to follow redirects or referrals to the updated links. To minimize breaking links, the API provider should invest in maintaining link consistency; a Link Lookup Resource can be used to do so.

Sometimes the data distribution reduces the number of messages exchanged. Different Linked Information Holders may be defined for data that changes at a different velocity. Clients then can request frequently changing data whenever they require the latest snapshot of it; they do not have to re-request slower changing data that is embedded with it (and therefore tightly coupled).

The pattern leads to modular API designs but also adds a dependency that must be managed. It potentially has performance, workload, and maintenance costs attached. The Embedded Entity pattern can be used instead if justified from a performance point of view. This makes sense if a few large calls turn out to perform better than many small ones due to network and endpoint processing capabilities or constraints (this should be measured and not guessed). It might be required to switch back and forth between Embedded Entity and Linked Information Holder during API evolution; with Two In Production, both designs can be offered at the same time, for instance, for experimentation with a potential change. The API refactorings "Inline Information Holder" and "Extract Information Holder" of the Interface Refactoring Catalog [Stocker 2021b] provide further guidance and step-by-step instructions.

Linked Information Holder is well suited when referencing rich information holders serving multiple usage scenarios: usually, not all message recipients require the full set of referenced data, for instance, when Master Data Holders such as customer profiles or product records are referenced from Operational Data Holders such as customer inquiries or orders. Following links to Linked Information Holders, message recipients can obtain the required subsets on demand.

The decision to use Linked Information Holder and/or to include an Embedded Entity might depend on the number of API clients and the level of similarity of their use cases. Another decision driver is the complexity of the domain model and the application scenarios it represents. For example, if one client with a specific use case is targeted, it usually makes sense to embed all data. However, if there are several clients, not all of them might appreciate the same comprehensive data. In such situations, Linked Information Holders pointing at the data used only by a fraction of the clients reduces the message sizes.

Related Patterns

LINKED INFORMATION HOLDERS typically reference INFORMATION HOLDER RESOURCES. The referenced INFORMATION HOLDER RESOURCES can be combined with LINK LOOKUP RESOURCE to cope with potentially broken links. By definition, OPERATIONAL DATA HOLDERS reference MASTER DATA HOLDERS; these references can either be included and flattened as EMBEDDED ENTITIES or structured and then progressively followed using LINKED INFORMATION HOLDERS.

Other patterns that help reduce the amount of data exchanged can be used alternatively. For instance, CONDITIONAL REQUEST, WISH LIST, and WISH TEMPLATE are eligible; PAGINATION is an option too.

More Information

"Linked Service" [Daigneau 2011] is a similar pattern but is less focused on data. "Web Service Patterns" [Monday 2003] has a "Partial DTO Population" pattern that solves a similar problem; DTO stands for Data Transfer Object.

See *Build APIs You Won't Hate*, Section 7.4 [Sturgeon 2016b], for additional advice and examples, to be found under "Compound Document (Sideloading)."

The backup, availability, consistency (BAC) theorem investigates data management issues further [Pardon 2018].

Client-Driven Message Content (aka Response Shaping)

In the previous section, we presented two patterns to handle references between data elements in messages. An API provider can choose between embedding or linking related data elements, and also combine these two options to achieve suitable message sizes. Depending on the clients and their API usage, their best usage may be clear. But usage scenarios of clients might be so different that an even better solution would be to let clients themselves decide at runtime which data they are interested in.

The patterns in this section offer two different approaches to optimize this facet of API quality further, *response slicing* and *response shaping*. They address the following challenges:

- **Performance, scalability, and resource use:** Providing all clients with all data every time, even to those that only have a limited or minimal information need, comes at a price. From a performance and workload point of view, it therefore makes sense to transmit only the relevant parts of a data set. However, the pre- and postprocessing required to rightsize the message exchanges also require resources and might harm performance. These costs have to be balanced against the expected reduction of the response message size and the capabilities of the underlying transport network.

- **Information needs of individual clients:** An API provider might have to serve multiple clients with different information needs. Usually, providers do not want to implement custom APIs or client-specific operations but let the clients share a set of common operations. However, certain clients might be interested in just a subset of the data made available via an API. The common operations might be too limited or too powerful in such cases. Other clients might be overwhelmed if a large set if data arrives at once. Delivering too little or too much data to a client is also known as *underfetching* and *overfetching*.

- **Loose coupling and interoperability:** The message structures are important elements of the API contract between API provider and API client; they contribute to the shared knowledge of the communication participants, which impacts the format autonomy aspect of loose coupling. Metadata to control data set sizing and sequencing becomes part of this shared knowledge and has to be evolved along with the payload.

- **Developer convenience and experience:** The developer experience, including learning effort and programming convenience, is closely related to understandability and complexity considerations. For instance, a compact format optimized for transfer might be difficult to document and understand, and to prepare and digest. Elaborate structures enhanced with metadata that simplify and optimize processing cause extra effort during construction (both at design time and at runtime).

- **Security and data privacy:** Security requirements (data integrity and confidentiality in particular) and data privacy concerns are relevant in any message design; security measures might require additional message payloads such as API Keys or security tokens. An important consideration is which payload can and should actually be sent; data that is not sent cannot be tampered with (at least not on the wire). The need for certain, data-specific security measures might actually lead to different message designs (for instance, credit card information might be factored out into a dedicated API endpoint with specifically secured operations). In the context of slicing and sequencing large data sets, all parts can be treated equally unless they have different protection needs. The heavy load caused by assembling and transmitting large data sets can expose the provider to denial-of-service attacks.

- **Test and maintenance effort:** Enabling clients to select which data to receive (and when) creates options and flexibility with regards to what the provider has to expect (and accept) in incoming requests. Therefore, the testing and maintenance effort increases.

The patterns in this section, Pagination, Wish List, and Wish Template, address these challenges in different ways.

Pattern:
PAGINATION

When and Why to Apply

Clients query an API, fetching collections of data items to be displayed to the user or processed in other applications. In at least one of these queries, the API provider responds by sending a large number of items. The size of this response may be larger than what the client needs or is ready to consume at once.

The data set may consist of identically structured elements (for example, rows fetched from a relational database or line items in a batch job executed by an enterprise information system in the backend) or of heterogeneous data items not adhering to a common schema (for example, parts of a document from a document-oriented NoSQL database such as MongoDB).

▼

How can an API provider deliver large sequences of structured data without overwhelming clients?

▲

In addition to the forces already presented in the introduction to this section, PAGINATION balances the following ones:

- **Session awareness and isolation:** Slicing read-only data is relatively simple. But what if the underlying data set changes while being retrieved? Does the API guarantee that once a client retrieves the first page, the subsequent pages (which may or may not be retrieved later) will contain a data set that is consistent with the subset initially retrieved? How about multiple concurrent requests for partial data?

- **Data set size and data access profile:** Some data sets are large and repetitive, and not all transmitted data is accessed all the time. This offers optimization potential, especially for sequential access over data items ordered from the most recent to the oldest, which may no longer be relevant for the client. Moreover, clients may not be ready to digest data sets of arbitrary sizes.

One could think of sending the entire large response data set in a single response message, but such a simple approach might waste endpoint and network capacity; it also does not scale well. The size of the response to a query may be unknown in advance, or the result set may be too large to be processed at once on the client side (or on the provider side). Without mechanisms to limit such queries, processing errors such as out-of-memory exceptions may occur, and the client or the endpoint implementation may crash. Developers and API designers often underestimate the memory requirements imposed by unlimited query contracts. These problems usually go unnoticed until concurrent workload is placed on the system or the data set size increases. In shared environments, it is possible that unlimited queries cannot be processed efficiently in parallel, which leads to similar performance, scalability, and consistency issues—only combined with concurrent requests, which are hard to debug and analyze anyway.

How It Works

▼

> Divide large response data sets into manageable and easy-to-transmit chunks (also known as pages). Send one chunk of partial results per response message and inform the client about the total and/or remaining number of chunks. Provide optional filtering capabilities to allow clients to request a particular selection of results. For extra convenience, include a reference to the next chunk/page from the current one.

▲

The number of data elements in a chunk can be fixed (its size then is part of the API contract) or can be specified by the client dynamically as a request parameter. METADATA ELEMENTS and LINK ELEMENTS inform the API client how to retrieve additional chunks subsequently.

API clients then process some or all partial responses iteratively as needed; they request the result data page by page. Hence, subsequent requests for additional chunks might have to be correlated. It might make sense to define a policy that governs how clients can terminate the processing of the result set and the preparation of partial responses (possibly requiring session state management).

Figure 7.4 visualizes a sequence of requests that use PAGINATION to retrieve three pages of data.

Variants The pattern comes in four variants that navigate the data set in different ways: page based, offset based, cursor or token based, and time based.

Page-Based Pagination (a somewhat tautological name) and *Offset-Based Pagination* refer to the elements of the data set differently. The page-based variant divides the data set into same-sized pages; the client or the provider specify the page size. Clients then request pages by their index (like page numbers in a book). With Offset-Based Pagination, a client selects an offset into the whole data set (that is, how many single elements to skip) and the number of elements to return in the next chunk (often referred to as *limit*). Both approaches may be used interchangeably (the offset

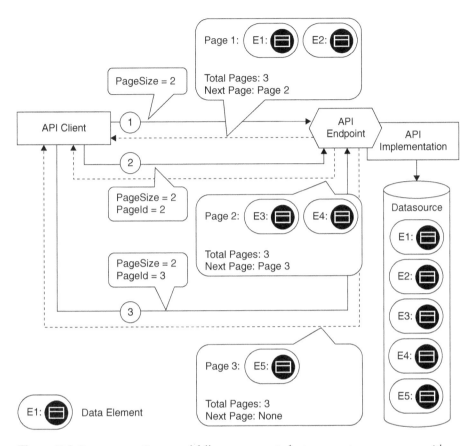

Figure 7.4 *PAGINATION: Query and follow-on requests for pages, response messages with partial results*

can be calculated by multiplying the page size with the page number); they address the problem and resolve the forces in similar ways. Page-Based Pagination and Offset-Based Pagination do not differ much with respect to developer experience and other qualities. Whether entries are requested with an offset and limit or all entries are divided into pages of a particular size and then requested by an index is a minor difference. Either case requires two integer parameters.

These variants are not well suited for data that changes in between requests and therefore invalidates the index or offset calculations. For example, given a data set ordered by creation time from most recent to oldest, let us assume that a client has retrieved the first page and now requests the second one. In between these requests, the element at the front of the data set is removed, causing an element to move from the second to the first page without the client ever seeing it.

The *Cursor-Based Pagination* variant solves this problem: it does not rely on the absolute position of an element in the data set. Instead, clients send an identifier that the provider can use to locate a specific item in the data set, along with the number of elements to retrieve. The resulting chunk does not change even if new elements have been added since the last request.

The remaining fourth variant, *Time-Based Pagination*, is similar to Cursor-Based Pagination but uses timestamps instead of element IDs. It is used in practice less frequently but could be applied to scroll through a time plot by gradually requesting older or newer data points.

Example

The Lakeside Mutual Customer Core backend API illustrates Offset-Based Pagination in its `customer` endpoint:

```
curl -X GET http://localhost:8080/customers?limit=2&offset=0
```

This call returns the first chunk of two entities and several control METADATA ELEMENTS. Besides the link relation [Allamaraju 2010] that points at the next chunk, the response also contains the corresponding `offset`, `limit`, and total `size` values. Note that `size` is not required to implement PAGINATION on the provider side but allows API clients to show end users or other consumers how many more data elements (or pages) may be requested subsequently.

```
{
  "offset": 0,
  "limit": 2,
  "size": 50,
  "customers": [
    ...
  ,
    ...
  ],
  "_links": {
    "next": {
      "href": "/customers?limit=2&offset=2"
    }
  }
}
```

The preceding example can easily be mapped to the corresponding SQL query `LIMIT 2 OFFSET 0`. Instead of talking about offsets and limits, the API could also use the page metaphor in its message vocabulary, as shown here:

```
curl -X GET http://localhost:8080/customers?page-size=2&page=0

{
  "page": 0,
  "pageSize": 2,
  "totalPages": 25,
  "customers": [
    ...
  ,
    ...
  ],
  "_links": {
    "next": {
      "href": "/customers?page-size=2&page=1"
    }
  }
}
```

Using Cursor-Based Pagination, the client first requests an initial page of the desired size 2:

```
curl -X GET http://localhost:8080/customers?page-size=2

{
  "pageSize": 2,
  "customers": [
    ...
  ,
    ...
  ],
  "_links": {
    "next": {
      "href": "/customers?page-size=2&cursor=mfn834fj"
    }
  }
}
```

The response contains a link to the next chunk of data, represented by the cursor value `mfn834fj`. The cursor could be as simple as the primary key of the database or contain more information, such as a query filter.

Discussion

PAGINATION aims to substantially improve resource consumption and performance by sending only the data presently required and doing so just in time.

A single large response message might be inefficient to exchange and process. In this context, data set size and data access profile (that is, the user needs), especially the number of data records required to be available to an API client (immediately and over time), require particular attention. Especially when returning data for human consumption, not all data may be needed immediately; then PAGINATION has the potential to improve the response times for data access significantly.

From a security standpoint, retrieving and encoding large data sets may incur high effort and cost on the provider side and therefore lead to a denial-of-service attack. Moreover, transferring large data sets across a network can lead to interruptions, as most networks are not guaranteed to be reliable, especially cellular networks. This aspect is improved with PAGINATION because attackers can only request pages with small portions of data instead of an entire data set (assuming that the maximum value for the page size is limited). Note that in a rather subtle attack, it could still be enough to request the first page; if a poorly designed API implementation loads a vast data set as a whole, expecting to feed the data to the client page by page, an attacker still is able to fill up the server memory.

If the structure of the desired responses is not set oriented, so that a collection of data items can be partitioned into chunks, PAGINATION cannot be applied. Compared to response messages using the PARAMETER TREE pattern without PAGINATION, the pattern is substantially more complex to understand and thus might be less convenient to use, as it turns a single call into a longer conversation. PAGINATION requires more programming effort than does exchanging all data with one message.

PAGINATION leads to tighter coupling between API client and provider than single message transfers because additional representation elements are required to manage the slicing of the result sets into chunks. This can be mitigated by standardizing the required METADATA ELEMENTS. For example, with hypermedia, one just follows a Web link to fetch the next page. A remaining coupling issue is the session that may have to be established with each client while the pages are being scanned.

If API clients want to go beyond sequential access, complex parameter representations may be required to perform random access by seeking specific pages (or to allow clients to compute the page index themselves). The Cursor-Based Pagination variant with its—from a client perspective, opaque—cursor or token usually does not allow random access.

Delivering one page at a time allows the API client to process a digestible amount of data; a specification of which page to return facilitates remote navigation directly within the data set. Less endpoint memory and network capacity are required to handle individual pages, although some overhead is introduced because PAGINATION management is required (discussed shortly).

The application of Pagination leads to additional design concerns:

- Where, when, and how to define the page size (the number of data elements per page). This influences the chattiness of the API (retrieving the data in many small pages requires a large number of messages).

- How to order results—that is, how to assign them to pages and how to arrange the partial results on these pages. This order typically cannot change after the paginated retrieval begins. Changing the order as an API evolves over its life cycle might make a new API version incompatible with previous ones, which might go unnoticed if not communicated properly and tested thoroughly.

- Where and how to store intermediate results, and for how long (deletion policy, timeouts).

- How to deal with request repetition. For instance, do the initial and the subsequent requests have to be idempotent to prevent errors and inconsistencies?

- How to correlate pages/chunks (with the original, the previous, and the next requests).

Further design issues for the API implementation include the caching policy (if any), the liveness (currentness) of results, filtering, as well as query pre- and post-processing (for example, aggregations, counts, sums). Typical data access layer concerns (for instance, isolation level and locking in relational databases) come into play here as well [Fowler 2002]. Consistency requirements differ by client type and use case: Is the client developer aware of the Pagination? The resolution of these concerns is context-specific; for instance, frontend representations of search results in Web applications differ from batch master data replication in Backend Integrations of enterprise information systems.

With respect to behind-the-scenes changes to mutable collections, two cases have to be distinguished. One issue that has to be dealt with is that new items might be added while the client walks through the pages. The second issue concerns updates to (or removal of) items on a page that has already been seen by the client. Pagination can deal with new items but will usually miss changes to already downloaded items that happened while a Pagination "session" was ongoing.

If the page size was set too small, sometimes the result of Pagination can be annoying for users (especially developers using the API), as they have to click through and wait to retrieve the next page even if there are only a few results. Also, human users may expect client-side searches to filter an entire data set; introducing Pagination may incorrectly result in empty search results because the matching data items are found in pages that have not yet been retrieved.

Not all functions requiring an entire record set, such as searching, work (well) with PAGINATION, or they require extra effort (such as intermediate data structures on the API client side). Paginating after searching/filtering (and not vice versa) reduces workload.

This pattern covers the download of large data sets, but what about upload? Such *Request Pagination* can be seen as a complementary pattern. It would gradually upload the data and fire off a processing job only once all data is there. Incremental State Build-up, one of the Conversation Patterns [Hohpe 2017], has this inverse nature. It describes a solution similar to PAGINATION to deliver the data from the client to the provider in multiple steps.

Related Patterns

PAGINATION can be seen as the opposite of REQUEST BUNDLE: whereas PAGINATION is concerned with reducing the individual message size by splitting one large message into many smaller pages, REQUEST BUNDLE combines several messages into a single large one.

A paginated query typically defines an ATOMIC PARAMETER LIST for its input parameters containing the query parameters and a PARAMETER TREE for its output parameters (that is, the pages).

A request-response correlation scheme might be required so that the client can distinguish the partial results of multiple queries in arriving response messages; the pattern "Correlation Identifier" [Hohpe 2003] might be eligible in such cases.

A "Message Sequence" [Hohpe 2003] also can be used when a single large data element has to be split up.

More Information

Chapter 10 of *Build APIs You Won't Hate* covers PAGINATION types, discusses implementation approaches, and presents examples in PHP [Sturgeon 2016b]. Chapter 8 in the *RESTful Web Services Cookbook* deals with queries in a RESTful HTTP context [Allamaraju 2010]. *Web API Design: The Missing Link* covers PAGINATION under "More on Representation Design" [Apigee 2018].

In a broader context, the user interface (UI) and Web design communities have captured PAGINATION patterns in different contexts (not API design and management, but interaction design and information visualization). See coverage of the topic at the Interaction Design Foundation Web site [Foundation 2021] and the UI Patterns Web site [UI Patterns 2021].

Chapter 8 of *Implementing Domain-Driven Design* features stepwise retrieval of a notification log/archive, which can be seen as Offset-Based Pagination [Vernon 2013]. RFC 5005 covers feed paging and archiving for Atom [Nottingham 2007].

Pattern:
WISH LIST

When and Why to Apply

API providers serve multiple different clients that invoke the same operations. Not all clients have the same information needs: some might use just a subset of the data offered by an endpoint and its operations; other clients might need rich data sets.

> How can an API client inform the API provider at runtime about the data it is interested in?

When addressing this problem, API designers balance performance aspects such as response time and throughput with factors influencing the developer experience such as learning effort and evolvability. They strive for data parsimony (or *Datensparsamkeit*).

These forces could be resolved by introducing infrastructure components such as network- and application-level gateways and caches to reduce the load on the server, but such components add to the complexity of the deployment model and network topology of the API ecosystem and increase related infrastructure testing, operations management, and maintenance efforts.

How It Works

> As an API client, provide a WISH LIST in the request that enumerates all desired data elements of the requested resource. As an API provider, deliver only those data elements in the response message that are enumerated in the WISH LIST ("response shaping").

Specify the WISH LIST as an ATOMIC PARAMETER LIST or flat PARAMETER TREE. As a special case, a simple ATOMIC PARAMETER may be included that indicates a verbosity level (or level of detail) such as `minimal`, `medium`, or `full`.

Figure 7.5 sketches the request and response messages used when introducing a Wish List:

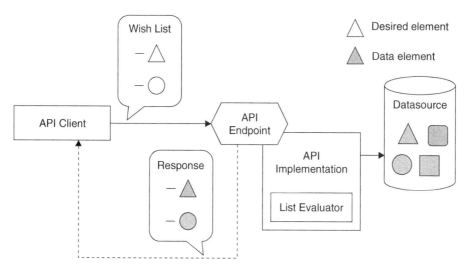

Figure 7.5 *Wish List: A client enumerates the desired data elements of the resource*

The List Evaluator in the figure has two implementation options. It often is translated to a filter for the data source so that only relevant data is loaded. Alternatively, the API implementation can fetch a full result set from the data source and select the entities that appear in the client wish when assembling the response data. Note that the data source can be any kind of backend system, possibly remote, or database. For instance, the wish translates into a WHERE clause of a SQL query when the data source is a relational database. If a remote system is accessed via an API, the Wish List might simply be passed on after having been validated (assuming that the downstream API also supports the pattern).

Variants   A common variant is to provide options for *expansion* in responses. The response to the first request provides only a terse result with a list of parameters that can be expanded in subsequent requests. To expand the request results, the client can select one or more of these parameters in the Wish List of a follow-on request.

Another variant is to define and support a wildcard mechanism, as known from SQL and other query languages. For instance, a star * might request all data elements of a particular resource (which could then be the default if no wishes are specified). Even more complex schemes are possible, such as cascaded specifications (for example, `customer.*` fetching all data about the customer).

Example

In the Lakeside Mutual Customer Core application, a request for a customer returns all of its available attributes.

```
curl -X GET http://localhost:8080/customers/gktlipwhjr
```

For customer ID `gktlipwhjr`, this would return the following:

```
{
  "customerId": "gktlipwhjr",
  "firstname": "Max",
  "lastname": "Mustermann",
  "birthday": "1989-12-31T23:00:00.000+0000",
  "streetAddress": "Oberseestrasse 10",
  "postalCode": "8640",
  "city": "Rapperswil",
  "email": "admin@example.com",
  "phoneNumber": "055 222 4111",
  "moveHistory": [ ],
  "customerInteractionLog": {
    "contactHistory": [ ],
    "classification": {
      "priority": "gold"
    }
  }
}
```

To improve this design, a WISH LIST in the query string can restrict the result to the fields included in the wish. In the example, an API client might be interested in only the `customerId`, `birthday`, and `postalCode`:

```
curl -X GET http://localhost:8080/customers/gktlipwhjr?\
fields=customerId,birthday,postalCode
```

The returned response now contains only the requested fields:

```
{
  "customerId": "gktlipwhjr",
  "birthday": "1989-12-31T23:00:00.000+0000",
  "postalCode": "8640"
}
```

This response is much smaller; only the information required by the client is transmitted.

Discussion

WISH LIST helps manage the different information needs of API clients. It is well suited if the network has limited capacity and there is a certain amount of confidence that clients usually require only a subset of the available data. The potential negative consequences include additional security threats, additional complexity, as well as test and maintenance efforts. Before introducing a WISH LIST mechanism, these negative consequences must be considered carefully. Often, they are treated as an afterthought, and mitigating them can lead to maintenance and evolution problems once the API is in production.

By adding or not adding attribute values in the WISH LIST instance, the API client expresses its wishes to the provider; hence, the desire for data parsimony (or *Datensparsamkeit*) is met. The provider does not have to supply specialized and optimized versions of operations for certain clients or to guess data required for client use cases. Clients can specify the data they require, thereby enhancing performance by creating less database and network load.

Providers have to implement more logic in their service layers, possibly affecting other layers down to data access as well. Providers risk exposing their data model to clients, increasing coupling. Clients have to create the WISH LIST, the network has to transport this metadata, and the provider has to process it.

A comma-separated list of attribute names can lead to problems when mapped to programming language elements. For instance, misspelling an attribute name might lead to an error (if the API client is lucky), or the expressed wish might be ignored (which might lead the API client to the impression that the attribute does not exist). Furthermore, API changes might have unexpected consequences; for instance, a renamed attribute might no longer be found if clients do not modify their wishes accordingly.

Solutions using the more complex variants introduced earlier (such as cascaded specifications, wildcards, or expansion) might be harder to understand and build than simpler alternatives. Sometimes existing provider-internal search-and-filter capabilities such as wildcards or regular expressions can be reused.

This pattern (or, more generally speaking, all patterns and practices sharing this common goal and theme of client-driven message content) is also known as *response shaping*.

Related Patterns

WISH TEMPLATE addresses the same problem as WISH LIST but uses a possibly nested structure to express the wishes rather than a flat list of element names. Both WISH LIST and WISH TEMPLATE usually deal with PARAMETER TREES in response messages because patterns to reduce message sizes are particularly useful when dealing with complex response data structures.

Using a WISH LIST has a positive influence on sticking to a RATE LIMIT, as less data is transferred when the pattern is used. To reduce the transferred data further, it can be combined with CONDITIONAL REQUEST.

The PAGINATION pattern also reduces response message sizes by splitting large repetitive responses into parts. The two patterns can be combined.

More Information

Regular expression syntax or query languages such as XPath (for XML payloads) can be seen as an advanced variant of this pattern. GraphQL [GraphQL 2021] offers a declarative query language to describe the representation to be retrieved against an agreed-upon schema found in the API documentation. We cover GraphQL in more detail in the WISH TEMPLATE pattern.

Web API Design: The Missing Link [Apigee 2018] recommends comma-separated WISH LISTS in its chapter "More on Representation Design." James Higginbotham features this pattern as "Zoom-Embed" [Higginbotham 2018].

"Practical API Design at Netflix, Part 1: Using Protobuf FieldMask" in the Netflix Technology Blog [Borysov 2021] mentions GraphQL field selectors and sparse fieldsets in JSON:API [JSON API 2022]. It then features Protocol Buffer `FieldMask` as a solution for gRPC APIs within the Netflix Studio Engineering. The authors suggest that API providers may ship client libraries with prebuilt `FieldMask` for the most frequently used combinations of fields. This makes sense if multiple consumers are interested in the same subset of fields.

Pattern: WISH TEMPLATE

When and Why to Apply

An API provider has to serve multiple different clients that invoke the same operations. Not all clients have the same information needs: some might need just a subset of the data offered by the endpoint; other clients might need rich, deeply structured data sets.

How can an API client inform the API provider about nested data that it is interested in? How can such preferences be expressed flexibly and dynamically?[3]

---

3. Note that this problem is very similar to the problem of the pattern WISH LIST but adds the theme of response data nesting.

An API provider that has multiple clients with different information might simply expose a complex data structure that represents the superset (or union) of what the client community wants (for example, all attributes of master data such as product or customer information or collections of operational data entities such as purchase order items). Very likely, this structure becomes increasingly complex as the API evolves. Such a one-size-fits-all approach also costs performance (response time, throughput) and introduces security threats.

Alternatively, one could use a flat WISH LIST that simply enumerates desired attributes, but such a simple approach has limited expressiveness when dealing with nested data structures.

Network-level and application-level gateways and proxies can be introduced to improve performance, for instance, by caching. Such responses to performance issues add to the complexity of the deployment model and network topology and come with design and configuration effort.

How It Works

Add one or more additional parameters to the request message that mirror the hierarchical structure of the parameters in the corresponding response message. Make these parameters optional or use Boolean as their types so that their values indicate whether or not a parameter should be included.

The structure of the wish that mirrors the response message often is a PARAMETER TREE. API clients can populate instances of this WISH TEMPLATE parameter with empty, sample, or dummy values when sending a request message or set its Boolean value to true to indicate their interest in it. The API provider then uses the mirrored structure of the wish as a template for the response and substitutes the requested values with actual response data. Figure 7.6 illustrates this design.

The Template Processor in the figure has two implementation options, depending on the chosen template format. If a mirror object is already received from the wire and structured as a PARAMETER TREE, this data structure can be traversed to prepare the data source retrieval (or to extract relevant parts from the result set). Alternatively, the templates may come in the form of a declarative query, which must be evaluated first and then translated to a database query or a filter to be applied to the fetched data (these two options are similar to those in the List Evaluator component of a WISH LIST processor shown in Figure 7.5). The evaluation of the template instance can be straightforward and supported by libraries or language concepts in the API implementation (for instance, navigating through nested JSON objects with JSONPath, XML documents with XPath, or matching a regular expression).

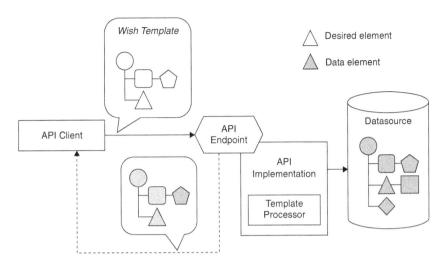

Figure 7.6 *WISH TEMPLATE components and processing steps*

For complex template syntaxes constituting a domain-specific language, the introduction of compiler concepts such as scanning and parsing might be necessary.

Figure 7.7 shows the matching input and output parameter structure for two top-level fields, aValue and aString, and a nested child object that also has two fields, aFlag and aSecondString. The output parameters (or response message elements) have integer and string types, and the mirror in the request message specifies matching Boolean values. Setting the Boolean to true indicates interest in the data.

Example
The following MDSL service contract sketch introduces a <<Wish_Template>> highlighted with a stereotype:

```
data type PersonalData P // unspecified, placeholder
data type Address P // unspecified, placeholder
data type CustomerEntity <<Entity>> {PersonalData?, Address?}

endpoint type CustomerInformationHolderService
  exposes
    operation getCustomerAttributes
      expecting payload {
        "customerId":ID, // the customer ID
        <<Wish_Template>>"mockObject":CustomerEntity
        // has same structure as desired result set
      }
      delivering payload CustomerEntity
```

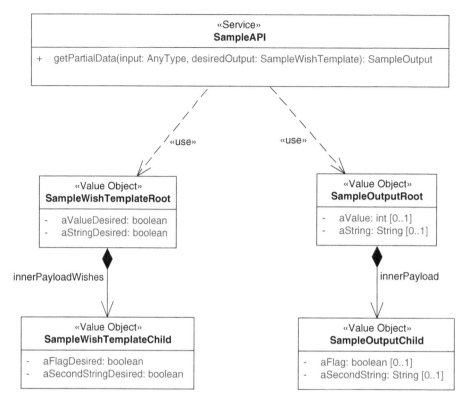

Figure 7.7 *Possible structure of mock/mirror object (WISH TEMPLATE)*

In this example of an API, the client can send a `CustomerEntity` mirror (or mock) object that may include `PersonalData` and/or `Address` attributes (this is defined in the `data type` definition `CustomerEntity`). The provider can then check which attributes were sent (ignoring the dummy values in the wish) and respond with a filled-out `CustomerEntity` instance containing `PersonalData` and/or `Address`.

Discussion

Data parsimony (or *Datensparsamkeit*) is an important general design principle in distributed systems that are performance- and security-critical. However, this principle is not always applied when iteratively and incrementally defining an API endpoint: it is typically easier to add things (here, information items or attributes) than to remove them. That is, once something is added to an API, it is often hard to determine whether it can be safely removed in a backward-compatible way (without breaking changes, that is) as many (maybe even unknown) clients might depend on it. By specifying selected attribute values in the WISH TEMPLATE instance and filling it with marker values or Boolean flags, the consumer expresses its wishes to the provider; thus, the desire for data parsimony and flexibility is met.

When implementing this pattern, several decisions have to be made, including how to represent and populate the template. The sibling pattern WISH LIST mentions a comma-separated list of wishes as one approach, but the PARAMETER TREES forming the WISH TEMPLATE are more elaborate and therefore require encoding and syntactic analysis. While highly sophisticated template notations might improve the developer experience on the client side and performance significantly, they also run the risk of turning into a larger, rather complex piece of middleware embedded into the API implementation (which comes with development, test, and maintenance effort as well as technical risk).

Another issue is how to handle errors for wishes that cannot be fulfilled, for example, because the client specified an invalid parameter. One approach could be to ignore the parameter silently, but this might hide real problems, for instance, if there was a typo or the name of a parameter changed.

The pattern is applicable not only when designing APIs around business capabilities but also when working with more IT-infrastructure-related domains such as software-defined networks, virtualization containers, or big data analysis. Such domains and software solutions for them typically have rich domain models and many configuration options. Dealing with the resulting variability justifies a flexible approach to API design and information retrieval.

GraphQL, with its type system, introspection, and validation capabilities, as well as its resolver concept can be seen as an advanced realization of this pattern [GraphQL 2021]. The WISH TEMPLATES of GraphQL are the query and mutation schemas providing declarative descriptions of the client wants and needs. Note that the adoption of GraphQL requires the implementation of a GraphQL server (effectively realizing the Template Processor in Figure 7.6). This server is a particular type of API endpoint located on top of the actual API endpoints (which become resolvers in GraphQL terms). This server has to parse the declarative description of queries and mutations and then call one or more resolvers, which in turn may call additional ones when following the data structure hierarchy.

Related Patterns

WISH LIST addresses the same problem but uses a flat enumeration rather than a mock/template object; both these patterns deal with instances of PARAMETER TREE in response messages. The WISH TEMPLATE becomes part of a PARAMETER TREE that appears in the request message.

WISH TEMPLATE shares many characteristics with its sibling pattern WISH LIST. For instance, without client- and provider-side data contract validation against a schema (XSD, JSON Schema), WISH TEMPLATE has the same drawbacks as the simple enumeration approach described in the WISH LIST pattern. WISH TEMPLATES can become more complex to specify and understand than simple lists of wishes; schemas and validators are usually not required for simple lists of wishes. Provider developers must be aware that complex wishes with deep nesting can strain and stress the communication infrastructure.[4] Processing can then also get more complex. Accepting the additional effort, as well as the complexity added to the parameter data definitions and their processing, only makes sense if simpler structures like WISH LISTS cannot express the wish adequately.

Using a WISH TEMPLATE has a positive influence on a RATE LIMIT, as less data is transferred when the pattern is used and fewer requests are required.

More Information

In "You Might Not Need GraphQL," Phil Sturgeon shows several APIs that implement response shaping and how they correspond to related GraphQL concepts [Sturgeon 2017].

Message Exchange Optimization (aka Conversation Efficiency)

The previous section offered patterns that allow clients to specify the partition of large data sets and which individual data points they are interested in. This lets API providers and clients avoid unnecessary data transfers and requests. But maybe the client already has a copy of the data and does not want to receive the same data again. Or they might have to send many individual requests that cause transmission and processing overhead. The patterns described here provide solutions to these two issues and try to balance the following common forces:

- **Complexity of endpoint, client, and message payload design and programming:** The additional effort needed to implement and operate a more complex API endpoint that takes data update frequency characteristics into account needs to be balanced against the expected reduction in endpoint processing and bandwidth usage. Reducing the number of requests does not imply that

---

4. Olaf Hartig and Jorge Pérez analyzed the performance of the GitHub GraphQL API and found an "exponential increase in result sizes" as they increased the query level depth. The API timed out on queries with nesting levels higher than 5 [Hartig 2018].

less information is exchanged. Hence, the remaining messages have to carry more complex payloads.

- **Accuracy of reporting and billing:** Reporting and billing of API usage must be accurate and should be perceived as being fair. A solution that burdens the client with additional work (for instance, keeping track of which version of data it has) to reduce the provider's workload might require some incentive from the provider. This additional complexity in the client-provider conversation might also have an impact on the accounting of API calls.

The two patterns responding to these forces are CONDITIONAL REQUEST and REQUEST BUNDLE.

 Pattern:
CONDITIONAL REQUEST

When and Why to Apply

Some clients keep on requesting the same server-side data repeatedly. This data does not change between requests.

> How can unnecessary server-side processing and bandwidth usage be avoided when invoking API operations that return rarely changing data?

In addition to the challenges introduced at the beginning of this section, the following forces apply:

- **Size of messages:** If network bandwidth or endpoint processing power is limited, retransmitting large responses that the client already has received is wasteful.

- **Client workload:** Clients may want to learn whether the result of an operation has changed since their last invocation in order to avoid reprocessing the same results. This reduces their workload.

- **Provider workload:** Some requests are rather inexpensive to answer, such as those not involving complex processing, external database queries, or other backend calls. Any additional runtime complexity of the API endpoint, for instance, any decision logic introduced to avoid unnecessary calls, might negate the possible savings in such cases.

- **Data currentness versus correctness:** API clients might want to cache a local copy of the data to reduce the number of API calls. As copy holders, they must decide when to refresh their caches to avoid stale data. The same considerations apply to metadata. On the one hand, when data changes, chances are that metadata about it has to change too. On the other hand, the data could remain the same, and only the metadata might change. Attempts to make conversations more efficient must take these considerations into account.

One might consider scaling up or scaling out on the physical deployment level to achieve the desired performance, but such an approach has its limits and is costly. The API provider or an intermediary API gateway might cache previously requested data to serve them quickly without having to recreate or fetch them from the database or a backend service. Such dedicated caches have to be kept current and invalidated at times, which leads to a complex set of design problems.[5]

In an alternative design, the client could send a "preflight" or "look before you leap" request asking the provider if anything has changed before sending the actual request. But this design doubles the number of requests, makes the client implementation more complex, and might reduce client performance when the network has a high latency.

How It Works

▼

Make requests conditional by adding METADATA ELEMENTS to their message representations (or protocol headers) and processing these requests only if the condition specified by the metadata is met.

▲

If the condition is not met, the provider does not reply with a full response but returns a special status code instead. Clients can then use the previously cached value. In the simplest case, the conditions represented by METADATA ELEMENTS could be transferred in an ATOMIC PARAMETER. Application-specific data version numbers or timestamps can be used if already present in the request.

---

5. As Phil Karlton (quoted by Martin Fowler) notes, "There are only two hard things in Computer Science: cache invalidation and naming things" [Fowler 2009]. Fowler provides tongue-in-cheek evidence for this claim.

Figure 7.8 illustrates the solution elements.

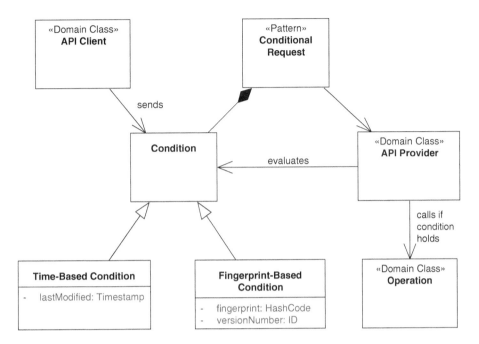

Figure 7.8 *CONDITIONAL REQUEST*

It is also possible to implement the CONDITIONAL REQUEST pattern within the communication infrastructure, orthogonal and complementary to the application-specific content. To do so, the provider may include a hash of the data served. The client can then include this hash in subsequent requests to indicate which version of the data it already has and for which data it wishes to receive only newer versions. A special `condition violated` response is returned instead of the complete response if the condition is not met. This approach implements a "virtual caching" strategy, allowing clients to recycle previously retrieved responses (assuming they have kept a copy).

Variants   Request conditions can take different forms, leading to different variants of this pattern:

- *Time-Based Conditional Request:* Resources are timestamped with a `last-modified` date. A client can use this timestamp in the subsequent requests so that the server will reply with a resource representation only if it is newer than the copy the client already has. Note that this approach requires some clock synchronization between clients and servers if it is supposed to work accurately (which might not always be required). In HTTP, the `If-Modified-Since` request header carries such a timestamp, and the `304 Not Modified` status code is used to indicate that a newer version is not available.

- *Fingerprint-Based Conditional Request:* Resources are tagged, that is, finger-printed, by the provider, using, for example, a hash function applied to the response body or some version number. Clients can then include the fingerprint to indicate the version of the data they already have. In HTTP, the entity tag (ETag), as described in RFC 7232 [Fielding 2014a], serves that purpose together with the If-None-Match request header and the previously mentioned 304 Not Modified status code.

Example

Many Web application frameworks, such as Spring, support CONDITIONAL REQUESTS natively. The Spring-based Customer Core backend application in the Lakeside Mutual scenario includes ETags—implementing the fingerprint-based CONDITIONAL REQUEST variant—in all responses. For example, consider retrieving a customer:

```
curl -X GET --include \
http::/localhost:8080/customers/gktlipwhjr
```

A response containing an ETag header could start with:

```
HTTP/1.1 200
ETag: "0c2c09ecd1ed498aa7d07a516a0e56ebc"
Content-Type: application/hal+json;charset=UTF-8
Content-Length: 801
Date: Wed, 20 Jun 2018 05:36:39 GMT
{
  "customerId": "gktlipwhjr",
...
```

Subsequent requests can then include the ETag received from the provider previously to make the request conditional:

```
curl -X GET --include --header \
'If-None-Match: "0c2c09ecd1ed498aa7d07a516a0e56ebc"' \
http://localhost:8080/customers/gktlipwhjr
```

If the entity has not changed, that is, If-None-Match occurs, the provider answers with a 304 Not Modified response including the same ETag:

```
HTTP/1.1 304
ETag: "0c2c09ecd1ed498aa7d07a516a0e56ebc"
Date: Wed, 20 Jun 2018 05:47:11 GMT
```

If the customer has changed, the client will get the full response, including a new ETag, as shown in Figure 7.9.

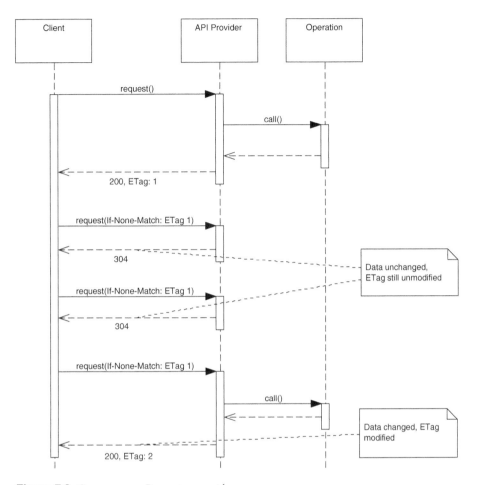

Figure 7.9 *Conditional Request example*

Note that the Customer Core microservice implements Conditional Request as a filter applied to the response. Using a filter means that the response is still computed but then is discarded by the filter and replaced with the `304 Not Modified` status code. This approach has the benefit of being transparent to the endpoint implementation; however, it only saves bandwidth and not computation time. A server-side cache could be used to minimize the computational time as well.

Discussion

Conditional Requests allow both clients and API providers to save bandwidth without assuming that providers remember whether a given client has already seen the latest version of the requested data. It is up to the clients to remind the server about their latest known version of the data. They cache previous responses and are responsible for keeping track of their timestamp or fingerprint and resending this information along with their next requests. This simplifies the configuration of the *data currentness interval*. Timestamps, as one way to specify the data currentness interval, are simple to implement even in distributed systems as long as only one system writes the data. The time of this system is the master time in that case.

The complexity of the provider-side API endpoint does not increase if the pattern is implemented with a filter, as shown in the preceding example. Further improvements, such as additional caching of responses, can be realized for specific endpoints to reduce provider workload. This increases the complexity of the endpoint, as they have to evaluate the conditions, filters, and exceptions, including errors that might occur because of the condition handling or filtering.

Providers also have to decide how CONDITIONAL REQUESTS affect other quality measures such as a RATE LIMIT and whether such requests require special treatment in a PRICING PLAN.

Clients can choose whether or not to make use of CONDITIONAL REQUESTS, depending on their performance requirements. Another selection criterion is whether clients can afford to rely on the server to detect whether the state of the API resources has changed. The number of messages transmitted does not change with CONDITIONAL REQUESTS, but the payload size can be reduced significantly. Rereading an old response from the client cache is usually much faster than reloading it from the API provider.

Related Patterns

Using a CONDITIONAL REQUEST may have a positive influence on a RATE LIMIT that includes response data volumes in the definition of the limit, as less data is transferred when this pattern is used.

The pattern can be carefully combined with either WISH LIST or WISH TEMPLATE. This combination can be rather useful to indicate the subset of data that is to be returned if the condition evaluates to `true` and the data needs to be sent (again).

A combination of CONDITIONAL REQUESTS with PAGINATION is possible, but there are edge cases to be considered. For example, the data of a particular page might not have changed, but more data was added, and the total number of pages has increased. Such a change in metadata should also be included when evaluating the condition.

More Information

Chapter 10 in the *RESTful Web Services Cookbook* [Allamaraju 2010] is dedicated to conditional requests. Some of the nine recipes in this chapter even deal with requests that modify data.

 **Pattern:**
REQUEST BUNDLE

When and Why to Apply

An API endpoint that exposes one or more operations has been specified. The API provider observes that clients make many small, independent requests; individual responses are returned for these requests. These chatty interaction sequences harm scalability and throughput.

How can the number of requests and responses be reduced to increase communication efficiency?

In addition to the general desire for efficient messaging and data parsimony (as discussed in the introduction to this chapter), the goal of this pattern is to improve performance:

- **Latency:** Reducing the number of API calls may improve client and provider performance, for instance, when the network has high latency or overhead is incurred by sending multiple requests and responses.

- **Throughput:** Exchanging the same information through fewer messages may lead to a higher throughput. However, the client has to wait longer until it can start working with the data.

One might consider using more or better hardware to meet the performance demands of the API clients, but such an approach has its physical limits and is costly.

How It Works

Define a REQUEST BUNDLE as a data container that assembles multiple independent requests in a single request message. Add metadata such as identifiers of individual requests (bundle elements) and a bundle element counter.

There are two options to design the response messages:

1. One request with one response: REQUEST BUNDLE with a *single bundled response*.

2. One request with multiple responses: REQUEST BUNDLE with *multiple responses*.

The REQUEST BUNDLE container message can, for instance, be structured as a PARAMETER TREE or a PARAMETER FOREST. In the first option, a message structure for the response container that mirrors the request assembly and corresponds to the bundled requests has to be defined. The second option can be implemented with support from the underlying network protocols to support suitable message exchange and conversation patterns. For example, with HTTP, the provider can delay the response until a bundle item has been processed. RFC 6202 [Saint-Andre 2011] presents details on this technique, which is called *long polling*.

Errors have to be handled both individually and on the container level. Different options exist; for instance, an ERROR REPORT for the entire batch can be combined with an associative array of individual ERROR REPORTS for bundle elements accessible via ID ELEMENTS.

Figure 7.10 shows a REQUEST BUNDLE of three individual requests, A, B, and C, assembled into a single remote API call. Here, a single bundled response is used (Option 1).

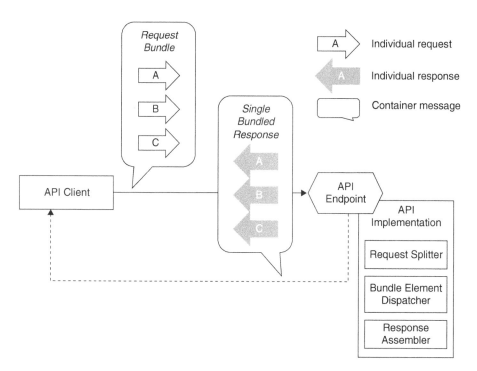

Figure 7.10 *REQUEST BUNDLE: Three independent requests, A, B, and C, are assembled in a container message. The provider processes the requests and replies with a Single Bundled Response*

The API implementation has to split the request bundle and assemble the response bundle. This can be as straightforward as iterating through an array that the provider-side endpoint hands over, but it also may require some additional decision and dispatch logic, for instance, using a control METADATA ELEMENT in the request to decide where in the API implementation to route the bundle elements to. The API client has to split a bundled response in a similar way if the provider returns a single bundled response.

Example

In the Lakeside Mutual Customer Core service, clients can request multiple customers from the customer's INFORMATION HOLDER RESOURCE by specifying an ATOMIC PARAMETER LIST of customer ID ELEMENTS. A path parameter serves as a bundle container. A comma (,) separates the bundle elements:

```
curl -X GET http://localhost:8080/customers/ce4btlyluu,rgpp0wkpec
```

This will return the two requested customers as DATA ELEMENTS, represented as JSON objects in a bundle-level array (using the single bundled response option):

```
{
  "customers": [
    {
      "customerId": "ce4btlyluu",
      "firstname": "Robbie",
      "lastname": "Davenhall",
      "birthday": "1961-08-11T23:00:00.000+0000",
      ...
      "_links": { ... }
    },
    {
      "customerId": "rgpp0wkpec",
      "firstname": "Max",
      "lastname": "Mustermann",
      "birthday": "1989-12-31T23:00:00.000+0000",
      ...
      "_links": { ... }
    }
  ],
  "_links": { ... }
}
```

This example implements the pattern option REQUEST BUNDLE with single bundled response, introduced earlier.

Discussion

By transmitting a bundle of requests at once, the number of messages can be reduced significantly if the client-side usage scenarios include batch or bulk processing (for instance, periodic updates to customer master data). As a consequence, the communication is sped up because less network communication is required. Depending on the actual use case, client implementation effort might also decrease because the client does not have to keep track of multiple ongoing requests. It can process all logically independent bundle elements found in a single response one by one.

The pattern adds to endpoint processing effort and complexity. Providers have to split the request messages and, when realizing REQUEST BUNDLE with multiple responses, coordinate multiple individual responses. Client processing effort and complexity can increase as well because clients must deal with the REQUEST BUNDLE and its independent elements, again requiring a splitting strategy. Finally, the message payload design and processing get more complex, as data from multiple sources has to be merged into one message.

Being independent of each other, individual requests in the REQUEST BUNDLE might be executed concurrently by the endpoint. Hence, the client should not make any assumptions about the order of evaluation of the requests. API providers should document this container property in the API DESCRIPTION. Guaranteeing a particular order of bundle elements causes extra work, for instance ordering a single bundled response in the same way as the incoming REQUEST BUNDLE.

The pattern is eligible if the underlying communication protocol cannot handle multiple requests at once. It assumes that data access controls are sufficiently defined and presented so that all bundle elements are allowed to be processed. If not, the provider must compose partial responses indicating to the client which commands/requests in the bundle failed and how to correct the corresponding input so that invocation can be retried. Such element-level access control can be challenging to handle on the client side.

Clients must wait until all messages in the bundle have been processed, increasing the overall latency until a first response is received; however, compared to many consecutive calls, the total communication time typically speeds up, as less network communication is required. The coordination effort might make the service provider stateful, which is considered harmful in microservices and cloud environments due to its negative impact on scalability. That is, it becomes more difficult to scale out horizontally when workload increases because the microservices middleware or the cloud provider infrastructure may contain load balancers that now have to make sure that subsequent requests reach the right instances and that failover procedures recreate state in a suited fashion. It is not obvious whether the bundle or its elements should be the units of scaling.

Related Patterns

The request and response messages of a REQUEST BUNDLE form PARAMETER FORESTS or PARAMETER TREES. Additional information about the structure and information that identifies individual requests comes as one or more ID ELEMENTS or METADATA ELEMENTS. Such identifiers might realize the "Correlation Identifier" pattern [Hohpe 2003] to trace responses back to requests.

A REQUEST BUNDLE can be delivered as a CONDITIONAL REQUEST. The pattern can also be combined with a WISH LIST or a WISH TEMPLATE. It must be carefully analyzed if enough gains can be realized to warrant the complexity of a combination of two or even three of those patterns. If the requested entities are of the same kind (for instance, several people in an address book are requested), PAGINATION and its variants can be applied instead of REQUEST BUNDLE.

Using a REQUEST BUNDLE has a positive influence on staying within a RATE LIMIT that counts operation invocations because fewer messages are exchanged when the pattern is used. This pattern goes well with explicit ERROR REPORTS because it is often desirable to report the error status or success per bundle element and not only for the entire REQUEST BUNDLE.

REQUEST BUNDLE can be seen as an extension of the general "Command" design pattern: each individual request is a command according to terminology from [Gamma 1995]. "Message Sequence" [Hohpe 2003] solves the opposite problem: to reduce the message size, messages are split into smaller ones and tagged with a sequence ID. The price for this is a higher number of messages.

More Information

Recipe 13 in Chapter 11 of the *RESTful Web Services Cookbook* [Allamaraju 2010] advises against providing a generalized endpoint to tunnel multiple individual requests.

Coroutines can improve performance when applying the REQUEST BUNDLE pattern in the context of batch processing (aka chunking). "Improving Batch Performance when Migrating to Microservices with Chunking and Coroutines" discusses this option in detail [Knoche 2019].

Summary

This chapter presented patterns concerned with API quality, specifically, finding the sweet spot between API design granularity, runtime performance, and the ability to support many diverse clients. It investigated whether many small or few large messages should be exchanged.

Applying the EMBEDDED ENTITY pattern makes the API exchange self-contained. LINKED INFORMATION HOLDER leads to smaller messages that can refer to other API endpoints and, therefore, will lead to multiple round-trips to retrieve the same information.

PAGINATION lets clients retrieve data sets piecewise, depending on their information needs. If the exact selection of details to be fetched is not known at design time, and clients would like the API to satisfy all of their desires, then WISH LISTS and WISH TEMPLATES offer the required flexibility.

Bulk messages in a REQUEST BUNDLE require only one interaction. While performance can be carefully optimized by sending and receiving payloads with the right granularity, it also helps to introduce CONDITIONAL REQUESTS and avoid resending the same information to clients who already have it.

Note that performance is hard to predict in general and in distributed systems in particular. Typically, it is measured under steady conditions as a system landscape evolves; if a performance control shows a negative trend that runs the risk of violating one or more formally specified SERVICE LEVEL AGREEMENTS or other specified runtime quality policies, the API design and its implementation should be revised. This is a broad set of important issues for all distributed systems; it becomes even more severe when a system is decomposed into small parts, such as microservices to be scaled and evolved independently of each other. Even when services are loosely coupled, the performance budget for meeting the response-time requirements of an end user performing a particular business-level function can be evaluated only as a whole and end-to-end. Commercial products and open-source software for load/performance testing and monitoring exist. Challenges include the effort required to set up an environment that has the potential to produce meaningful, reproducible results as well as the ability to cope with change (of requirements, system architectures, and their implementations). Simulating performance is another option. There is a large body of academic work on predictive performance modeling of software systems and software architectures (for example, "The Palladio-Bench for Modeling and Simulating Software Architectures" [Heinrich 2018]).

Next up is API evolution, including approaches to versioning and life-cycle management (Chapter 8, "Evolve APIs").

Chapter 8

Evolve APIs

This chapter covers patterns eligible when APIs change over time. Most successful APIs do evolve; compatibility and extensibility are somewhat conflicting requirements that have to be balanced during the API life cycle. Clients and providers might not agree on the most efficient mix. Keeping multiple versions supported is costly; full backward compatibility might be desired. However, it is usually harder to achieve in practice as it seems. Poor evolution decisions might disappoint customers (and their API clients) and stress providers (and their developers).

We first motivate the need for evolution patterns and then present those we found in practice: two patterns for versioning and compatibility management and four patterns describing different life-cycle management guarantees.

This chapter corresponds to the Refine phase of the Align-Define-Design-Refine (ADDR) process.

Introduction to API Evolution

By definition, an API is not a static standalone product but part of an open, distributed, and interconnected system. APIs are intended to provide a rock-solid foundation on which to build client applications. Still, over long periods of time, like ocean waves that shape the rocky cliffs above them, APIs do change, especially when they are used by wave after wave of clients.

As APIs evolve to adapt to a changing environment, new features are added, bugs and defects get fixed, and some features are discontinued. Our evolution patterns help introduce API changes in a controlled way, deal with their consequences, and manage the impact of these changes on API clients. They support API owners, designers, and their customers when answering the following question:

What are the governing rules balancing stability and compatibility with maintainability and extensibility during API evolution?

Challenges When Evolving APIs

Our evolution patterns are concerned with the following desired qualities directly or indirectly:

- **Autonomy:** Allowing the API provider and the client to follow different life cycles; a provider can roll out new API versions without breaking existing clients.

- **Loose coupling:** Minimizing the impact on the client forced by API changes.

- **Extensibility:** Making it possible for the provider to improve and extend the API and change it to accommodate new requirements.

- **Compatibility:** Guaranteeing that API changes do not lead to semantic "misunderstandings" between client and provider.

- **Sustainability:** Minimizing the long-term maintenance effort to support old clients.

The different and independent life cycles, deployment frequencies, and schedules of providers and clients of APIs make it necessary to plan API evolution early and then continuously. They forbid making arbitrary changes to an already published API. This problem becomes more severe as an increasing number of clients start to use and depend on the API. The provider's influence on the clients or ability to manage them may shrink if many clients exist (or the provider does not know its clients). Public APIs are particularly challenging to evolve: if alternative providers exist, clients might prefer the most stable API being offered. However, even if no competing provider is available, API clients might not be able to adapt to new API versions at all and thus rely on the provider to evolve the API fairly. This is especially the case if clients are known to have been implemented in a project by some contracted developer who is not available anymore. For example, a small company might have paid an external consultant to integrate their online shop with a payment provider via a payment API. By the time the API moves to a new version, this external consultant might have moved on to another assignment.

Compatibility and *extensibility* are typically conflicting quality requirements. Many considerations in the evolution of an API are driven by compatibility considerations. Compatibility is a property of the relation between a provider and a client. The two parties are compatible if they can conduct their message exchange and correctly interpret and process all messages according to the semantics of the respective API version. For instance, the provider of API version n and clients written for this version are compatible by definition (assuming the interoperability tests have passed). If the client for API version n is compatible with the API provider for version n−1, the provider is *forward-compatible* with the new client version. If the client for API version n is compatible with the provider version n+1, the provider is *backward-compatible* with the old API version.

Compatibility is easy to achieve—or at least assumed to exist—at the time of the initial deployment of an API provider and its clients. An initial version exists and is documented in the API Description, so that API clients and providers agree on and share the same knowledge; interoperability can be designed and tested for. While the API evolves, the shared understanding may begin to vaporize; clients and provider drift apart simply because only one side may actually get a chance to change.

Compatibility considerations become more relevant and more difficult to achieve when the life cycle of all API providers and all clients can no longer be synchronized. With the move of many applications to cloud computing, the number of remote clients has increased significantly and client-provider relationships keep changing dynamically. In modern architecture paradigms such as microservices, an important characteristic is the ability to scale independently (to run multiple instances of a service at the same time, that is), and to deploy new versions with zero downtime. The latter is achieved by having multiple service instances running at the same time and switching them to the new version one after another until all instances have been upgraded. At least during such transition time, multiple versions of the API are offered. This means that when designing how to evolve an API and guaranteeing its compatibility, the possibility of having multiple client versions interact with multiple API versions must be taken into account.

Extensibility is the ability to offer new functionality in an API. For example, the current version of an API may expose response messages that contain a single Data Element (Chapter 6, "Design Request and Response Message Representations") called "price" representing money amounts, and the API Description may explain that the currency of the price is US dollar. In a future version of the API, multiple currencies shall be supported. Implementing such an extension can easily break existing clients because they can handle only US dollar values; if a new Metadata Element called "currency" is introduced, they will not be able to process it until they are updated. Thus, extensibility sometimes conflicts with maintaining compatibility.

The evolution patterns in this chapter are concerned with conscious decisions about the level of commitment and life-cycle support and with keeping or breaking compatibility under different circumstances. They also describe how to communicate breaking and nonbreaking changes.

Differing life cycles, deployment frequencies, and deployment dates of providers and clients occur frequently in practice, especially in PUBLIC API and COMMUNITY API scenarios (two patterns featured in Chapter 4, "Pattern Language Introduction"). This makes it necessary to plan API evolution before any software releases because it is difficult—or sometimes even impossible—to change an already published API arbitrarily. Depending on the ratio of API providers and clients, it is worthwhile to burden the provider (for maintaining older API versions) or the client (for migrating to new API versions more often). Political factors—such as how important a customer is—influence the solution space: to avoid losing dissatisfied clients, the provider will invest more effort to support old API versions. In case of a more powerful position of the provider, clients can be forced to migrate to newer API versions more often by shortening support periods of APIs or features within an API.

Sometimes APIs are released without a strategy for maintaining and updating them. Such an ad hoc approach leads to problems down the road resulting in broken clients and unavailability of those clients to their users. Even worse, problems may go unnoticed when no measures are taken to prevent clients from misinterpreting a message, which—while keeping an identical or at least similar syntax—has changed semantics in a new API version (for instance, does a price element include value added tax or not, and what is the rate?). Versioning an entire API with all its endpoints, operations, and messages is a rather coarse-grained strategy and leads to many—perhaps too many—released versions. Much effort may have to be spent on the client side to track and adapt a new API version.

If no explicit guarantees are given, clients often implicitly expect an API to be offered forever (which, in most cases, is not what a provider wants). When an API eventually sunsets, but the client expected it to be available for eternity (especially in the case of PUBLIC APIs with anonymous clients) or perhaps even had negotiated for lifetime extensions, the provider's reputation is damaged.

Sometimes providers want to change versions too often. This can result in problems with maintaining multiple versions in parallel or forcing upgrades upon their clients. It is important to avoid customer churn from too many versions that do not add enough value to invest the time and resources to upgrade. Moreover, some APIs must assume that API client developers are not available all the time; in that case, the API provider often has to support previous versions of its API. Such a situation occurs, for example, if client developers were hired for a small business Web site that must keep running, and they will never be paid to upgrade to a new API version. The Stripe API [Stripe 2022] for accepting online payments might have such small business clients. Student term projects often use public APIs; breaking changes to these APIs cause the project results to stop working, often after the projects ended.

Patterns in This Chapter

Figure 8.1 shows the pattern map for this chapter.

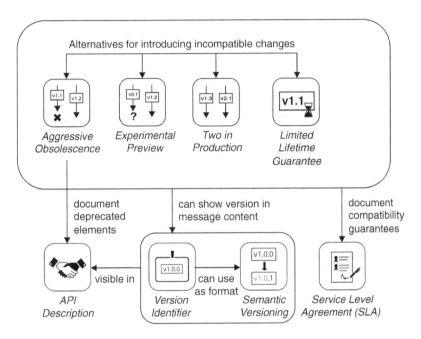

Figure 8.1 *Pattern map for this chapter (API evolution)*

Introducing an explicit Version Identifier that is visible to and correctly validated by message recipients helps clients and providers distinguish compatible and incompatible changes; such an identifier is also useful for API monitoring and support. A three-part Version Identifier following the Semantic Versioning pattern describes the compatibility between changes and thus conveys more information than simple version numbers.

Limited Lifetime Guarantee imposes a timeframe in which an API is supported. This time is communicated when the API is published, allowing clients to plan necessary API migrations in a timely manner. When the Two in Production pattern is applied, providers offer multiple versions of an API to avoid semantic misunderstandings that are based on poorly implemented backward or forward compatibility and give clients freedom of choice; each version running in production has a separate

VERSION IDENTIFIER. This is a middle-ground solution allowing for a gradual transition. Sometimes an API provider explicitly does not want to make any guarantees, for example, when developing an API and still fine-tuning its exact message structure and endpoint design. In such situations, the EXPERIMENTAL PREVIEW pattern can be used, which gives no guarantees but allows future clients to learn about and experiment with the API under development. With AGGRESSIVE OBSOLESCENCE, an API provider can deprecate and phase out APIs (or parts of them) at any time without offering multiple API versions at once.

Versioning and Compatibility Management

The two patterns in this section are VERSION IDENTIFIER and SEMANTIC VERSIONING.

 Pattern:
VERSION IDENTIFIER

When and Why to Apply

An API that runs in production evolves. New versions with improved functionality are offered over time. Eventually, the changes in a new version are no longer backward compatible; this causes existing clients to break.

How can an API provider indicate its current capabilities as well as the existence of possibly incompatible changes to clients in order to prevent malfunctioning of clients due to undiscovered interpretation errors?

- **Accuracy and exact identification:** When releasing a new API version, no problems with semantic mismatches or other differences between the new and the older API versions should occur. Clients must be able to rely on the syntax and semantics of an API version, even if that version is improved, extended, or otherwise modified.

- **No accidental breakage of compatibility:** If versions are called out in the messages to and from the API, communication participants can reject a request or response if they are confronted with an unknown or incompatible version number. This way, it is impossible to break backward compatibility accidentally, which might happen when the semantics of an existing representation element change without notice.

- **Client-side impact:** Breaking changes to an API require changes to the clients. These changes usually do not add any business value. Therefore, clients appreciate a stable API that they can rely on, an API that does not cause hidden costs for frequent maintenance releases that keep up with API changes.

- **Traceability of API versions in use:** API providers can monitor which and/ or how many clients depend on a specific API version. This data can be used to plan further governance actions, for instance, retiring old API versions or prioritizing feature enhancements.

Sometimes organizations roll out APIs without planning how to manage their life cycles. They might think that such planning can be just as effectively done after rollout. However, lack of governance and versioning is one of the factors that have caused some service-oriented architecture initiatives and projects to fail in the past [Joachim 2013].

How It Works

Introduce an explicit version indicator. Include this VERSION IDENTIFIER in the API DESCRIPTION and in the exchanged messages. To do the latter, add a METADATA ELEMENT to the endpoint address, the protocol header, or the message payload.

The explicit VERSION IDENTIFIER often takes a numeric value to indicate evolution progress and maturity. It can be included in dedicated representation elements, attribute/element name suffixes, parts of the endpoint addresses such as URLs, domain names, XML namespaces, or the HTTP content type header. To avoid consistency issues, the VERSION IDENTIFIER should appear in one and only one place in all message exchanges supported by an API, unless clients or middleware strongly desire to see it in several places.

To mint identifiers, the three-part SEMANTIC VERSIONING pattern is frequently used. By referring to such a structured VERSION IDENTIFIER, communication parties can check whether they can understand and correctly interpret the message; incompatibilities are straightforward to spot and distinguish from feature extensions.

By indicating a new version with a different VERSION IDENTIFIER, the receiving party can abort the interpretation of the message before any further problems occur and report an incompatibility error (for example, in an ERROR REPORT). The API DESCRIPTION can reference features that were introduced at a particular point in time (such as at the release of a certain version) or that are available only in certain

API versions but have been decommissioned in later versions, for example, when using the AGGRESSIVE OBSOLESCENCE pattern.

Note that the schema of request and response message (for instance, defined as custom media types in HTTP resource APIs) can also be versioned, possibly only loosely aligned with the endpoint/operation versioning. Alexander Dean and Frederick Blundun call this approach *SchemaVer* in [Dean 2014].

Also note that API evolution and implementation evolution are two different things, as the implementation can evolve separately from the interface (and be updated more frequently). This might lead to the use of multiple version identifiers, one for the remote API and one for each implementation of it.

All implementation dependencies should be included in the versioning concept (and/or backward compatibility of the dependencies must be ensured): if lower-layer components such as a database that underpins stateful API calls have a schema that cannot be evolved as fast as the API itself, this might slow down the release frequency. It must be clear which of the two (or more) API versions in production use which version of backend systems and other downstream dependencies. A "roll forward" strategy, or adding a facade that decouples implementation versioning from API versioning, may be considered.

Example

In HTTP resource APIs, the version of different features can be indicated as follows. The version of specific representation formats supported by the client appears in the content-type negotiation headers of HTTP such as the `Accept` header [Fielding 2014c]:

```
GET /customers/1234
Accept: text/json+customer; version=1.0
...
```

The version of specific endpoints and operations becomes part of the resource identifier:

```
GET v2/customers/1234
...
```

The version of the whole API can also be specified in the host domain name:

```
GET /customers/1234
Host: v2.api.service.com
...
```

In SOAP/XML-based APIs, the version is usually indicated as part of the name-space of the top-level message element:

```
<soap:Envelope>
  <soap:Body>
    <ns:MyMessage xmlns:ns="http://www.nnn.org/ns/1.0/">
    ...
    </ns:MyMessage>
  </soap:Body>
</soap:Envelope>
```

Another possibility is to specify the version in the payload, as in the following JSON example. In the initial version 1.0 of the billing API, the prices were defined in euros:

```
{
  "version": "1.0",
  "products": [
    {
      "productId": "ABC123",
      "quantity": 5;
      "price": 5.00;
    }
  ]
}
```

With a new version, the requirement of multicurrency was realized. This leads to the new data structure and the new contents of the version element "version": "2.0":

```
{
  "version": "2.0",
  "products": [
    {
      "productId": "ABC123",
      "quantity": 5;
      "price": 5.00;
      "currency": "USD"
    }
  ]
}
```

If no VERSION IDENTIFIER or any other mechanism to indicate a breaking change had been used, old software interpreting the version 2.0 of the message would assume that the product costs five euros, although it costs five US dollars. This is because a new attribute has changed the semantics of an existing one. Passing the version in the HTTP content type, as shown earlier, can eliminate this problem. While it would be possible to introduce a new field, `priceInDollars`, to avoid this problem, such changes lead to technical debt, which aggregates over time, especially in less trivial examples.

Discussion

Use of the VERSION IDENTIFIER pattern allows the provider to clearly communicate API, endpoint, operation, and message compatibility and extensibility. It reduces the likelihood of problems due to undetected semantic changes between API versions accidentally breaking compatibility. It also enables tracing which message payload versions are actually used by clients.

APIs that work with LINK IDENTIFIERS, such as hypermedia controls in HTTP resource APIs, require special attention when versioning them. Endpoints and APIs that are rather tightly coupled with each other, such as those forming an API product, should be versioned together (in a coordinated fashion, that is). APIs that are rather loosely coupled, such as those exposed by microservices owned and maintained by different teams in an organization, are more challenging to evolve. In the Lakeside Mutual case, if version 5 of the Customer Management backend API returns LINK IDENTIFIERS that refer to policy INFORMATION HOLDER RESOURCES residing in the Policy Management backend, which policy endpoint version does Customer Management backend assume? It may not know the Policy Management backend API version that the API client receiving the policy links, which reside in the Customer Self-Service frontend, is capable of handling (the mentioned components of the Lakeside Mutual architecture were introduced in Figure 2.6).

When the VERSION IDENTIFIER changes, clients might be required to migrate to a new API version even though the functionality that they rely on has not changed; this increases the effort for some API clients.

Introducing VERSION IDENTIFIERS does not allow providers to make arbitrary changes to the API, nor does it minimize the changes necessary to support old clients. However, it makes it possible to apply patters that have these benefits, for example, when offering TWO IN PRODUCTION. The pattern itself does not support the decoupling of the provider and client life cycle, either, but it is required by other patterns that do so. For example, implementing TWO IN PRODUCTION and AGGRESSIVE OBSOLESCENCE is simplified when versions are explicitly signaled.

This pattern describes a simple but effective mechanism to indicate breaking changes, especially those changes that a "Tolerant Reader" [Daigneau 2011] would be able to parse successfully but would fail to understand and use correctly. By making the version explicit, providers can force the client to reject a message of a newer version or can refuse to process an outdated request. This provides a mechanism to make incompatible changes safely. However, it forces the clients to migrate to a new, supported API version. Patterns like Two in Production can provide a grace period in which clients can migrate to the new version.

When opting for explicit versioning, it must be decided on what level the versioning takes place: in a Web Services Description Language (WSDL), the whole contract can be versioned (by changing the namespace, for example), as can its individual operations (for instance, by having a version suffix) and representation elements (schemas). HTTP resource APIs can also be versioned differently: for example, content types, URLs, and version elements in the payload can be used to indicate the version (as shown earlier). Versioning scope ("subject") and versioning solution ("means") should not be confused; for instance, representation elements can carry version information but also be subject to versioning themselves.

Using smaller units of versioning, for instance, single operations, decreases coupling between provider and client: consumers might use only features of an API endpoint that are not impacted by a change. Instead of providing a separate API endpoint per client, fine-grained versioning (on the level of operations or message representation elements) can limit the change impact. However, the more elements of an API are versioned, the higher the governance and test effort is. Both provider and client organizations need to keep track of the possibly many versioned elements and their active versions. Offering APIs specialized for special clients or different client types might be a better design choice in such circumstances.

Using a Version Identifier can lead to unnecessary change requests for software components such as the API client. This may happen if the code needs to be changed whenever the API version is changed. For example, changes to an XML namespace require changes and new deployments of clients. When using primitive code generation (for instance, JAXB [Wikipedia 2022f] without any customizations), this can be a problem because a change in the namespace results in a change in the Java package name, which affects all generated classes and references in the code to those classes. At a minimum, the code generation should be customized (or more robust and stable mechanisms to access the data be used) so that the impact of such technical changes is reduced and contained.

Different integration technologies offer different mechanisms for versioning and have different corresponding practices that are accepted by the respective communities. If SOAP is used, versions are usually indicated by different namespaces of the exchanged SOAP messages, although some APIs use a version suffix to the top-level message element. In contrast, parts of the REST community condemn the use of explicit Version Identifiers, and others encourage the use of HTTP accept and content-type headers (for instance, see [Klabnik 2011]) to convey the version. However, in practice, many applications also use Version Identifiers in the exchanged JSON/XML or the URL to indicate the version.

Related Patterns

A Version Identifier can be seen as a special type of Metadata Element. The Version Identifier can be further structured, for example, by using the Semantic Versioning pattern. The life-cycle pattern Two in Production requires explicit versioning; the other life-cycle patterns (Aggressive Obsolescence, Experimental Preview, Limited Lifetime Guarantee) may also use it.

The visibility and role of an API drive related design decisions. For instance, the different life cycles, deployment frequencies, and release dates of providers and clients in a Public API for Frontend Integration scenario might make it necessary to plan API evolution before making design decisions. Such scenarios usually do not allow providers to make arbitrary ad hoc changes to already published APIs due to the impact of such changes on clients (for example, downtimes, resultant test and migration effort); some or all of these clients might not even be known. A Community API providing Backend Integration capabilities between a few stable communication parties that are maintained on the same release cycle (and share a common roadmap) might be able to employ more relaxed versioning tactics. Finally, a Solution-Internal API for Frontend Integration connecting a mobile app frontend with a single backend owned, developed, and operated by the same agile team might fall back to an ad hoc, opportunistic approach to evolution that relies on frequent, automated unit and integration tests within a continuous integration and delivery practice.

More Information

Because versioning is an important aspect of API and service design, there is much discussion about it in different development communities. The strategies differ widely and are debated passionately. Opinions reach from no explicit versioning at all because an API should always be backward compatible, according to "Roy Fielding on Versioning, Hypermedia, and REST" [Amundsen 2014], to the different versioning strategies compared by Mark Little [Little 2013]. James Higginbotham describes the available options in "When and How Do You Version Your API?" [Higginbotham 2017a] and in *Principles of Web API Design* [Higginbotham 2021].

Chapter 11 of *SOA in Practice* [Josuttis 2007] introduces a service life cycle in the context of service-oriented architecture (SOA) design; Chapter 12 discusses versioning.

Chapter 13 of *Build APIS You Won't Hate* [Sturgeon 2016b] discusses seven options for versioning (with the VERSION IDENTIFIER in URLs being one of these options) and their advantages and disadvantages. It also gives implementation hints.

Chapter 15 of SOA with REST [Erl 2013] deals with service versioning for REST.

Pattern:
SEMANTIC VERSIONING

When and Why to Apply

When adding VERSION IDENTIFIERS to request and response messages or publishing version information in the API DESCRIPTION, it is not necessarily clear from a single number how significant the changes between different versions are. As a consequence, the impact of these changes is unknown and has to be analyzed by every client (for instance, by inspecting the API documentation in depth or running special compatibility tests). Consumers would like to know the impact of a version upgrade beforehand so that they can plan the migration without having to invest much effort or take unnecessary risk. In order to fulfill any guarantees made to clients, providers must manage different versions and thus have to unveil and disclose whether the planned API interface and implementation changes are compatible or will break client functionality.

▼

How can stakeholders compare API versions to detect immediately whether they are compatible?

▲

- **Minimal effort to detect version incompatibility:** When APIs change, it is important for all parties, especially the clients, to know what the impact of the rollout of the new version is. Clients want to know what level of compatibility is achieved so that they can decide whether to simply use the new version straight away or to plan and execute a necessary migration.

- **Clarity of change impact:** Whenever a new API interface version is released, it should be clear to the developers of the API provider as well as of the API clients what the change impact and the guarantees—especially with regard to compatibility—are. To plan API client development projects, the effort and risk of accommodating the new API version have to be known.

- **Clear separation of changes with different levels of impact and compatibility:** In order to make the change impact clear and address the needs of different clients, it is often necessary to separate changes with different levels of backward compatibility. For example, many implementation-level bug fixes can be accomplished with backward compatibility preserved; fixing design bugs or closing conceptual gaps often requires breaking changes in the clients.

- **Manageability of API versions and related governance effort:** Managing an API, and especially multiple API versions, is difficult and binds resources. The more guarantees have been made to the clients and the more APIs and API versions are made available, the higher the effort for managing those APIs usually is. Providers usually strive to keep these management tasks to a minimum.

- **Clarity with regard to evolution timeline:** Multiple parallel versions of an API might be created—for example, when using the TWO IN PRODUCTION pattern. In such cases, it is necessary to keep careful track of the evolution of each API. One version might carry bug fixes only while another contains restructured messages that break the compatibility of the API. The API publication date is not meaningful in such cases because successor versions are released at different times, thereby making the date information meaningless with respect to guarantees to either client or provider.

When marking a new version of an API—regardless of whether explicit VERSION IDENTIFIERS are added to messages or versions are indicated elsewhere—the easiest solution is to use simple, single numbers as versions (version 1, version 2, and so on). However, this versioning scheme does not indicate which versions are compatible with each other (for example, version 1 might be compatible with version 3, but version 2 is a new development branch and will be further developed in versions 4 and 5). Thus, branching APIs—for example in a TWO IN PRODUCTION case—with a plain, single-number versioning scheme is hard because an invisible compatibility graph and several API branches have to be followed. This is because a single version represents the chronological order of releases but does not address any other concerns.

Another option is to use the commit ID of the API revision as the VERSION IDENTIFIER (depending on the source control system, this ID might not be numeric, as, for example, in Git). While this frees API designers and developers from having to assign version numbers manually, not every commit ID is deployed, and no indication of branches and compatibility might be visible to the API client.

How It Works

Introduce a hierarchical three-number versioning scheme x.y.z, which allows API providers to denote different levels of changes in a compound identifier. The three numbers are usually called major, minor, and patch versions.

Figure 8.2 illustrates a common numbering scheme.

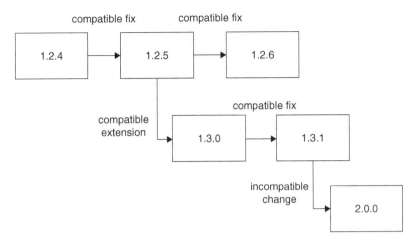

Figure 8.2 *SEMANTIC VERSIONING. Version numbers indicate whether or not a change is compatible*

The common numbering scheme in SEMANTIC VERSIONING works with three numbers:

1. *Major version.* This number is incremented for incompatible, breaking changes, such as removing an existing operation. For example, a breaking change to version 1.3.1 will result in a new version 2.0.0.

2. *Minor version.* This number is incremented if a new version provides new functionality (such as a new operation to an API or a new optional data element to the messages of an existing operation) in a compatible manner. For example, a compatible extension to version 1.2.5 will result in a new version 1.3.0.

3. *Patch version* (also called fix version). This number is incremented for compatible bug fixes, such as changing and clarifying the documentation in an API contract or changing the API implementation to fix a logic error. For example, a compatible bug fix to version 1.2.4 will result in a new version 1.2.5.

SEMANTIC VERSIONING only describes how VERSION IDENTIFIERS are constructed, not how these identifiers are placed and used. This remark applies both to the versioned object (for example, whole API, individual endpoints and operations, and message data types) and to the places where identifiers are visible (for example, namespace, attribute contents, and attribute names). SEMANTIC VERSIONING can be applied both to versions that are not communicated to clients and to those that are.

Note the difference between API versions (visible to clients) and API revisions (chosen and handled internally by providers) that James Higginbotham explains in "A Guide for When (and How) to Version Your API" [Higginbotham 2017b]. Chapter 14 in *Principles of Web API Design* [Higginbotham 2021] covers this topic in depth.

Example

A startup wants to establish itself as a stock exchange data provider in the market. Its first API version (version 1.0.0) offers a search operation, which searches for a substring of the stock symbol and returns the list of matching stocks, including their full names and their prices in USD. Upon customer feedback, the startup decides to offer a historic search function. The existing search operation is extended to option- ally accept a time range to provide access to historical price records. If no time range is supplied, the existing search logic is executed and the last known quote is returned. This version is fully backward compatible with the old version; old clients can call this operation and interpret its results. Thus, this version is called version 1.1.0.

A bug is discovered in the search function of version 1.1.0: not all stocks con- taining a supplied search string are found—only those that *start* with the string are returned. The API contract is correct but not fully implemented and not sufficiently tested. The API implementation is fixed and rolled out as version 1.1.1.

International customers are attracted to the services offered by the startup and request the support of international stock exchanges. As such, the response is extended to include a mandatory currency element. This change is incompatible from a client point of view, so the new version is numbered 2.0.0.

Note that this example is technology-independent on purpose. The supplied data can be transferred in any format, for example, as JSON or XML objects, and oper- ations can be implemented using any integration technology (HTTP, gRPC, etc.). This pattern deals with the conceptual problem of issuing version identifiers based on the type of change introduced to the API interface and/or its implementation.

Discussion

SEMANTIC VERSIONING offers high clarity with regard to expressing the impact on compatibility of changes between two API versions. However, it increases the effort to assign accurate VERSION IDENTIFIERS because sometimes it is hard to decide to what category a change belongs. Such discussions about compatibility are especially difficult, but they provide important insights into the changes being made. If, how- ever, the pattern is not applied consistently, breaking changes might sneak into minor updates; such violations should be watched for and discussed in daily standups, code reviews, and so on.

The clear separation of breaking and nonbreaking changes is achieved by the semantics of major versus minor/patch version numbers. This separation allows both API clients and providers to better assess the impact of changes, and thus the application of Semantic Versioning increases the transparency of changes.

Additional aspects include manageability of API versions and related governance effort. The pattern lays the foundation for resolving this rather broad and cross-cutting force. By offering a means to clearly signal the extent of compatibility, additional patterns and measures can be applied.

A simplified version of the pattern uses only two numbers, `n.m`. For instance, Higginbotham suggests using a simplified major.minor semantic versioning scheme [Higginbotham 2017a]. Another option is to use three numbers but hide the third one from clients and use it only internally—perhaps as an internal revision number. Not disclosing patch versions avoids accidental coupling with clients that interpret the third version number received in messages—a number they were not meant to receive and use.

Both the API (and its contract) and the API implementation can and probably will be versioned one way or the other. Care must be taken and differences be communicated clearly because the version numbers of an interface and its implementation(s) usually will not match. When official standards evolve slowly, the version of the API and the versions of its implementations often differ. For example, a clinic management system might implement version 3 of the HL7 standard [International 2022] in its system software versions 6.0, 6.1, and 7.0.[1]

APIs that support replays of messages, for instance, those provided by distributed transaction logs such as Apache Kafka, require special attention during versioning. Distributed log transactions must be backward compatible should the client choose to replay the message history. Incompatible versions of a message would break the client. Hence, all message versions must be constantly in sync to support processing future and historical messages. The same holds for backup-and-restore capabilities in microservices-based systems (assuming that older, incompatible versions of data are restored and then re-exposed in the API) [Pardon 2018].

Related Patterns

Semantic Versioning requires a Version Identifier. The three-digit Version Identifier may travel as a single string (with formatting constraints) or as an Atomic Parameter List with three entries. API Description and/or Service Level Agreement can carry the part of the versioning information that matters to clients.

---

1. HL7 defines how systems exchange medical data.

The introduction of a RATE LIMIT often is an example of breaking change, requiring response messages to carry new ERROR REPORTS indicating that a limit has been passed.

All life-cycle patterns that differ in the level of commitment given by the API provider are related: LIMITED LIFETIME GUARANTEE, TWO IN PRODUCTION, AGGRESSIVE OBSOLESCENCE, and EXPERIMENTAL PREVIEW. When applying these patterns, SEMANTIC VERSIONING helps distinguish past, present, and future versions, calling out the compatibility guarantees and how they change.

To improve compatibility between versions, especially minor ones, the "Tolerant Reader" pattern can be used [Daigneau 2011].

More Information

More information on implementing SEMANTIC VERSIONING can be found online at Semantic Versioning 2.0.0 [Preston-Werner 2021].

For additional information on how to use semantic versioning in REST, the REST CookBook Web site [Thijssen 2017] includes a chapter on versioning. The API Stylebook Web site also covers governance and versioning [Lauret 2017].

The Apache Avro specification [Apache 2021a] distinguishes the writer's schema from the reader's schema and identifies the cases in which these schemas match and do not match. The latter cases indicate incompatibility and/or interoperability issues, requiring a new major version.

Alexander Dean and Frederick Blundun introduce a structure and semantics for schema versioning [Dean 2014]. It utilizes the three version numbers of this pattern, specifically defining their meanings in the context of data structures. The first number is called *model* and is changed if all data readers break. The second is *revision,* which is incremented if some data readers break. The third is called *addition* and is incremented if all changes are backward compatible.

LinkedIn defines breaking and nonbreaking changes in its "API Breaking Change Policy" [Microsoft 2021].

Life-Cycle Management Guarantees

This section presents four patterns that explain when and how to publish and decommission API versions: EXPERIMENTAL PREVIEW, AGGRESSIVE OBSOLESCENCE, LIMITED LIFETIME GUARANTEE, and TWO IN PRODUCTION.

Pattern:
EXPERIMENTAL PREVIEW

When and Why to Apply

A provider is developing a new API or a new API version that differs significantly from the published version(s) and is still under intensive development. As a result, the provider wants to be freely able to make any necessary modifications. However, the provider also wants to offer its clients early access so that these clients can start integrating against the emerging API and comment on the new API features.

How can providers make the introduction of a new API, or new API version, less risky for their clients and obtain early adopter feedback without having to freeze the API design prematurely?

- **Innovations and new features:** Early access to emerging features raises customer awareness of a new API (or version), and gives customers time to decide whether to use the new API and initiate development projects. An iterative and incremental, or even agile, integration development process is supported; agile practices recommend releasing early and often.

- **Feedback:** Providers desire feedback from early clients and/or key accounts to make sure they expose the right features with adequate qualities in their APIs. Many customers want to influence the API design by providing comments and suggestions about the developer experience.

- **Focus efforts:** Providers do not want to document, manage, and support API prototypes with the same level of rigor as official versions. This helps focus their efforts and saves resources.

- **Early learning:** Consumers want to learn about new APIs or API versions early so that they can plan ahead and build innovative products that leverage the new features.

- **Stability:** Consumers appreciate stable APIs in order to minimize change efforts caused by frequent updates that they cannot benefit from (yet).

The provider could just release a new full-fledged API version when the development is finished. However, this means that clients cannot start developing and testing against the API until the release date. Developing the first client implementations might take several months; during this time, the API cannot be used, which results in revenue losses (for commercial API providers).

One way to counter these problems is to release API versions frequently. While this practice allows the client to sneak a peek at an API, the provider has to manage many versions. The provider will probably release many incompatible changes, which increases the governance effort further and makes it difficult for clients to closely track the latest API version.

How It Works

Provide access to an API on a best-effort basis without making any commitments about the functionality offered, stability, and longevity. Clearly and explicitly articulate this lack of API maturity to manage client expectations.

Figure 8.3 illustrates the pattern.

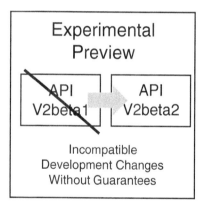

Figure 8.3 *Changes in EXPERIMENTAL PREVIEW sandbox and production*

By releasing an unstable version as an EXPERIMENTAL PREVIEW in an ungoverned development sandbox, the provider makes an API version available to clients outside of the normal management process. For instance, the preview might not be governed by a SERVICE LEVEL AGREEMENT but still be documented by a draft API DESCRIPTION. Consumers volunteer to test and experiment with the new API version knowing that they cannot rely on its availability, stability, or any other quality level. By definition, the EXPERIMENTAL PREVIEW API might disappear suddenly or be available for a short and fixed amount of time only. Having early access to the API preview is especially beneficial for clients who have to estimate the effort required to integrate with the final version or who would like to jumpstart their own development while the API development is ongoing.

The EXPERIMENTAL PREVIEW, which covers the prerelease guarantees, often is complemented by an application of TWO IN PRODUCTION for governing the life cycle of production APIs. The EXPERIMENTAL PREVIEW can be made available to all known or unknown clients; alternatively, a closed user group can be selected for it (to limit support and communication effort).

Example

Let us assume that a fictitious software tools company wants to create a new product that lets it leave its comfort zone because it goes beyond the functionality offered in existing products. The company has been active in the development of a continuous build and deployment solution, currently offered as a cloud software service with a Web-based online user interface. Development teams at customers of the software tools company use the service to build their software by fetching a revision from a repository and deploying the built artifacts to configurable servers. Large customers have now requested an API to better trigger and manage builds and receive notifications about build states besides the Web interface. Because the software tools company has not yet offered any APIs for its products and thus lacks related knowledge and experience, the developers choose an EXPERIMENTAL PREVIEW of the API and improve it continuously by incorporating feedback from the customers who decide to adopt it early.

Discussion

EXPERIMENTAL PREVIEWS grant clients early access to API innovations and receive the opportunity to influence the API design. This is faithful to agile values and principles such as welcoming change and responding to it continuously. Providers have the flexibility to change the API freely and rapidly before declaring it stable. Learning and helping the provider to try out a new API and its features is different from writing production applications. Providers can introduce a grace period to ease the transition from preview to the production version. Early adopters perform a sort of acceptance testing, as they might find inconsistencies and missing functionality in this API version, resulting in changes without requiring the provider to follow a full-blown governance process.

As a downside, providers may find it difficult to attract clients due to a lack of long-term commitment to the experimental API, being perceived as immature. Clients have to keep changing their implementation until a stable version is released. Clients might face a total loss of investment if a stable API is never released and/or the preview disappears suddenly.

By offering an API in a nonproduction environment that is closely linked to the current development version, providers can offer peek previews into a new API or API version to interested clients. For this environment, different—and usually very lax—service levels (for example, regarding availability) are guaranteed. Consumers can intentionally decide to use this relatively unstable environment for giving feedback on the new API design and its functionality and to start development. However, clients can also choose to wait for the new production version of the API or stick to the current officially supported version (that is still provided with the standard service levels and thus is usually more stable and reliable).

When applied at the right time and with the right scope, EXPERIMENTAL PREVIEW allows and/or deepens the collaboration between providers and their clients and enables clients to more quickly roll out software that utilizes new API functionality. However, the provider organization must operate an additional runtime environment, for instance, providing different API endpoints in the same or another physical or virtual hosting location; the additional access channel might add systems management effort and has to be secured properly. It also makes its development progress on new APIs more transparent. This includes changes (and mistakes) that are not part of the final API, which become visible to external parties.

Related Patterns

EXPERIMENTAL PREVIEW is similar to traditional beta (testing) programs. This is the weakest support commitment given by an API provider (followed by AGGRESSIVE OBSOLESCENCE). When transitioning the API to a productive environment, another life-cycle governance pattern must be chosen, for instance, TWO IN PRODUCTION and/or LIMITED LIFETIME GUARANTEE. When the N in Production variant of TWO IN PRODUCTION is applied, an EXPERIMENTAL PREVIEW can be combined with any of these patterns.

The EXPERIMENTAL PREVIEW may have a VERSION IDENTIFIER but does not have to. An API DESCRIPTION should clearly state which version is experimentally previewed and which one is productive. Specific API KEYS can be assigned to grant certain clients access to the preview/the beta version.

More Information

Vimal Maheedharan shares tips and tricks on beta testing in his article "Beta Testing of Your Product: 6 Practical Steps to Follow" [Maheedharan 2018].

James Higginbotham advises keeping supported and unsupported operations separate and getting feedback early and often. He recommends the following stability states of API operations: experimental, prerelease, supported, deprecated, and retired [Higginbotham 2020].

Pattern:
AGGRESSIVE OBSOLESCENCE

When and Why to Apply

Once an API has been released, it evolves, and new versions with added, removed, or changed functionality are offered. In order to reduce effort, API providers no longer want to support certain functionalities for clients, for instance, because they are no longer used regularly or have been superseded by alternative versions.

> How can API providers reduce the effort for maintaining an entire API or its parts (such as endpoints, operations, or message representations) with guaranteed service quality levels?

- **Minimizing the maintenance effort:** Allowing the provider to discontinue support of rarely used parts of an API or an API as a whole helps reduce the maintenance effort. Supporting old clients can be particularly painful; for instance, the required skills and experience (regarding notations, tools, and platforms in certain versions) might differ from those required to evolve the current version.

- **Reducing forced changes to clients in a given time span as a consequence of API changes:** It is often not possible to just switch off an old version. Clients usually do not follow the same life cycle as their providers: even within the same organization, it is often difficult or impossible to roll out upgrades to two systems at the same point in time, for instance, if different teams own these systems. The problem becomes worse if different organizations own the systems; in this case, the API provider might not even know the client developers. Therefore, it is often necessary to decouple the life cycles of clients and providers. This decoupling can be achieved by giving clients time to make any necessary changes. To reduce the impact of changes to clients, it is also useful to be able to remove only certain obsolete parts of an API (for instance, operations or message elements in requests and responses), not the entire API version. Removing only parts of an API reduces the impact of API changes to clients compared to withdrawing support of an entire API version. The removal might not affect those clients that do not depend on the particular discontinued feature(s).

- **Respecting/acknowledging power dynamics:** Organizational units and teams may influence each other in various ways, from formal or informal hearings to official voting and approvals. Political factors influence the design decisions. For example, high-profile customers often have good leverage with competing providers that can be swapped in and out easily because their APIs are similar or identical. In contrast, a monopolist offering a unique API can impose changes on millions of clients without involving them much—as they have nowhere else to turn. Depending on the ratio of API clients per provider, it might be worthwhile to shift more implementation effort to one or the other.

- **Commercial goals and constraints:** Removing obsolete APIs or API features might have monetary consequences if a commercial Pricing Plan is in place. There is a risk that the API product becomes less valuable if features are cut but the price remains the same (or increases). Providers might try to motivate clients to move over to another offering, such as a new product line, to reducing maintenance costs for the old product. To do so, clients can be asked to pay extra fees for certain old features or be offered discounts for the new ones.

One could give no guarantees or assure a rather short Limited Lifetime Guarantee, but such weak commitments do not always minimize the impact of changes as desired. One could declare an API to be an Experimental Preview, but this is an even weaker commitment that clients might not receive well.

How It Works

Announce a decommissioning date to be set as early as possible for the entire API or its obsolete parts. Declare the obsolete API parts to be still available but no longer recommended to be used so that clients have just enough time to upgrade to a newer or alternative version before the API parts they depend on disappear. Remove the deprecated API parts and the support for it as soon as the deadline has passed.

Aggressive Obsolescence makes old API versions as a whole—or parts thereof—unavailable rather quickly, for instance, within a year (or even less) for an enterprise application API.

When releasing an API, the provider should clearly communicate that it follows such an Aggressive Obsolescence strategy, which means that a particular feature might be deprecated and subsequently decommissioned anytime in the future (removed from support and maintenance, that is). When an API, operation or representation element is to be removed, the provider declares this element of the API as deprecated and specifies a point in time when the feature will be removed completely. Depending on their market position and the availability of alternatives, clients can then choose to upgrade or switch to a different provider.

When a provider releases an API, it reserves the right to deprecate and then remove parts of it later. The parts may be entire endpoints, operations exposing certain functionality, or specific representation elements in the request and response messages (such as a particular in or out parameter). Hence, planning obsolescence and removal involves three steps. Figure 8.4 illustrates them.

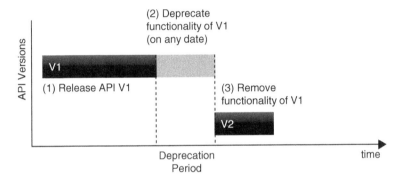

Figure 8.4 *Stepwise approach to* AGGRESSIVE OBSOLESCENCE: *The API provider first releases V1 of API functionality. While this version is available, the provider deprecates and then removes it*

The three steps are as follows:

1. *Release.* An API version is used in production (V1 in the figure). Clients happily use it.

2. *Deprecate.* The provider announces the deprecation of an API or some of its parts within an API version and indicates when these parts will be removed (for example, when the next version of the API is published, V2 in the figure). Clients receive the announcement and can start the migration to the new version—or, in extreme cases, switch to alternative providers.

3. *Remove/decommission.* The provider deploys a new API version that no longer supports the deprecated parts (V2 in the figure). The old version is taken down; requests to the old endpoint either fail or are redirected to the new version. When the removal/decommissioning takes place, clients who depend on any removed parts of the API (because they did not migrate to a newer version) will no longer have access to those parts.

The AGGRESSIVE OBSOLESCENCE strategy is eligible when the needs of the provider outweigh those of the clients. By clearly announcing the deprecation and removal schedule for old versions of APIs or API parts, the provider can reduce and limit effort for supporting API parts that are not support-worthy in a broad sense, such as economically, because a feature is too costly to maintain (for example, rarely used features), or legally, because some functionality becomes unavailable. For instance, the introduction of the International Bank Account Number (IBAN) to identify bank accounts replaced old account numbers, and the introduction of the euro currency replaced many other currencies; APIs dealing with accounts and currencies had to be changed accordingly.

The notification of a deprecation and later decommissioning date allows clients to plan the required effort and schedules for continuing to use the old API while they migrate to an alternative way of achieving the required functionality. Communicating which entities are deprecated and when they will be removed may require adding special "sunset" markers, for instance, in protocol headers or METADATA ELEMENTS. An alternative, simple solution is sending client developers an email reminding and warning them that they are still depending on API features that will disappear soon.

Sometimes AGGRESSIVE OBSOLESCENCE might be the only option for API providers that have not yet declared any life-cycle policies. If no guarantees are given, deprecating features and announcing—possibly generous—transition periods might be a proper way to be able to introduce incompatible changes.

Example

A payment provider offers an API that allows clients to instruct payments from their accounts to other accounts. Accounts can be identified by old-fashioned, country-specific account and bank numbers or by IBANs.[2] Because IBANs are the new standard and the old account and bank numbers are rarely used, the API provider decides not to support the old numbers anymore. This allows the provider to delete parts of its implementation, thereby reducing maintenance effort.

In order to allow old clients to migrate to the IBAN scheme, the provider publishes a removal announcement on its API documentation Web page, marks the account and bank number as deprecated in the API documentation, and notifies its registered clients. The announcement states that the old, country-specific functionality will be removed after one year.

After one year, the payment provider deploys a new implementation of the API that has no support for the old account and bank numbers and removes the old,

---

2. IBANs originally were developed in Europe but are now used in other parts of the world as well. They have become an ISO standard [ISO 2020].

country-specific attributes from its API documentation. Calls using the old and removed functionality will fail from now on.[3]

Discussion

This pattern allows a rather fine-grained way to change APIs: in the best case, clients do not have to change at all if functionality that becomes obsolete is not used, while the provider code base is kept small and thus simple to maintain. The pattern can be applied not only proactively but also reactively during API maintenance.

Providers must announce which features are deprecated and when these features will be decommissioned. However, clients that rely on rarely used features or take full advantage of all API features are forced to change by implementing modifications within a schedule that might have been unknown when the decision to use a particular API was made. The decommissioning time is communicated to the clients upon deprecation and not during the API release (in contrast to the LIMITED LIFETIME PATTERN); therefore, it might or might not fit the client's release roadmap. Furthermore, deprecation times and decommissioning periods might differ per API part. Another challenge is that clients must be notified about obsolete parts, which might be challenging in some PUBLIC API scenarios. Rightsized, pragmatic API governance helps in this case.

AGGRESSIVE OBSOLESCENCE can be used to enforce a coherent and secure ecosystem around the APIs offered: for example, replacing weak cryptographic algorithms, out-phased standards, or inefficient libraries can help in achieving a better overall experience for all involved parties.

The AGGRESSIVE OBSOLESCENCE pattern emphasizes the reduction of effort on the provider side but burdens clients. Essentially, it requires the clients to evolve continuously with the API. In turn, clients stay current with the newest functions and improvements and thus benefit from switching away from old versions; for instance, they are forced to use new or updated (improved) security procedures. Depending on the deprecation period, clients can plan and follow API changes but are required to remain rather active.

Depending on the API and API endpoint types and their versioning policies, explained in the VERSION IDENTIFIER and SEMANTIC VERSIONING patterns, it is not straightforward to come up with a suited deprecation and decommissioning approach. Master data, for instance, might be harder to be removed from message representations than operational data. It takes effort to maintain a precise list of deprecated parts in the API DESCRIPTION, and it is important to plan when these parts will eventually be removed from the API.

---

3. Note that in this case, legislature also had specified a transition period to the IBAN system, in effect deprecating the old, country-specific account number scheme.

In in-house scenarios in particular, the knowledge of which systems are currently using an API (or the deprecated subset of an API) is of great help when deciding if—and which—features or APIs should be removed. Intercompany services are usually more restrictive and are designed to ensure that other systems continue to work properly. Thus, additional care must be taken before an API or functionality is finally removed. Knowing the relationships between systems and establishing dependency traceability can help with this problem in both scenarios. DevOps practices and supporting tools can be leveraged for such tasks (for instance, for monitoring and distributed log analysis). Enterprise architecture management may provide insights regarding active and stale system relationships.

In some business contexts, external clients are not supported with great care because their API usage is not very important to the API provider (for instance, commodity services that validate data or convert it from one notation or language to another). In such circumstances, using the PRICING PLAN pattern (or at least some metering mechanisms) can help identify services to be deprecated and eventually removed. PRICING PLANS can help to financially measure the economic value of an API that can be compared with the maintenance and development effort, thereby deriving an economic decision about prolonging the API lifetime.

Related Patterns

Several strategies for discontinuation of API parts can be employed, as portrayed in the TWO IN PRODUCTION and LIMITED LIFETIME GUARANTEE patterns. The AGGRESSIVE OBSOLESCENCE pattern can be used in a fine-grained way. While other strategies are attached to entire APIs, endpoints, or operations, only certain representation elements might get deprecated and removed in AGGRESSIVE OBSOLESCENCE, thereby allowing less obstructive changes.

Another difference to other patterns is that AGGRESSIVE OBSOLESCENCE always uses relative timeframes for removing functionality: because functionality becomes obsolete during the lifetime of an API, it is flagged as deprecated within its active period, and the deprecation period runs from this time onward. In contrast, TWO IN PRODUCTION or LIMITED LIFETIME GUARANTEE can be used with absolute timeframes based on the initial release date.

AGGRESSIVE OBSOLESCENCE may or may not use a VERSION IDENTIFIER. If present, an API DESCRIPTION or a SERVICE LEVEL AGREEMENT should indicate its use.

More Information

Managed Evolution [Murer 2010] shares general information on service governance and versioning, for instance, how to define quality gates and how to monitor traffic. Chapter 7 discusses ways to measure the managed evolution.

Planned obsolescence is discussed in "Microservices in Practice, Part 1" [Pautasso 2017a]. Here, the plan foresees a rather short lifetime.

Pattern:
LIMITED LIFETIME GUARANTEE

When and Why to Apply

An API has been published and made available to at least one client. The API provider cannot manage or influence the evolution roadmaps of its clients, or it considers the financial or reputation damage caused by forcing clients to change their implementation to be high. Therefore, the provider does not want to make any breaking changes in the published API but still wants to improve the API in the future.

> How can a provider let clients know for how long they can rely on the published version of an API?

- **Make client-side changes caused by API changes plannable:** When clients have to modify their code because an API changes in an incompatible manner, the modification should be plannable well ahead of the publication of the new API version. This allows clients to align their development roadmap and allocate resources in their project planning, thereby reducing late migration problems. Some clients cannot (or do not want to) migrate to newer API versions—at least for a considerable time span.

- **Limit the maintenance effort for supporting old clients:** Providers strive for low costs for development and operations. Refactoring an API may make it easier to use and lower the development and maintenance effort [Stocker 2021a]. However, other factors increase the effort for the provider. These factors include the support of older or less used API parts.

How It Works

> As an API provider, guarantee to not break the published API for a fixed time-frame. Label each API version with an expiration date.

Figure 8.5 sketches the timeline resulting from such a LIMITED LIFETIME GUARANTEE.

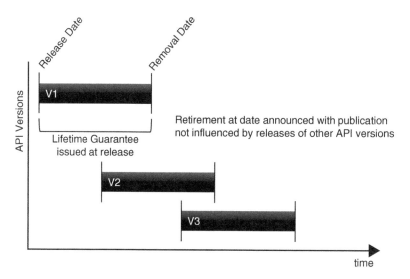

Figure 8.5 *API life cycle when using* LIMITED LIFETIME GUARANTEE. *Removal time is stated at publication time*

The provider promises to keep the API usable for a defined, limited but considerably long time and retires it after that. This practice keeps the client safe from unwanted negative impact or outages. It also sets a fixed expiration deadline that the client can plan for each time a version is published.

The advantage of a fixed time window serving as LIMITED LIFETIME GUARANTEE (instead of fixing the number of active versions, which is the approach taken in the TWO IN PRODUCTION pattern) is that no further coordination between the provider and client organization is necessary. When using an API version for the first time, the client already knows when it has to adapt and release a version of its application that is compatible with the then current API version.

The LIMITED LIFETIME GUARANTEE pattern stresses the stability for the client side via a built-in expiration time; outdated versions can be decommissioned right away when the time comes. The provider guarantees that the API will never change in an incompatible manner in the preannounced time span and agrees to implement any reasonable measure to keep the API up and running in a backward-compatible manner during that time.

In practice, guaranteed timeframes often are multitudes of 6 months (for instance, 6, 12, 18, or 24 months), which seems to provide a good balance for provider and client needs.

Example

One example for a LIMITED LIFETIME GUARANTEE was the introduction of the IBAN in Europe. The limited lifetime was specified in a 2012 resolution of the European Parliament [EU 2012] granting a period until 2014 after which the old, national account numbers had to be replaced by the new standard; the use of IBANs became compulsory after that. This regulatory requirement naturally had an impact on software systems that have to identify accounts. The services offered by such systems had to issue a LIMITED LIFETIME GUARANTEE for the old API operations, which used the old account numbers. This example shows that versioning and evolution strategies not only are decided by the API provider alone but can also be influenced or even mandated by external forces (such as legislation or industry consortia).

Discussion

In general, this pattern allows planning well ahead due to fixed time windows that are known in advance. It does so by limiting the provider's ability to respond to urgent change requests if they impact compatibility.

Customers are forced to upgrade their API clients at a well-defined, fixed point in time that might conflict with their own roadmap and life cycle. This can be a problem if API clients that are still in use are no longer actively maintained. Changing existing clients might not even be possible, for instance, if a software vendor no longer actively maintains its products.

This pattern is applicable if the provider can constrain the API evolution to include only backward-compatible changes during the fixed lifetime guarantee. Over time, effort to do so will increase, and the API will build up technical debt by introducing changes in a backward-compatible way that the client can still interpret. This debt increases the effort on the provider side, for instance, for regression testing and maintaining the API; the provider has to live with this added debt until it is permitted to change or revoke the API.

While the LIMITED LIFETIME GUARANTEE is usually part of the SERVICE LEVEL AGREEMENT between provider and client, it has large implications on the provider. The longer the guarantee is valid, the higher the burden is on the provider development organization. To keep the published API stable, the provider will usually first try to make all changes in a backward-compatible manner. This might lead to unclean interfaces with awkward names put in place in order to support both older and newer clients. If changes cannot be (efficiently) made to the existing version, a new API version might be developed. This new version must run in parallel with the old version in order to fulfill the guarantee.

Furthermore, the API freeze caused by the guarantee might inhibit progress and integration of new technologies and features on the provider side that in turn may also hinder clients.

In some settings, providers may want to get rid of clients who do not upgrade when the lifetime guarantee expires. For example, due to mistakes in the API design or progress in the area of cryptography, security risks to the whole ecosystem of the provider and all clients might arise. Introducing the Limited Lifetime Guarantee pattern offers an institutionalized way of enforcing timely client updates.

Related Patterns

More lenient approaches give the provider more freedom with respect to releasing incompatible updates; they are presented in the Aggressive Obsolescence and Two in Production patterns. The Limited Lifetime Guarantee pattern shares some properties with Aggressive Obsolescence. In both cases, the API must not change in an incompatible way within the announced time span. The fixed time span here in Limited Lifetime Guarantee implies an implicit deprecation notification; the end of the guarantee is the decommissioning time. After the guaranteed time span has expired, the provider may make any changes, including breaking ones, or may discontinue the expired API version altogether.

A Limited Lifetime Guarantee usually has an explicit Version Identifier. The API Description and, if present, a Service Level Agreement should indicate the actual expiration date for the API version in order to inform API clients of the upcoming need to take action and upgrade.

More Information

Managed Evolution [Murer 2010] gives rich advice on service versioning and service management processes, for instance, including quality gates. Section 3.6 mentions service retirement.

 Pattern:
Two in Production

When and Why to Apply

An API evolves and new versions with improved functionality are offered regularly. At some point in time, the changes to a new version are no longer backward compatible, thereby breaking existing clients. However, API providers and their clients, especially those of a Public API or a Community API, evolve at different speeds; some of them cannot be forced to upgrade to the latest version in a short timeframe.

How can a provider gradually update an API without breaking existing clients but also without having to maintain a large number of API versions in production?

- **Allow the provider and the client to follow different life cycles:** When changing an API over time, one of the main problems is how (and for how long) to support clients of older API versions. Keeping old API versions alive usually requires additional resources for operations and maintenance—for instance, bug fixes, security patches, upgrades of external dependencies, and subsequent regression testing cause work required for each version. This inflicts cost and binds developer resources.

  It is not always possible to simply switch off an old version, because the life cycles and evolution of API clients and their providers often differ. Even within the same company, it is difficult or even impossible to roll out multiple systems that depend on each other at the same point in time, especially if they are owned by different organizational units. The problem becomes worse if multiple clients are owned by different organizations or if the clients are unknown to the provider (for instance, in Public API scenarios). Thus, it is often necessary to decouple the life cycles of the client and the provider. Enabling such autonomous life cycles is one of the core tenets of microservices [Pautasso 2017a].

  Under independent life cycles with different API publication frequencies and release dates of API provider implementations and their clients, it becomes necessary to plan API evolution from the very beginning of API design and development because it is impossible to make arbitrary changes to an already published API.

- **Guarantee that API changes do not lead to undetected backward-compatibility problems between clients and the provider:** Introducing only changes that are backward compatible is hard, particularly if done without tools that automatically check for incompatibilities. There is a risk that changes will quietly introduce problems—for instance, when changing the meaning of existing elements in requests and responses without making the changes visible in the message syntax. An example is the decision to include the value added tax in a price, without changing parameter name or type. Such semantic change cannot be detected by message receivers easily, even in API tests.

- **Ensure the ability to roll back if a new API version is designed badly:** When redesigning or restructuring an API thoroughly, the new design might not work as expected. For example, functionality still required by some clients might unintentionally be removed. Being able to fall back and undo a change helps to avoid breaking those clients for a while.

- **Minimize changes to the client:** Clients in general appreciate API stability. When an API is released, it can be assumed to work as intended. Updates bind resources and cost money (which would be better spent on delivering more business value). However, providing a highly stable API requires upfront effort on the provider side; provider-side agility may trigger frequent client-side changes that might come unexpectedly and might not always be welcome.

- **Minimize the maintenance effort for supporting clients relying on old API versions:** Any life-cycle management strategy not only must take the client effort into consideration but also must balance it with the effort on the provider side to maintain multiple API versions, including versions supporting infrequently used (and therefore unprofitable) features.

How It Works

Deploy and support two versions of an API endpoint and its operations that provide variations of the same functionality. These TWO IN PRODUCTION do not have to be compatible with each other. Update and decommission the versions in a rolling, overlapping fashion.

Such a rolling, overlapping support strategy can be realized in the following way:

- Choose how to identify a version, for instance, by using the VERSION IDENTIFIER pattern.

- Offer a fixed number (usually two, as indicated in the pattern name) of API versions in parallel and inform your clients about this life-cycle choice.

- When releasing a new API version, retire the oldest one that still runs in production (which is the second last one by default) and inform remaining clients (if any) about their migration options. Continue to support the previous version.

- Redirect calls to the retired version, for instance, by leveraging protocol-level capabilities such as those in HTTP.

By following these steps, a sliding window of active versions is created (see Figure 8.6). Thereby, providers allow clients to choose the time of migration to a newer version. If a new version is released, the client can continue to use the previous version and migrate later. They can learn about the API changes and required client-side modifications without risking the stability of their own primary production system.

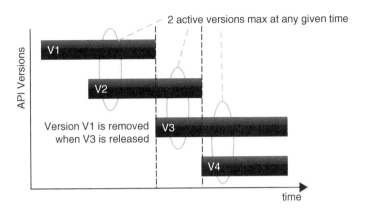

Figure 8.6 *Version lifetimes when using* TWO IN PRODUCTION. *Clients always have a choice between two versions*

Variant   Although typically two versions are offered in parallel, this pattern can also be applied in a slightly changed variant: In N *in Production* more than two versions are supported.

In N in Production, the sliding window of active versions is increased to N (with N greater than 2). This strategy gives clients more time and more options to upgrade but places more maintenance effort and operational cost on the provider side, obviously.

Example

A business software vendor releases version 1 of a payroll API for its enterprise resource planning (ERP) system. In the continued development of this ERP system, the payroll API is extended with new pension plan management features. At some point, the new features break the API because their data retention policies are incompatible with the previously used ones; a new major version, version 2, is published. Because the vendor supports TWO IN PRODUCTION, it releases its software with the old API (version 1) and the new API with pension plan management features (version 2). Customers who use version 1 can update the ERP system and then start migrating to version 2. New customers who need the pension plan management feature can start to use the API version 2 right away.

With the next release of the ERP system, the software vendor again publishes a new API (version 3) and removes support for version 1; versions 2 and 3 are now the TWO IN PRODUCTION. Customers that still use version 1 are cut off until they have migrated to version 2 or 3 (that they can be redirected to). Clients using version 2 can continue to use it until version 4 comes out. Version 5 brings end of life for version 3, and so on.

Discussion

TWO IN PRODUCTION disentangles the life cycle of provider and client. API clients do not have to release their software every time the provider does so in a breaking way. Instead, they are granted a time window in which they can migrate, test, and release their software updates. However, clients must move eventually, as they cannot rely on an eternal lifetime guarantee for the API. This means that they have to plan and allocate resources for upgrading their software over its lifetime as the two versions in production come and go.

The provider can use this pattern to make brave changes in a new API version because existing clients will stay on the old version until they migrate. This gives the provider more freedom to refine the API incrementally.

When TWO IN PRODUCTION is used, the effort of providers and clients are balanced: customers have a defined time window to migrate their API clients to a new API version, while API providers do not have to support an unlimited number of versions for an undefined, possibly inappropriately long amount of time. As a result, this pattern also clarifies the responsibilities of both parties to plan their life cycle: the provider can introduce new and possibly incompatible versions but must support multiple versions, whereas the client must migrate to a new version in a limited time but can plan its release schedule rather freely and flexibly.

For clients, however, it might be difficult to know when development activity is required: unlike in the LIMITED LIFETIME GUARANTEE pattern, the removal of API versions is dynamic and depends on other API releases. Therefore, it cannot be planned as easily (unless the patterns are combined).

Related Patterns

The use of this pattern usually requires the VERSION IDENTIFIER pattern in order to distinguish the API versions that are currently active and supported concurrently. Fully compatible versions, for instance, as indicated by the patch version in SEMANTIC VERSIONING, can replace active versions without violating the TWO IN PRODUCTION constraints; the TWO IN PRODUCTION are two major versions. This should be reported in the API DESCRIPTION and/or the SERVICE LEVEL AGREEMENT.

AGGRESSIVE OBSOLESCENCE can be applied to one of the TWO IN PRODUCTION to force clients to stop using the older API version and migrate to a newer one so that the provider can introduce an even newer API version. If the client requires more guarantees on the expiration date of the old API version, it might be better to combine TWO IN PRODUCTION with a LIMITED LIFETIME GUARANTEE.

An EXPERIMENTAL PREVIEW can be one of the two (or N) versions running in production when following this pattern.

More Information

Managed Evolution covers life-cycle management on a general level, but also dives into API versioning. Section 3.5.4 reports a combined usage of Semantic Versioning and Two in Production. Three versions are reported to have proven to be a good compromise between provider complexity and adaptation pace [Murer 2010].

"Challenges and Benefits of the Microservice Architectural Style," a two-part article on the IBM Developer portal [Fachat 2019], recommends this pattern.

Summary

This chapter presented six patterns that are concerned with the evolution of APIs. Two patterns covered versioning and compatibility management: Version Identifier and Semantic Versioning. It is much easier to detect the presence and the impact of changes if each API revision is properly identified. The Version Identifier should clearly indicate whether or not the new version is compatible with previous ones. Major, minor, and patch versions should be distinguished.

The remaining four patterns focused on the API life cycle by balancing the client desire for stability and the provider need to restrict maintenance effort. Experimental Preview helps introduce changes and get feedback about them from interested clients without committing to their stability, as in an official release. Two In Production eases the migration of clients by offering them two or more versions of the API at the same time. Aggressive Obsolescence and Limited Lifetime Guarantee make it explicit that no API lasts forever and clients should be aware that someday their dependencies will cease to function (at least in part). Obsolescence can be declared at any time, with a grace period granted (called deprecation period); by definition, a lifetime guarantee is established at API publication time.

A rather extreme solution for an API provider would be an *experimental preview in production*, which could also be called "living at head" or "surfing the latest wave." No guarantees for compatibility are given, and clients that intend to continue working over long periods must stay in sync with the most current API version. However, doing so requires effort and often is not a viable option.

In contrast to most other patterns in this book, only a few of the evolution patterns directly affect the syntax of request and response messages: a Version Identifier may be placed in the message and use an Atomic Parameter serving as a Metadata Element to transmit the version—whether it follows the Semantic Versioning scheme or not.

The versioned subject can reside on different levels of abstraction: entire API, endpoints, individual operations, and/or data types used in the request and response messages. The same is true for the life-cycle guarantees offered in an AGGRESSIVE OBSOLESCENCE policy. Operations applying the REQUEST BUNDLE pattern are a special case, posing the question whether all requests packaged in the request container must have the same version. Mixing versions might be desirable but complicates provider-side request dispatching.

OPERATIONAL DATA HOLDERS that implement mission-critical, innovative features often are often exposed to test clients and early adopters in an EXPERIMENTAL PREVIEW; they might also realize AGGRESSIVE OBSOLESCENCE and be replaced with a newer API and API implementation frequently. MASTER DATA HOLDERS tend to give longer LIMITED LIFETIME GUARANTEES than other types of information holders. Their clients benefit from a TWO IN PRODUCTION policy particularly well. REFERENCE DATA HOLDERS might rarely evolve; if they do, TWO IN PRODUCTION is eligible in this scenario, too. A long-running PROCESSING RESOURCE with STATE TRANSITION OPERATIONS representing business activities might not only have to migrate API and API implementation (including database definitions) when upgrading the VERSION IDENTIFIER to a new major version but also have to upgrade all process instances.

Evolution strategies should be documented in the API DESCRIPTION and SERVICE LEVEL AGREEMENT of the API. RATE LIMITS and PRICING PLANS have to be changed as the API evolves; changes in these artifacts might also trigger version upgrades.

Service Design Patterns [Daigneau 2011] includes a chapter called "Evolution." Two of its six patterns (*Breaking Changes, Versioning*) are not available online but are presented in the book. *Tolerant Reader* and *Consumer-Driven Contracts* deal with evolution; the remaining two patterns (*Single Message Argument, Dataset Amendment*) focus on message construction and representation, which have an impact on evolution. One particular life-cycle model is described in an IBM Redpiece covering an API management solution [Seriy 2016].

Chapter 13 of the *RESTful Web Services Cookbook* [Allamaraju 2010] is devoted to extensibility and versioning in the context of RESTful HTTP. It presents seven related recipes—for example, how to maintain URI compatibility and how to implement clients to support extensibility. Roy Fielding expresses his views on versioning, hypermedia, and REST in an InfoQ interview [Amundsen 2014]. James Higginbotham covers the topic in "When and How Do You Version Your API?" [Higginbotham 2017a]. The microservices movement suggests nontraditional approaches to life-cycle management and evolution; see "Microservices in Practice: Part 2" [Pautasso 2017b] for a discussion.

Next up is Chapter 9, "Document and Communicate API Contracts," covering API contracts and descriptions, including both technical and business aspects.

Chapter 9

Document and Communicate API Contracts

This final chapter of Part 2 collects patterns for capturing technical API specifications and sharing them with client developers and other stakeholders. We also cover business aspects that API product owners are concerned with, including pricing and usage constraints. Documenting software engineering artifacts might not be a popular task, but it is key to promoting API interoperability and understandability. Charging for API usage and limiting resource usage protects the current and future health of an API. Failing to do so might not cause any major problems in the short term (depending on the API status and criticality), but it increases business and technical risk, possibly harming the success of the API in the long run.

Unlike previous chapters, this one does not correspond to a single phase in Align-Define-Design-Refine (ADDR). Due to their cross-cutting nature, API specifications and supplemental documentation artifacts can be introduced and then gradually enhanced at any time; therefore, ADDR has a separate documentation step covering related activities [Higginbotham 2021]. The patterns in this chapter are eligible in this extra ADDR step.

Introduction to API Documentation

Chapters 4 to 8 covered the roles and responsibilities of API endpoints and operations, dived into message structures that help us achieve certain quality goals, and featured API versioning and long-term evolution strategies. One might think that by deliberately choosing and applying the selected patterns, the success of the API is more or less guaranteed. Unfortunately, just building a decent technical product is not enough to ensure its success. API providers also must communicate their offerings to existing and prospective clients so that these clients can decide whether a particular offering matches their own technical and commercial expectations. A joint understanding of the API capabilities is required in all stages of the API evolution, both during development and at runtime. Without that understanding, developer experience and software interoperability suffer. To address these concerns, the patterns in this chapter help API product owners answer the following question:

> *How can the functional capabilities, quality properties, and business-related aspects of an API be documented, communicated, and enforced?*

Challenges When Documenting APIs

The amount of documentation required at the code level often is the subject of intense discussions among developers. One agile value, for instance, is to prefer "working software over comprehensive documentation" [Beck 2001]. However, if the subject of the documentation is the API—and assuming that clients do not have access to the API implementation code—providing adequate, sufficiently rich documentation is paramount. Introductory material helps getting started quickly without roadblocks.[1] The amount of documentation required depends on the client-provider relationship. If the same individual or the same agile team develops both API client and API provider implementations, it might be okay to rely on tacit knowledge for some time. If the client developers belong to other teams or organizations or are not known at all, detailed, comprehensive documentation makes sense and justifies its investment.

Documentation primarily targets humans; if it is machine-readable too, tools can transform it (for instance, into Web displays) and generate test data and client code for different programming languages.

The following questions arise when documenting an API:

- **Interoperability:** How can API client and API provider make explicit their agreement on the functional aspects of service invocation? For example, which data transfer representations are expected and delivered? Do any prerequisites for successful invocation exist? And how can such functional information be amended with other technical specification elements (such as protocol headers, security policies, fault records) and business-level documentation (for instance, operation semantics, API owner, billing information, support procedures, versioning)? Should the documentation be platform-independent or offer protocol-level precision?

---

1. In Chapter 1, we defined *developer experience* via four pillars: function, stability, ease of use, and clarity.

- **Compliance:** How can a client learn about a provider's compliance with government regulations, security and privacy rules, and other legal obligations?

- **Information hiding:** What is the right level of detail for quality-of-service (QoS) specifications, both avoiding underspecification (which may lead to tension between clients and providers) and overspecification (which may cause a lot of effort in development, operations, and maintenance)?

API documentation has to answer the following questions as well:

- **Economic aspects:** How can an API provider select a pricing model that balances its economic interests with those of its customers and the competition?

- **Performance and reliability:** How can the provider maintain a satisfying performance for all clients while properly economizing its resources? How can a provider offer reliable, cost-efficient services without overly restricting the ability of clients to use its services?

- **Meter granularity:** How accurately and fine-grained should API consumption be metered to satisfy client information needs without incurring unnecessary performance penalties or reliability issues?

- **Attractiveness from a consumer point of view:** How can an API provider communicate the attractiveness, availability, and performance goals of its services to clients (assuming that more than one provider offers a certain functionality) without making unrealistic promises that may cause client dissatisfaction or financial losses?

API clients might state that they want a service with a 100 percent uptime guarantee, unlimited resources, and stellar performance at minimal or no cost. Of course, this is not realistic. An API provider must strike a balance between economizing its available resources and making a profit—or keep costs at a minimum (for example, when providing open government offerings).

Patterns in This Chapter

An API Description is created to initially specify the API and provide a mechanism to not only define its syntactical structure but also cover organizational matters such as ownership, support, and evolution strategies. The level of detail of such descriptions may vary from minimal to elaborate.

Providers can define a PRICING PLAN for the API usage to bill clients or other stakeholders. Common options are simple flat-rate subscriptions and more elaborate consumption-based pricing.

API clients might use excessively many resources, thus negatively influencing the service for other clients. To limit such abuse, providers can establish a RATE LIMIT to restrain specific clients. The client can stick to the RATE LIMIT by avoiding unnecessary calls to the API.

Clients have to know that a provider can deliver acceptable service quality, and providers want to deliver high-quality services while at the same time using their available resources economically. A SERVICE LEVEL AGREEMENT (SLA) expresses the resulting compromise in targeted service-level objectives and associated penalties. SLAs often focus on availability but can also refer to any other nonfunctional quality property.

Figure 9.1 shows the relations between the patterns of this chapter.

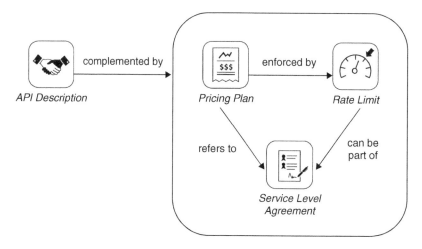

Figure 9.1 *Pattern map for this chapter (API documentation)*

Documentation Patterns

Our final four patterns explain how to specify API contracts and how to communicate and/or enforce agreed-upon API usage terms: API DESCRIPTION, PRICING PLAN, RATE LIMIT, and SERVICE LEVEL AGREEMENT.

Pattern:
API Description

When and Why to Apply

An API provider has decided to expose one or more operations in an API endpoint. Developers of clients (such as Web and mobile app developers implementing Front-end Integrations or the system integrators writing adapters for Backend Integrations) are not yet able to code operation invocations and do not know what to expect in responses. Supplemental interface descriptions are missing as well, including informal explanations of the meaning of the API operations (for example, parameters in message representations, effects on application state in the API implementation) and related qualities (including idempotency and transactionality).

Which knowledge should be shared between an API provider and its clients? How should this knowledge be documented?

High-level forces to be resolved and balanced when defining shared knowledge in distributed systems include the following:

- **Interoperability:** Platform autonomy is one of multiple dimensions of loose coupling which, in turn, is a key SOA principle and microservices tenet [Zimmermann 2017]. Clients and servers may be written in different programming languages and run on different operating systems, which requires them to agree on a common, programming-language-independent encoding and serialization format of the messages being exchanged at runtime. In addition, clients have to agree with providers on a common representation format for API descriptions themselves so that the interoperability of development tools for building APIs and their clients can be achieved. This can be seen as an aspect of format autonomy, another dimension of loose coupling [Fehling 2014].

- **Consumability (including understandability, learnability, and simplicity):** Any guesswork that is required to understand and use an API effectively increases the effort and cost of consuming an API. It should take minutes rather than hours or days to write a first API client that successfully exchanges messages with the API implementation on the provider side; programmers prefer quick wins and a continued sense of achievement to many frustrating trial-and-error iterations. Reading lengthy tables listing parameters with their effects and meanings and reverse-engineering the structure from sample responses usually takes longer than copy-pasting a code example or digesting a well-defined, validatable interface description that can also be used to generate code and test cases (which, by the way, is seen as an antipattern by parts of the community). Generally speaking, tools and their documentation should be "honest." API descriptions and supporting tools should not hide the fact that remote network communication takes place, and they should not take away control (and responsibility) from client and provider programmers. The more honest an API and its description are, the more consumable they become, as unpleasant surprises are avoided, for instance, during testing and maintenance. Simple descriptions and their implementations are usually easier to comprehend than accidentally complex ones.

- **Information hiding:** Providers have certain expectations on how clients will use their APIs. Clients make assumptions on how to invoke operations correctly. These assumptions might concern required presence and permitted values of parameters, invocation sequencing, call frequency, and so forth. If client assumptions match provider expectations, the interaction will be successful. However, providers should not leak their secret implementation details into interfaces, and successful interactions should not depend on clients guessing which assumptions should be made.

- **Extensibility and evolvability:** Clients and providers evolve at different paces; one provider may have to satisfy present and future needs of multiple clients, which differ in their use cases and in their technology choices. This might lead to the introduction of optional features and representation elements (that are supposed to promote compatibility but might also harm it). Speed of bug fixing and enhancing capabilities matter. Our evolution patterns cover these forces in depth. When APIs evolve, the corresponding documentation has to be updated to reflect the changes. This bears risk and cost.

One could choose to provide only basic information such as network addresses and examples of API calls and responses, and many public APIs do just this. Such an approach leaves room for interpretation and is a source of interoperability problems. It offloads work of the API team on the provider side because less information has to be updated during service evolution and maintenance. This comes at the expense of creating extra learning, experimentation, development, and testing effort on the client side.

How It Works

Create an API DESCRIPTION that defines request and response message structures, error reporting, and other relevant parts of the technical knowledge to be shared between provider and client.

In addition to static and structural information, also cover dynamic or behavioral aspects including invocation sequences, pre- and postconditions, and invariants.

Complement the syntactical interface description with quality management policies as well as semantic specifications and organizational information.

Make the API DESCRIPTION both human- and machine-readable. Specify it either in plain text or in a more formal language, depending on the supported usage scenario, development culture, and maturity of the development practices.

Make sure that the semantic specification is business-aligned but also technically accurate; it must unveil the supported business capabilities in domain terms so that it is understandable for business analysts (aka domain subject matter experts) but also cover data management concerns such as consistency, freshness, and idempotency. Cover licensing and terms and conditions or factor out this information and define a SERVICE LEVEL AGREEMENT (for example, for business- and mission-critical APIs).

Consider using a recognized functional contract description language such as OpenAPI Specification (formerly known as Swagger) for the technical contract part of HTTP resource APIs. Note that OpenAPI Specification (OAS) Version 3.0 has an attribute to share license information.

Variants   Two variants are popular in practice: *Minimal Description* and *Elaborate Description*. They represent opposite ends of a spectrum; hybrid forms can be found as well.

- *Minimal Description.* At a minimum, clients need to know the API endpoint addresses, the operation names, and the structure and meaning of the request and response message representations, as defined in our domain model introduced in Chapter 1, "Application Programming Interface (API) Fundamentals." This minimal description forms the technical API contract. In HTTP resource APIs, the operation names are constrained by the HTTP verbs/methods (with the usage of these verbs being defined implicitly/by convention). Together with the data contract, they still have to be specified explicitly. Figure 9.2 shows this variant.

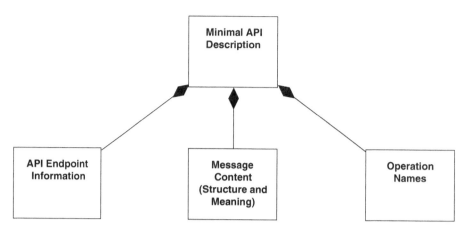

Figure 9.2 *Minimal API DESCRIPTION variant*

- *Elaborate Description.* More elaborate API DESCRIPTIONS add usage examples; feature detailed tables explaining parameter meanings, data types, and constraints; enumerate error codes and error structures in responses; and may even include test cases to check provider compliance, as shown in Figure 9.3. See Chapter 1 as well as Recipes 3.14 and 14.1 in the *RESTful Web Services Cookbook* [Allamaraju 2010] for related advice.

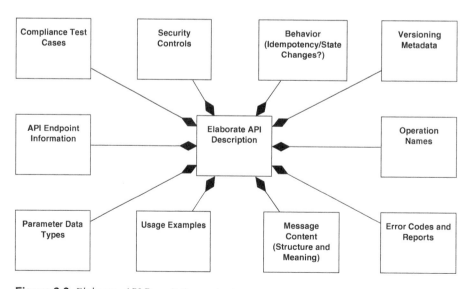

Figure 9.3 *Elaborate API Description variant*

Example

The "Template for Elaborate API Descriptions" in Figure 9.4 covers both business information and functional-technical API design concerns.

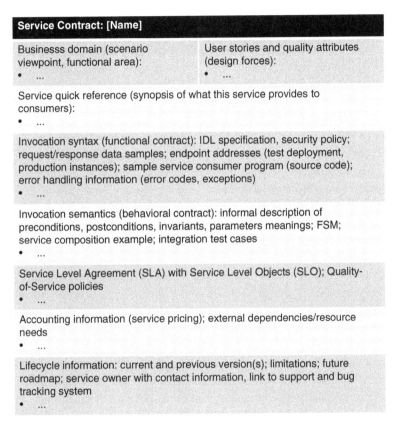

Service Contract: [Name]	
Businesss domain (scenario viewpoint, functional area): • ...	User stories and quality attributes (design forces): • ...
Service quick reference (synopsis of what this service provides to consumers): • ...	
Invocation syntax (functional contract): IDL specification, security policy; request/response data samples; endpoint addresses (test deployment, production instances); sample service consumer program (source code); error handling information (error codes, exceptions) • ...	
Invocation semantics (behavioral contract): informal description of preconditions, postconditions, invariants, parameters meanings; FSM; service composition example; integration test cases • ...	
Service Level Agreement (SLA) with Service Level Objects (SLO); Quality-of-Service policies • ...	
Accounting information (service pricing); external dependencies/resource needs • ...	
Lifecycle information: current and previous version(s); limitations; future roadmap; service owner with contact information, link to support and bug tracking system • ...	

Figure 9.4 *Template for Elaborate API Descriptions (also known as service contracts). IDL: interface description language; FSM: finite-state machine*

In practice, descriptions of APIs are often made available via developer portals, project wikis, or service documentation Web sites. MDSL, introduced in Appendix C, "Microservice Domain-Specific Language (MDSL)," supports the API DESCRIPTION pattern natively.

Discussion

A MINIMAL DESCRIPTION is compact and easy to evolve and maintain. ELABORATE DESCRIPTIONS are expressive. They promote interoperability.

A Minimal Description might cause client developers to guess or reverse-engineer provider-side behavior; such implicit assumptions cause the information-hiding principle to be violated and sometimes become invalid in the long run. Furthermore, ambiguities may harm interoperability; testing and maintenance efforts increase if new versions that are not backward compatible are not indicated as such. Elaborate Descriptions might introduce inconsistencies due to their intrinsic redundancy where the same elements are mentioned in different parts of the specification. If they disclose provider-side implementation details such as downstream (outbound) dependencies, they violate the information-hiding principle. They cause maintenance effort when evolving, primarily the need to systematically update the descriptions (and then consistently implement the changes).

The amount of effort required for API DESCRIPTIONS that meet the information need of the clients depends on the chosen specification depth and level of detail that is required to make meaningful and correct communication possible. If a contract is overspecified, it is hard to consume and maintain (and is considered anti-lean because it is seen as unnecessary documentation that qualifies as waste to be eliminated). If it is underspecified, it is easy to read and update but still might not lead to interoperable client-server conversations that also produce the desired results at runtime. Missing information has to be guessed, assumed, or simply reverse-engineered—for example, server-side effects of calls (state changes, data accuracy and consistency), handling of erroneous input, security enforcement policies, and so on—with no guarantees by the provider on the correctness of the assumptions made by the client. One might consider explaining QoS policies, for example, regarding availability, in an explicit SERVICE LEVEL AGREEMENT.

While informal API descriptions are widely used in practice, the value of machine-readable technical API contracts that can be used to generate proxy and stub code has been discussed controversially. The success of notations such as API Blueprint [API Blueprint 2022], JSON:API [JSON API 2022], and OpenAPI Specification [OpenAPI 2022] and tools such as the Apigee console and API Management Gateways suggests that there is a need for machine-readable technical API contracts in most (if not all) integration scenarios. Many REST books and articles admit that there always is a contract—sometimes called the *uniform contract* [Erl 2013]. It just looks different and is created and maintained by different stakeholders.

It is subject to debate whether contracts are really negotiated and agreed upon in practice or simply dictated by the API provider. Business contexts and API usage scenarios differ: a small startup or a thesis project team consuming the cloud APIs of one of the dominating cloud providers has little hope of being able to request features or negotiate terms and conditions. On the other end of the spectrum, large software vendors and corporate users with enterprise-level agreements (ELAs) do exactly this in their strategic outsourcing deals and cloud partnerships, for instance, when rolling out multitenant, business-critical applications. Market dynamics and development culture will determine the amount of effort invested in scope and quality of an API Description. Client developers can (and should) consider the accuracy and usability of these descriptions in the decision-making process when selecting an API and its provider.

Related Patterns

All other patterns in this book are related to this one way or another. Depending on mission criticality and market dynamics, an API Description can be completed with a Service Level Agreement to specify quality goals—and the consequences of not meeting them. Version information and evolution strategies can be included (see, for instance, Version Identifier and Two in Production patterns).

"Service Descriptor" [Daigneau 2011] and "Interface Description" [Voelter 2004] cover the technical part of the API Description.

More Information

An online API Stylebook collects and references related documentation advice in a dedicated "design topic" [Lauret 2017]. Recipe 14.1 in the *RESTful Web Services Cookbook* [Allamaraju 2010] discusses how to document RESTful Web services. The "Engagement Perspective" in *Perspectives on Web Services* [Zimmermann 2003] collects WSDL (and SOAP) best practices; much of the given advice also applies to other API contract syntaxes. Chapter 13 in *Principles of Web API Design* [Higginbotham 2021] covers different API description formats and other components of an effective API documentation.

The "Microservices Canvas" template proposed by Chris Richardson creates Elaborate Descriptions when filled out completely. The template includes implementation information, service invocation relationships, and events produced/subscribed to [Richardson 2019].

The notion of Design-by-Contract was established by Bertrand Meyer in the context of object-oriented software engineering [Meyer 1997]; his advice can also be adopted when defining remote API contracts. The specific role of data in interface contracts is explained by Pat Helland in "Data on the Outside versus Data on the Inside" [Helland 2005].

The practice collection *Design Practice Reference* (DPR) features a Stepwise Service Design activity and an API Description artifact [Zimmermann 2021b]. MDSL implements the pattern [Zimmermann 2022].

Pattern:
PRICING PLAN

When and Why to Apply

An API is an asset of the organizations or individuals that have built it. From the viewpoint of commercial organizations, this means that it has both monetary and immaterial value. The development and operations of this asset have to be funded somehow. The API clients can be charged for API usage, but the API provider can also sell advertisements or find other means of raising funds.

> How can the API provider meter API service consumption and charge for it?

When metering and billing, the following concerns are challenging to resolve in a way that is acceptable both for API customers and for their providers:

- **Economic aspects:** Deciding on a pricing model is a decision that touches on many aspects of an organization: visibility of the organization, perceived fairness of the pricing, branding, perception of the company in the market, monetization, customer acquisition strategy (free trials, upselling, etc.), competitors, customer satisfaction. Another factor is the effort and cost required to meter and charge customers, which must be contrasted with the benefits of metering and charging.

- **Accuracy:** API users expect to be billed only for the services they consume. They might even want to gain a certain amount of control over spending limits. Detailed metering reports and bills increase the confidence of the API user, but such deep accounting of each API call might also incur an unnecessary performance penalty.

- **Meter granularity:** Metering can be performed and reported at different levels of verbosity. For example, an API provider might offer continuous metering with real-time reporting, while another might just report daily aggregated numbers. When the metering is down, the provider loses money.

- **Security:** Metering and charging data may contain sensitive information about users that has to be protected (for example, to adhere to data privacy regulations). Providers must also charge the correct customer. Impersonating another customer's identity or using somebody else's API KEYS must be prevented. In multitenant systems such as cloud offerings, tenants should not even know that others exist (not even in error situations in which detailed Error Reports are collected). Those other tenants might include competitors or business partners; nondisclosure agreements might have been signed. While tenants might be interested in performance data of other tenants, sharing such data deliberately or accidentally is unethical (or even illegal).

One could just invoice the customer a one-off sign-up fee, but such an approach might treat hobbyists and high-volume corporate users equally. This is a valid solution in some cases but might also oversimplify the picture and be too cheap for certain user segments and too expensive for others.

How It Works

Assign a Pricing Plan for the API usage to the API Description that is used to bill API customers, advertisers, or other stakeholders accordingly.

Define and monitor metrics for measuring API usage, such as API usage statistics per operation.

Variants   Several variants of Pricing Plans exist. The most common ones are *subscription-based pricing* and *usage-based pricing*. A *market-based allocation* is seen less often (also known as *auction-style allocation* of resources). These plans can be combined with a *freemium model* where a particular low or hobbyist usage level is free. Payment comes into effect for higher usages or once an initial trial period expires. Combinations of different plans are also possible, for example, a monthly base *flat-rate subscription* fee for a base package and extra *usage-based pricing* for additionally consumed services.

- *Subscription-based Pricing (see Figure 9.5).* In subscription-based or flat-rate pricing, the customer is billed a recurring (for example, monthly or yearly) fee that is independent of the actual usage of the service, sometimes in combination with a Rate Limit to ensure fair use. Within these boundaries, the subscription typically allows customers near-unlimited usage and requires less bookkeeping than usage-based pricing. Alternatively, a provider can offer different billing levels, from which a user can choose the one that best matches its expected usage. If a customer exceeds its allowance, it can be offered an upgrade to a more expensive billing level. If a customer is not willing to upgrade, further calls will be blocked (or be responded to with a lower service level).

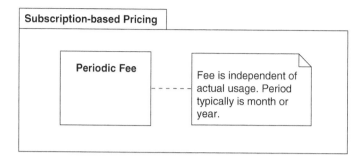

Figure 9.5 *Subscription-based Pricing variant*

- *Usage-based Pricing (see Figure 9.6)*. A usage-based pricing policy bills the customer only for actual usage (for example, API calls or amount of data transferred) of the service resources. The pricing can be varied for different API operations; for instance, a simple reading of a resource might cost less than creating a resource. This usage can then be billed periodically. An alternative is to offer prepaid packages (as is sometimes done in mobile telephony contracts) with credits that are then spent.[2]

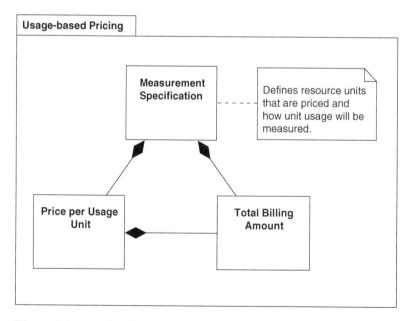

Figure 9.6 *Usage-based Pricing variant*

---

2. For example, when using CloudConvert, a document-conversion SaaS, customers can purchase packages of conversion minutes that can then be spent over time.

- *Market-based Pricing (see Figure 9.7).* Elastic market-based pricing is a third variant. For a market to emerge, the price of a resource may have to move in line with the demand for the service. A customer then places a bid to use the service at a specific maximum price, and when the market price falls to or below the bid price, the customer is allocated the service until the price rises above the bidding price again.

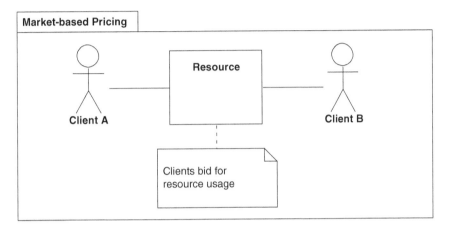

Figure 9.7 *Market-based Pricing variant*

These variants of Pricing Plans differ in the effort required to define and update the prices; they have an impact on attracting and retaining customers. They also differ in their ambitions to make sustainable profits. Finally, they may differ in their scope: entire API endpoint versus individual operations and API access versus back-end services (for example, actual computing/data retrieval/communication) are two such scoping dimensions.

Client developers and application owners are advised to read the fine print and run some trials to familiarize themselves with the billing granularity and operational procedures before committing to using a particular offering. Some experimentation might be necessary to find an API consumption profile that is both technically and financially satisfying for them.

Example

Imagine a fictitious provider offering an API to programmatically send and receive e-mails, liberating clients from working with the SMTP and POP/IMAP protocols directly. The provider decided to implement a usage-based Pricing Plan, with a freemium level for low usage and different pricing levels depending on how many e-mails per month are sent, as shown in Table 9.1.

Table 9.1 *Usage-Based PRICING PLAN of a Fictitious API Provider with Different Billing Levels.*

E-Mails per Month (up to)	Pricing per Month
100	Free
10,000	$20
100,000	$150
1,000,000	$1,000

A competitor of the provider, trying to differentiate itself and keep the monitoring at a minimum, might instead decide to go with a flat-rate subscription fee of $50 per month that offers unlimited e-mails to customers.

Discussion

By using a PRICING PLAN, customers and their provider reach a clear agreement about incurring costs and their mutual obligations (for example, with regard to invoicing and payment settlement). A PRICING PLAN is sometimes also called a Rate Plan.

Writing and publishing sensible PRICING PLANS is challenging. It requires much knowledge about the customers' interests and business models on both sides. The API product owner and developers must work together closely to pick a variant that balances effort and benefit. API clients have to be identified by an API KEY or some other means of authentication. Usage-based pricing requires detailed monitoring and measurement of client actions. To avoid disputes, customers will want detailed reporting to track and monitor their API usage. This requires more effort on the provider's side. Limits can be put in place that trigger a notification when exceeded.

Another consideration is how to deal with outages of the metering functions of the PRICING PLAN implementation: if metering cannot be performed, it is impossible to bill the customer for its consumption later. Consequently, the API has to be shut down until the metering system is available again, or its services have to be provided free of charge during the outage.

Subscription-based pricing is much easier to implement than usage-based pricing; development should inform nontechnical stakeholders (such as product owners) about the consequences of the more expensive implementation option. If possible, one can start with subscription-based pricing and implement usage-based pricing at a later stage.

Security requirements have to be satisfied by the underlying API implementation and operational infrastructure.

Related Patterns

A Pricing Plan can use Rate Limits to enforce different billing levels. If used, the Pricing Plan should refer to the Service Level Agreement.

To identify the client making a request, an API Key (or another authentication practice) can be used. A Wish List or a Wish Template can help to keep costs low if the amount of data transferred is part of the Pricing Plan definition.

More Information

"API Gateway" [Richardson 2016] and the systems management patterns in *Enterprise Integration Patterns* [Hohpe 2003], "Wire Tap" and "Message Store" in particular, can be used to implement metering and serve as enforcement points. A Wire Tap can be inserted between the source and destination of a message to copy incoming messages to a secondary channel or a Message Store that is used to count the requests per client without having to implement this at the API endpoint.

Pattern:
Rate Limit

When and Why to Apply

An API endpoint and the API contract exposing operations, messages, and data representations have been established. An API Description has been defined that specifies message exchange patterns and protocol. Clients of the API have signed up with the provider and have agreed to the terms and conditions that govern the usage of the endpoint and operations. Some APIs might not require any contractual relation, for example, when offered as an open data service or during a trial period.

How can the API provider prevent API clients from excessive API usage?[3]

When preventing excessive API usage that may harm provider operations or other clients, solutions to the following design issues have to be found:

- **Economic aspects:** Preventing API clients from abuse requires resources to be implemented and maintained. Clients might react negatively to quotas and

---

3. The API provider defines what exactly is deemed excessive. A paid flat-rate subscription typically imposes different limitations than a free usage plan. See the Pricing Plan pattern for a detailed discussion of the trade-offs of different subscription models.

their enforcement because of the extra work involved (for example, to stay aware of its allowances). This can be a criterion for the client to move to a competitor. Measures thus should only be taken if impact and severity of API abuse are judged as sufficiently high to warrant the costs and business risks.

- **Performance:** The API provider typically wants, or might be required by contract or regulation, to maintain a high quality of its service for all its API clients. The exact details might be defined in the respective SERVICE LEVEL AGREEMENT.

- **Reliability:** If any API client abuses the service deliberately or accidentally, actions must be taken to stop harm to other clients. Individual requests can be rejected or access to the API revoked. If a provider is too restrictive, it runs the risk of dissatisfying prospective consumers; if it is too relaxed, it gets overwhelmed and the response times perceived by other consumers (for example, paying consumers) might suffer. Those other clients might start looking for alternatives in that case.

- **Impact and severity of risks of API abuse:** The possible negative consequences of API clients abusing the service deliberately or accidentally have to be analyzed and assessed. These consequences have to be weighed against the costs of any measure taken to prevent abuse. For example, the foreseeable usage patterns might indicate a low probability of negative consequences of abuse and/or a low impact of such abuse (for example, economic impact or reputation damage). If the remaining risks can be mitigated or accepted, the API provider might decide not to take any action to prevent API clients from excessive API usage.

- **Client awareness:** Responsible clients will want to manage their allowance. They monitor their usage so they do not risk being locked out for exceeding their limit.

To prevent clients that exhibit excessive usage from harming other API clients, one could simply add more processing power, storage space, and network bandwidth. Often this is not economically viable.

How It Works

Introduce and enforce a RATE LIMIT to safeguard against API clients that overuse the API.

Formulate this limit as a certain number of requests that are allowed per time window. If the client exceeds this limit, further requests can either be declined, be processed in a later period, or be served with best-effort guarantees, allocating a smaller amount of resources. Figure 9.8 illustrates such interval-based RATE LIMIT with periodic resets.

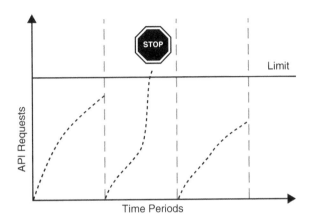

Figure 9.8 *RATE LIMIT: Once the client exceeds the allowed number of requests per time period, all further requests are declined*

Set the scope of the RATE LIMIT, which can be the entire API, a single endpoint, a group of operations, or an individual operation. Requests do not have to be treated uniformly. Endpoints can have varying operational costs, and token usage can thus differ.[4]

Define an appropriate time period, for example, daily or monthly, per API operation or group of API operations after which the RATE LIMIT is reset. This interval may be rolling. Keep track of client calls in the defined time period through monitoring and logging.

A RATE LIMIT may also restrict the amount of concurrency allowed, that is, the number of concurrent requests a client is allowed to make. For example, under a free billing plan, clients could be limited to just a single concurrent request. When a client has exceeded its RATE LIMIT, the provider can stop serving the client altogether or slow it down (or, for commercial offerings, offer to upgrade to a higher-cost plan). This latter case is sometimes also described as *throttling*. Note that the exact terminology differs by providers, and often RATE LIMIT and throttling are used interchangeably.

---

4. For example, retrieving a simple ID costs a single token (unit) in the YouTube API, whereas a video upload consumes approximately 1,600 units.

If a client hits the RATE LIMIT too often, the account or corresponding API KEY can be suspended and put on a "deny list."[5]

Example

GitHub uses this pattern to control access to its RESTful HTTP API: once a RATE LIMIT is exceeded, subsequent requests are answered with HTTP status code `429 Too Many Requests`. To inform clients about the current state of each RATE LIMIT and to help clients manage their allowance of tokens, custom HTTP headers are sent with each rate-limited response.

The following code listing shows an excerpt of such a rate-limited response from the GitHub API. The API has a limit of 60 requests per hour, of which 59 remain:

```
curl -X GET --include https://api.github.com/users/misto
HTTP/1.1 200 OK
...
X-RateLimit-Limit: 60
X-RateLimit-Remaining: 59
X-RateLimit-Reset: 1498811560
```

The `X-RateLimit-Reset` indicates the time when the limit will be reset with a UNIX timestamp.[6]

Discussion

A RATE LIMIT gives the provider control over the API consumption of clients. By implementing a RATE LIMIT, an API provider can protect its offering from malicious clients, such as unwelcome bots, and preserve the quality of its service. The provider can better provision resources due to capped maximal usage, thereby improving performance and reliability for all clients.

Deciding on appropriate limits is not easy. If the RATE LIMIT is set too high, it will not have the desired effect. Overly aggressive limits will annoy API users. Finding the right levels requires some experimentation and tuning. For example, a provider's PRICING PLAN might allow for 30,000 requests per month. With no additional restrictions, a client could consume all these requests in a short burst of time, probably overwhelming the provider. To mitigate this particular problem, the provider could additionally restrict clients to just one request per second. Clients need to control

---

5. A deny list, or blocklist, is an access control mechanism that bars certain blocked elements but lets all others pass. This is in contrast to an allow list, or welcome list, where only elements that are on the list can pass.

6. UNIX timestamps count the number of seconds since January 1, 1970.

their usage and manage the case of hitting the Rate Limit, for example, by tracing their API usage and/or by queuing requests. This can be achieved by caching and prioritizing API calls. A Rate Limit makes the API implementation stateful, which has to be taken into account when scaling out.

Paid offerings offer a better way to manage Rate Limits with multiple subscription levels and, accordingly, different limits. Excessive API usage can even be seen as something positive (because it leads to increased revenue). However, a free service does not have to give all of its clients the same Rate Limit either. It can instead take into account other metrics to accommodate clients of various sizes and stages. For example, Facebook grants API calls proportional to the number of users that have the client app installed.

In order to measure and enforce the Rate Limit metrics, the provider has to identify the client or user. For identification purposes, the API client has obtained a means to identify itself at the endpoint (more precisely, at the security policy enforcement point[7] within the API), for instance, with an API Key or an authentication protocol. If no sign-up is required, for example, in a free service, the endpoint has to establish another way to identify the client, such as by IP address.

Related Patterns

The details of a Rate Limit can be part of a Service Level Agreement. A Rate Limit can be dependent on the client's subscription level, which is described further in the Pricing Plan pattern. In such cases, the Rate Limit is used to enforce different billing levels of the Pricing Plan.

Wish List or a Wish Template can help to ensure that data-bound Rate Limits are not violated. The current state of the Rate Limit, for example, how many requests remain in the current billing period, can be communicated via an explicit Context Representation in the message payload.

More Information

"Leaky Bucket Counter" [Hanmer 2007] offers a possible implementation variant for Rate Limit. Chapter 21 in *Site Reliability Engineering* [Beyer 2016] covers strategies for handling overload.

The systems management patterns published by [Hohpe 2003] can help to implement metering and can thus also serve as enforcement points. For example, a "Control Bus" can be used to increase or decrease certain limits dynamically at runtime

---

7. In the eXtensible Access Control Markup Language (XACML) [OASIS 2021], the policy enforcement point protects a resource from unauthorized access. It consults a policy decision point in the background while doing so.

and "Message Store" can help implement continuous monitoring of resource usage over time.

The Cloud Architecture Center [Google 2019] presents different strategies and techniques for the realization of Rate Limits.

Pattern:
Service Level Agreement

When and Why to Apply

An API Description defines one or more API endpoints, including the functional interface of operations with their request and response messages. The dynamic invocation behavior of these operations has not been articulated precisely yet in terms of qualitative and quantitative QoS characteristics. Furthermore, the support of the API services along its life cycle, including guaranteed lifetime and mean time to repair, has not yet been specified either.

> How can an API client learn about the specific quality-of-service characteristics of an API and its endpoint operations?
>
> How can these characteristics, and the consequences of not meeting them, be defined and communicated in a measurable way?

Partially conflicting concerns make it hard to specify QoS characteristics in a way that is acceptable for both clients and providers. Specifically, the following concerns have to be addressed:

- **Business agility and vitality:** The business model of an API client might rely on the availability of a particular API service (and on some other of the previously mentioned qualities, such as scalability or privacy). Business agility and vitality might rely on guarantees about the former three qualities, as violations to those might disrupt the client.

- **Attractiveness from the consumer point of view:** Assuming that more than one API is available that offers a required functionality, guaranteeing service characteristics can be an expression of confidence of the provider in its own capabilities (including API implementation and downstream systems). For example, when choosing between two functionally similar offerings with different availability guarantees, consumers are more likely to go for the offering that has a higher availability guarantee (unless other factors such as price have higher priority and favor the API offering the lower guarantee).

- **Availability:** The API client is usually interested in a high uptime of the API provider services. Uptime matters in many domains and empowers API clients to give certain guarantees to their own consumers .

- **Performance and scalability:** The API client is usually interested in a low latency, and high throughput is desired on the provider side.

- **Security and privacy:** If an API deals with confidential or private data, the API client is interested in the means and measures taken by the provider to ensure security and privacy.

- **Government regulations and legal obligations:** Government regulations have to be met, for example, related to personal data protection[8] or mandating that data be stored locally.[9] Such regulations might prohibit local companies from using the offerings of a foreign provider unless the provider complies with that regulation. For example, a Swiss startup may use the services of a US provider that complies with the Swiss-US Privacy Shield Framework. A guarantee by the API provider can be a way to document compliance.

- **Cost-efficiency and business risks from a provider point of view:** A provider wants to economize its available resources and typically also aims at being profitable (or keep costs at a minimum—for example, in open government offerings). Offering an unrealistically high service level guarantee or agreeing to pay punitive penalties would require careful consideration and must be in line with risk management strategies on the provider side. Offering any kind of guarantees at all, if they have no clear values, is not advisable because of the high risks and costs for implementing them and mitigating violations of the guarantees.

The client could simply trust the provider to make commercially and technically reasonable efforts to provide a satisfying API usage experience, and in many public APIs as well as solution-internal APIs, this option is chosen. However, if API usage is business critical for the client, the resulting risk might not be tolerable. One might rely on unstructured, freeform text that states the commercial and technical terms and conditions of API usage only informally; many public APIs provide such documents. However, such natural language documents (just like oral ad hoc agreements) are ambiguous and leave room for interpretations that might lead to misunderstandings and, in turn, to critical project situations. They might no longer be sufficient when competitive pressure increases. When no alternative is available or there is

---

8. The EU General Data Protection Regulation [EU 2016] regulates how companies must protect individuals' data that they process.

9. For instance, laws in Brazil and Russia require providers to store data locally [The Economist 2015].

no room for negotiating a customized agreement, deciding on using an API simply comes down to trusting the provider and/or predicting its future QoS characteristics based on historical data and previous experiences.

How It Works

As an API product owner, establish a quality-oriented SERVICE LEVEL AGREEMENT that defines testable service-level objectives.

In any SERVICE LEVEL AGREEMENT, define at least one service-level objective (SLO) as well as penalties, compensation credits or actions, and reporting procedures for violations of the SLA. An SLA and its SLOs must identify the API operations they pertain to. API client developers can then study the SLA and its SLOs carefully before committing to use a particular API endpoint and its operations. The SLA structure should be recognizable, ideally even standardized across offerings; the writing style should be assertive and unambiguous. Figure 9.9 shows the structure of an SLA with its SLOs.

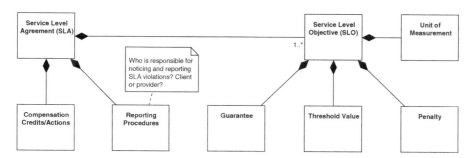

Figure 9.9 *Structure and content of a SERVICE LEVEL AGREEMENT*

Derive the SLOs for each controlled service from specific and measurable quality attributes that are relevant to the API and ideally have been specified during analysis and design [Cervantes 2016]. SLOs can also arise from regulatory guidelines; for example, personal data protection laws such as the General Data Protection Regulation [EU 2016] might mandate that data is erased once it is no longer needed. SLOs can be broadly grouped into categories; for example, the European Commission's SLA guidelines [C-SIG 2014] categorize SLOs into performance, security, data management, and personal data protection categories.

In each SLO that corresponds to a particular quality attribute, specify a *threshold* value and the unit of measurement. Give a *guarantee* (that is, minimum percentage) for how much of the time it will be met and a *penalty* if it is not achieved. For example, an SLO might state that 99 percent of the time (guarantee), requests should be answered in less than 500 milliseconds (threshold, unit of measurement) over a 30-day window. If this SLO cannot be met, customers will get a 10 percent discount on their next bill (penalty).

It is important to state clearly how the measurement will be performed and interpreted. This avoids confusion and unrealistic expectations. For example, in the previous example, it is important to clarify that the 99 percent is calculated over a 30-day window.

When defining the SLA, all relevant internal and external stakeholders must be involved early (for example, C-level executives, legal department, and security officer). API providers should let the SLA specification be reviewed and approved by a well-defined set of these stakeholders (for example, the legal department). Several iterations are typically required, which might be rather time consuming due to busy schedules; agreeing on SLA content and wording is a negotiation process that can be rather intense and has a large human factor.[10]

Example

Lakeside Mutual offers a self-service application for customers to request quotations for different kinds of insurance. As part of its new growth strategy, the company started offering white-label insurance products. Third parties can include Lakeside Mutual products under their own branding on their Web sites, with Lakeside Mutual taking a small cut from the insurance premiums. To increase confidence in this offering, the following SLA was defined:

> The White-Label Insurance API service has a response time of maximally 0.5 seconds.

The response time might need some clarification:

> The response time is measured from the time the request arrives at the API endpoint until the response has been sent out.

Note that this does not include the time it takes for the request and response to travel across the network from the API provider to the client. Furthermore, the provider assures:

> The White-Label Insurance SLO will be met for 99 percent of the requests, measured over a 30-day window; otherwise, the customer will receive a discount credit of 10 percent on the current billing period. To receive a credit, the customer must submit a claim, including the dates and times of the incident, to the customer support center.

---

10. Think about procurement and decision making in everyday life!

Discussion

The primary target audience for this pattern is the API product owner on the provider side rather than the developers of API endpoints and operations. An SLA often is part of the terms and conditions (of services) or a master service agreement, along with other policies such as an acceptable use policy or a privacy policy.

Clients establish a shared understanding with the provider concerning service levels and quality levels that can be expected. An SLA may target all provided services or a specific set of operations exposed at a particular API endpoint. For example, SLOs relating to a personal data protection regulation will likely be handled in an overall SLA, but data management objectives—for example, data backup frequency—might differ per endpoint and/or operation. Well-crafted SLAs with measurable SLOs are an indicator of service maturity and transparency. Notably, many public APIs and cloud offerings do not expose any, or only rather weak, SLAs. This can be attributed to market dynamics and lack of regulation.

The provider can be held accountable for failing to provide the service. Sometimes organizations do not want to be held accountable for their failures. Establishing clearly defined obligations like a SERVICE LEVEL AGREEMENT might therefore trigger internal organizational resistance caused by fear.

It only makes sense to define SLAs and precise SLOs, and publish them to clients if this is required (and paid for) by clients—or if providers consider it beneficial from a business point of view. Otherwise, SLAs might cause an unnecessary business risk, as they are often legally binding. It might be hard to fulfill them at all times; if not asked for, why offer strong guarantees? SLAs require substantial effort to be designed, implemented, and monitored; mitigating SLA violations also causes work. Maintaining operations personnel to quickly deal with SLA violations is expensive. The business risks related to SLAs can be mitigated by limiting the liability of the API provider, for example, to offer service credits as the only penalty for SLA violations.

Alternatives to an SLA with measurable SLOs, as described in this pattern, are to define no SLAs or to set quality goals in loose terms (that is, in an SLA with informally specified SLOs). An SLA might contain both measurable SLOs about certain qualities and specify others only informally. Security aspects, for example, are hard to capture formally without becoming overly complex and either unrealistic or hard to validate. A provider might therefore agree to make "commercially reasonable efforts" to secure its API.

SLAs can be beneficial to the API provider even in the form of an internal SLA—yielding a variant of the pattern in which the API provider uses the SLA to specify and measure its own performance on relevant qualities but does not share this information with clients external to the organization. This approach may be part of *Site Reliability Engineering* [Beyer 2016].

Related Patterns

A Service Level Agreement accompanies the API contract or the API Description (which would refer to the Service Level Agreement). SLAs may govern the use of instances of many patterns in this pattern language, such as those in the representation and quality categories of this pattern language.

The details of Rate Limits and Pricing Plans can be included in a Service Level Agreement.

More Information

Site Reliability Engineering [Beyer 2016] devotes an entire chapter to SLOs, including their measurements, called "Service Level Indicators" (SLIs).

Jay Judkowitz and Mark Carter cover SLA, SLO, and SLI management in a blog post in the Google Cloud Platform Blog [Judkowitz 2018].

Summary

This chapter presented four patterns that are concerned with the documentation of APIs both from a technical and from a business point of view: API Description, Pricing Plan, Rate Limit, and Service Level Agreement.

While an API Description focuses on capturing the API functionality, a complementary Service Level Agreement states the qualities that clients can expect from the API explicitly. Pricing Plan brings these two aspects together, as it defines how much clients are supposed to pay for accessing different subsets of the API functionality with a certain level of quality. A Rate Limit can prevent clients from exploiting the API provider resources beyond what they pay for.

Naturally, the four patterns have strong connections to many of those in Chapters 5 to 7. The API Description should make the API endpoint role explicit: Information Holder Resources are data-oriented, and this data differs in terms of its usage, lifetime, and linking; Processing Resources are activity-oriented, on granularity levels that range from simple actions to complex business processes. The same holds for the operation responsibilities within these types of endpoints that differ in the way they access provider-side application state: State Creation Operation (write access), Retrieval Operation (read access), State Transition Operation (read and write access), and Computation Function (no access). These endpoint roles and operation responsibilities influence the need for and the content of a Pricing Plan and a Rate Limit, and of a Service Level Agreement as well. For example, an Information Holder Resource may charge clients depending on the amount of data transferred and stored, while a Processing Resource may want to limit how many concurrent activity requests clients may initiate and how computing-intense such requests may be. The conventions for naming endpoints and their operations in the API documentation should make their roles and responsibilities clear at first glance.

Both RATE LIMITS and PRICING PLANS often make use of API KEYS to identify clients. The RATE LIMIT is affected when patterns such as REQUEST BUNDLE that change message size and exchange frequency are applied. If a PRICING PLAN is in place, clients expect certain service-level guarantees—for instance, regarding performance, availability, and API stability.

Finally, the versioning approach and the lifetime guarantees discussed in Chapter 8, "Evolve APIs," are part of API DESCRIPTIONS and/or SERVICE LEVEL AGREEMENTS. It is likely that the combination of PRICING PLAN with EXPERIMENTAL PREVIEW makes less sense than charging for the consumption of APIs applying TWO IN PRODUCTION and/or LIMITED LIFETIME GUARANTEE.

We are done with the pattern catalog! The next chapter applies them to larger, real-world examples.

Part 3

<hr>

Our Patterns in Action (Now and Then)

Part 3 returns to the big picture of API design and evolution.

Now that our 44 patterns have been introduced and discussed in depth, we can apply them jointly to larger, real API designs, presented in Chapter 10, "Real-World Pattern Stories." It is also time to reflect and share our outlook on the future of APIs in Chapter 11, "Conclusion."

Chapter 10

Real-World Pattern Stories

This chapter investigates API design and evolution in real-world business domains and application genres. We present two existing API-centric systems with their contexts, requirements, and design challenges as larger, domain-specific examples of pattern use. Both system have been running in production for a long time.

We return to the questions, options, and criteria for pattern selection from Chapter 3, "API Decision Narratives." To do so, the chapter applies the patterns from Chapters 4 to 9 in combination, focusing on

- When to apply which pattern, and why.
- When to prefer which alternatives, and why.

The first pattern story, "Large-Scale Business Process Integration in the Swiss Mortgage Business," is about an existing e-government and business process digitalization solution. The second one, "APIs for Offering and Ordering Processes in the Building Construction Domain," presents Web APIs supporting business processes in the construction industry (construction of physical real-world buildings, that is!).

After you have read this chapter, you should be able to combine patterns from the previous ones and employ a business-context-specific and quality-attribute-driven approach to API design. The two sample cases provide larger and real examples of pattern usage and explain the rationale behind it.

Large-Scale Process Integration in the Swiss Mortgage Business

In this section, we present the Terravis case and its use of patterns.

Business Context and Domain

Terravis [Lübke 2016] is a large process-based integration platform developed and used in Switzerland. It connects and integrates land registries, notaries, banks, and other parties for conducting land registry and mortgage-based business processes fully electronically. The project started in 2009 and resulted in an award-winning product [Möckli 2017].

While the domain of land registries, parcels, mortgages, and (parcel) owners has been well established for several centuries, it remained a *refugio* for paper-based processing for a long time. Here, the federated structure of Switzerland led to different cantons (member states of the Swiss Confederation) using different processes, data models, and laws governing land registry businesses. In 2009, the Swiss Federation introduced a law that laid the foundation for the digitization of Swiss land registry businesses. For the first time, (1) a common data model with Swiss-wide unique identifiers for parcels, called *EGRID* (the EGRID identifier is an electronic parcel ID), and rights, called *EREID* (electronic rights ID); and (2) a Land Register data access interface called *GBDBS* [Meldewesen 2014][1] to access this data were defined and declared mandatory to use. This API and data model have to be offered by all Swiss land registries.

In the eight context dimensions defined by Philippe Kruchten [Kruchten 2013], the Terravis platform can be characterized as follows:

1. *System size:* From a business perspective, Terravis offers three services to institutional clients and cantonal offices: (1) *Query,* allowing unified access to Swiss Land Register data (subject to access permissions and auditing), (2) *Process Automation,* fully digitizing end-to-end processes between different partners, and (3) *Nominee,* allowing banks to outsource mortgage administration. Technically, Terravis consists of approximately one hundred (micro-) services performing different tasks such as document generation or an implementation of a business rule. Terravis integrates hundreds of partner systems and is expected to connect to approximately one thousand systems when all partners will be participating.

---

1. In German: *Grundbuchdatenbezugsschnittstelle.*

2. *System criticality:* Terravis is deemed critical for the financial infrastructure in Switzerland.

3. *System age:* The system was first released in 2009 and has been under continuous development since then.

4. *Team distribution:* The team is based in a single office in Zurich, Switzerland.

5. *Rate of change:* Terravis is still adding more and more processes to its Process Automation and Nominee components and better data integration in the Query component. The sprint length is one month. A recent analysis of changes in the processes modeled in the Business Process Execution Language (BPEL) showed that the processes constantly evolve [Lübke 2015].

6. *Preexistence of a stable architecture:* Terravis is a first-of-its-kind application. Although it had to conform to some prior in-house architectural constraints (for instance, use of proprietary, internal frameworks from its parent company SIX Group), generally it was started as a greenfield project.

7. *Governance:* Terravis was established as a public-private partnership project at the SIX Group. It has governance bodies that represent the Swiss Federation, cantons as representatives of the land registries, banks, and notaries. Thus, the governance reflects all stakeholders in the system and is equally complex as the technical environment.

8. *Business model:* Terravis is marketed as a fee-based software-as-a-service offering, allowing institutional and administrative partners to use the platform.

While the initial scope of the project was to build only the Query component that allows important participants in land registry business processes to access relevant federated master data, it was quickly decided that more value can be offered by digitizing entire business processes. This led to the definition of Terravis-owned APIs that allow banks, notaries, and so on, to interface with Terravis, while the Land Register API is owned by the Swiss Federation. This diversity also becomes evident in different naming conventions and different release cycles in the APIs. Terravis must not store nor cache Land Register data in its Query component to honor the federated, cantonal ownership of this master data.

Technical Challenges

Many of Terravis's technical challenges originate from its complex business environment [Berli 2014]. Different partners using different software systems connect via APIs to Terravis. This leads to technical integration problems—intensified by the different life cycles of all the partner systems. Synchronized deployments are impossible; implementation and update frequencies are measured in months and years and not in weeks. Thus, appropriate API evolution was one challenge.

The technical integration also was made more complex by a rather generic Land Register API that references many details of the common Land Register data model and thus requires clients to have intimate knowledge of this data model. Differences between one-to-many and one-to-one relationships became apparent in workshops. Thus, Terravis decided to offer APIs based on a new, easier-to-use data model to gain acceptance.

While integration was planned to be a partner-to-partner or machine-to-machine integration only, it became clear quickly that not all partners would be able to change their systems to implement the Terravis APIs. For others, the update frequency would not be as high as that of Terravis. Thus, Terravis decided to also offer a Web-based user interface called *Portal*. Terravis allows every partner to work with business process instances in the portal or via their integrated systems in parallel. This way, partners that implement only limited functionality of an older API can use newer functionality via the portal if required.

Trust is an essential success factor for Terravis: by demonstrating that the project was able to (1) deliver a platform that was difficult to build, (2) maintain a high pace of releases, and (3) deliver its services with high reliability and security, Terravis became a respected mediator between the banks, notaries, land registries, and other involved parties.

To establish trust with the cantons as owners of the land registries, Terravis was obliged not to become a loophole for a central Swiss-wide land registry. Although the platform is supposed to provide transparent access to data regardless of the master Land Register, this obligation implied that Terravis must neither cache nor store Land Register data. This constraint causes issues with response times for data queries, which potentially must contact all Swiss land registries to deliver a result.

Many important requirements are concerned with long-term maintainability (for instance, by accommodating different life cycles, as discussed previously) and security. Security includes using transport-level security between Terravis and all partners, full auditability of transactions and business process steps being performed, and non-reputability of instructions via the platform. Terravis was the first platform to offer centralized signing servers that fulfilled all requirements for legally binding electronic signatures in Switzerland; this allows parties to sign documents and thus conduct their processes fully digitally.

At the time of writing, the platform handles more than 500,000 end-to-end land registry business processes annually and processes even more parcel queries.

Role and Status of API

Because Terravis is heavily focused on business and technical integration of its partners to enable digitized business processes, APIs are highly important artifacts. Due to their connector role (motivated in Chapter 1, "Application Programming Interface (API) Fundamentals"), APIs are the enablers of integration, and better API designs lead to better Terravis services.

While the APIs for the Query component are comparatively stable, the APIs for the Process Automation component change more frequently. More and more supported business processes and business process variants are added to it over time.

Whenever a major change to a business process is made or a new one is implemented as a digitized process, the API definition is one of the two most important parts of the document along with the business process documentation. Thus, expressiveness of API contracts and clear meaning and semantics of API operations are key qualities of the Terravis APIs and key success factors for the entire product.

Pattern Usage and Implementation

Terravis applied many patterns from this book. In this section, we first describe the patterns applied to all components. We then provide a component walkthrough.

Patterns Applied to All Components

Terravis distinguishes between COMMUNITY API and SOLUTION-INTERNAL API, as shown in Figure 10.1. Because only institutional partners are legally allowed to use Terravis services, no PUBLIC API is offered. Parties such as banks and notaries have to register, demonstrate that they are legally entitled to use the service, and sign a contract. Having completed this process, they can then use the available COMMUNITY APIs. In addition, Terravis uses SOLUTION-INTERNAL APIs because many large components are broken down into smaller microservices, which communicate internally. These decisions are shielded from the partners; they are treated as implementation details by Terravis and are subject to change at the team's discretion. Thus, to prevent unwanted coupling, the SOLUTION-INTERNAL APIs are neither published nor made available to partners.

Services are function-specific (for example, document generation and mortgage creation process) but usually do not offer any user interface directly. Especially because Terravis aims to be a fully automated process integration platform, user interfaces are not necessary for all partners. For instance, when land registries work with Terravis, they use the API integration of their software suppliers. There is another reason to separate the user interface part (Terravis Portal) from the backend

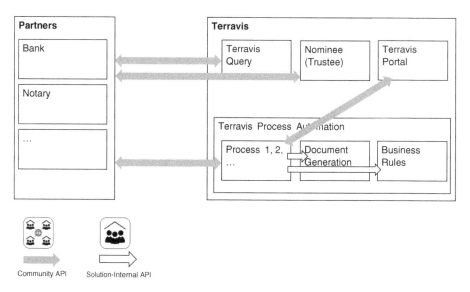

Figure 10.1 *High-level overview of APIs in Terravis*

and process logic (Terravis Process Automation): as illustrated in Figure 10.1, the Terravis Portal uses only COMMUNITY APIs to connect to backend services. The Terravis Portal serves as a substitute for a partner system, which supports all functions of the platform. Terravis Portal enables human users to use the system but cannot gain the efficiency of a direct system integration. As discussed previously, partners that are unable to quickly integrate had to be accommodated. This design yielded an important additional function: it serves as a reference implementation of all Terravis APIs and therefore helps in validating the API design during development. From the point of view of the backend services, the Portal is just another partner system.

All APIs are documented in an API DESCRIPTION, which consists of a Web Services Description Language (WSDL) with corresponding XML Schemas and—where required—a document with samples and graphical models for the data types. However, documentation within the WSDL and XML Schemas is preferred so that there is only a single source for all API-related information. In addition to the API DESCRIPTION, Terravis defines SERVICE LEVEL AGREEMENTS as part of the partner contract that is mandatory for partners to sign to get access to the COMMUNITY APIs. Such SERVICE LEVEL AGREEMENTS define, for instance, availability, security, and confidentiality guarantees. One part of the interface contract is that all parties have to validate the received and sent SOAP messages against the respective XML Schemas. Correct interpretation of data is crucial because legally binding activities are triggered based on it. Full XML validation ensures that no syntactic interoperability problems arise. It also reduces the risk of semantic misinterpretations between systems. Validation can be easily enabled in commonly used frameworks such as Spring and is one layer of quality assurance and interoperability enforcement in Terravis.

Terravis does not use the API Key pattern for transferring authentication information in a request message. Instead, it fully relies on Two-Way-SSL to authenticate API requests via the supplied client certificate.

As outlined earlier, allowing many partner systems to co-evolve with Terravis is a critical success factor. Thus, many evolution patterns are used in Terravis: Terravis makes a Two-In-Production guarantee for every API that it offers. However, the third API version is not immediately phased out. Instead, a modified version of the Limited Lifetime Guarantee pattern is used: from the time a third API version is released, the oldest one is scheduled for decommission within a year. This approach strikes a balance between Terravis's needs to reduce maintenance effort for old API versions while still allowing partners with rare deployments the opportunity to keep pace with API changes.

Terravis uses a customized variant of the Semantic Versioning scheme n.m.o for assigning version numbers to API releases. The semantic of the middle number, that is, the minor version, is relaxed to mean that two API versions with the same major versions but different minor versions are semantically compatible in a business sense and messages of both API versions can be transformed into each other without loss. This relaxed definition allows for structural refactoring—if and only if semantics remain completely unchanged. Fix versions (indicated by the third number) are also used to add new minor functionality if it does not break compatibility.

Terravis uses the Version Identifier pattern to convey version information both in the XML namespace and as an element in the header of a message. The namespace contains only the major and minor versions and thus guarantees compatibility for fix versions. Initially, it was deemed appropriate to also transmit the full version as information that must not be used in business logic but can be used for diagnostic information. Thus, the full version was stored in the separate header element. However, inevitably, according to Hyrum's law [Zdun 2020], partners eventually relied on this version number as on any other part of the API and implemented business logic based on the transmitted information.

Across all APIs and components, the Error Report pattern is used. Terravis utilizes a common data structure in all APIs to signal errors in a way that it is machine readable (error codes such as `MORTGAGE_NOT_FOUND`). This data structure contains context information (error details, for example, the mortgage that was not found), and a default English error description in case the error should be presented directly to a user or operator, for example, "Mortgage CH12345678 not found."

Query Component

The first developed component, which also is a prerequisite for the Process Automation component added later, is the Query component, illustrated in Figure 10.2.

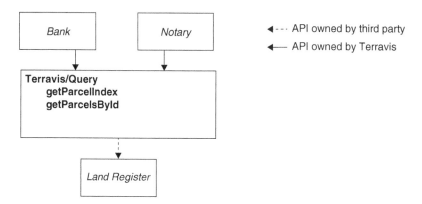

Figure 10.2 *Overview of Terravis Query with corresponding APIs*

The Query API has two main operations: getParcelIndex and get-ParcelsById, which can, for example, be called by banks and notaries. The request messages of these two RETRIEVAL OPERATIONS provide a CONTEXT REPRESENTATION as part of the payload, which contains a message ID. During problem analysis, this ID serves as a "Correlation Identifier" [Hohpe 2003] between incoming requests (from Terravis partners) and outgoing calls to the land registry. getParcelIndex is used to search for parcel IDs by a limited number of query criteria such as community, canton-specific legacy parcel number, or an electronic rights ID (EREID). It returns a list of parcel IDs (EGRIDs) that can be used to fetch the master data via getParcelsById.

Both operations function as a facade because they do not contain business logic but, following the "Message Router" pattern [Hohpe 2003], serve as a technical routing component dispatching incoming requests to land registry systems. Because Terravis is not allowed to cache Land Register data, it has a limited set of mappings (for instance, which land registry serves which community or which EGRIDs or EREIDs are known to be hosted by a certain land registry) to pinpoint a land registry system. However, if no entry is found in these mappings, a Swiss-wide search dispatching the request to every land registry system must be performed. The main benefit of Query is the central routing: partners are not required to legally and technically clarify and set up access to Land Register data, which is a daunting task with more than one hundred different systems. Instead, Terravis serves as an access point from which requests are dispatched.

The `getParcelsById` operation also utilizes the MASTER DATA HOLDER and WISH LIST patterns: it allows read-only access to master data stored in the land registries. An enumeration defines three possible result data sizes that can be selected according to the current needs of the partner and on the basis of its permissions. For example, not all partners are allowed to access the historical data of a land registry. Only up to ten parcels may be queried at once; therefore, no additional safeguards such as PAGINATION against excessive usage are implemented. As a facade, this operation can enforce a global RATE LIMIT on Swiss-wide requests to manage the load on the Terravis system. Such requests are handled in their own queue, which is capped by the number of simultaneous active requests, while searches that could be narrowed in advance to one land registry are handled without a RATE LIMIT.

Providing access to Land Register data is a commercial service. A PRICING PLAN is in place. To create monthly invoices according to this plan, API requests by partners are logged in a dedicated fee table in the database. Terravis charges its own service fee as well as the land registration fees, which are then forwarded to the corresponding land registry.

Query is a read-only service. All operations changing Land Register data are clearly separated into the Process Automation component, which is described in the following section. Terravis thereby follows command and query responsibility separation (CQRS) as initially described in *Object-Oriented Software Construction* [Meyer 1997].

Process Automation Component

Terravis's Process Automation component offers over 20 long-running business processes involving multiple parties/partners, eventually changing Land Register data. Its most sophisticated and value-driven APIs are PROCESSING RESOURCES serving as technical equivalents of business processes that encapsulate end-to-end logic of processes related to land registries. Figure 10.3 shows a simplified architecture. Partners such as those shown in the figure access the system via SOAP and Two-Way SSL. The requests are authenticated and authorized in a reverse proxy; additional infrastructure services route and transform messages. Terravis also sends outgoing requests via similar infrastructure components such as an enterprise service bus (ESB), which encapsulate the routing to partner endpoints and the transformation to the partner's API version (indicated by the bidirectional arrows in Figure 10.3); they offer this logic to all business processes. Every business process is modeled in the Business Process Execution Language (BPEL) and deployed as a single process artifact.

All request messages of all APIs concerning process automation contain a special header implementing the CONTEXT REPRESENTATION pattern. This header contains a unique business process ID (an instance of the ID ELEMENT pattern) generated by Terravis, a message ID generated by the client, the Terravis partner ID, the associated user (sent for auditing purposes), and the full version of the API implemented by the client (support purposes).

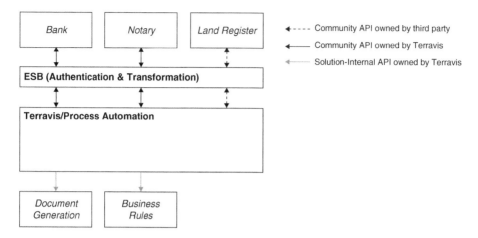

Figure 10.3 *Overview of Terravis Process Automation with selected partners and internal services. Each arrowhead indicates an API provider, for example Banks are both API clients and providers of callback operations*

Business processes are started by using a STATE CREATION OPERATION. The names of these operations begin with "start"—for example, `startNewMortgage` for a business process that creates a new mortgage. Figure 10.4 shows selected parts, such as a bank as an example of a partner. Names of operations that trigger a business activity implementing the STATE TRANSITION OPERATION pattern in its BUSINESS ACTIVITY PROCESSOR variant start with "request." Such operations always have a callback operation: if, for example, Terravis requests an action from a bank, the bank will send the result via a callback to Terravis (or vice versa). Names of callback operations start with "confirm" or "reject" depending on the outcome of the business activity. Operation names starting with "do" signal a request for an activity that is not supervised by Terravis. For example, sending documents is initiated by such operations for which Terravis cannot verify whether or not they have been performed. Similarly, there are "notify" operations (not shown in the figure), which will signal partial results of the business process. Both do and notify operations will likely also be implemented as STATE TRANSITION OPERATIONS but require no response to the original client. As such, the final implementation design is left to the API provider. Finally, the process end is signaled by an "end" operation, which is sent to all participating partners to close their respective business cases and signal success or failure in reaching the business process goal. Thus, Terravis realizes its business process implementations as PROCESSING RESOURCES in the BPM services variant.

By definition, business process services are stateful, and the design goal was to move all state to the processes. However, there are shared stateless services that aid the processes. For example, certain electronic documents are generated in many

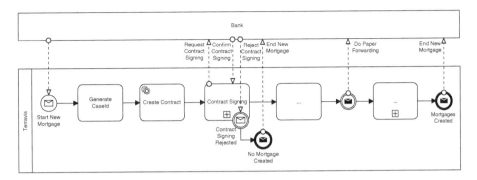

Figure 10.4 *Skeleton of a business process with a partner bank*

processes that must be digitally signed later. Such operations are offered as Computation Functions via Solution-Internal APIs.

Process Metadata Elements, such as the current process state or pending payments, are exposed via an API that utilizes the Pagination pattern for chunking
responses to reasonable sizes. Because one requirement was to display the number
of total hits, proprietary SQL extensions of Microsoft SQL Server are used to fetch
both the requested page and the total number of results in a single query. This design
speeds up the response to these APIs significantly.

The Terravis Portal that provides Web-based access to the functionality of the
Process Automation component has additional Solution-Internal APIs. This
includes the management of pending tasks via an API that also uses Pagination.

Nominee Component

The newest component of Terravis is its Nominee service. Nominee is part of the
trustee offering to banks for handling all register-based mortgages (as opposed to
paper mortgages). This component requires a bookkeeping service, which implements the Operational Data Holder pattern, the State Creation Operation
pattern to add register mortgages to the system, the State Transition Operation
pattern to change information about a register mortgage, and other State Transition Operations for marking register mortgages for approval and so on.

Whenever queries that can result in an unlimited number of response records
are offered via an API, the Pagination pattern is applied in this component as well.
Because mortgages might be moved in large batches between different owners, a variant of such a transfer operation is offered as a version implementing the Request
Bundle pattern. This pattern allows moving hundreds of thousands of mortgages
between different owners in a single API operation call.

Pattern Implementation Technologies

The Terravis APIs are based on WS-* technologies: interfaces are designed using WSDL and XML Schema. While HTTP can be used for service calls between containers on the same host, HTTPS is used for all cross-machine communication. API calls are additionally secured with Two-Way SSL (client certificates). For example, connections from partners to the incoming reverse proxy are secured with client machine certificates. The same holds for the connections from the reverse proxy to the respective service.

There is a wide range of possible technology choices for implementing SOAP clients and providers. Initially, JAX-WS was used for implementing services offering business logic. Later, Terravis migrated to Spring-WS.

To efficiently extract and handle information from the message, the CONTEXT REPRESENTATION in particular, interceptors were defined that populate the logging and request context so that authorization and logging logic is simplified and thus less error prone. These interceptors are used in all services implemented in Java.

Infrastructure components, especially the transformation components in the enterprise service bus, are implemented using more general technologies such as XML DOM [W3C 1998], XSLT [W3C 2007], or XQuery [W3C 2017]. These XML-specific languages allow higher developer efficiency when implementing infrastructure components.

Retrospective and Outlook

Terravis has been successful in part because of its business process and corresponding API design. Managing both environmental and technical complexity is a challenging task that can be made easier if interfaces are defined in an accessible manner and with clear semantics. API design is heavily influenced by both business requirements and technical constraints, and coordinating API design with such a high number of partners can be daunting. However, this task gets easier over time as all parties—both technical and business stakeholders—get to better know each other and the underlying design principles.

In the beginning, the Terravis APIs were larger and partitioned by the partner type. For example, the Process Automation component offered one large API for banks and another one for notaries, but each API included all operations required for every business process. Thus, an API did span across different technical components but, more important, across different domains: these coarse-grained, stakeholder-group-oriented API designs led to an undesired coupling that was resolved by using the interface segregation principle [Martin 2002]. Newly defined APIs are partitioned on the basis of the partner role and the business process, leading to more but smaller APIs that are easier to discuss and communicate. Smaller and more task-focused APIs are also easier to evolve: if a change is made, only clients using that particular API are impacted. This eliminates the effort for unaffected clients; it also eases change impact analysis by affected parties because the change scope is narrower and more clearly defined.

The initial idea to convey the full version information, including the fix version, in a separate field failed in practice. While it was repeatedly stressed that no logic must depend on this field, partners started to do exactly this.

The data structures implementing the ERROR REPORT pattern were extended to allow full support for machine-readable errors and the capability to present errors in multiple languages—a feature that fits well with Switzerland's four official languages. The required change from unstructured errors to structured error messages had to be introduced incrementally in different APIs. It is now done by default for any new API or API version. The takeaway is that structured data for signaling errors enhances the clarity of the communication. It also helps to carefully design error conditions and other important information for the clients.

The PAGINATION pattern has been used more extensively over time. Initially, some operations were designed without thinking about minimizing payload and required processing time and resources. Problems at runtime were analyzed, identified, and mitigated, for instance, by using this pattern. Using the full potential of the underlying database server to not require a second count query (instead of an object-relational mapper such as Java Persistence API or Hibernate) resulted in a major performance improvement.

The project found a substantial difference between generically designed APIs and task-specific APIs: the Land Register API is designed very generically. Thus, only two versions were released in over 10 years; the API is syntactically very stable. For requesting updates to Land Register data, a message with generic, command-like data structures is created and sent. This reduces the number of exposed operations to one but moves complexity into the message payload. Due to the generic structure, the API is difficult to learn, understand, implement, and test. In contrast, Terravis-owned schemas are designed very specifically in the context of supported business processes in a contract-first design, driven by stakeholder demand. These APIs are much easier to understand and implement. However, they expose many operations and change more frequently. In hindsight, the task-specific, domain-driven APIs turned out to be more suitable.

Overall, Terravis has been a successful platform, in part because its API design allows full integration among many different stakeholders. Use of the patterns presented in this book, as well as of other patterns such as "Enterprise Integration Patterns," helped to produce well-designed APIs. While the business setting is uncommon and complex due to the types and numbers of involved systems and organizations, the integration of many different systems is a common challenge. Hence, the lessons learned on this project can benefit others.

Offering and Ordering Processes in Building Construction

This section presents patterns used as part of an internal system at the concrete column manufacturer SACAC who built an internal microservice landscape to improve its offering and ordering processes.

Business Context and Domain

SACAC is a Swiss company producing concrete columns for construction companies. Each column is tailored specifically for a particular construction site. The offering process for such concrete columns is much more complex than one would expect. Depending on the required column strength and size, different materials, such as steel, and/or different variations of the concrete column ends are required to ensure the stability of a newly constructed building. Furthermore, SACAC offers to adjust the shape of the concrete column to suit the architect's ideas of an aesthetically appealing building. This vast product flexibility requires many calculations and designs and must adhere to many business rules. The market is competitive; construction companies might request offers for the same concrete columns for the same building from competing producers on behalf of the property owner.

To support the offering process, different existing software systems, for example, the enterprise resource planning (ERP) and computer-aided design (CAD) systems, have to work together. New functionality, for example, a configuration system for creating the offers, has been developed in a new system. With respect to the project dimensions defined by Philippe Kruchten [Kruchten 2013], the SACAC offer and order system can be described as follows:

1. *System size:* The system comprises 15 services designed as vertical microservices running on one virtual machine. Each service is a Ruby application implemented with Ruby on Rails [Ruby on Rails 2022] or Sinatra [Sinatra 2022], which includes the user interface, business logic, and access to a message bus and a MongoDB database.

2. *System criticality:* The system is highly critical for the company because certain core processes are executable only via the new system.

3. *System age:* The system has been released 10 years ago and has been under continuous development since then.

4. *Team distribution:* The development started in Switzerland, but as the project progressed, more and more work was done by a remote team located in Germany.

5. *Rate of change:* The system is still being maintained and developed. In the beginning, approximately 20 versions per year were released. This number later went down to six releases per year. The development team also changed over time: there were up to three developers plus one tester and one IT staff member. In total, twelve people were involved.

6. *Preexistence of a stable architecture:* The company had no governing IT architecture, so this was a greenfield project.

7. *Governance*: The project team itself was required to define all architectural constraints and management rules, but they had direct contact with the CEO.

8. *Business model:* The initial focus of this project was process improvement aimed at reducing the error rate, establishing more process awareness, removing copy-and-paste redundancies, and automating processes.

The system was instrumental in achieving a 100 percent increase in sales volume in two years and offering lower prices by having more accurate cost estimates and thus being able to offer the concrete columns with smaller risk margins. After that success, the project morphed into a business process improvement initiative to further decrease overall process cost and process cycle time.

Technical Challenges

The key requirement for SACAC is the correctness of all calculations and thus the final offer. Having to change technical decisions to more expensive options would lead to increased costs and fewer profits or to customers not placing an order.

The dynamic environment of the project was a challenge. Because for the first-time core processes have been improved and digitized, many changes and stakeholders were to be managed, and new ideas came up over time. Extracting correct requirements and understanding the current business processes were required prior to optimizing them and developing corresponding software support. This also included a transition from a "buy software" to "develop custom software for a specific need" mentality as well as a shift to thinking of "an integrated application landscape" instead of "single software systems."

The offer process spans multiple collaborating roles such as customer, engineer, drawer, planner, and so on. The customer requests an offer by specifying constraints that have a great influence on the concrete column and thus the pricing. This data must be used in CAD and structural analysis systems for designing and evaluating the solution. Prior to this project, the business process was human-driven and supported by standalone software. This landscape was transitioned into an integrated software landscape using HTTP and WebDAV APIs as well as asynchronous messaging following a microservice-oriented architecture.

The main architectural choices include browser-based integration, RESTful HTTP APIs, and decoupling by using hypermedia and JSON home documents [Nottingham 2022]. All microservices are governed by a set of common naming conventions and architectural constraints, such as when to use synchronous or asynchronous messaging technologies [Hohpe 2003].

Role and Status of API

The solution consists of different microservices organized by domains, for example, offer management, order management, difference calculation, and production planning.

The custom-developed part of the SACAC software is organized as microservices providing and consuming RESTful HTTP APIs realized with HTTPS and JSON as the message exchange format, as shown in Figure 10.5. Commercial-off-the-shelf software is integrated using their respective interfaces, mainly based on file transfers.

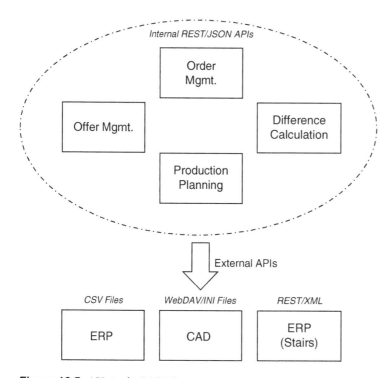

Figure 10.5 *APIs in the SACAC ecosystem*

The CAD system, which is a standalone application, was required for designing the concrete columns. Being a standalone system with no server components, integration was challenging: the chosen solution was to offer configuration files for this application via a virtual WebDAV [Dusseault 2007] share. WebDAV is usually used as a file-sharing network protocol for saving and reading files on a remote server. The files in this WebDAV implementation can be read and written like normal files, but they also trigger business logic. For example, an upload of a valid concrete column CAD file to the WebDAV share triggers further processing of an order process, such as moving it to the next action.

In addition to providing file-based interfaces, the CAD integration had to map the data model of the application. This data model is very specific to concrete columns, while the CAD data model is a generic one designed for any type of CAD work. Closing this semantic gap required discussions with many stakeholders before a correct export and import of CAD data could be achieved. Another external system was an ERP system, which lacked easy-to-consume APIs for external integration. Thus, it was decided to use CSV files published via WebDAV to transfer data. The third external system was integrated later. It was a different ERP system that is used for planning concrete stairs (in response to a product scope increase) that offered suitable Web APIs using XML payload.

APIs offered by the system itself are only meant to be used by other microservices and therefore are Solution-Internal APIs both for Frontend Integration and for Backend Integration. One development team is responsible for all microservices, which allows for easy negotiation of API changes. In general, APIs are meant to be stable. APIs might be moved from one microservice to another; however, the technical contract part of the API Description must remain compatible.

Location transparency is achieved by serving a central home document that contains endpoints for all APIs. Because this project uses REST principles for integration, endpoints of resources are published in this central document. If APIs are rearranged or new versions in a Two in Production scenario are deployed, these are published in the central home document, which allows other microservices to still work without redeployment.

The use of APIs is restricted, as shown in Figure 10.6. Operations that change data must be called only by the same microservice. Calls across microservices must use read-only APIs exclusively. But how is data changed, then? Integration of different microservices is achieved by *transclusion*. Transclusion means including HTML fragments, served by a certain microservice, in another page, possibly served by another microservice. These transcluded pages thus might have content originating from the other microservice, which is permitted to change data concerning orders.

In such a system, much central information is stored, which contains shared information about an order that is used everywhere. Instead of replicating this data

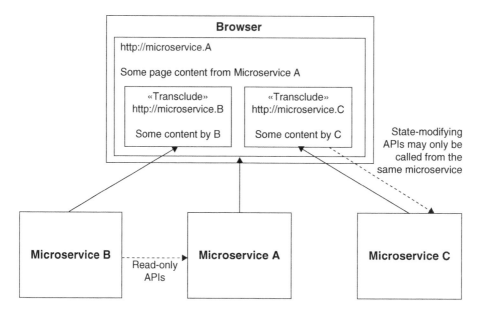

Figure 10.6 *HTML transclusion and API restrictions*

into read models residing in the database of each microservice, a read-only view in a shared database was created. More complex solutions would not have provided sufficient benefit given the team structure and project size. Microservices still have a dedicated database for data, which they exclusively own.

Pattern Usage and Implementation

Many different patterns are used in this solution. First, the main API usage is a FRONTEND INTEGRATION that allows HTML pages and transcluded page fragments to invoke business logic on their originating microservices. These APIs allow for read and write operations, with the latter being STATE CREATION OPERATIONS (write) and STATE TRANSITION OPERATIONS (read and write). The write operations are constrained to pages or parts of pages delivered by the same microservice. Furthermore, BACKEND INTEGRATION is used with read-only APIs between different microservices. Examples of operations in these APIs are RETRIEVAL OPERATIONS for fetching various domain objects as well as complex COMPUTATION FUNCTIONS, for example, for calculating metrics for structural engineering.

The API as a whole was not versioned. Sometimes different versions were required to support old and new types of business processes. In these cases, the necessary old APIs were made available via the Two in Production pattern, and their URLs were distinguished by a Version Identifier.

To improve the user experience, many results were displayed in increments. Thus, the data Retrieval Operations support the Pagination pattern. This is commonly done when customer, offer, and appointment domain object representations are returned. Another pattern used to reduce message payload sizes is Conditional Request. Its application avoids returning data that has not changed since the last request for it.

Because a business process, as well as individual interactions with the system, might consist of multiple steps and thus multiple calls to the system, a Context Representation is passed with all API calls and HTML page requests: this includes common elements like security information. A common requirement also addressed in the Context Representation is the impersonation of a user by an administrative or support account. The business context is also included, which might be a particular process step, an order, or any other business object. These context elements are identified by their respective universally unique identifiers (UUIDs), which is in line with the Id Element pattern, and passed on in the context. The request context might include a "from" and a "to" jump point allowing users to easily navigate the system. Nondefault URLs for the user to follow or to return to can be specified. This is implemented by using Link Elements. Due to using REST and relying on hypermedia for business process navigation as well as selecting correct API versions, Link Elements are an important type of information passed in messages. As explained previously, these are amended by a central JSON home document that, in our pattern terms, serves as a Link Lookup Resource bringing location transparency for API endpoints.

Requests might fail for various reasons, such as technical outages, insufficient permissions, or simple errors in the business logic. At first, only simple HTTP error codes were returned. Over time, important user-facing error messages were improved by returning an Error Report providing more information about the problem.

The system has been implemented in Ruby using Ruby on Rails. This framework allows the easy implementation of some patterns. For example, Conditional Requests are supported by the framework itself. Ruby on Rails also supports HTTP, JSON, and REST-styled APIs well. For integrating external systems via WebDAV, a custom library, RailsDAV, has been developed and open-sourced.

For better and easier management of the request context and transcluded content, all microservices are accessible under one TCP/IP domain that is served by a reverse proxy. The reverse proxy uses the URL to route requests to the correct microservices.

This way, all assets and scripts are served from the same domain, and problems with security measures on the browser side (for example, related to same-origin policies) can be avoided.

Retrospective and Outlook

In summary, the project has been a success and the software was the main building block for realizing many business benefits at SACAC and led to competitive advantages. API-based integration within the solution as well as to external systems was crucial for realizing end-to-end business process support. In hindsight, some more APIs to export data for statistics and business intelligence purposes would have been useful. Overall, the solution integrates data and systems well; no focus was placed on also exporting data to other systems and integrating with external use cases because this need only became apparent later on.

One of the lessons learned is that well-accepted user interfaces have to be supported by well-aligned APIs driven by the user requirements and thus the business (and not the technology). In this book, the responsibility patterns serve as a bridge.

While microservices have been used, the question remains whether a well-structured monolith would have been the more efficient development model. However, this is hard to assess after the fact; enforcing structure and boundaries is promoted by microservices, and these boundaries provide an excellent tool for software architects.

This project was started before many of the technologies were available in mainstream libraries. For example, transclusion can be achieved by standard means today. If the project started from scratch today, many functionalities would not have to be implemented in custom code but could be reused from libraries. To improve reliability as well as user experience, more actions would likely be processed in an asynchronous fashion.

This project could draw on an experienced project team and stay focused on business value and benefits, making it ultimately successful. It extended the responsibilities of developers to also serve as business consultants and business process engineers—working hand in hand with business owners to realize a digital transformation in a real-world domain that is more software-intensive than one would think.

Summary

This chapter presented two large examples of real-world API designs that (knowingly or unknowingly) applied patterns from this book. Both systems run in production and evolved over time.

The first pattern story featured a large-scale business process integration hub and portal for the Swiss mortgage business. We saw that many quality patterns, including WISH LIST and CONTEXT REPRESENTATION, were applied. The evolution patterns VERSION IDENTIFIER and TWO IN PRODUCTION also played an important role in this scenario that involves many parties, businesses, and government organizations. Using its COMMUNITY APIs must be paid for under a PRICING PLAN.

The second pattern story involved building architects in addition to software architects and API designers. It described a Web-based offer and order management system to custom design concrete columns for building construction sites. API patterns from this book, including many of those found in the first story (for example, ERROR REPORT) as well as endpoint role patterns such as LINK LOOKUP RESOURCE, helped craft a flexible and resource-efficient software design.

Note that even if patterns are chosen and applied well, the API implementations can still harm qualities such as extensibility, performance, consistency, and availability. Such quality-related forces and patterns addressing them have numerous many-to-many relationships among each other and with other critical success factors. Patterns always have to be adopted *and* adapted to the project context; good software engineering practices for development and testing have to be applied along the way.

We are almost done now. A summary and outlook follow to conclude the book.

Chapter 11

Conclusion

Let us recapitulate the book content and reflect on the patterns for API design and evolution as we presented them across its three parts. This chapter also points to related research and contains our—somewhat speculative and risky—take on the future of APIs and related architectural knowledge.

Distributed systems are the norm today. In such systems, a number of services work together and communicate through remote APIs. When being assembled into distributed applications, APIs and their implementations must satisfy rather diverse integration requirements—different APIs may use different communication protocols and message exchange formats, their implementation components may reside in different security zones and/or run in different locations, and so on. Different options are available to fine-tune the message and endpoint design according to desired qualities and existing constraints. For instance, APIs often must be responsive, scalable and reliable but also readily developer-friendly and evolvable. Many of them automate business processes and activities involving customers, products, and business partners; such business activities and their supporting software frequently change in response to changes in their functional requirements and quality goals.

The purpose of the pattern language presented in this book is to help integration architects, API developers, and other roles involved with API design and evolution make more informed, adequate, and sound decisions when crafting APIs for a particular client community with its goals and domain contexts. Our patterns provide proven design options for these decisions.

Short Retrospective

We presented 44 patterns for API design and evolution, including rather common ones such as PAGINATION (Chapter 7) and API DESCRIPTION (Chapter 9) but also less obvious ones such as CONTEXT REPRESENTATION (Chapter 6) and TWO IN PRODUCTION (Chapter 8). Chapter 4 provided a language overview and patterns to scope APIs and structure messages, including FRONTEND INTEGRATION and PARAMETER TREE.

We assume that the APIs that apply these patterns exchange plain text messages rather than remote objects. They may do so over synchronous communication channels or asynchronous, queue-based ones. Selected patterns are implemented in the Lakeside Mutual sample application introduced in Chapter 2 and in the two real-world cases featured in Chapter 10. While many motivating examples and known uses of the patterns came from microservice-oriented systems, all software systems that contain remote APIs may benefit from applying them.

Did we miss some patterns? Certainly. For instance, reactive, long-running, event-driven API designs were only touched upon—these topics could fill an entire book. It would also be interesting to mine patterns on advanced composite structures that carry certain domain-specific semantics such as resource reservations, overview-details presentations, or case management activities. One could think of turning Martin Fowler's *Analysis Patterns* [Fowler 1996] into pre-canned API designs. Books on data modeling [Hay 1996] could provide input to such effort, and common data definition initiatives such as microformats [Microformats 2022] and Schema.org[1] would have their role to play too. Business responsibility-driven design could take a prominent place in such "domain API" undertaking.

On the API realization level, we could distinguish aggregated, mediating "guard resources" calling other APIs from self-contained "ground resources" that do not depend on other APIs provided elsewhere. We could also continue to work on patterns about API orchestration flows or conversations [Pautasso 2016]. Another time—maybe. While we hinted at API implementation options, we did not cover topics such as system transactions versus business-level compensation (ACID guarantees versus various forms of BASE properties) much; "Sagas" [Richardson 2018] or "Try-Confirm/Cancel" steps [Pardon 2011] could possibly support business-level compensation.

We only touched upon protocol specifics in examples and discussion sections; the recipes in the *RESTful Web Services Cookbook* [Allamaraju 2010] and many other books provide detailed advice regarding RESTful HTTP. The preface provided information about related pattern languages and other good reads.

---

1. https://schema.org.

We also did not put much emphasis on operating API implementations; just like any application deployment, API implementations have to be managed at runtime. There are many deployment and hosting options for API implementations and service-oriented systems, including serverless functions and other cloud computing offerings. API endpoints and, possibly, API gateways, have to be configured, secured, accounted for, and monitored (for instance, with regard to faults and performance). These activities fall under *API management*, a term that summarizes a suite of practices and tools complementary to API design and evolution.[2]

API Research: Refactoring to Patterns, MDSL, and More

"API first" design on a greenfield is one thing, but what if production APIs encounter quality problems? A survey conducted by two of us showed that quality deficits and changes in functional requirements might trigger API changes just as existing and new requirements do [Stocker 2021a].

One approach to improving the quality aspects of a software system and preparing for functional changes is *refactoring*. Refactoring is the practice of improving a software system without changing its external, observable behavior. A code refactoring cleans up a piece of code, for instance, renaming classes and methods to increase their understandability or breaking up a long piece of code into several parts for better maintainability.

API refactoring extends the notion of code refactoring (and stretches the meaning of the term somewhat):

An API refactoring evolves the remote interface of a system without changing its feature set and its semantics to improve at least one quality attribute.

An "Interface Refactoring Catalog" [Stocker 2021b] is emerging at the time of writing. The purpose of a refactoring can (but does not have to) be the alignment of the software with a design pattern [Kerievsky 2004]; not surprisingly, the Interface Refactoring Catalog references and suggests many of the patterns from this book. Examples of refactorings to API patterns in the catalog are "Add Wish List," "Introduce Pagination," and "Externalize Context."

Many of the refactorings from the catalog are supported in the *Microservice Domain Specific Language (MDSL) Tools*. This is possible because, as shown in Appendix C, MDSL starts from our API domain model (introduced in Chapter 1) and features all of our patterns (from Chapters 4 to 9) one way or another, often as

---

2. It seems that we just had the second round of buzzword bingo in this book. Do you remember the first one?

decorators of specification elements such as API endpoints, operations, and message representation elements.

Four of us worked on patterns on the relation of APIs to domain-driven design (DDD); two examples are "Domain Model Facade as API" and "Aggregate Roots as API Endpoints" [Singjai 2021a; Singjai 2021b; Singjai 2021c]. To support this transition, research on approaches for modeling APIs in relation to domain models and detecting the API-to-DDD mapping patterns in models is ongoing. API analytics research is another promising direction, yielding new patterns such as "Mutable Collection Resource" [Serbout 2021].

The Future of APIs

It is well known that it is hard to predict the future. At the time of writing, it is difficult to imagine that HTTP will go away. HTTP/2, a major revision of the original protocol, has been under standardization since 2015, and HTTP/3, the next proposed successor, reached the status of a "Proposed Standard" in June 2022 as well. In the last few years, we also saw additional protocols being introduced, some of which use HTTP/2 internally; gRPC is one prominent example. Even if protocols change, message verbosity and service granularity, and coupling/decoupling of communicating parties, will continue to keep API designers busy, particularly those of APIs and their clients operating in resource-constrained environments. Hardware improves, but history has taught us that client expectations grow with the progress that the hardware makes.

Message exchange formats seem to come and go more frequently than protocols; for example, XML went out of fashion, and JSON dominates at the time of writing. However, there was a time when XML was considered the ultimate and final stage of the evolution of markup languages. Will we ever abandon JSON, and if so, what comes next? We do not have answers to these questions but are quite confident that patterns related to message design, for instance, EMBEDDED ENTITY and LINKED INFORMATION HOLDER, will continue to be relevant—also to API design leveraging the next generations of formats (if any).[3]

OpenAPI Specification is the dominant API description language for HTTP-based APIs at present. AsyncAPI is gaining importance as a similar approach to describe message-based APIs. MDSL has bindings and generator support for OpenAPI Specification and AsyncAPI, as well as for other contemporary API description languages. Will additional API description languages emerge and sustain, covering the two prevailing integration camps (synchronous and asynchronous communication) as well

---

3. Maybe some semi-intelligent, format-autonomous tools can automate their application in the future?

as other integration technologies and protocols? Is there a chance for a unified language? Time will tell, and we look forward to finding known uses of our patterns in these languages and API designs using them.

Additional Resources

The Web site companion to this book provides pattern summaries and additional background information:

https://api-patterns.org

The Interface Refactoring Catalog is available here:

https://interface-refactoring.github.io

The "Stepwise Service Design" activity proposed in the software and service *Design Practice Reference* (DPR) leverages many of the patterns from this book [Zimmermann 2021b]. DPR also comes as an open-source repository of methods and practices that are applicable to service analysis and design:

https://socadk.github.io/design-practice-repository

Final Remarks

While IT buzzwords and technology concepts come and go, integration styles and design patterns stay. Patterns are not final solutions but can help you do better and avoid common mistakes—so that you have an opportunity to make new ones, which then become lessons learned and, eventually, lead to new patterns or antipatterns. Please view our patterns as a starting point for your design endeavors, not as their destination!

We are confident that the architectural knowledge captured in this book and its patterns has the potential to guide architectural decisions on your real-world API design and development projects. If this actually happens, we will be happy to get your feedback on how the patterns helped you craft awesome APIs.

Thanks for buying, reading, and making it to the end of our book!

Olaf, Mirko, Daniel, Uwe, and Cesare

June 30, 2022

Appendix A

Endpoint Identification and Pattern Selection Guides

This appendix provides guidance on when to apply which pattern in the form of a cheat sheet. It also connects our pattern language with responsibility-driven design (RDD), domain-driven design (DDD), and the Align-Define-Design-Refine (ADDR) process.

Cheat Sheet for Pattern Selection

The cheat sheet provides issue-pattern tables to indicate when a particular pattern is eligible. Please note that this is a gross simplification of a set of complex design problems and considerations. The decision models in Part 1 and the pattern texts in Part 2 discuss context, forces, and consequences of related solutions in much more depth. Chapter 4 provides several more entry points for book content and pattern language.

Getting Started with API Design

Foundation patterns address the early and basic API scoping issues. Table A.1 lists such issues and corresponding patterns.

The selection of these patterns is driven by criteria such as type of client, business model, product/project vision, and project/product context. The client portfolio (that is, number and location of clients, information needs of these clients), and security requirements are important criteria to consider. Chapters 1, 3, and 4 collect many more decision drivers and desired qualities.

Table A.1 *Eligibility of API Foundation Patterns (Covered in Chapter 4)*

Issue	Patterns to Consider
An end-user application wants data from or activity in a backend	Realize a FRONTEND INTEGRATION API
Two backends have to collaborate to fulfill a business requirement	Realize a BACKEND INTEGRATION API
A new API should be broadly accessible	Introduce a PUBLIC API
The visibility of a new API should be restricted to a group of clients	Introduce a COMMUNITY API
A new API targets a single application only, for instance to decompose it into services	Introduce a SOLUTION-INTERNAL API

Next up, in Table A.2, responsibility patterns can jumpstart API endpoint design.

Table A.2 *How to Identify and Classify API Endpoints by Role (from Chapter 5)*

Issue	Pattern(s)
Identify API endpoint candidates	Apply DDD and/or stepwise API design practice such as ADDR or one of those compiled in *Design Practice Reference* [Zimmermann 2021b]
Model a business capability that is action-oriented (representing business activities or commands)	Define a PROCESSING RESOURCE and realize the required activities as well as coordination and state management in its operations (see Table A.3)
Model a business capability that is data-oriented	Define an INFORMATION HOLDER RESOURCE, being aware of the coupling introduced and provide suited create, read, update, delete, and search operations for it (Table A.3)
Let applications exchange transient data without coupling them directly	Define a DATA TRANSFER RESOURCE and add API clients to the applications
Decouple provider locations from clients	Provide a LINK LOOKUP RESOURCE as an directory serving dynamic endpoint references
Expose short-lived, transactional data	Mark an INFORMATION HOLDER RESOURCE as OPERATIONAL DATA HOLDER
Expose long-lived, mutable data	Mark an INFORMATION HOLDER RESOURCE as MASTER DATA HOLDER
Expose long-lived data not mutable for clients	Mark an INFORMATION HOLDER RESOURCE as REFERENCE DATA HOLDER

During endpoint identification, one might decide to define one API or one API endpoint for each "Bounded Context" from DDD if logic and data are highly cohesive [Singjai 2021a]. If fine-grained decomposition is desired and possible, "Aggregate" may initiate API and API endpoint identification [Singjai 2021b; Singjai 2021c].

The operations exposed by API endpoints differ in the way they touch (or do not touch) provider-side state: read, write, read-write, or neither read nor write (Table A.3).

Table A.3 *How to Classify Operations (from Chapter 5)*

Issue	Pattern(s)
Allow API client to initialize provider-side state (including domain-layer entities)	Mark an operation as write-only STATE CREATION OPERATION
Allow API client to query and read provider-side state	Mark an operation as read-only RETRIEVAL OPERATION
Allow API client to update or delete provider-side state	Mark an operation as read-write STATE TRANSITION OPERATION (variants: full/partial state replacement, state deletion)
Allow API client to invoke a state-agnostic operation	Mark an operation as COMPUTATION FUNCTION

Designing Request and Response Message Structures

Once the roles and responsibilities of API endpoints and their operations have been characterized, it is time to specify the data contract (the structure of headers and body in request and response messages, that is). Table A.4 shows the different options.

Table A.4 *Basic Message Structure Patterns (from Chapter 4)*

Issue	Pattern(s)
Data is simple	Design ATOMIC PARAMETER and/or ATOMIC PARAMETER LIST for request and response messages
Data is complex	Design PARAMETER TREE, possibly arranged as PARAMETER FOREST for requests and responses; PARAMETER TREES may contain others and ATOMIC PARAMETERS or ATOMIC PARAMETER LISTS as leaves

Table A.5 shows how, in message payload design, both basic and structured message elements may receive certain stereotypical roles.

Table A.5 *Element Stereotypes (from Chapter 6)*

Issue	Pattern(s)
Exchange structured data (for instance, domain entity representations)	Add DATA ELEMENT with EMBEDDED ENTITIES to message payload (following entity relationships)
Distinguish representation elements or other API parts	Add ID ELEMENT to message payload (locally or globally unique)
Make operation flow flexible	Upgrade from ID ELEMENT to LINK ELEMENT to support the REST principle of hypertext as the engine of application state (hypermedia controls); links may refer to PROCESSING RESOURCES or INFORMATION HOLDER RESOURCES
Annotate payload to ease processing	Add METADATA ELEMENTS (control, provenance, aggregated metadata)

Improving API Quality

Patterns related to API quality can help solve interoperability issues and size message representations right if the goal is to achieve data transfer parsimony (Table A.6).

Table A.6 *When to Apply Which Quality Improvement (from Chapters 6, 7, and 9)*

Issue	Pattern(s)
API clients report interoperability and usability problems	Switch from minimal to elaborate API DESCRIPTION
	Add METADATA ELEMENTS to PARAMETER TREES
	Introduce a CONTEXT REPRESENTATION in the payload encapsulating control metadata such as quality-of-service properties
API usage mistakes and other faults are difficult to analyze and fix	Add an ERROR REPORT to response representations to describe failures in detail
API clients report performance problems	Switch from EMBEDDED ENTITIES to LINKED INFORMATION HOLDERS to adjust message size and service granularity (the two patterns can be combined flexibly)
	Reduce the amount of transferred data with a WISH LIST or a WISH TEMPLATE
	Consider other quality patterns improving data transfer parsimony (for instance, CONDITIONAL REQUEST or REQUEST BUNDLE)
	Introduce PAGINATION
Access control is needed	Introduce API KEYS or more advanced security solutions

API Support and Maintenance

API providers have to deal with change and must balance compatibility and extensibility. The evolution patterns in Table A.7 cover strategies and tactics for doing so.

Table A.7 *When to Apply Which Evolution Pattern (from Chapter 8)*

Issue	Pattern(s)
Indicate changes that are not backward compatible	Introduce a new major API version with a new, explicit Version Identifier
Communicate the impact and significance of changes from version to version	Apply Semantic Versioning to distinguish major, minor, and patch versions
Maintain several versions of API endpoints and their operations	Offer Two in Production (variant: N in Production)
Avoid having to support multiple versions of API endpoints and their parts (including message structure elements)	Announce an Aggressive Obsolescence strategy and announce a decommissioning/removal date at any time (but grant an intermediate deprecation period)
Commit to keeping API available and supported for a fixed amount of time	Give a Limited Lifetime Guarantee and communicate it at API publication time
Avoid committing to stability and future existence of API	Position API as an Experimental Preview

API Release and Productization

Once an API goes into production, documentation and governance tasks come into play. Table A.8 introduces some common issues and applicable patterns.

Table A.8 *API Specification and Documentation (from Chapter 9)*

Issue	Pattern(s)
Clients need to know how to call the API	Create and publish a minimal or elaborate API Description
Ensure fair use of the API	Enforce a Rate Limit
Charge for API usage	Establish a Pricing Plan
Communicate quality-of-service characteristics	Issue a Service Level Agreement or informal specification

"Driven" API Design

This section provides background information on RDD, summarizes how to leverage DDD to craft APIs, and revisits the complementary nature of the ADDR process (introduced at the beginning of Part 2) and our patterns.

RDD Concepts

To order and structure the endpoint and operation design space (or, in ADDR, the Define phase), we adopt some of the terminology and the role stereotypes from RDD [Wirfs-Brock 2002]. RDD was originally created for the context of object-oriented analysis and design (OOAD), which becomes apparent in its core definitions:

- An *application* is a set of interacting objects.
- An *object* is an implementation of one or more roles.
- A *role* groups related responsibilities.
- A *responsibility* is an obligation to perform a task or know information.
- A *collaboration* may be an interaction of objects or roles, or a combination of both.
- A *contract* is an agreement outlining the terms of a collaboration.

In our experience, RDD works equally well on the code level and on the architecture level. As API design has both architectural and developmental ramifications, the *role stereotypes* in RDD are a natural choice to express API behavior. For instance, all API endpoints can be seen to have (remote) interfacers that provide and protect access to service providers, controllers/coordinators, and information holder roles. The read-write operations exposed by API endpoints correspond to responsibilities. The API DESCRIPTION specifies the RDD contract, and collaborations arise from calls to API operations.

The patterns in Chapter 5 pick up these terms and concepts for the context of API design.

DDD and API Design

DDD [Evans 2003; Vernon 2013] and our patterns are also related in several ways:

- DDD "Services" are good candidates for remote API exposure.
- A DDD "Bounded Context" may correspond to a single API (with several endpoints).

- A DDD "Aggregate" can also be exposed via an API (possibly having several endpoints, starting with the root "Entity"). Depending on the nature of an Aggregate, a Processing Resource is often preferred over an Information Holder Resource; see the discussions in these two patterns for rationale.

- DDD "Repositories" deal with entity life-cycle management, which involves read and write access to API provider-side application state (as defined by our operation responsibility patterns). For instance, repositories usually provide lookup capabilities, which may turn into API-level Retrieval Operations. Special-purpose repositories may yield Link Lookup Resources. DDD "Factories" also deal with life-cycle management and may donate additional API operations (unless their functionality should remain an API-implementation detail).

- DDD "Value Objects" can be exposed as data transfer representations (DTRs) in the Published Language established by the data part of the API Description. Data Element from Chapter 6 is a related pattern.

In DDD, the Aggregate and Entity patterns often expose process-like properties (as they represent groups of domain concepts that have an identity and a life cycle at runtime). Hence, these patterns can help identify State Creation Operation and State Transition Operation candidates during endpoint identification. However, it is important not to expose the entire domain model as Published Language on the API level because this creates an undesired tight coupling between the API clients and the provider-side API implementation.

DDD does not distinguish between master data and operational data in its tactic patterns; both operational data and master data may be part of the Published Language and appear in dedicated Bounded Contexts and Aggregates as Entities (see [Vernon 2013]). In DDD, domain event sourcing [Fowler 2006] is the recommended practice to integrate Aggregates (both within the same and in different Bounded Contexts) because it decouples them and allows replaying events up to the current state in case of failures that lead to consistency issues. APIs may support this.

In *Principles of Web API Design*, James Higginbotham reminds us that "resources are not data models" and "resources are not objects or domain models" [Higginbotham 2021], with resources corresponding to endpoints in our technology-neutral terminology. And "REST was never about CRUD" either. That said, data and domain models may still serve as API design *input* when taken with a grain of salt.

ADDR and Our Patterns

Principles of Web API Design [Higginbotham 2021] also is the source of the ADDR process that we roughly followed in Part 2.

Table A.9 summarizes the correspondences between ADDR phases/steps and the patterns from this book. It also provides application examples from our sample case (note that some of the pattern selection decisions appeared in the narratives in Chapter 3).

Table A.9 *ADDR to Pattern Mapping (with Examples)*

Phase/Step	Pattern(s)	Example
Align		
1. Identify Digital Capabilities	Foundation patterns (Chapter 4)	User story about "contact information updates" in Chapter 2
2. Capture Activity Steps	n/a	The agile practice of story splitting *could* be applied; same for event storming (examples available online)[*]
Define		
3. Identify API Boundaries	Foundation patterns (Chapter 4)	Lakeside Mutual domain model and context map in Chapter 2
	Responsibility patterns (Chapter 5)	For example, PROCESSING RESOURCE, INFORMATION HOLDER RESOURCE usage in Lakeside Mutual
4. Model API Profiles	Foundation patterns (Chapter 4)	See interludes in Chapter 3
	Responsibility patterns (Chapter 5)	See interludes in Chapter 3
	Initial SERVICE LEVEL AGREEMENT (Chapter 9)	See interludes in Chapter 3
Design		
5. High-Level Design	Basic structure patterns (Chapter 4)	See interludes in Chapter 3
	Element stereotype patterns (Chapter 6)	See interludes in Chapter 3
	EMBEDDED ENTITY and LINKED INFORMATION HOLDER patterns (Chapter 7)	The HTTP resource APIs for Lakeside Mutual, implemented in Java, provide examples of pattern use (see Appendix B)
	Technology realization of patterns (for instance, as HTTP resources)	See Appendix B
Refine		
6. Refine the Design	Quality patterns (Chapters 6 and 7)	WISH LIST in operations of Customer Information Holder in Lakeside Mutual
7. Document the API	API DESCRIPTION, RATE LIMIT (Chapter 9)	See OpenAPI snippet in Appendix B for a minimal technical contract
	Evolution patterns such as VERSION IDENTIFIER (Chapter 8)	See sample decisions in Chapter 3

[*] https://ozimmer.ch/categories/#Practices.

More details on the **Identify API Boundaries step.** Our messages are very much in line with James Higginbotham's advice; for instance, our patterns help avoid the antipatterns he discusses [Higginbotham 2021, p. 70 ff.]. By considering our endpoint role patterns from Chapter 5 when deciding between activity- or data-oriented semantics of endpoints and being aware of the differences in the responsibilities of their operations, antipatterns like the "Mega All-In-One API," "Overloaded API," and "Helper API" can be avoided.

More details on the **Model API Profiles step.** This is an ADDR step in which many of our patterns are eligible. For instance, the LINK ELEMENT pattern and related METADATA ELEMENTS from Chapter 6 may be used to describe the "resource taxonomies" (independent/dependent/associative resources) [Higginbotham 2021, p. 87], and the "operation safety classification" (safe/unsafe/idempotent operations) [p. 91] can be expressed with the operation responsibilities from Chapter 5.

More details on the **High-Level Design step.** This ADDR step is complementary to our Chapters 4, 5, and 7; the patterns from these chapters fit here. A RATE LIMIT (Chapter 9) can be part of the "API Management Layer." Deciding whether to include related or nested resources, discussed in the context of "hypermedia serialization" [Higginbotham 2021, p. 127], is covered by our EMBEDDED ENTITY and LINKED INFORMATION HOLDER patterns. Our WISH TEMPLATE pattern provides complementary advice on "query-based APIs."

More details on the **Refine the Design step.** Note that optimizing for performance on a platform-neutral level (as our Chapters 6 and 7 patterns do) is not covered as such in ADDR. That said, our Chapters 6 and 7 patterns belong to this phase and step in ADDR. Higginbotham's process and our patterns complement each other here.

Appendix B

Implementation of the Lakeside Mutual Case

In this appendix, we return to the fictitious case we introduced in Chapter 2, "Lakeside Mutual Case Study." Many examples from the case are provided in Part 2. Here, we feature selected specification and implementation details.

Pattern Application

Many of the patterns from this book were applied in the Lakeside Mutual case. Some examples follow:

- The class `InsuranceQuoteRequestProcessingResource.java` in the Policy Management microservice is an activity-oriented PROCESSING RESOURCE, which is indicated by its name suffix. The data-oriented `CustomerInformationHolder.java` in the Customer Core service is an INFORMATION HOLDER RESOURCE.

- The representation element `customerProfile` in `CustomerDto.java` applies DATA ELEMENT and EMBEDDED ENTITY.

- A RATE LIMIT realization can be found in `RateLimitInterceptor.java` in the Customer Self-Service microservice.

A more complete overview is available in the GitHub repository of Lakeside Mutual.[1] In the following, we provide two different views on the `getCustomers` RETRIEVAL OPERATION of the Customer Core INFORMATION HOLDER RESOURCE.

---

1. https://github.com/Microservice-API-Patterns/LakesideMutual/blob/master/MAP.md.

463

Java Service Layer

Figure 2.4 in Chapter 2 shows a domain model of the realized insurance business concepts; the Java Service Layer featured here implements parts of this domain model. Due to space constraints, we show only parts of each artifact here; a more complete implementation can be found in the GitHub repository.

This is the `CustomerInformationHolder` class that serves as a Spring `@RestController`:

```java
@RestController
@RequestMapping("/customers")
public class CustomerInformationHolder {
/**
 * Returns a 'page' of customers.
 *
 * The query parameters {@code limit} and {@code offset} can be
 * used to specify the maximum size of the page and the offset of
 * the page's first customer.
 *
 * The response contains the customers, limit and offset of the
 * current page, as well as the total number of customers
 *(data set size).
 * Additionally, it contains HATEOAS-style links that link to the
 * endpoint addresses of the current, previous, and next page.
 */
 @Operation(summary =
     "Get all customers in pages of 10 entries per page.")
 @GetMapping // operation responsibility: Retrieval Operation
 public ResponseEntity<PaginatedCustomerResponseDto>
     getCustomers(
   @RequestParam(
     value = "filter", required = false, defaultValue = "")
   String filter,
   @RequestParam(
     value = "limit", required = false, defaultValue = "10")
   Integer limit,
   @RequestParam(
     value = "offset", required = false, defaultValue = "0")
   Integer offset,
   @RequestParam(
     value = "fields", required = false, defaultValue = "")
```

```
    String fields) {

  String decodedFilter = UriUtils.decode(filter, "UTF-8");

  Page<CustomerAggregateRoot> customerPage = customerService
    .getCustomers(decodedFilter, limit, offset);

  List<CustomerResponseDto> customerDtos = customerPage
    .getElements()
    .stream()
    .map(c -> createCustomerResponseDto(c, fields))
    .collect(Collectors.toList());

  PaginatedCustomerResponseDto response =
    createPaginatedCustomerResponseDto(
      filter,
      customerPage.getLimit(),
      customerPage.getOffset(),
      customerPage.getSize(),
      fields,
      customerDtos);

  return ResponseEntity.ok(response);
}
```

OpenAPI Specification and Sample API Client

Stepping back from the implementation details, the following OpenAPI specification (shortened for clarity) of the getCustomers operation from the Java Service Layer provides another view of the API design:

```
openapi: 3.0.1
info:
  title: Customer Core API
  description: This API allows clients to create new customers
    and retrieve details about existing customers.
  license:
    name: Apache 2.0
  version: v1.0.0
servers:
```

```yaml
  - url: http://localhost:8110
    description: Generated server url
paths:
  /customers:
    get:
      tags:
        - customer-information-holder
      summary: Get all customers in pages of 10 entries per page.
      operationId: getCustomers
      parameters:
        - name: filter
          in: query
          description: search terms to filter the customers by
            name
          required: false
          schema:
            type: string
            default: ''
        - name: limit
          in: query
          description: the maximum number of customers per page
          required: false
          schema:
            type: integer
            format: int32
            default: 10
        - name: offset
          in: query
          description: the offset of the page's first customer
          required: false
          schema:
            type: integer
            format: int32
            default: 0
        - name: fields
          in: query
          description: a comma-separated list of the fields
            that should be included in the response
          required: false
          schema:
            type: string
            default: ''
      responses:
```

```
        '200':
          description: OK
          content:
            '*/*':
              schema:
                $ref: "#/components/schemas\
                        /PaginatedCustomerResponseDto"
components:
  schemas:
    Address:
      type: object
      properties:
        streetAddress:
          type: string
        postalCode:
          type: string
        city:
          type: string
    CustomerResponseDto:
      type: object
      properties:
        customerId:
          type: string
        firstname:
          type: string
        lastname:
          type: string
        birthday:
          type: string
          format: date-time
        streetAddress:
          type: string
        postalCode:
          type: string
        city:
          type: string
        email:
          type: string
        phoneNumber:
          type: string
        moveHistory:
          type: array
          items:
```

```
        $ref: '#/components/schemas/Address'
    links:
      type: array
      items:
        $ref: '#/components/schemas/Link'
Link:
  type: object
  properties:
    rel:
      type: string
    href:
      type: string
AddressDto:
  required:
    - city
    - postalCode
    - streetAddress
  type: object
  properties:
    streetAddress:
      type: string
    postalCode:
      type: string
    city:
      type: string
  description: the customer's new address
PaginatedCustomerResponseDto:
  type: object
  properties:
    filter:
      type: string
    limit:
      type: integer
      format: int32
    offset:
      type: integer
      format: int32
    size:
      type: integer
      format: int32
    customers:
```

```
        type: array
        items:
          $ref: '#/components/schemas/CustomerResponseDto'
      links:
        type: array
        items:
          $ref: '#/components/schemas/Link'
```

When querying the endpoint using `curl`, the following HTTP response is returned:

```
curl -X GET --header \
'Authorization: Bearer b318ad736c6c844b' \
http://localhost:8110/customers\?limit\=2

{
  "limit": 2,
  "offset": 0,
  "size": 50,
  "customers": [ {
    "customerId": "bunlo9vk5f",
    "firstname": "Ado",
    "lastname": "Kinnett",
    "birthday": "1975-06-13T23:00:00.000+00:00",
    "streetAddress": "2 Autumn Leaf Lane",
    "postalCode": "6500",
    "city": "Bellinzona",
    "email": "akinnetta@example.com",
    "phoneNumber": "055 222 4111",
    "moveHistory": [ ]
  }, {
    "customerId": "bd91pwfepl",
    "firstname": "Bel",
    "lastname": "Pifford",
    "birthday": "1964-02-01T23:00:00.000+00:00",
    "streetAddress": "4 Sherman Parkway",
    "postalCode": "1201",
    "city": "Genf",
    "email": "bpiffordb@example.com",
    "phoneNumber": "055 222 4111",
    "moveHistory": [ ]
```

```
    } ],
  "_links": {
    "self": {
      "href": "/customers?filter=&limit=2&offset=0&fields="
    },
    "next": {
      "href": "/customers?filter=&limit=2&offset=2&fields="
    }
  }
}
```

Appendix C

Microservice Domain-Specific Language (MDSL)

This appendix introduces as much of the *Microservice Domain-Specific Language (MDSL)* as required to understand the examples in Parts 1 and 2 of the book. MDSL is applicable irrespective of any architectural styles and supporting technologies; hence, MDSL may stand for *Message and Data Specification Language* as well.

MDSL allows API designers to specify API contracts, their data representations, and bindings to technologies. The language supports the domain model and patterns from this book in its syntax and semantics. Its tools provide generators for interface description and service programming languages such as OpenAPI, gRPC protocol buffers, GraphQL, Application-Level Profile Semantics (ALPS), and Jolie (which also brings support for Web Services Description Language [WSDL] and XML Schema conversion).

The MDSL language specification and supporting tools are available online.[1]

Getting Started with MDSL

First and foremost, MDSL supports the API DESCRIPTION pattern from Chapter 9. To specify such API contracts, MDSL picks up domain model concepts such as *API endpoint, operation, client,* and *provider,* as introduced in Chapter 1.

The patterns from this book are integrated into the language natively. For instance, ATOMIC PARAMETERS and PARAMETER TREES from Chapter 4 structure the data definitions. Moreover, the roles and responsibilities introduced in Chapter 5 can be assigned

---

1. https://microservice-api-patterns.github.io/MDSL-Specification.

to endpoints and operations. On the message representation level, MDSL includes decorators for the element stereotypes and quality patterns from Chapters 6, 7, and 9; an example is <<Pagination>>. Finally, the evolution patterns from Chapter 8 are integrated into the language as well: API providers and their SERVICE LEVEL AGREEMENTS may disclose lifecycle guarantees such as EXPERIMENTAL PREVIEW or LIMITED LIFETIME GUARANTEE; many language elements may receive a VERSION IDENTIFIER.

Design Goals

As a contract language for service and API design, MDSL aims at facilitating *agile modeling practices, API sketching*, and API *design workshops*. It is supposed to be readable for all stakeholder groups involved in API design and evolution. MDSL should support partial specifications that can be refined iteratively. To be usable in tutorials and publications such as this book, its syntax must be compact so that a nontrivial API contract still fits on one book page or presentation slide (or less).

MDSL can be used in *top-down* API design from requirements (for instance, user stories for integration scenarios and API sketches) down to code and deployment artifacts and in *bottom-up* discovery of internal interfaces in existing systems, possibly wrapped in public, community, or solution-internal remote APIs. One example of a top-down design process is Align-Define-Design-Refine (ADDR) [Higginbotham 2021], as introduced at the beginning of Part 2; a discovery tool with MDSL support is the domain-driven Context Mapper [Kapferer 2021].

MDSL aims at *platform independence* of API designs. API DESCRIPTIONS created with MDSL are not limited to HTTP or any other single protocol or message exchange format. The HTTP protocol design deviates from most interface definition languages and RPC-style communication protocols in many ways. Hence, MDSL has to provide configurable provider-to-technology bindings that surmount protocol differences—without losing either generality or specificity.

"Hello World" (API Edition)

The "Hello World" of MDSL and service API design look as follows:

```
API description HelloWorldAPI

data type SampleDTO {ID<int>, "someData": D<string>}

endpoint type HelloWorldEndpoint
exposes
  operation sayHello
```

```
    expecting payload "in": D<string>
    delivering payload SampleDTO

API provider HelloWorldAPIProvider
  offers HelloWorldEndpoint
  at endpoint location "http://localhost:8000"
  via protocol HTTP
    binding resource HomeResource at "/"
      operation sayHello to POST
```

There is a single endpoint type, `HelloWorldEndpoint`, that exposes an operation `sayHello`. This operation has a single inlined request parameter, `"in"`: `D<string>`, and returns an unnamed data transfer object (DTO) called `SampleDTO` as output. This DTO is modeled explicitly so that its specification can be reused. The sample DTO is a PARAMETER TREE, `{ID<int>, "someData": D<string>}`, which is flat in this case. The DATA ELEMENT D in the tree is called `"someData"` and has a string type; the unnamed `ID` parameter, an ID ELEMENT, is of type integer.

Each endpoint type describes a platform-independent API contract, possibly provided multiple times. In addition to the endpoint type `HelloWorldEndpoint`, the example contains an API provider instance `HelloWorldAPIProvider` exposing an API implementation that binds the abstract endpoint type to HTTP. The endpoint type is bound to a single HTTP resource `HomeResource` in the example. The single endpoint operation `sayHello` is bound to the POST method in this single resource. The resource URI is assembled from two parts marked with the keyword `at`, one on the endpoint level and one on the resource level. The request parameters could be bound individually and explicitly to QUERY or PATH or other parameter types defined in the HTTP RFCs; this is not shown in the example, and a default binding to the request BODY is assumed.

It is possible to specify data types preliminarily:

```
data type SampleDTOStub {ID, "justAName"}
```

`SampleDTOStub` is specified incompletely. The first element in this flat PARAMETER TREE has an identifier role ID, but it does not have a name yet and its type is unknown still. The role and type of the second parameter have not been specified either; it merely consists of `"justAName"`. Such incomplete, preliminary specifications are useful when only sketching interfaces at early design stages or when the details in a given modeling context are not of concern.

The online "Primer: Getting Started with MDSL"[2] and the project repository provide additional examples.

---

2. https://microservice-api-patterns.github.io/MDSL-Specification/primer.

MDSL Reference

Let us now walk through the language concepts in depth.

API Endpoint Types (with Message Specifications)

The grammar of MDSL is inspired by the domain model from Chapter 1. An API DESCRIPTION in MDSL features one or more *endpoint* types, which expose *operations*. These operations expect and deliver request and/or response *messages*. The request and response messages sent and received by operations consist of simple or structured data. A comprehensive example looks as follows:

```
API description CustomerRelationshipManagementExample

endpoint type CustomerRelationshipManager
  serves as PROCESSING_RESOURCE
data type Customer P
exposes
  operation createCustomer
    with responsibility STATE_CREATION_OPERATION
    expecting payload "customerRecord": Customer
    delivering payload "customerId": D<int>
    compensated by deleteCustomer
  // no GET operation yet
  operation upgradeCustomer
    with responsibility STATE_TRANSITION_OPERATION
    expecting payload "promotionCode": P // partially specified
    delivering payload P // response unspecified
  operation deleteCustomer
    with responsibility STATE_DELETION_OPERATION
    expecting payload "customerId": D<int>
    delivering payload "success": MD<bool>
    transitions from "customerIsActive" to "customerIsArchived"
  operation validateCustomerRecord
    with responsibility COMPUTATION_FUNCTION
    expecting
      headers "complianceLevel": MD<int>
      payload "customerRecord": Customer
    delivering
      payload "isCompleteAndSound": D<bool>
    reporting
      error ValidationResultsReport
        "issues": {"code":D<int>, "message":D<string>}+
```

The CustomerRelationshipManager API exposes and serves as a PROCESSING_RESOURCE (or, following our layout convention for pattern names, as a Processing Resource). This is one of the responsibility patterns in Chapter 5. Its four operations differ in their read-write characteristics; this is expressed by the with responsibility decorators. For instance, upgradeCustomer is a STATE_TRANSITION_OPERATION. All operations in this example have request and response messages (which is not mandatory in MDSL, as message exchange patterns may vary). The header and payload content of request and response messages is modeled via MDSL data transfer representations, introduced in the section "Data Types and Data Contracts" that follows.

Some of the operations define undo operations (compensated by) and state transitions (transitions from ... to). The operation validateCustomerRecord can return an Error Report, which is a pattern from Chapter 6. Note that one or more issues can be reported in ValidationResultsReport due to its "at least one" cardinality, indicted with the plus symbol, "+". This operation also features a request header, "complianceLevel": MD<int>, which has a metadata role and an integer type.

See "Service Endpoint Contracts in MDSL" in the online language specification for more explanations [Zimmermann 2022].

Data Types and Data Contracts

Throughout the book, we emphasized the importance of data modeling; the Published Language of an API contains data representations in several places, which may be flat or nested:

- Endpoint types define operations, which have request and (optionally) response messages containing payload content and metadata headers. The structure of these messages has to be specified unambiguously and agreed upon to achieve interoperability as well as accuracy, and it must ensure a positive client developer experience.

- When certain data structures are used by multiple operations, these operations may refer to shared data transfer representations (which are message-level pendants to DTOs internal to programs). Such representations become part of one or more API endpoint contracts.

- APIs may be used to emit and receive events. Such events also require data definitions.

API data definitions have a strong impact on the success of an API because the amount of coupling between client and provider is influenced by these definitions.

MDSL supports data modeling in several ways, addressing the preceding usage scenarios. The MDSL data types are inspired—and generalize from—message exchange formats such as JSON. Here are two examples:

```
data type SampleDTO {ID, D<string>}

data type Customer {
  "name": D<string>,
  "address": {"street": D<string>, "city": D<string>}*,
  "birthday": D<string> }
```

The basic structure patterns from Chapter 4, ATOMIC PARAMETER and PARAMETER TREE in particular, provide the type system of MDSL. In the example, "name": D<string> is an ATOMIC PARAMETER, and Customer is a nested PARAMETER TREE, containing an inner PARAMETER TREE representing one or more "address" elements. This is indicated by the asterisk * at the end of its definition.

Parameter Trees and Forests

Nesting is supported to realize the PARAMETER TREE pattern. The structure is expressed in an object- or block-like syntax: {...{...}}. This syntax is similar to objects in data representation languages such as JSON.

The preceding example features two trees; one of these trees is inlined in the message specification:

```
  "address": {"street": D<string>, "city": D<string>}
```

Usage of the PARAMETER FOREST pattern is indicated by square brackets [...]:

```
data type CustomerProductForest [
  "customers": { "customer": CustomerWithAddressAndMoveHistory}*;
  "products": { "product": ID<string> }
]
```

Atomic Parameters (Full or Partial Specification)

Full ATOMIC PARAMETERS are defined as *Identifier-Role-Type* triples: "aName":D<String>

- The optional *identifier* "aName" corresponds to the variable names in programming languages and data representation languages such as JSON. Identifiers must be embedded in double quotes: "somePayloadData". They may contain blanks: " " or underscores "_".

- The mandatory *role* can be `D` (data), `MD` (metadata), `ID` (identifier), or `L` (link). These roles directly match the four element stereotype patterns from Chapter 6: DATA ELEMENT, METADATA ELEMENT, ID ELEMENT, and LINK ELEMENT.

- The base *types* are `bool`, `int`, `long`, `double`, `string`, `raw`, and `void`. This type information is optional.

For instance, `D<int>` is an integer data value and `D<void>` is an empty representation element.

Rationale for Identifier-Role-Type Triple Concept

The primary specification element is the role within a message payload taken by a particular part of a header or payload (or a representation element in our domain model terminology); identifiers and data type are optional. Making identifier and type optional supports the early use of MDSL when an API design is not yet complete:

```
operation createCustomer
  expecting payload "customer": D
  delivering payload MD
```

The three-part specification is a bit different from the identifier-type pairs typically used in programming languages. As stated earlier, only the role is mandatory. This makes it possible to create rather compact specifications during agile API modeling. An abstract, unspecified element can be represented as `P` (for parameter or payload placeholder). `P` may take the place of the Role-Type elements in the Identifier-Role-Type triple; the placeholder can also replace the entire triple:

```
operation upgradeCustomer
  expecting payload "promotionCode": P // placeholder
  delivering payload P // response unspecified
```

A `"nameOnly"` may also specify a generic placeholder parameter (which has no role and no type).

Multiplicity

The cardinality classifiers `"*"`, `"?"`, and `"+"` turn a type definition into a collection (`"*"`: zero or more, `"?"`: one or none, `"+"`: at least one). The default, which does not have to be specified, is `"!"` (exactly one).

The online language reference provides more explanations under "Data Contracts and Schemas in MDSL" [Zimmermann 2022].

Providers and Protocol Bindings (HTTP, Other Technologies)

MDSL by design generalizes and abstracts from concepts in other API contract languages. This is rather straightforward for most of them (and has been done before in other interface definition languages). For HTTP resource APIs, additional concepts and an intermediate step are required because MDSL endpoints do not map to resources and their URIs one-to-one. In particular, dynamic endpoint addressing, as promoted by RFC6570 "URI Templates" [Fielding 2012] and used in HTTP path parameters, is specific to HTTP. Moreover, it is not obvious how to express complex request payloads of retrieval operations—HTTP GET and request bodies do not go well together.[3] HTTP also handles addressing, request and response parameters, errors, and security concerns in specific ways (for good reasons).

The missing mapping information can be specified in an explicit provider-level *HTTP binding*:

```
API provider CustomerRelationshipManagerProvider version "1.0"
offers CustomerRelationshipManager
  at endpoint location "http://localhost:8080"
via protocol HTTP binding
  resource CustomerRelationshipManagerHome
    at "/customerRelationshipManagerHome/{customerId}"
    operation createCustomer to PUT // POST taken
      element "customerRecord" realized as BODY parameter
    // no GET yet
    operation upgradeCustomer to PATCH
      element "promotionCode" realized as BODY parameter
    operation deleteCustomer to DELETE
      element "customerId" realized as PATH parameter
    operation validateCustomerRecord to POST
      element "customerRecord" realized as BODY parameter
provider governance TWO_IN_PRODUCTION
```

To generate OpenAPI and, later on, server-side stubs and client-side proxies from MDSL specifications, not all of the required binding information can be derived from the abstract endpoint types. A particularly important example is the mapping of MDSL operations to HTTP verbs such as GET, POST, PUT, and so on. Hence, additional mapping details, for instance, whether a payload parameter is transferred in the QUERY string or the message BODY (or the URI PATH or a HEADER or a

---

3. The protocol specifications are not fully explicit and precise here; that said, many tools and protocol runtimes do not support this combination.

COOKIE), can also be provided (as motivated earlier). Error reports and security policies can also be bound, and media type information can be provided.

See "Protocol Bindings for HTTP, gRPC, Jolie, Java" in the online language specification for more explanations [Zimmermann 2022].

Summary of Support for Microservice API Patterns

MDSL supports the Microservice API Patterns (MAP) presented in this book in several ways:

1. The basic representation elements serve as MDSL grammar rules in the data contract part. PARAMETER TREE and ATOMIC PARAMETER are the main constructs; ATOMIC PARAMETER LISTS and PARAMETER FORESTS are supported as well. PARAMETER TREES correspond to JSON objects {...}; the set cardinalities "*" and "+" indicate that an API that uses JSON as its message exchange format should send or receive a JSON array [...]. Base types such as `int`, `string`, and `bool` can also be found in MDSL.

2. Foundation patterns may appear as decorator annotations for the entire API description, for instance, `PUBLIC_API` and `FRONTEND_INTEGRATION`. The other visibility and direction patterns from Chapter 4 are supported as well: `PUBLIC_API`, `COMMUNITY_API`, `SOLUTION_INTERNAL_API`.

3. Role and responsibility decorators exist on endpoint and operation levels. Some patterns serve as decorators on the API endpoint level, for example, expressing `PROCESSING_RESOURCE` and `MASTER_DATA_HOLDER` roles. Other responsibility patterns appear as decorators representing operation responsibilities, for instance, `COMPUTATION_FUNCTION` and `RETRIEVAL_OPERATION` (Chapter 5).

4. Representation element stereotypes provide the options for the role part of the Identifier-Role-Type triples defining ATOMIC PARAMETERS: `D` (data), `MD` (metadata), `L` (link), and `ID` (identifier).

5. Explicit data types and inlined representation elements can be annotated with pattern decorators as well. Examples of stereotypes decorating representation elements are `<<Context Representation>>` and `<<Error_Report>>` from Chapter 6 as well as `<<Embedded_Entity>>` and `<<Wish_List>>` from Chapter 7.

The following elaborate example features all five types of MAP support in MDSL:

```
API description CustomerManagementExample version "1.0.1"
usage context SOLUTION_INTERNAL_API
  for FRONTEND_INTEGRATION


data type Customer <<Data_Element>> {ID, D} // preliminary

endpoint type CustomerRelationshipManager
 serves as INFORMATION_HOLDER_RESOURCE
 exposes
  operation findAll with responsibility RETRIEVAL_OPERATION
    expecting payload "query": {
      "queryFilter":MD<string>*,
      "limit":MD<int>,
      "offset":MD<int> }
    delivering payload
     <<Pagination>> "result": {
        "responseDTR":Customer*,
        "offset-out":MD<int>,
        "limit-out":MD<int>,
        "size":MD<int>,
        "self":Link<string>,
        "next":L<string> }*
```

The PAGINATION pattern (Chapter 7) usage is indicated in the `findAll` operation; the message design in the specification of `CustomerRelationshipManager` follows the solution sketch in the pattern with pattern-specific representation elements such as `"limit"`. In line with the pattern description, the client specifies a `"limit"` and an `"offset"` in offset-based pagination.

The example contains instances of all four types of element stereotypes such as METADATA ELEMENT and LINK ELEMENT. Both long and short names may specify data elements; both options are used in the example (see `"self"` and `"next"`):

- `Data` or `D`, representing a plain/basic data/value role. `D` corresponds to DATA ELEMENT.

- `Identifier` or `ID` for identifiers, corresponding to the pattern ID ELEMENT.

- `Link` or `L` for identifiers that are also network-accessible (as, for instance, URIs links are) as described in the LINK ELEMENT pattern.

- `Metadata` or `MD` representing control, provenance, or aggregate METADATA ELEMENTS.

The element role stereotypes can be combined with the base types to yield precise specifications of ATOMIC PARAMETERS.

Using the MDSL decorator annotations and stereotypes is optional. If present, they make the API description more expressive and can be processed by tools such as API linters/contract validators, code/configuration generators, MDSL to OpenAPI converters, and so on.

MDSL Tools

An Eclipse-based editor and API linter, also offering transformations for rapid, goal-driven API design ("API first") and refactoring to many of the patterns from this book is available. Not only can MDSL specifications be validated, but platform-specific contracts (OpenAPI, gRPC, GraphQL, and Jolie) can be generated. A prototypical MDSL-Web[4] tool is available as an open-source project. A command-line interface (CLI) offers most of the IDE functionality; therefore, it is not imperative to work with Eclipse when creating and using MDSL specifications.

An intermediate generator model and API exist so that support for other target languages and integration with other tools can be added. Template-based reporting is available via Apache Freemarker. One of the available sample templates turns the MDSL into Markdown.

See "MDSL Tools: Users Guide" for updates [Zimmermann 2022].

Online Resources

The definite, up-to-date language reference can be found online.[5] An MDSL primer, a tutorial, and a quick reference are available on the MDSL Web site as well.

The Interface Refactoring Catalog introduced in Chapter 11 specifies many of its API refactorings with before-after MDSL snippets:

https://interface-refactoring.github.io

Step-by-step instructions and demos of MDSL Tools are available as blog posts:

https://ozimmer.ch/categories/#Practices

---

4. https://github.com/Microservice-API-Patterns/MDSL-Web.

5. https://microservice-api-patterns.github.io/MDSL-Specification.

Bibliography

[Allamaraju 2010] S. Allamaraju, *RESTful Web Services Cookbook*. O'Reilly, 2010.

[Alur 2013] D. Alur, D. Malks, and J. Crupi, *Core J2EE Patterns: Best Practices and Design Strategies*, 2nd ed. Prentice Hall, 2013.

[Amundsen 2011] M. Amundsen, *Building Hypermedia APIs with HTML5 and Node*. O'Reilly, 2011.

[Amundsen 2013] M. Amundsen, "Designing & Implementing Hypermedia APIs." Slide presentation at QCon New York, June 2013. https://www.slideshare.net/rnewton/2013-06q-connycdesigninghypermedia.

[Amundsen 2014] M. Amundsen, "Roy Fielding on Versioning, Hypermedia, and REST." *InfoQ*, December 2014. https://www.infoq.com/articles/roy-fielding-on-versioning/.

[Amundsen 2020] M. Amundsen, *Design and Build Great Web APIs: Robust, Reliable, and Resilient*. Pragmatic Bookshelf, 2020.

[Amundsen 2021] M. Amundsen, L. Richardson, and M. W. Foster, "Application-Level Profile Semantics (ALPS)." Internet Engineering Task Force, Internet-Draft, May 2021. https://datatracker.ietf.org/doc/html/draft-amundsen-richardson-foster-alps-07.

[Apache 2021a] "Apache Avro Specification." Apache Software Foundation, 2021. https://avro.apache.org/docs/current/spec.html#Schema+Resolution.

[Apache 2021b] "Apache Thrift." Apache Software Foundation, 2021. https://thrift.apache.org/.

[API Academy 2022] "API Academy GitHub Repositories." API Academy, accessed June 24, 2022. https://github.com/apiacademy.

[API Blueprint 2022] "API Blueprint. A Powerful High-Level API Description Language for Web APIs." API Blueprint, accessed June 24, 2022. https://apiblueprint.org/.

[Apigee 2018] Apigee, *Web API Design: The Missing Link*. Apigee, 2018, EPUB. https://cloud.google.com/apigee/resources/ebook/web-api-design-register/index.html/.

[Arlow 2004] J. Arlow and I. Neustadt, *Enterprise Patterns and MDA: Building Better Software with Archetype Patterns and UML*. Addison-Wesley, 2004.

[Atlassian 2022] "Bitbucket Cloud Reference." Atlassian Developer, accessed June 24, 2022. https://developer.atlassian.com/cloud/bitbucket/rest/intro/#serialization.

[Baca 2016] M. Baca, *Introduction to Metadata*, 3rd ed. Getty Publications, 2016. http://www.getty.edu/publications/intrometadata.

[Beck 2001] K. Beck et al., "Manifesto for Agile Software Development." 2001. https://agilemanifesto.org/.

[Bellido 2013] J. Bellido, R. Alarcón, and C. Pautasso, "Control-Flow Patterns for Decentralized RESTful Service Composition." *ACM Transactions on the Web (TWEB)* 8, no. 1 (2013): 5:1–5:30. https://doi.org/10.1145/2535911.

[Belshe 2015] M. Belshe, R. Peon, and M. Thomson, "Hypertext Transfer Protocol Version 2 (HTTP/2)." RFC 7540; RFC Editor, May 2015. https://doi.org/10.17487/RFC7540.

[Berli 2014] W. Berli, D. Lübke, and W. Möckli, "Terravis—Large-Scale Business Process Integration between Public and Private Partners." In *Proceedings of INFORMATIK 2014*, Gesellschaft für Informatik e.V., 2014, 1075–1090.

[Beyer 2016] B. Beyer, C. Jones, J. Petoff, and N. R. Murphy, *Site Reliability Engineering: How Google Runs Production Systems*. O'Reilly, 2016.

[Bishop 2021] M. Bishop, "Level 3 REST." Draft, 2021. https://level3.rest/.

[Borysov 2021] A. Borysov and R. Gardiner, "Practical API Design at Netflix, Part 1: Using Protobuf FieldMask." Netflix Technology Blog, 2021. https://netflixtechblog.com/practical-api-design-at-netflix-part-1-using-protobuf-fieldmask-35cfdc606518.

[Brewer 2012] E. Brewer, "CAP Twelve Years Later: How the 'Rules' Have Changed." *Computer* 45, no. 2 (2012): 23–29.

[Brown 2021] K. Brown, B. Woolf, C. D. Groot, C. Hay, and J. Yoder, "Patterns for Developers and Architects Building for the Cloud." Accessed June 24, 2022. https://kgb1001001.github.io/cloudadoptionpatterns/.

[Buschmann 1996] F. Buschmann, R. Meunier, H. Rohnert, P. Sommerlad, and M. Stal, *Pattern-Oriented Software Architecture—Volume 1: A System of Patterns*. Wiley, 1996.

[Buschmann 2007] F. Buschmann, K. Henney, and D. Schmidt, *Pattern-Oriented Software Architecture: A Pattern Language for Distributed Computing*. Wiley, 2007.

[Cavalcante 2019] A. Cavalcante, "What Is DX?" October 2019. https://medium.com/swlh/what-is-dx-developer-experience-401a0e44a9d9.

[Cervantes 2016] H. Cervantes and R. Kazman, *Designing Software Architectures: A Practical Approach*. Addison-Wesley, 2016.

[Cisco Systems 2015] "API Design Guide." Cisco DevNet, 2015. https://github.com/CiscoDevNet/api-design-guide.

[Coplien 1997] J. O. Coplien and B. Woolf, "A Pattern Language for Writers' Workshops." *C Plus Plus Report* 9 (1997): 51–60.

[C-SIG 2014] C-SIG, "Cloud Service Level Agreement Standardisation Guidelines." Cloud Select Industry Group, Service Level Agreements Subgroup; European Commission, 2014. https://ec.europa.eu/newsroom/dae/redirection/document/6138.

[Daigneau 2011] R. Daigneau, *Service Design Patterns: Fundamental Design Solutions for SOAP/WSDL and RESTful Web Services*. Addison-Wesley, 2011.

[Daly 2021] J. Daly, "Serverless." 2021. https://www.jeremydaly.com/serverless/.

[DCMI 2020] "Dublin Core Metadata Initiative Terms." DublinCore, 2020. https://www.dublincore.org/specifications/dublin-core/dcmi-terms/.

[Dean 2014] A. Dean and F. Blundun, "Introducing SchemaVer for Semantic Versioning of Schemas." *Snowplow Blog*, 2014. https://snowplowanalytics.com/blog/2014/05/13/introducing-schemaver-for-semantic-versioning-of-schemas/.

[Dubuisson 2001] O. Dubuisson and P. Fouquart, *ASN.1: Communication between Heterogeneous Systems*. Morgan Kaufmann Publishers, 2001.

[Dusseault 2007] L. M. Dusseault, "HTTP Extensions for Web Distributed Authoring and Versioning (WebDAV)." RFC 4918; RFC Editor, June 2007. https://doi.org/10.17487/RFC4918.

[Erder 2021] M. Erder, P. Pureur, and E. Woods, *Continuous Architecture in Practice: Software Architecture in the Age of Agility and DevOps*. Addison-Wesley, 2021.

[Erl 2013] T. Erl, B. Carlyle, C. Pautasso, and R. Balasubramanian, *SOA with REST: Principles, Patterns and Constraints for Building Enterprise Solutions with REST*. Prentice Hall, 2013.

[EU 2012] European Parliament and Council of the European Union, "Technical Requirements for Credit Transfers and Direct Debits in Euros." Regulation (EU) 260/2012, 2012. https://eur-lex.europa.eu/legal-content/EN/TXT/?uri=CELEX:52012AP0037.

[EU 2016] European Parliament and Council of the European Union, "General Data Protection Regulation." Regulation (EU) 2016/679, 2016. https://eur-lex.europa.eu/eli/reg/2016/679/oj.

[Evans 2003] E. Evans, *Domain-Driven Design: Tackling Complexity in the Heart of Software*. Addison-Wesley, 2003.

[Evans 2016] P. C. Evans and R. C. Basole, "Revealing the API Ecosystem and Enterprise Strategy via Visual Analytics." *Communications of the ACM 59*, no. 2 (2016): 26–28. https://doi.org/10.1145/2856447.

[Fachat 2019] A. Fachat, "Challenges and Benefits of the Microservice Architectural Style." IBM Developer, 2019. https://developer.ibm.com/articles/challenges-and-benefits-of-the-microservice-architectural-style-part-2/.

[Fehling 2014] C. Fehling, F. Leymann, R. Retter, W. Schupeck, and P. Arbitter, *Cloud Computing Patterns: Fundamentals to Design, Build, and Manage Cloud Applications*. Springer, 2014.

[Ferstl 2006] O. K. Ferstl and E. J. Sinz, *Grundlagen der wirtschaftsinformatik*. Oldenbourg, 2006.

[Fielding 2012] R. T. Fielding, M. Nottingham, D. Orchard, J. Gregorio, and M. Hadley, "URI Template." RFC 6570; RFC Editor, March 2012. https://doi.org/10.17487/RFC6570.

[Fielding 2014c] R. T. Fielding and J. Reschke, "Hypertext Transfer Protocol (HTTP/1.1): Semantics and Content." RFC 7231; RFC Editor, June 2014. https://doi.org/10.17487/RFC7231.

[Fielding 2014a] R. T. Fielding and J. Reschke, "Hypertext Transfer Protocol (HTTP/1.1): Conditional Requests." RFC 7232; RFC Editor, June 2014. https://doi.org/10.17487/RFC7232.

[Fielding 2014b] R. T. Fielding and J. Reschke, "Hypertext Transfer Protocol (HTTP/1.1): Authentication." RFC 7235; RFC Editor, June 2014. https://doi.org/10.17487/RFC7235.

[Foundation 2021] "Split the Contents of a Website with the Pagination Design Pattern." Interaction Design Foundation, 2021. https://www.interaction-design.org/literature/article/split-the-contents-of-a-website-with-the-pagination-design-pattern.

[Fowler 1996] M. Fowler, *Analysis Patterns: Reusable Object Models*. Addison-Wesley, 1996.

[Fowler 2002] M. Fowler, *Patterns of Enterprise Application Architecture*. Addison-Wesley, 2002.

[Fowler 2003] M. Fowler, "AnemicDomainModel." November 25, 2003. https://martinfowler.com/bliki/AnemicDomainModel.html.

[Fowler 2006] M. Fowler, "Further Patterns of Enterprise Application Architecture." Updated July 18, 2006. https://martinfowler.com/eaaDev/.

[Fowler 2009] M. Fowler, "TwoHardThings." July 14, 2009. https://martinfowler.com/bliki/TwoHardThings.html.

[Fowler 2011] M. Fowler, "CQRS." July 14, 2011. https://martinfowler.com/bliki/CQRS.html.

[Fowler 2013] M. Fowler, "GiveWhenThen." August 21, 2013. https://www.martinfowler.com/bliki/GivenWhenThen.html.

[Fowler 2016] S. J. Fowler, *Production-Ready Microservices: Building Standardized Systems across an Engineering Organization*. O'Reilly, 2016.

[Furda 2018] A. Furda, C. J. Fidge, O. Zimmermann, W. Kelly, and A. Barros, "Migrating Enterprise Legacy Source Code to Microservices: On Multitenancy, Statefulness, and Data Consistency." *IEEE Software* 35, no. 3 (2018): 63–72. https://doi.org/10.1109/MS.2017.440134612.

[Gambi 2013] A. Gambi and C. Pautasso, "RESTful Business Process Management in the Cloud." In *Proceedings of the 5th ICSE International Workshop on Principles of Engineering Service-Oriented Systems (PESOS)*. IEEE, 2013, 1–10. https://doi.org/10.1109/PESOS.2013.6635971.

[Gamma 1995] E. Gamma, R. Helm, R. Johnson, and J. Vlissides, *Design Patterns: Elements of Reusable Object-Oriented Software*. Addison-Wesley, 1995.

[Good 2002] J. Good, "A Gentle Introduction to Metadata." 2002. http://www.language-archives.org/documents/gentle-intro.html.

[Google 2008] "Protocol Buffers." Google Developers, 2008. https://developers.google.com/protocol-buffers/.

[Google 2019] "Rate-Limiting Strategies and Techniques." Google Cloud Architecture Center, 2019. https://cloud.google.com/architecture/rate-limiting-strategies-techniques.

[GraphQL 2021] "GraphQL Specification." GraphQL Foundation, 2021. https://spec.graphql.org/.

[gRPC] gRPC Authors, "gRPC: A High Performance, Open Source Universal RPC Framework." Accessed June 24, 2022. https://grpc.io/.

[gRPC-Gateway 2022] gRPC-Gateway Authors, "gRPC-gateway." Accessed June 24, 2022. https://grpc-ecosystem.github.io/grpc-gateway/.

[GUID 2022] "The Quick Guide to GUIDs." Better Explained, 2022. https://betterexplained.com/articles/the-quick-guide-to-guids/.

[Gysel 2016] M. Gysel, L. Kölbener, W. Giersche, and O. Zimmermann, "Service Cutter: A Systematic Approach to Service Decomposition." In *Proceedings of the European Conference on Service-Oriented and Cloud Computing (ESOCC)*. Springer-Verlag, 2016, 185–200.

[Hanmer 2007] R. Hanmer, *Patterns for Fault Tolerant Software*. Wiley, 2007.

[Hardt 2012] D. Hardt, "The OAuth 2.0 Authorization Framework." RFC 6749; RFC Editor, October 2012. https://doi.org/10.17487/RFC6749.

[Harrison 2003] N. B. Harrison, "Advanced Pattern Writing Patterns for Experienced Pattern Authors." In *Proceedings of the Eighth European Conference on Pattern Languages of Programs (EuroPLoP)*. UVK - Universitaetsverlag Konstanz, 2003, 1–20.

[Hartig 2018] O. Hartig and J. Pérez, "Semantics and Complexity of GraphQL." In *Proceedings of the World Wide Web Conference (WWW)*. International World Wide Web Conferences Steering Committee, 2018, 1155–1164. https://doi.org/10.1145/3178876.3186014.

[Hay 1996] D. C. Hay, *Data Model Patterns: Conventions of Thought*. Dorset House, 1996.

[Heinrich 2018] R. Heinrich et al., "The Palladio-Bench for Modeling and Simulating Software Architectures." In *Proceedings of the 40th International Conference on Software Engineering (ICSE)*. Association for Computing Machinery, 2018, 37–40. https://doi.org/10.1145/3183440.3183474.

[Helland 2005] P. Helland, "Data on the Outside versus Data on the Inside." In *Proceedings of the Second Biennial Conference on Innovative Data Systems Research (CIDR)*. 2005, 144–153. http://cidrdb.org/cidr2005/papers/P12.pdf.

[Hentrich 2011] C. Hentrich and U. Zdun, *Process-Driven SOA: Patterns for Aligning Business and IT*. Auerbach Publications, 2011.

[Higginbotham 2017a] J. Higginbotham, "When and How Do You Version Your API?" Tyk Blog, 2017. https://tyk.io/blog/when-and-how-do-you-version-your-api/.

[Higginbotham 2017b] J. Higginbotham, "A Guide for When (and How) to Version Your API." Tyk Blog, 2017. https://tyk.io/blog/guide-version-api/.

[Higginbotham 2018] J. Higginbotham, "REST was NEVER about CRUD." Tyk Blog, 2018. https://tyk.io/blog/rest-never-crud/.

[Higginbotham 2019] J. Higginbotham, "How to Add Upsert Support to Your API." Tyk Blog, 2019. https://tyk.io/blog/how-to-add-upsert-support-to-your-api/.

[Higginbotham 2020] J. Higginbotham, "Tyk Tips Limit Breaking Changes." Tyk Blog, 2020. https://tyk.io/blog/tyk-tips-limit-breaking-changes/.

[Higginbotham 2021] J. Higginbotham, *Principles of Web API Design: Delivering Value with APIs and Microservices.* Addison-Wesley, 2021.

[Hohpe 2003] G. Hohpe and B. Woolf, *Enterprise Integration Patterns: Designing, Building, and Deploying Messaging Solutions.* Addison-Wesley, 2003.

[Hohpe 2007] G. Hohpe, "Conversation Patterns: Interactions between Loosely Coupled Services." In *Proceedings of the 12th European Conference on Pattern Languages of Programs (EuroPLoP).* UVK - Universitaetsverlag Konstanz, 2007, 1–45.

[Hohpe 2016] G. Hohpe, I. Ozkaya, U. Zdun, and O. Zimmermann, "The Software Architect's Role in the Digital Age." *IEEE Software* 33, no. 6 (2016): 30–39. https://doi.org/10.1109/MS.2016.137.

[Hohpe 2017] G. Hohpe, "Conversations between Loosely Coupled Systems." Last updated 2017. https://www.enterpriseintegrationpatterns.com/patterns/conversation/.

[Hornig 1984] C. Hornig, "A Standard for the Transmission of IP Datagrams over Ethernet Networks." RFC 894; RFC Editor, April 1984. https://doi.org/10.17487/RFC0894.

[IANA 2020] "Link Relations." Internet Assigned Numbers Authority, 2020. https://www.iana.org/assignments/link-relations/link-relations.xhtml.

[International 2022] HL7 International, "Health Level 7 International." Accessed June 24, 2022. http://www.hl7.org.

[ISO 2005] International Organization for Standardization, *Industrial Automation Systems and Integration—Product Data Representation and Exchange—Part 1179: Application Module: Individual Involvement in Activity,* ISO 10303-1179: 2005. ISO, 2005.

[ISO 2020] International Organization for Standardization, *Financial Services—International Bank Account Number (IBAN)—Part 1: Structure of the IBAN,* ISO 13616-1:2020. ISO, 2020.

[Joachim 2013] N. Joachim, D. Beimborn, and T. Weitzel, "The Influence of SOA Governance Mechanisms on IT Flexibility and Service Reuse." *Journal of Strategic Information Systems* 22, no. 1 (2013): 86–101. https://doi.org/https://doi.org/10.1016/j.jsis.2012.10.003.

[Jones 2012] M. Jones and D. Hardt, "The OAuth 2.0 Authorization Framework: Bearer Token Usage." RFC 6750; RFC Editor, Oct. 2012. https://doi.org/10.17487/RFC6750.

[Jones 2015] M. Jones, J. Bradley, and N. Sakimura, "JSON Web Token (JWT)." RFC 7519; RFC Editor, May 2015. https://doi.org/10.17487/RFC7519.

[Josefsson 2006] S. Josefsson, "The Base16, Base32, and Base64 Data Encodings." RFC 4648; RFC Editor, October 2006. https://doi.org/10.17487/RFC4648.

[Josuttis 2007] N. Josuttis, *SOA in Practice: The Art of Distributed System Design.* O'Reilly, 2007.

[JSON API 2022] JSON API, "JSON:API: A Specification for Building APIs in JSON." 2022. https://jsonapi.org/.

[Judkowitz 2018] J. Judkowitz and M. Carter, "SRE Fundamentals: SLIs, SLAs and SLOs." Google Cloud Platform Blog, 2018. https://cloudplatform.googleblog.com/2018/07/sre-fundamentals-slis-slas-and-slos.html?m=1.

[Julisch 2011] K. Julisch, C. Suter, T. Woitalla, and O. Zimmermann, "Compliance by Design–Bridging the Chasm between Auditors and IT Architects." *Computers & Security* 30, no. 6 (2011): 410–426.

[Kapferer 2021] S. Kapferer and O. Zimmermann, "ContextMapper: A Modeling Framework for Strategic Domain-Driven Design." Context Mapper, 2021. https://contextmapper.org/.

[Kelly 2016] M. Kelly, "JSON Hypertext Application Language." Internet Engineering Task Force; Internet Engineering Task Force, Internet-Draft, May 2016. https://datatracker.ietf.org/doc/html/draft-kelly-json-hal-08.

[Kerievsky 2004] J. Kerievsky, *Refactoring to Patterns*. Pearson Higher Education, 2004.

[Kimball 2002] R. Kimball and M. Ross, *The Data Warehouse Toolkit: The Complete Guide to Dimensional Modeling*, 2nd ed. Wiley, 2002.

[Kircher 2004] M. Kircher and P. Jain, *Pattern-Oriented Software Architecture, Volume 3: Patterns for Resource Management*. Wiley, 2004.

[Klabnik 2011] S. Klabnik, "Nobody Understands REST or HTTP." 2011. https://steveklabnik.com/writing/nobody-understands-rest-or-http#representations.

[Knoche 2019] H. Knoche, "Improving Batch Performance When Migrating to Microservices with Chunking and Coroutines." *Softwaretechnik-Trends* 39, no. 4 (2019): 20–22.

[Krafzig 2004] D. Krafzig, K. Banke, and D. Slama, *Enterprise SOA: Service-Oriented Architecture Best Practices (the COAD Series)*. Prentice Hall, 2004.

[Kruchten 2000] P. Kruchten, *The Rational Unified Process: An Introduction*, 2nd ed. Addison-Wesley, 2000.

[Kruchten 2013] P. Kruchten, "Contextualizing Agile Software Development." *Journal of Software: Evolution and Process* 25, no. 4 (2013): 351–361. https://doi.org/10.1002/smr.572.

[Kubernetes 2022] Kubernetes, "The Kubernetes API." Accessed June 24, 2022. https://kubernetes.io/docs/concepts/overview/kubernetes-api/.

[Lanthaler 2021] M. Lanthaler, "Hydra Core Vocabulary—A Vocabulary for Hypermedia-Driven Web APIs." Unofficial draft, July 2021. http://www.hydra-cg.com/spec/latest/core/.

[Lauret 2017] A. Lauret, "API Stylebook: Collections of Resources for API designers." 2017. http://apistylebook.com/.

[Lauret 2019] A. Lauret, *The Design of Web APIs*. Manning, 2019.

[Leach 2005] P. J. Leach, R. Salz, and M. H. Mealling, "A Universally Unique IDentifier (UUID) URN Namespace." RFC 4122; RFC Editor, July 2005. https://doi.org/10.17487/RFC4122.

[Lewis 2014] J. Lewis and M. Fowler, "Microservices: A Definition of This New Architectural Term." martinFowler.com, 2014. https://martinfowler.com/articles/microservices.html.

[Leymann 2000] F. Leymann and D. Roller, *Production Workflow: Concepts and Techniques*. Prentice Hall, 2000.

[Leymann 2002] F. Leymann, D. Roller, and M.-T. Schmidt, "Web Services and Business Process Management." *IBM System Journal* 41, no. 2 (2002): 198–211. https://doi.org/10.1147/sj.412.0198.

[Little 2013] M. Little, "The Costs of Versioning an API." *InfoQ*, 2013. https://www.infoq.com/news/2013/12/api-versioning/.

[Lübke 2015] D. Lübke, "Using Metric Time Lines for Identifying Architecture Shortcomings in Process Execution Architectures." In *Proceedings of the 2nd International Workshop on Software Architecture and Metrics (SAM)*. IEEE Press, 2015, 55–58.

[Lübke 2016] D. Lübke and T. van Lessen, "Modeling Test Cases in BPMN for Behavior-Driven Development." *IEEE Software* 33, no. 5 (2016): 15–21. https://doi.org/10.1109/MS.2016.117.

[Maheedharan 2018] V. Maheedharan, "Beta Testing of Your Product: 6 Practical Steps to Follow." *dzone.com*, 2018. https://dzone.com/articles/beta-testing-of-your-product-6-practical-steps-to.

[Manikas 2013] K. Manikas and K. M. Hansen, "Software Ecosystems—A Systematic Literature Review." *Journal of Systems and Software* 86, no. 5 (2013): 1294–1306. https://doi.org/10.1016/j.jss.2012.12.026.

[Martin 2002] R. C. Martin, *Agile Software Development: Principles, Patterns, and Practices*. Prentice Hall, 2002.

[Meldewesen 2014] eCH-Fachgruppe Meldewesen, "GBDBS XML Schema." Accessed June 24, 2014. https://share.ech.ch/xmlns/eCH-0173/index.html.

[Melnikov 2011] A. Melnikov and I. Fette, "The WebSocket Protocol." RFC 6455; RFC Editor, December 2011. https://doi.org/10.17487/RFC6455.

[Mendonça 2021] N. C. Mendonça, C. Box, C. Manolache, and L. Ryan, "The Monolith Strikes Back: Why Istio Migrated from Microservices to a Monolithic Architecture." *IEEE Software* 38, no. 5 (2021): 17–22. https://doi.org/10.1109/MS.2021.3080335.

[Meyer 1997] B. Meyer, *Object-Oriented Software Construction*, 2nd ed. Prentice Hall, 1997.

[Microformats 2022] Microformats Web site. Accessed June 24, 2022. http://microformats.org.

[Microsoft 2021] Microsoft, "LinkedIn API Breaking Change Policy." *Microsoft Docs,* 2021. https://docs.microsoft.com/en-us/linkedin/shared/breaking-change-policy.

[Moats 1997] R. Moats, "URN Syntax." RFC 2141; RFC Editor, May 1997. https://doi.org/10.17487/RFC2141.

[Möckli 2017] W. Möckli and D. Lübke, "Terravis—the case of process-oriented land register transactions digitization." In *Digital Government Excellence Awards 2017: An Anthology of Case Histories,* edited by D. Remenyi. Academic Conferences and Publishing, 2017.

[Monday 2003] P. B. Monday, *Web Services Patterns: Java Edition.* Apress, 2003.

[Murer 2010] S. Murer, B. Bonati, and F. Furrer, *Managed Evolution—A Strategy for Very Large Information Systems.* Springer, 2010.

[Neri 2020] D. Neri, J. Soldani, O. Zimmermann, and A. Brogi, "Design Principles, Architectural Smells and Refactorings for Microservices: A Multivocal Review." *Software-Intensive Cyber Physical Systems* 35, no. 1 (2020): 3–15. https://doi.org/10.1007/s00450-019-00407-8.

[Neuman 2005] C. Neuman, S. Hartman, K. Raeburn, and T. Yu, "The Kerberos Network Authentication Service (V5)." RFC 4120; RFC Editor, July 2005. https://doi.org/10.17487/RFC4120.

[Newman 2015] S. Newman, "Pattern: Backends for Frontends." Sam Newman & Associates, 2015. https://samnewman.io/patterns/architectural/bff/.

[Nottingham 2007] M. Nottingham, "Feed Paging and Archiving." RFC 5005; RFC Editor, September 2007. https://doi.org/10.17487/RFC5005.

[Nottingham 2017] M. Nottingham, "Web Linking." RFC 8288; RFC Editor, October 2017. https://doi.org/10.17487/RFC8288.

[Nottingham 2022] M. Nottingham, "Home Documents for HTTP APIs." Network Working Group, Internet-Draft, 2022. https://datatracker.ietf.org/doc/html/draft-nottingham-json-home-06.

[Nygard 2011] M. Nygard, "Documenting Architecture Decisions." Cognitect, 2011. https://www.cognitect.com/blog/2011/11/15/documenting-architecture-decisions.

[Nygard 2018a] M. Nygard, *Release It! Design and Deploy Production-Ready Software,* 2nd ed. Pragmatic Bookshelf, 2018.

[Nygard 2018b] M. Nygard, "Services by Lifecycle." Wide Awake Developers, 2018. https://www.michaelnygard.com/blog/2018/01/services-by-lifecycle/.

[Nygard 2018c] M. Nygard, "Evolving Away from Entities." Wide Awake Developers, 2018. https://www.michaelnygard.com/blog/2018/04/evolving-away-from-entities/.

[OASIS 2005] OASIS, *Security Assertion Markup Language (SAML) v2.0.* Organization for the Advancement of Structured Information Standards, 2005.

[OASIS 2021] OASIS, *eXtensible Access Control Markup Language (XACML) version 3.0.* Organization for the Advancement of Structured Information Standards, 2021.

[OpenAPI 2022] OpenAPI Initiative, "OpenAPI Specification." 2022. https://spec.openapis.org/oas/latest.html.

[OpenID 2021] OpenID Initiative, "OpenID Connect Specification." 2021. https://openid.net/connect/.

[OWASP 2021] "OWASP REST Security Cheat Sheet." OWASP Cheat Sheet Series, 2021. https://cheatsheetseries.owasp.org/cheatsheets/REST_Security_Cheat_Sheet.html.

[Pardon 2011] G. Pardon and C. Pautasso, "Towards Distributed Atomic Transactions over RESTful Services." In *REST: From Research to Practice*, edited by E. Wilde and C. Pautasso. Springer, 2011, 507–524.

[Pardon 2018] G. Pardon, C. Pautasso, and O. Zimmermann, "Consistent Disaster Recovery for Microservices: The BAC theorem." *IEEE Cloud Computing* 5, no. 1 (2018): 49–59. https://doi.org/10.1109/MCC.2018.011791714.

[Pautasso 2016] C. Pautasso, A. Ivanchikj, and S. Schreier, "A Pattern Language for RESTful Conversations." In *Proceedings of the 21st European Conference on Pattern Languages of Programs*. Association for Computing Machinery, 2016.

[Pautasso 2017a] C. Pautasso, O. Zimmermann, M. Amundsen, J. Lewis, and N. M. Josuttis, "Microservices in Practice, Part 1: Reality Check and Service Design." *IEEE Software* 34, no. 1 (2017): 91–98. https://doi.org/10.1109/MS.2017.24.

[Pautasso 2017b] C. Pautasso, O. Zimmermann, M. Amundsen, J. Lewis, and N. M. Josuttis, "Microservices in Practice, Part 2: Service Integration and Sustainability." *IEEE Software* 34, no. 2 (2017): 97–104. https://doi.org/10.1109/MS.2017.56.

[Pautasso 2018] C. Pautasso and O. Zimmermann, "The Web as a Software Connector: Integration Resting on Linked Resources." *IEEE Software* 35, no. 1 (2018): 93–98. https://doi.org/10.1109/MS.2017.4541049.

[Preston-Werner 2021] T. Preston-Werner, "Semantic Versioning 2.0.0." 2021. https://semver.org/.

[Reschke 2015] J. Reschke, "The 'Basic' HTTP Authentication Scheme." RFC 7617; RFC Editor, September 2015. https://doi.org/10.17487/RFC7617.

[Richardson 2016] C. Richardson, "Microservice Architecture." Microservices.io, 2016, http://microservices.io.

[Richardson 2018] C. Richardson, *Microservices Patterns*. Manning, 2018.

[Richardson 2019] C. Richardson, "Documenting a Service Using the Microservice Canvas," Chris Richardson Consulting Blog, 2019, https://chrisrichardson.net/post/microservices/general/2019/02/27/microservice-canvas.html.

[Riley 2017] J. Riley, *Understanding Metadata: What Is Metadata, and What Is It For? A Primer.* NISO, 2017. https://www.niso.org/publications/understanding-metadata-2017.

[Rosenberg 2002] M. Rosenberg, *Nonviolent Communication: A Language of Life.* PuddleDancer Press, 2002.

[Rozanski 2005] N. Rozanski and E. Woods, *Software Systems Architecture: Working with Stakeholders Using Viewpoints and Perspectives.* Addison-Wesley, 2005.

[Ruby on Rails 2022] Ruby on Rails Web site. Accessed June 24, 2022. https://rubyonrails.org/.

[Saint-Andre 2011] P. Saint-Andre, S. Loreto, S. Salsano, and G. Wilkins, "Known Issues and Best Practices for the Use of Long Polling and Streaming in Bidirectional HTTP." RFC 6202; RFC Editor, April 2011. https://doi.org/10.17487/RFC6202.

[Schumacher 2006] M. Schumacher, E. Fernandez-Buglioni, D. Hybertson, F. Buschmann, and P. Sommerlad, *Security Patterns: Integrating Security and Systems Engineering.* Wiley, 2006.

[Serbout 2021] S. Serbout, C. Pautasso, U. Zdun, and O. Zimmermann, "From OpenAPI Fragments to API Pattern Primitives and Design Smells." In *Proceedings of the 26th European Conference on Pattern Languages of Programs (EuroPLoP).* Association for Computing Machinery, 1–35, 2021. https://doi.org/10.1145/3489449.3489998.

[Seriy 2016] A. Seriy, *Getting Started with IBM API Connect: Scenarios Guide.* IBM Redbooks, 2016.

[Sermersheim 2006] J. Sermersheim, "Lightweight Directory Access Protocol (LDAP): The Protocol." RFC 4511; RFC Editor, June 2006. https://doi.org/10.17487/RFC4511.

[Simpson 1996] W. A. Simpson, "PPP Challenge Handshake Authentication Protocol (CHAP)." RFC 1994; RFC Editor, August 1996. https://doi.org/10.17487/RFC1994.

[Sinatra 2022] Sinatra Web site. Accessed June 24, 2022. http://sinatrarb.com/.

[Singjai 2021a] A. Singjai, U. Zdun, and O. Zimmermann, "Practitioner Views on the Interrelation of Microservice APIs and Domain-Driven Design: A Grey Literature Study Based on Grounded Theory." In *Proceedings of the 18th International Conference on Software Architecture (ICSA),* IEEE, 2021, 25–35. https://doi.org/10.1109/ICSA51549.2021.00011.

[Singjai 2021b] A. Singjai, U. Zdun, O. Zimmermann, and C. Pautasso, "Patterns on Deriving APIs and Their Endpoints from Domain Models." In *Proceedings of the European Conference on Pattern Languages of Programs (EuroPLoP),* Association for Computing Machinery, 2021, 1–15.

[Singjai 2021c] A. Singjai, U. Zdun, O. Zimmermann, M. Stocker, and C. Pautasso, "Patterns on Designing API Endpoint Operations." In *Proceedings of the 28th Conference on Pattern Languages of Programs (PLoP),* Hillside Group, 2021. http://eprints.cs.univie.ac.at/7194/.

[Siriwardena 2014] P. Siriwardena, *Advanced API Security: Securing APIs with OAuth 2.0, OpenID Connect, JWS, and JWE.* Apress, 2014.

[Sookocheff 2014] K. Sookocheff, "On Choosing a Hypermedia Type for Your API - HAL, JSON-LD, Collection+JSON, SIREN, Oh My!" March 2014. https://sookocheff.com/post/api/on-choosing-a-hypermedia-format/.

[Stalnaker 1996] R. Stalnaker, "On the Representation of Context." In *Proceeding from Semantics and Linguistic Theory,* vol. 6. Cornell University, 1996, 279–294.

[Stettler 2019] C. Stettler, "Domain Events vs. Event Sourcing: Why Domain Events and Event Sourcing Should Not Be Mixed Up." innoQ Blog, January 15, 2019. https://www.innoq.com/en/blog/domain-events-versus-event-sourcing.

[Stocker 2021a] M. Stocker and O. Zimmermann, "From Code Refactoring to API Refactoring: Agile Service Design and Evolution." in *Proceedings of the 15th Symposium and Summer School on Service-Oriented Computing (SummerSOC)*, Springer, 2021, 174–193.

[Stocker 2021b] M. Stocker and O. Zimmermann, Interface Refactoring Catalog Web site. 2021. https://interface-refactoring.github.io/.

[Stripe 2022] "API Reference." Stripe API, 2022. https://stripe.com/docs/api.

[Sturgeon 2016a] P. Sturgeon, "Understanding RPC vs REST for HTTP APIs." *Smashing Magazine,* 2016. https://www.smashingmagazine.com/2016/09/understanding-rest-and-rpc-for-http-apis/.

[Sturgeon 2016b] P. Sturgeon, *Build APIs You Won't Hate*. LeanPub, 2016. https://leanpub.com/build-apis-you-wont-hate.

[Sturgeon 2017] P. Sturgeon, "You Might Not Need GraphQL." Runscope Blog, 2017. https://blog.runscope.com/posts/you-might-not-need-graphql.

[Swiber 2017] K. Swiber et al., "Siren: A Hypermedia Specification for Representing Entities." kevinswiber / siren, April 2017. https://github.com/kevinswiber/siren.

[Szyperski 2002] C. Szyperski, *Component Software: Beyond Object Oriented Programming,* 2nd ed. Addison Wesley, 2002.

[Tanenbaum 2007] A. S. Tanenbaum and M. Van Steen, *Distributed Systems: Principles and Paradigms*. Prentice Hall, 2007.

[The Economist 2015] "New EU Privacy Rules Could Widen the Policy Gap with America." *The Economist,* 2015. https://www.economist.com/international/2015/10/05/new-eu-privacy-rules-could-widen-the-policy-gap-with-america.

[Thijssen 2017] J. Thijssen, "REST CookBook." restcookbook.com: How to Do Stuff Restful, 2017. https://restcookbook.com/.

[Thoughtworks 2017] "APIs as a Product." Thoughtworks, 2017. https://www.thoughtworks.com/radar/techniques/apis-as-a-product.

[Tödter 2018] K. Tödter, "RESTful Hypermedia APIs." Online slide deck, SpeakerDeck, 2018. https://speakerdeck.com/toedter/restful-hypermedia-apis.

[Torres 2015] F. Torres, "Context Is King: What's Your Software's Operating Range?" *IEEE Software* 32, no. 5 (2015): 9–12. https://doi.org/10.1109/MS.2015.121.

[Twitter 2022] Twitter Ads API Team, "Pagination." Twitter Developer Platform, 2022. https://developer.twitter.com/en/docs/twitter-ads-api/pagination.

[UI Patterns 2021] "Pagination Design Pattern." UI Patterns: User Interface Design Pattern Library, 2021. http://ui-patterns.com/patterns/Pagination.

[Vernon 2013] V. Vernon, *Implementing Domain-Driven Design*. Addison-Wesley, 2013.

[Vernon 2021] V. Vernon and T. Jaskula, *Strategic Monoliths and Microservices: Driving Innovation Using Purposeful Architecture*. Pearson Education, 2021.

[Voelter 2004] M. Voelter, M. Kircher, and U. Zdun, *Remoting Patterns: Foundations of Enterprise, Internet, and Realtime Distributed Object Middleware*. Wiley, 2004.

[Vogels 2009] W. Vogels, "Eventually Consistent." *Communications of the ACM 52*, no. 1 (2009): 40–44. https://doi.org/10.1145/1435417.1435432.

[Vollbrecht 2004] J. Vollbrecht, J. D. Carlson, L. Blunk, B. D. Aboba, and H. Levkowetz, "Extensible Authentication Protocol (EAP)." RFC 3748; RFC Editor, June 2004. https://doi.org/10.17487/RFC3748.

[W3C 1998] W3C, *Level 1 Document Object Model Specification*. World Wide Web Consortium, 1998. https://www.w3.org/TR/REC-DOM-Level-1/.

[W3C 2004] W3C, *Web Services Addressing*. World Wide Web Consortium, 2004. https://www.w3.org/Submission/ws-addressing/.

[W3C 2007] W3C, *XSL Transformations (XSLT), Version 2.0*. World Wide Web Consortium, 2007. https://www.w3.org/TR/xslt20/.

[W3C 2010] W3C, *XML Linking Language (XLink), Version 1.1*. World Wide Web Consortium, 2010. https://www.w3.org/TR/xlink11/.

[W3C 2013] W3C, *SPARQL 1.1 Query Language*. World Wide Web Consortium, 2013. https://www.w3.org/TR/sparql11-query/.

[W3C 2017] W3C, *XQuery 3.1: An XML Query Language*. World Wide Web Consortium, 2017. https://www.w3.org/TR/xquery-31/.

[W3C 2019] W3C, *JSON-LD 1.1: A JSON-Based Serialization for Linked Data*. World Wide Web Consortium, 2019.

[Webber 2010] J. Webber, S. Parastatidis, and I. Robinson, *REST in Practice: Hypermedia and Systems Architecture*. O'Reilly, 2010.

[White 2006] A. White, D. Newman, D. Logan, and J. Radcliffe, "Mastering Master Data Management." Gartner Group, 2006.

[Wikipedia 2022a] Wikipedia, s.v. "Wicked Problem." Last edited August 24, 2022. https://en.wikipedia.org/wiki/Wicked_problem.

[Wikipedia 2022b] Wikipedia, s.v. "Reference Data." Last edited December 23, 2021. http://en.wikipedia.org/w/index.php?title=Reference%20data&oldid=1000397384.

[Wikipedia 2022c] Wikipedia, s.v. "Metadata." Last edited December 23, 2021. http://en.wikipedia.org/w/index.php?title=Metadata&oldid=1061649487.

[Wikipedia 2022d] Wikipedia, s.v. "Metadata Standard." Last edited December 6, 2021. http://en.wikipedia.org/w/index.php?title=Metadata%20standard&oldid=1059017272.

[Wikipedia 2022e] Wikipedia, s.v. "Uniform Resource Name." Last edited November 27, 2021. http://en.wikipedia.org/w/index.php?title=Uniform%20Resource%20Name&oldid=1057401001.

[Wikipedia 2022f] Wikipedia, s.v. "Jakarta XML Binding." Last edited November 13, 2021. http://en.wikipedia.org/w/index.php?title=Jakarta%20XML%20Binding&oldid=1055101833.

[Wikipedia 2022g] Wikipedia, s.v. "Compensating Transaction." Last edited July 5, 2021. https://en.wikipedia.org/wiki/Compensating_transaction.

[Wikipedia 2022h] Wikipedia, s.v. "Open Data." Last edited January 4, 2022. https://en.wikipedia.org/wiki/Open_data.

[Wilde 2013] E. Wilde, "The 'profile' Link Relation Type." RFC 6906; RFC Editor, March 2013. https://doi.org/10.17487/RFC6906.

[Wirfs-Brock 2002] R. Wirfs-Brock and A. McKean, *Object Design: Roles, Responsibilities, and Collaborations*. Pearson Education, 2002.

[Wirfs-Brock 2011] "Agile Architecture Myths #2 Architecture Decisions Should Be Made at the Last Responsible Moment" (posted by Rebecca). wirfs-brock.com, January 18, 2011. http://wirfs-brock.com/blog/2011/01/18/agile-architecture-myths-2-architecture-decisions-should-be-made-at-the-last-responsible-moment/.

[Wirfs-Brock 2019] R. Wirfs-Brock, "Cultivating Your Design Heuristics." Online slide deck, wirfs-brock.com, 2019. https://de.slideshare.net/rwirfs-brock/cultivating-your-design-heuristics.

[Yalon 2019] E. Yalon and I. Shkedy, "OWASP API Security Project." OWASP Foundation, 2019. https://owasp.org/www-project-api-security/.

[Zalando 2021] Zalando, *RESTful API and Event Guidelines.* Zalando SE Opensource, 2021. https://opensource.zalando.com/restful-api-guidelines.

[Zdun 2013] U. Zdun, R. Capilla, H. Tran, and O. Zimmermann, "Sustainable Architectural Design Decisions." *IEEE Software* 30, no. 6 (2013): 46–53. https://doi.org/10.1109/MS.2013.97.

[Zdun 2018] U. Zdun, M. Stocker, O. Zimmermann, C. Pautasso, and D. Lübke, "Guiding Architectural Decision Making on Quality Aspects in Microservice APIs." In *Service-Oriented Computing: 16th International Conference, ICSOC 2018, Hangzhou, China, November 12–15, 2018, Proceedings.* Springer, 2018, 73–89. https://doi.org/10.1007/978-3-030-03596-9_5.

[Zdun 2020] U. Zdun, E. Wittern, and P. Leitner, "Emerging Trends, Challenges, and Experiences in DevOps and Microservice APIs." *IEEE Software* 37, no. 1 (2020): 87–91. https://doi.org/10.1109/MS.2019.2947982.

[Zeng 2015] M. L. Zeng, Metadata Basics Web site. 2015. https://www.metadataetc.org/metadatabasics/types.htm.

[Zimmermann 2003] O. Zimmermann, M. Tomlinson, and S. Peuser, *Perspectives on Web Services: Applying SOAP, WSDL and UDDI to Real-World Projects.* Springer, 2003.

[Zimmermann 2004] O. Zimmermann, P. Krogdahl, and C. Gee, "Elements of Service-Oriented Analysis and Design." Developer Works, IBM Corporation. 2004.

[Zimmermann 2007] O. Zimmermann, J. Grundler, S. Tai, and F. Leymann, "Architectural Decisions and Patterns for Transactional Workflows in SOA." In *Proceedings of the Fifth International Conference on Service-Oriented Computing (ICSOC).* Springer-Verlag, 2007, 81–93. https://doi.org/10.1007/978-3-540-74974-5.

[Zimmermann 2009] O. Zimmermann, "An Architectural Decision Modeling Framework for Service-Oriented Architecture Design." PhD thesis, University of Stuttgart, Germany, 2009. http://elib.uni-stuttgart.de/opus/volltexte/2010/5228/.

[Zimmermann 2015] O. Zimmermann, "Architectural Refactoring: A Task-Centric View on Software Evolution." *IEEE Software* 32, no. 2 (2015): 26–29. https://doi.org/10.1109/MS.2015.37.

[Zimmermann 2017] O. Zimmermann, "Microservices Tenets." *Computer Science–Research and Development* 32, no. 3–4 (2017): 301–310. https://doi.org/10.1007/s00450-016-0337-0.

[Zimmermann 2021a] O. Zimmermann and M. Stocker, "What Is a Cloud-Native Application Anyway (Part 2)?" Olaf Zimmermann (ZIO), 2021. https://medium.com/olzzio/what-is-a-cloud-native-application-anyway-part-2-f0e88c3caacb.

[Zimmermann 2021b] O. Zimmermann and M. Stocker, *Design Practice Reference: Guides and Templates to Craft Quality Software in Style*. LeanPub, 2021. https://leanpub.com/dpr.

[Zimmermann 2021c] O. Zimmermann, "Architectural Decisions—The Making Of." Olaf Zimmermann (ZIO), 2021. https://ozimmer.ch/practices/2020/04/27/ArchitectureDecisionMaking.html.

[Zimmermann 2022] O. Zimmermann, "Microservice Domain Specific Language (MDSL) Language Specification." Microservice-API-Patterns, 2022. https://microservice-api-patterns.github.io/MDSL-Specification/.

Index